THEATRE IN BELFAST, 1736–1800

Theatre in Belfast, 1736–1800

John C. Greene

Lehigh
University
Press

Bethlehem: Lehigh University Press
London: Associated University Presses

Associated University Presses
440 Forsgate Drive
Cranbury, NJ 08512

Associated University Presses
16 Barter Street
London WC1A 2AH, England

Associated University Presses
P. O. Box 338, Port Credit
Mississauga, Ontario
Canada L5G 4L8

The paper used in this publication meets the requirements of the American National Standard for Permanence of Paper for Printed Library Materials Z39.48-1984.

Library of Congress Cataloging-in-Publication Data

Greene, John C., 1946-
    Theatre in Belfast, 1736-1800 / John C. Greene
        p. cm.
    Includes bibliographical references and indexes.
    ISBN 0-934223-53-X (alk.paper)
    1. Theater--Northern Ireland--Belfast--History--18th century.
    2. Theater--Northern Ireland--Belfast--Calendars. I. Title

    PN2602.B4 G74 2000
    792'.09416'709033--dc21

                                                    00-032744

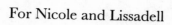

For Nicole and Lissadell

TABLE OF CONTENTS

ACKNOWLEDGMENTS

The performance data used in preparing this book was derived mainly from *The Belfast Newsletter* Index, 1737–1800, an online database prepared under my supervision with funding from The British Library, the Economic and Social Research Council, the Action for Community Employment Scheme, and Enterprise Ulster. The index data was compiled under the auspices of the Institute of Irish Studies, the Queen's University of Belfast between 1982 and 1988. I wish to thank Dr. Ronald Buchanan, former director of the Institute of Irish Studies, for his support of that project. Grateful thanks also to Drs. Gary Marotta, Doris Meriwether, Richard C. Cusimano, and David Barry of The University of Louisiana at Lafayette for granting the release time to finish this work. Special thanks to Ms. Leslie Donoghue Schilling of the ULL Humanities Resource Center, who prepared the camera-ready copy of this book, and to Mr. Lee Johnson, formerly of the ULL Engineering Department, for the many hours he dedicated to helping me with my computer problems.

KEY TO ABBREVIATIONS AND SYMBOLS

BD *A Biographical Dictionary of Actors, Actresses, Musicians, Dancers, Managers and Other Stage Personnel in London, 1660–1800*. Philip H. Highfill, *et. al.* 16 vols. Carbondale and Edwardsville: Southern Illinois University P., 1973–93.

BM *The Belfast Mercury.*

BNL *The Belfast Newsletter.*

Clark *The Irish Stage in the County Towns, 1720–1800* (Oxford: Clarendon P, 1965).

HM *The Hibernian Magazine* (Dublin).

NS The Belfast *Northern Star.*

PRFJ *The Public Register; or, Freeman's Journal* (Dublin).

REPERTORY SYMBOLS

A number inside parentheses, e.g. (2), denotes the number of times a piece is actually billed to be performed in a season. This number does not include performances not actually listed in playbills. If, for example, a playbill states that a play is being performed for the "third time" and corroborating evidence exists for only two performances, the putative performance is not included in these totals.

† = first recorded performance of the play in Belfast, but no explicit claim for a first performance is made in the playbills.

* or ⏭ = "never acted here." The claim in a playbill that a play was "never acted here" is ambiguous. It can mean either that the play had never before been acted in Belfast, or, simply, that the play had never before been acted at a particular theatre. Since the performance record is obviously fragmentary, a distinction is made here between plays for which no previous performance is recorded and for which an explicit statement that the piece was "never acted here" (denoted by the *) and those known to have been acted in Belfast previously, but which are being performed for the first time at a specific theatre (denoted by ⏭).

Θ = never performed before anywhere.
● = "never acted in this kingdom."
■ = announced as a long-term revival (longer than five years).
□ = never performed in Belfast and produced "as performed in London."
▣ = never performed in Belfast and produced "as performed in Dublin."

CHRONOLOGY OF BELFAST THEATRES

1730	1766	1768	1770	1778	1783	1792	1800

THE VAULTS

MILL GATE

RYDER'S MILL ST.

ANN STREET

ROSEMARY STREET

ARTHUR STREET

THEATRE IN BELFAST, 1736–1800

INTRODUCTION

This book provides the first comprehensive daily record of surviving evidence relating to nearly seven-hundred theatrical performances that took place in Belfast, Ireland, from the earliest recorded staging of a play there, in 1736, through the year 1800. At the heart of the work is the daily calendar of performances, each entry of which includes date of performance, titles of main- and afterpieces, cast lists and roles enacted, scenery, costume, specialty acts, dances, songs, and other music, as well as commentary on theatre management and any other information that helps to illuminate the kind and scope of theatre entertainment available to Belfast audiences during the era.

The headnote to each season includes lists of all theatre personnel known to have been working in Belfast during that season followed by biographical sketches of the actors. The reader will see that considerable space has been devoted to biography and to descriptions of members of the acting companies that performed in the Belfast theatres. The theatre personnel merit so much attention because relatively little was known previously about their activities, and particularly about those of performers who had not acted in London, and who, thus, were excluded from biographical treatment in Highfill, Langhans and Burnim, *Biographical Dictionary of Actors, Actresses, . . .* [etc.], *1660–1800.*

The actors' biographies have been grouped together by season and by company rather than listed alphabetically in an appendix so as to enable the reader to see relationships between the personnel present in Belfast each season. Many of the biographical sketches of actors (particularly Irish actors) found below are the first to be written, and it is hoped that this information about their lives and careers will help to illuminate the Irish theatre generally.

In keeping with current practice, each performance entry in the daily record of performances may represent a condensation and conflation of materials garnered from numerous sources, although the bulk of the evidence about the Belfast theatres survives only in the theatre playbills published in *The Belfast Newsletter (BNL)*, the principal newspaper of Belfast between the years 1737 and 1800. Commonly, the same or similar program information was repeated in several issues of the newspaper with varying amounts of detail. Unless otherwise indicated, the source date at the end of each entry indicates the issue of *The Belfast Newsletter* containing the greatest amount of information about that performance.

17

The orthography of the original playbills has been retained here, except for actors' names. In this case, if variant spellings appeared, the spelling has been regularized throughout to the one preferred by the authors of the *BD*, or, when the individual is not included in that work, to the spelling used most frequently in Belfast and Dublin playbills.

Appended to the calendar are several indexes: an author/play/performance date index; a complete list of Belfast actors, actresses, and other stage personnel, cross-referenced with roles (if specified) and performance dates; and a general index, which includes listings of songs, dances, and other entertainments, but excludes information found in the other two indexes.

James Magee was the principal Belfast printer of dramatic works during this era, and I have included in the calendar the Belfast publication dates by Magee of the pertinent plays.

This calendar supplements and corrects the performance information relating to Belfast presented in William S. Clark's excellent (though long out-of-print) history of the theatres of provincial Ireland, *The Irish Stage in the County Towns, 1720–1800* (Oxford: Clarendon P, 1965).

Portions of what is presented here may also be found in Clark, either in the historical narrative or in his two useful appendices: "Plays acted outside Dublin" and "Actors and Actresses Outside Dublin." However, with the passage of time and the publication of such invaluable research tools as *The London Stage, 1660–1800* and *A Biographical Dictionary of Actors, Actresses* . . . . etc., theatre researchers have become increasingly aware of several shortcomings of Clark's book. Most importantly, Clark excluded a substantial amount of the information about theatrical performances that was available to him. Also, *The Irish Stage in the County Towns* is difficult to use as a reference book due to its narrative format.

Three examples will serve to illustrate the point. First, Clark's narrative history tends to comment only on unusual or especially important occurrences and performances and makes no attempt to provide a day-by-day reconstruction of the Belfast theatrical milieu. Furthermore, Clark gives only a partial record of the stage activities of the many actors who appeared in Belfast. Thus, in his appendix, "Actors and Actresses Outside Dublin," he cites only the first and last appearances of the actors at each theatre in each season and ignores those which took place in the interim. For example, Clark indicates that in 1753 Mrs. Tobias Gemea acted for the first time on 29 June and for the last time on 7 September (359). He does not, however, record eight other performances that Mrs. Gemea gave that season.

A second shortcoming of Clark's book is that, with the exception of the relatively few named parts cited in the historical narrative, he does not record the roles enacted by the performers. One unfortunate consequence of these omissions is that our knowledge about the professional training and repertoire of many actors, as illustrated by the characters they played and the frequency with which they played them, is so much the less. A biographer interested in tracing the career of a particular actor would, in general, find in Clark only the terminal dates when his subject appeared in Belfast, but would find scant information about the roles his subject enacted.

Finally, Clark does not, except in a few cases, include the titles of entr'acte entertainments included in the theatre programs, and he makes virtually no mention of the many dancers, singers, musicians and other performers who increased the enjoyment of Belfast audiences.

By including the materials overlooked or ignored by Clark, I hope to provide here the most complete listing of performance information relating to the Belfast theatres between 1736 and 1800 available to date.

To provide continuity for the calendar, I include, where appropriate, brief commentary about the important theatrical, social, and political events which affected the theatre. In the interest of conciseness, I usually have cited in the calendar only the main titles of plays and afterpieces, except in the cases in which a play has its world premiere in Belfast or in which confusion may result from more than one play having the same or similar titles.

The Theatres

Prior to 1603 and the final defeat of the O'Neills, the village of Belfast consisted of little more than a dilapidated fort protecting the ford at the mouth of the River Lagan. After 1603, with the influx of Scots and English settlers eager to occupy the lands forfeited by the vanquished Irish clans, the settlement gradually became "a flourishing market town and a prospering port," rivaling in size and importance its neighboring towns of Carrickfergus, Newry and Londonderry (Bardon 1982, 11).

However, the general indifference of the region's dominant landowners, the Chichester family (later the Earls of Donegall), and the economic strength of Ireland's principal ports, Dublin and Cork, tended to suppress expansion of trade in the north of Ireland. Consequently, during the first half of the eighteenth century, the population of the town of Belfast remained small. In 1660, for example, it is estimated that only about 1,000 people resided there (20).

Such a number would not have attracted the attention of any British or Irish theatrical touring company. Although by 1688 Belfast had become the principal port of the north and the population had doubled to 2,000, the potential audience base remained small. Population figures for Belfast during the early decades of the eighteenth century are lacking, but it seems likely that by 1736, the year in which the earliest theatrical activity is recorded there, the number of inhabitants had risen to about 5,000. However, the growth of the city remained slow for the first half of the century, due mainly to the neglect of the Fourth Earl of Donegall, whose policy of insisting on short leases for his land discouraged improvement and forced many to emigrate to America.

When the Fifth Earl succeeded to the title the reforms he instituted after 1752 resulted in an expansion of the town and a sharp rise in population: 8,500 in 1757, 13,000 in 1782, and 20,000 by the end of the century, making Belfast the fifth or sixth largest city in Ireland (20, 31). But even a city of 20,000 inhabitants would hardly comprise enough regular theatre-goers to maintain a resident, professional theatre company, and it is not surprising that at no time during the eighteenth century did Belfast support a company of the sort found in Dublin. For the first fifty years of our period the city depended upon the occasional visits of strolling and touring companies of actors for its dramatic entertainment, and even after Michael Atkins acquired what was to become a *de facto* monopoly over theatre activity in Belfast in 1780, theatregoers were rarely offered two full, consecutive seasons of performances. Nevertheless, Belfast had a surprising active theatre life for a town of its size.

The Vaults (ca. 1730–1765)

The earliest evidence of professional theatrical activity in Belfast comes from an entry in the Funeral Register of the First Presbyterian Church, dated 18 June 1731 (*Town Book* 1892, xii). The burial entry reads simply: "Mrs. Johnes, play howse," implying that a Mrs. Johnes or Jones was in some way associated with a theatre that is presumably located in Belfast.

The theatre with which Mrs. Johnes was connected may have been "The Vaults" (suggesting converted wine vaults). This structure has long been thought to be the one advertised for lease in 1795 by Francis and John Turnly who advertise "that well situated Tenement in Weigh-house Lane, denominated the Old Vaults—with the stores thereon"(*BNL* 13 Apr 1795). However, this assumption is based solely on the fact that the building that the Turnleys owned was called "the Old Vaults." It now seems unlikely that "the Old Vaults in Weigh-house Lane" is the same structure as the theatre called "the Vaults." Advertisements in *The Belfast Newsletter* reveal that during this period several structures in Belfast town center were denominated "vaults," and several advertisements in *BNL* issues in August 1756, for example, indicate that "the Old Vaults" were occupied by a retail furniture merchant and an upholsterer (*BNL* 6, 13, 20 Aug. 1756). Since we know that the Vaults were certainly being used as a theatre (possessing both a pit and gallery) in 1754–55 and 1757–58, it is improbable that the commercial establishment would have been converted for use as a theatre and then back again with such alacrity. The Weigh-house Lane site was being used by furniture merchants as late as 1788 (*BNL* 11–18 Jan. 1788). Thus, we remain ignorant of the location of the theatre called the Vaults.

Record of the theatrical use of the Vaults is sometimes suppositious and nearly as intermittent as the visits of the strolling companies who acted in it. The first recorded (but almost certainly not the first actual) performance to take place there is noticed in a Dublin weekly newspaper, which mentions a production at "the Vaults" on Friday, 17 July 1736, when members of Dublin's Smock Alley Theatre company visited Belfast and performed *The Beaux' Stratagem* to a fashionable audience (*Weekly Oracle*, 24 July 1736; later noted by Hitchcock 1788–94, 1:114). We can only assume that the performances in the spring or summer of 1741, when the Smock Alley Company again visited Belfast, and another which took place after a hiatus of nearly ten years, on 3 January 1749/50, also occurred at the Vaults.

The next explicit mention of the venue appears in an undated Harvard playbill announcing a performance of *The Merry Wives of Windsor* "At the Vaults in Belfast" by a touring company of "Comedians from the Theatres of London and Dublin" headed by Mr. and Mrs. James Love. This company was active in the Irish provinces around the year 1751, and evidently remained in Belfast for at least a part of the 1751–52 season. The playbill also reveals that at this time the Vaults had a pit and one gallery, to which admission was 2s. 2d. and 1s. 1d., respectively.

Between 1753 and 1765 various strolling companies visited Belfast and presumably performed at the Vaults, although the bills are silent as to venue. During the 1754–55 season a company headed by the Dublin actor Richard Elrington performed in the city, but Elrington's playbills refer to the performance site as simply "The Theatre." The next overt reference to the Vaults occurs in 1758 when Sherriffe brought his "Drogheda Company of Comedians" to Belfast. Although no playbills for this season survive, the *BNL* 12 May 1758 prints an epilogue that was spoken "at the Vaults" on 5 May 1758. Dublin companies acted at "the Vaults" in 1761 and again in January 1763. The last performance known to have taken place at the Vaults occurred on 7 March 1766 when a company under the direction of Richard Knipe visited Belfast for a short winter season.

The Theatre in Mill Gate (or the "new" Theatre, Mill Street) 1768–69; then intermittently from 1771 to 1779.

It is perhaps remarkable that the Vaults was the only theatre in existence is Belfast during the first half of the eighteenth century, but it is worth remembering that at the beginning of the century the population of Belfast probably numbered no more than 2,500 and by mid-century the growth of the city was "almost imperceptible," as a recent historian has observed (Bardon 1982, 31). By 1757, however, the population had quadrupled almost overnight to about 8,500, largely as the result of the recent growth of the cotton and linen industries and related commerce. By 1782 the number of inhabitants had increased to 13,000 and then to 20,000 by the end of the century (31). A result of the burgeoning prosperity and population was the rapid boom of building that occurred in Belfast following the 1752 act of Parliament that allowed for longer leases and called for development of the land which had lain derelict for decades under the Fourth Earl of Donegall and his predecessors.

We must assume that the Vaults had fallen into disrepair by the summer of 1768 when James Parker, the itinerant actor-manager who was performing in Tralee as early as 1756, brought a company of "Comedians from the Theatres Royal of London, Dublin, and Edinburgh" to Belfast. Clark (1965, 226) speculates that Parker "fixed up a small unpretentious theatre" in the city, the precise location of which is unknown. The gate in Belfast's old city walls normally denominated "Mill Gate," as Clark observes, was located "near the junction of Mill and Castle Streets at the ancient town wall, an area then called Mill Gate" (226). A 1685 map of the city of Belfast places the Mill Gate at the southwest corner of the city walls. The land outside the gate quickly becomes rural, but for a distance of two hundred yards on the north side Mill Street is occupied by the mill and its adjacent pond and is also lined with a few dozen cottages. The map shows that a neat row of larger houses with gardens had been built on the south side of the street.

A contributory factor to the building of a new theatre may have been the "constructive" policy of the Fifth Earl of Donegall who demanded that all of the old leases in the town of Belfast be surrendered, and who, on 20 July 1767, granted new leases "for almost every holding in the town" with the requirement that the lessees built "to a higher standard than had previously been known (Brett 1967, 3). Many of the new leases mandated that the lessee raze and rebuilt the structures on the present site within a stipulated number of years. When Parker decided to open a new theatre, therefore, it seems likely that he (or the merchants from whom he may have leased the theatre) would have had to raze or renovate an existing structure.

Little is known about the physical characteristics of the new playhouse, except that contemporaries described it as relatively small, and that, like the Vaults, it had a pit and gallery. At Mill Gate theatre access to these seating areas was by separate, external doors. The facts that Parker played at the Mill Gate theatre for only a few months and that at virtually the same time he was constructing a new theatre in Newry make it unlikely that Parker actually owned the Mill Gate theatre building.

Parker performed at the Mill Gate theatre three times weekly for a short season that lasted from 23 August 1768 until late January 1769. He closed his theatre at the end of January 1769 and left Belfast to perform with his company in other provincial towns. Later that month he and his company are found acting in Newry, where he opened a "New Theatre" in High Street, and in August he is acting in Kilkenny.

The actor-manager Thomas Ryder had been a popular favorite with Irish audiences since 1757 and was to dominate the Dublin stage during the decade of the 1770s. Long a mainstay of Dublin's Smock Alley company, the ambitious Ryder had little chance for advancement in Dublin during the era of the Barry-Mossop rivalry, and it is probably for this reason that, in 1767, he assembled a touring company and struck out on his own. For three years Ryder's company performed in many Irish provincial towns, including Kilkenny, Waterford, Sligo, Galway, and Derry.

Ryder's company seems to have visited many of the same towns as Parker's at different times of the year. When James Parker's company left Belfast in 1769 to perform in Kilkenny and elsewhere, Ryder evidently spied an opportunity. In the *BNL* 20 April 1770 appeared the notice: "The Theatre which Mr. Ryder is erecting in Mill Gate is getting forward with the utmost expedition and will be opened as soon as possible. . . ."

Whether Ryder's theatre was an entirely new structure or a major refurbishment of Parker's older theatre remains a matter for conjecture. The above advertisement and two others from the previous week in which Ryder revealed his intention to "erect a Place, on such a Plan, as will not only be extremely commodious to the Audience, but will also leave him proper Room to shew, to the utmost Advantage, his entire Set of Scenes," suggests, as Clark observes, "that Ryder did not take over, as he might have been expected to do, Parker's playhouse of the preceding year" (1965, 229).

Nevertheless, the fact that both theatres were located in the same area, that neither had box seats, and that the two were never used simultaneously is, as Clark also states, "a tantalizing coincidence" (1965, 229). Whatever the case, it is clear from later references to the building that only one such structure continued to be used as a theatre in Mill Gate. In June of 1783, for example, Myrton Hamilton would state that "The old house in Mill Street being a disgrace to the drama, he therefore flatters himself this second improvement will meet with their approbation" (*BNL* 13–17 June 1783).

"Mr. Ryder's New Theatre in Mill Gate," consisting of a pit and one gallery, evidently suited Ryder's requirements for a theatre of considerable space. The first recorded performance took place there on 30 April 1770. His main attraction was a series of new, spectacular, pantomimes with large casts and elaborate scenery by the Dublin scenemaster Whitemore and machinery by Geoghagen. Even with the more spacious accommodation the stage area was evidently very crowded, and Ryder was forced, reluctantly, to restrict admittance behind the scenes.

The company performed in Belfast for fifteen weeks, then Ryder closed his theatre on 15 August 1770 and returned to Dublin for the regular Smock Alley season after a hiatus of three years. Ryder was to assume the management of Smock Alley the following spring. Parker returned to Belfast in the summer of 1771, and the preseason playbills announced that "the Theatre in Mill Street is repairing," a statement which throws no light upon whether he used the old playhouse he had abandoned in 1769 or took over Ryder's new theatre (*BNL* 16 July 1771).

Parker and his company acted in the Mill Gate theatre from November 1771 through January 1772, when his association with Belfast theatricals ends. At this time he evidently turned over his interest in Mill Gate Theatre to the provincial actor Michael Atkins, who took over Parker's company. It was probably James Parker (and not George) who acted in the Dublin theatres from the 1773–74 season through 1777–78 and who lead a company billed as "His Majesty's Company of Comedians" and composed of actors from the Dublin theatres to Kilkenny in 1776.

After leaving the theatre dark for the 1772–73 season, Atkins reopened it on 6 September 1773 for a season of six months. Thereafter, he used the Mill Gate theatre in Belfast in alternate seasons (1775–76, 1777–78), performing in the new theatre he had built in Derry in the intervening years. At the end of the 1778–79 season, Atkins signed articles to act with Ryder's Crow Street company and performed in Dublin and Cork. (The *BD* errs in finding Atkins in Dublin for the 1779–80 season). The direction of the Belfast theatre passed for a time into the hands of Atkins's erstwhile protégé, Myrton Hamilton, who moved the company to the new Ann Street theatre.

The last known use of the Mill Gate playhouse occurred in March 1779, when a Mr. Bisset opened the "Old Theatre in Mill Street" for a short season of equilibres and exhibitions of his "Bird of Knowledge," although, as we have seen, the building was still standing and known as "The old house in Mill Street" as late as 1783 (*BNL* 13–17 June 1783).

Ann Street Theatre (1778–1783).

During the summer of 1778 Michael Atkins (acting at the Mill Gate Theatre) evidently determined to retire from provincial management for a period, and he was engaged at Dublin's Crow Street Theatre for both the

1778–79 and 1779–80 seasons. The separation between manager and company was evidently sudden and acrimonious. His "abandoned" company, resolved to survive without him, and, led by Myrton Hamilton, acted in a new playhouse in Ann Street, in central Belfast. Again, the precise location of the playhouse is unknown, although tradition has it that it stood at the corner of Church Lane and Ann Street. Clark thinks it more likely that it was built "further westwards between Crown Entry and Wilson's Entry (now Wilson's Court) on the north side of Ann Street" (1965, 238).

The prologue spoken by Hamilton on the opening night of his Ann Street Theatre on 23 October 1778 in which he says: "By venturing my all, —the Toil of years—/To build a little frigate—See she appears!" suggests that Hamilton has invested his own money in the building (*HM* Appendix 1778, 751). It was probably not a very impressive structure; certainly by 1783 a visiting actor described it as "small, infirm, and inconvenient" (Bernard 1830, 1:199). Playbills indicate that the seating was confined to a pit, one gallery and boxes.

Hamilton and his company continued to use the Ann Street venue for the 1778–79 and 1779–80 seasons. The following season, however, Hamilton left Belfast and was engaged at Dublin's Smock Alley theatre, where he played secondary and tertiary parts. Then, at the end of the 1779–80 season, Hamilton organized a strolling company that toured the Irish provinces.

During Hamilton's absence Michael Atkins returned to Belfast and resumed management of the Belfast theatre, a position he was to retain without interruption until the end of the century. At the beginning of the 1780–81 season, Atkins's company performed at the Ann Street playhouse, which he may have leased from Hamilton. The company continued there for all or part of a further three seasons, when, in the summer of 1783 Atkins undertook to move to the Rosemary Lane Theatre.

Atkins's reasons for leaving Ann Street are not clear, but circumstances strongly suggest that Hamilton again was challenging him for the direction of Belfast stage and that there was a struggle for possession of the theatre. In *BNL* 13–17 June 1783 the following advertisement appeared:

> Theatre Ann Street Belfast. Myrton Hamilton with the utmost respect begs leave to inform the ladies and gentlemen of Belfast that as the theatre in Ann Street being at times too small for the reception of the audience proposes to enlarge it by subscription on the following plan. That each subscriber shall pay ten guineas for which he shall be entitled to one transferable ticket to admit one person to the pit for each performance for ten years the benefits excepted. No more than twenty subscribers to be received. The proprietor binds himself to make the theatre ten feet wider and five feet higher than it

now is and to have it boxed round after the manner of Smock Alley Theatre with a box-room in the front for servants to wait in. The subscription-money to be deposited in the hands of one of the subscribers as the proprietor of said theatre at his sole expence prepared it in the best manner the size would admit of for the reception of the publick. The old house in Mill Street being a disgrace to the drama he therefore flatters himself this second improvement will meet with their approbation.

Hamilton clearly still owned the Ann Street theatre and hoped to re-establish himself as a proprietor in Belfast. This advertisement suggests that the Ann Street company was playing to packed houses (under Atkins) and needed to be enlarged to accommodate the growing audiences. It is clear from the proposed improvements that the theatre had only a limited number of boxes (suggesting a more genteel audience was demanding such seating) and those were probably located at the back of the pit area and did not extend around the pit, as was the case at Smock Alley theatre in Dublin.

In the event, Hamilton was unable to attract the subscription money he needed, and he gave up the idea, returning to England in the autumn. Atkins, no longer interested in Hamilton's property, moved to Rosemary Street. The Ann Street theatre continued to be used occasionally for amateur theatricals and other forms of entertainment until the summer of 1785.

Rosemary Lane Theatre (1784–1792).

By June 1783, at the very time that Hamilton was starting his subscription drive, Atkins arranged with two Belfast merchants, John Ewing and John Holmes, to lease from them a new theatre. These businessmen agreed to build the outside structure; Atkins was to finish the interior (*Drennan*, letter no. 85, 17 June 1783). Atkins raised the money he needed for his part of the project by subscription, and in mid-June he informs his subscribers that he has "taken a lot of ground in Rosemary Lane an exellent and central situation and assures them that the theatre will be opened early in the ensuing winter. From his experience of the liberality of the Belfast audience he is determined to spare no trouble or expence to render the building for beauty and convenience equal to any house in the kingdom. He will also make the capital engagement in regard to his performers. It shall be his constant study by the most attention to prove himself as deserving as possible of so respectable a countenance as that of the inhabitants of Belfast" (*BNL* 13–17 June 1783).

Mulholland's 1788 "Map of the Town of Belfast" indicates that the "Theatre" was located on the south side of Rosemary Lane almost directly across from the present First Presbyterian Church. To enter the theatre one walked through what was later called the "Old Playhouse Gate" and down a passage on the east side of the building to the door, which seems to have been located at the south end of the theatre. The probable dimensions of the theatre were "95 feet long and 32 feet wide in the clear" (*BNL* 16–19 Oct. 1792).

On 3 March 1784 the Rosemary Lane Theatre opened, admission to the boxes 3s., pit 2s. and gallery 1s. A correspondent who attended the opening night wrote in *The Belfast Mercury* of 5 March that "The Theatre when lit up has a beautiful appearance; a delicate taste is displayed in the ornamental panels around the audience part of the house. . . ." The scenery and the stage finishing surpasses "anything of the kind the city of Dublin can at present exhibit." The building was not without defect, however. A writer in *The Belfast Newsletter* observed: "The entrance is not as convenient as might be wished, and there is only one passage thro' the pit, and that one too narrow for the present mode of female dress" (*BNL* 5 Mar. 1784).

Just as Atkins was preparing to open the Rosemary Lane theatre for the 1784–85 season it was rumored that a wind storm had damaged its roof, and Atkins was forced to delay performing for several weeks. He employed the Belfast architects Dunlap and Mulholland to survey the building, and they certified to the public in the newspaper that the building was "perfectly secure" (*BNL* 16 Nov. 1784). Atkins used the opportunity that closing afforded to add a new "lattice" or gallery-level box on each side of the stage, and he also augmented the stage decorations and scenery (*BNL* 10 Dec. 1784). Later that season he undertook some further refurbishment of the building, perhaps in anticipation of the impending visit of the popular actress Sarah Siddons. The net effect was a theatre "vastly handsomer than many of the Dublin Theatres" (*BNL* 7 June 1785).

For several years thereafter, Atkins went back to his earlier policy of performing in the Derry and Belfast theatres in alternate seasons: the 1785–86, 1787–88, and 1789–90 seasons in Derry, returning to the Rosemary Lane theatre in 1786–87, 1788–89, and 1790–91 seasons.

When Atkins reopened the theatre in October 1790 the public began to complain about the dilapidated and unclean state of the playhouse. The ladies's gowns were being soiled or destroyed by "the quantities of dirt and dust which are suffered to remain for months." The lighting is poor and messy: "The chandeliers are too few, and so contrived that the tallow runs out of them." Those in the boxes are regularly spattered with "quantities of punch and other liquors" which fall "in copious showers" on their unoffending heads from the "ill-ceiled" gallery. The seats in the boxes "consist of ill planed boards, destitute of covering. In short, everything in the boxes is finished in the shabbiest style . . . the boxes being a number of dark caverns without any illumination from the rear. . . and hung with some dirty stuff the color of which is no longer to be ascertained . . . ." (*BNL* 2 Nov. 1790). Atkins promised to remedy the situation in the newspaper (*BNL* 5 Nov. 1790).

Instead of going to Derry as was his custom, Atkins remained in Belfast for the 1791–92 season. Despite his promises the previous autumn to make substantial improvements to the Rosemary Street playhouse, it is now seems clear that he was already well advanced with plans to abandon that theatre for a new one in Arthur Street. Atkins continued to stage plays at the Rosemary Lane playhouse to the end of that season, the last performance there being recorded for 30 March 1792.

The *BD*, 1:166 says: "After a survey determined that structural defects in the Rosemary Lane house were irreparable, Atkins once more canvassed the town for support and laid the foundations stone of the Arthur Street Theatre on 7 September 1791." Neither Lawrence, Clark nor I can find any record of such a "survey." Perhaps this is a confusion with the collapse of the floor of the Arthur Street theatre in 1794 (*BNL* 28 Nov.–1 Dec. 1794).

Two months later, Atkins offered to lease the "shell of the Theatre in Rosemary Lane" along with the yard, house, and lofts (*BNL* 11–15 May 1792). Evidently, Atkins was successful in transferring his lease, for in the *BNL* 16–19 Oct. 1792 one David Tomb inserts an advertisement offering: "To be let from the 1st of November next for such term of years as may be agreed on, the old play-house in Rosemary Lane which being a very extensive building 95 feet long and 32 feet wide in the clear would answer well for carrying on the cotton manufacture or a warehouse." Again, in *BNL* 31 Jan. 1800 "the lease of the Old Theatre" located "in the rear" of a dwelling house in the Parade "adjoining the present residence of Gen. Drummond" was offered to the public indicating that the building was still in existence at that time (see also *BNL* 25 Feb. 1800).

Arthur Street Theatre (1793–1871).

By 13 September 1791, when the *Belfast Newsletter* formally announced the laying of the cornerstone of the Arthur Street playhouse, Atkins had raised a substantial amount of money for that purpose by offering private subscriptions to Belfast's civic leaders. In exchange for a subscription of £100 each, they were to receive a silver token granting admission to the boxes in perpetuity (Lawrence, "The Old Belfast Stage").

Similar to the arrangement he had made years earlier with the Rosemary Lane theatre, Atkins contracted to lease from the builders, John Ewing and John Holmes, "the new messuage or tenement, then lately erected, the same . . . intended for a Playhouse and Theatre and Dressing

Rooms and Apartments," for the annual rent of £66. 9s. 3d. plus "four Passes or Tickets to the Play on every night of entertainment during the said term, or in default of rendering the said Passes or Tickets, at the yearly rent of £100." The lease was to run for a period of seventy-eight years from 1 May 1792 (*NS* 2 Mar. 1793). Atkins evidently paid for the decoration of the interior of the building with his own and his subscribers' money.

A correspondent in the *BNL* 9–13 Sept. 1791 describes the laying of the cornerstone:

> New Theatre. On Wednesday last [7 September] the first stone was laid of an elegant new theatre in this town. The situation is excellent the front of the building being in Arthur Street extending sixty feet and containing two very handsome entrances for the box and pit audiences. The approach to the gallery and stage are to be in Castle Lane which side of the theatre will extend eighty four feet. Mr. Atkins seems determined to spare no expence to render it not only very commodious but in very respect one of the handsomest buildings of its kind in the kingdom. The boxes, lattices, pit, gallery, halls, passages, lobbies, staircases are all contrived in a superior stile so as to conduce to the convenience of both audience and actors. There are eight dressing-rooms and a large convenient green-room. The pit is admirably contrived as to its entrance, and on the most crouded night persons sitting on the first seat cannot be prevented from seeing by others standing before them as the passage by the orchestra is considerably below the platform or floor which contains the seats. The scenery and machinery will move on the construction of those in London; they will be very large and give ample scope for the display of Mr. Atkins pencil.

But in the early spring of 1792 Atkins's new theatre and even his managership in Belfast came under threat from the Dublin proprietor, Richard Daly. In 1786 Daly had secured a patent from the Lord Lieutenant entitling him to be sole proprietor of the theatre in Dublin. He soon acquired control of the Cork, Limerick, Waterford and Newry playhouses, and evidently had his eye on the one in Belfast. A petition in the correspondence of the Earl of Charlemont, the Lord Lieutenant of the day, written by Dr. Haliday, one of the principal Belfast subscribers, indicates that Atkins and the Arthur Street subscribers sought to preempt Daly's invasion by requesting a patent of their own for the Belfast theatre. Haliday argues not about the legality of Daly's attempt but only that Daly is a theatrical "Tyrant eager to invade foreign Territories" and that, on the other hand, Atkins is "universally esteem'd as a good and just man, and a humane, liberal manager. . . " (Charlemont, No. 75). Whether this carried any weight in the matter is not now known. Atkins did not receive a patent, but Daly did not take over the Belfast theatre either.

Compared to the speed with which the former Belfast theatres were constructed, work on the Arthur Street playhouse proceeded very slowly. Nearly eighteen months after the ground-breaking the *Northern Star* of 6 February 1793 describes the new Arthur Street Theatre:

> As this building is nearly finished, and will in a few days be opened with great eclat, we present our readers with the following description of it: The front of the Theatre facing Ann Street is in length sixty feet, and the side or depth of it in Castle Lane is eighty five. The approaches to it every way are extremely convenient for carriages, and the several entrances for the audience and actors are well contrived, as the box and pit doors are in the front, and the gallery and stage doors are in the side of the house, so that in going in or coming out, the people will not in the least incommode each other. The amphitheatre (or part which contains the audience) is laid out with great taste and judgment. It forms a perfect semicircle, and so contrived that from the very last or uppermost seat of the gallery, the spectator has as good a view as from the front of the boxes or pit. The boxes are roomy and comfortable, and the geometrical staircases to the lattices or upper boxes are very handsome and convenient. The paintings and ornaments are in an entire new style and are executed with great neatness. The stage boxes, in particular, are very elegant and commodious. The Stage is large, and great taste has been displayed in the erection of the scenery; and when the house is lighted (which we hear will be done by glass lustres), it must have a most elegant and brilliant effect.

Atkins opened the Arthur Street Theatre for the first time on 25 February 1793. The opening night was inauspicious, being disturbed by repeated calls from the gallery for "*Ça ira*," the French revolutionary song. Although Atkins apparently tried to remain aloof from the current political turmoil, the recent decision by the Dublin administration to disband the Belfast Volunteers because of their overt support for the French Revolution lead to frequent disruption of performances for the remainder of the season and caused Atkins to decide against opening his new theatre for the 1793–94 season, preferring to act in Derry instead.

At the beginning of the 1794–95 season the newspapers announced that Atkins was "retouching and adding to the decorations of his beautiful theatre" (*NS* 25 Sept. 1794). Perhaps this was in response to the sentiments expressed in a letter to *The Belfast Newsletter* soon after the theatre's opening in which it was remarked that: "The manner in which Mr. Atkins has prepared his new theatre does much honour to his taste, as no expense has been spared in its decoration. The stair leading to the Boxes is, however, quite too narrow, an error which he will no doubt endeavour to correct.

Were a second stair practicable, the inconvenience arising from the present one might be obviated" (26 Mar. 1793).

Scarcely had the season got under way when Atkins was forced to make further, unexpected repairs to his theatre. *BNL* 7–10 Nov. 1794 reports that

> on Friday the Theatre being extremely crowded the flooring of a great part of the pit gave way and sunk to the level of the ground. The confusion occasioned by it in every part of the house may be easily conceived. Happily no limbs were broken though the risque was great. The passages leading to the boxes and gallery as well as the door into the pit should as far as possible be widened as a press of people in cases of alarm might have serious consequences. In the present instance the audience chiefly remained in their places. We cannot entertain a doubt that the pit will be rebuilt in such a manner as forever to prevent a similar disaster and we would think it advisable for the manager after it is done to publish the opinion of an architect as to the strength both of it and of the galleries for the purpose of doing away the fears of any who will not themselves examine them. It is alleged that the present gloom of the boxes might be removed by sinking the chandeliers some inches lower than their present stations.

Atkins closed the playhouse for about a week after the collapse of the pit floor, and, preliminary to opening again on 19 November, he took the advise of the correspondent in the newspaper and called in architects to vouch for the safety of the theatre. Evidently, they were not happy with what they found during their first inspection, but the *BNL* 28 Nov.–1 Dec. 1794 printed the following statement:

> Being called on to inspect into the security of the Belfast theatre and to give such instructions as we could see necessary for the safety of the audience we now on a second examination find everything done according to the directions given. [signed] Roger Mulholland and Hugh Dunlap.

On the same day Atkins told the public that he was making all necessary repairs to guarantee the safety of the public and also the suggested lowering of the candelabra or lustres which, he states, will add "to the Brilliancy of the Amphitheatre" (*NS* 1 Dec. 1794).

Because of increasing civil disorder in Belfast during the summer and autumn of 1795, Atkins evidently decided again to delay the opening of the Arthur Street theatre, preferring to act in Derry. When he finally commenced performing in Belfast on 17 February 1796 it was for an abbreviated season. The following autumn Belfast was in a violently disordered state, which only worsened the following year, when marshall law was declared. The Belfast theatre was dark for three full seasons, and was not opened until 9 December for the 1799–1800 season, when, again, performances were frequently disrupted by political agitation.

Michael Atkins continued to manage the Arthur Street playhouse until the end of the 1805 season when he sold his interest in the theatre and company to Thomas Ludford Bellamy. The Arthur Street Theatre continued in use until well into the nineteenth century and was only demolished in 1871.

Admission Prices

The cost of admission to the theatres in Belfast remained fairly constant over the course of the century. Small theatres that had only a pit and gallery, such as the Vaults and Mill Gate, charged 2s. 2d. and 1s. 1d., respectively, for places. The Ann Street Theatre charged 2s. 3d. for its boxes, 1s. 6d. for the pit, and 9d. for the gallery. At Rosemary Lane boxes and lattices cost 3s. 3d., pit 2s. 2d., and gallery 1s. 1d. For special occasions, such as charity benefits or the visits of "stars," the prices were advanced to boxes 5s. 5d., pit 3s. 3d., gallery 2s. 2d. Arthur Street ordinary admission prices were boxes 3s. 3d., pit 2s. 2d., gallery 2s. 2d., which prices held until the end of the century.

Curtain Time

The first mention of performance time is at the beginning of the 1754–55 season at the Vaults when it is stressed that the "The ladies and gentlemen may depend upon the curtain being drawn up punctually at seven o'clock." Succeeding notices indicate that as a rule the doors opened at 6 and the play began at 7 o'clock. Occasionally, the program began earlier, as was the case in July 1770 when Thomas Ryder announced that on his benefit night on which a long program would be presented "the curtain will rise at a quarter before seven and the performance will be over at eleven." Similarly, in the spring of 1776, at a time of year when in Ireland daylight is of longer duration, an advertisement for a Masonic benefit states: "On account of the extraordinary length of the entertainments the door will be opened at half an hour after five and the curtain will rise precisely half an hour past seven o'clock to whatever company shall be then in the House."

The Theatrical Season

Belfast rarely enjoyed a regular theatre season of the kind typical in Dublin or London, where plays were performed from mid-October until mid-June, Monday through Saturday, excluding Holy Week and other important religious holidays. Strolling companies tended to visit Belfast for a few weeks or months before moving on to other provincial towns, and no pattern is discernable in their nights of performing. Late in the century Michael Atkins's relatively permanent company generally tended to act most frequently on Monday, Wednesday and Thursday.

Acting Companies

Although the terms are often used synonymously by theatre historians, in Ireland a distinction must be made between "strolling" and "touring" theatre companies. Strolling companies were comprised of actors, usually of the second or third rate (and often novices), who had little or no "regular" employment at major theatres in Dublin or in Britain and who lived a peripatetic existence between the medium-sized towns of Ireland, and the British provinces, performing sporadically in whatever venues they could hire for a few nights. Judging from the few surviving Irish playbills, these companies usually numbered from 12 to 15 performers with the ratio of men to women being about 3 to 1, and had at their head a person of some reputation who functioned as actor-manager and whose notoriety could be depended on to attract audiences. The actresses were almost always married and acted with their husbands.

Not surprisingly, most strolling companies were ephemeral. The short-lived strolling companies to visit Belfast during this period were those headed by James Love (1751–52 and 1752–53); Richard Elrington (1754–55); William Dawson (1757–58); Bloomer (1762–63); and Richard Knipe (1765–66; 1771–72). The company of actors "from the Theatres of Dublin" that William Dawson brought to Belfast in the summer of 1761 is perhaps somewhat problematical in this regard because few of the actors had actually worked in Dublin. Thomas Ryder, who came to Belfast for only one season (1769–70), had, nevertheless, headed a company of strollers that traveled between Drogheda, Waterford, Kilkenny, Sligo, Galway, Derry, Cork and Newry between 1765 and 1770.

The touring company was a different phenomenon. In its purest form the touring company is typified by the troupes that Dublin-based managers, such as Henry Mossop, Richard Daly and Frederick Jones, sent on an annual circuit to theatres that they owned or leased in Cork, Waterford, Limerick and elsewhere. Normally, they spent the bulk of the summer and autumn in the larger city of Cork, paying visits of a few weeks to the other cities, usually at the time of the annual horse races or assizes, when the towns could reasonably expected to be full.

Touring companies were usually composed of actors who were regular employees of the Dublin Theatres Royal. These stock actors were frequently augmented by visiting "stars" from London or provincial British theatres. In general, touring companies were larger than strolling companies, comprising about 25 actors, or about one-half of the regular Dublin company.

The absence of a proprietary relationship between the Belfast theatre and the Dublin Theatres Royal usually precluded the visits of the touring companies of the type just described, but not of a second form of touring company, as seen in James Parker's company of "Comedians from the Theatres Royal of London, Dublin, and Edinburgh" (1768–69; 1770–71). While it might be argued that Parker's actors were really only a better class of stroller, it is nevertheless true that the bulk of the actors he engaged had played at a major theatre in an earlier season and were to return to a major urban company soon thereafter.

Michael Atkins's company, which had a monopoly on Belfast theatricals from 1771 to the end of the century, is yet a third type of theatre company. Atkins's company acted in the theatres that he had built in both Belfast and Derry, and, as a rule, performed in one or the other of these towns (with short visits to neighboring towns, such as Lisburn) in alternate seasons. Starting with an established core of regulars who performed almost exclusively in the north of Ireland, the manager attracted to Belfast actors who had not been engaged by the touring company of the Dublin Theatre Royal and also the occasional "star," who, as a part of his or her own tour of Ireland and provincial Britain, was usually en route to or from Scotland via Belfast. Later in the century, actors under contract to the Theatre Royal sometimes received permission from the Dublin manager to make limited engagements of a week or two in Belfast during the regular season.

Conditions of Employment

Very little evidence has survived about the contractual arrangements that pertained between performers and managers in Belfast, and most of what follows is surmise based on contemporary custom and practice elsewhere. In Dublin and London, actors above the rank of supernumerary (who were paid daily wages) signed formal articles with the manager. These generally stipulated the duration of the engagement (usually the entire season), the number of nights each week the actor would perform, and the nightly or weekly salary. Specified in the articles, too, was the number of benefits to which the actor was entitled, whether the benefit was to be shared, and the approximate date for which the benefit would be scheduled.

Principal actors generally received one or two benefits each season, secondary actors one benefit, to be taken shortly before Easter (the recipient to pay his own advertising costs), and tertiary actors took one benefit, shared with one or two others of their status. Principal actors generally chose their own benefit plays, while lesser personnel were assigned theirs by the manager.

Strolling companies generally could not exact such rigid commitments as these, and it seems that in lieu of regular salaries strolling players received shares of the nightly receipts, prorated to their standing in the company and after deductions for operating expenses (the manager usually taking the lion's share). The relatively large number of benefit performances that have survived for Belfast (they make up a significant proportion of the surviving record) indicates that in general most actors, of whatever rank, were entitled to an individual benefit, the profits from which must have constituted the bulk of the emolument they received from their time in the city.

The Repertory

Many more performances took place in the Belfast theatres than are recorded. We can only speculate about how many more because Belfast managers placed relatively few advertisements in newspapers, and, as I observed above, Belfast did not have a regular theatre season or set nights of performance from which we might deduce a number of evenings of playing. Evidently, the relatively small size of the Belfast theatre audience allowed the theatre managers to content themselves with advertising their programs by means of ephemera, such as handbills, broadsides, and announcements after performances, with the result that the performance record is commensurately incomplete.

The repertory for the Belfast theatre is generally too fragmentary to yield much to analysis, and the few seasons for which the performance record is relatively abundant cannot be considered typical. In the seasonal entries in the calendar below, I have discussed any plays or events that I have found to be interesting or unusual. Nevertheless, a few cautious generalizations about the Belfast repertory may be made.

An analysis of the 280 different, named mainpieces (ca. 140) and afterpieces (ca. 140) performed in Belfast during the eighteenth century indicates that from the outset the audiences expected the program to consist of a mainpiece, an afterpiece and entr'acte entertainments, as had been the case in Dublin since the 1720s. Here it should also be noted that Belfast advertisements were sometimes imprecise about the titles of plays and afterpieces that were to be performed, and the calendar includes about 40 unnamed mainpieces and over 65 unnamed afterpieces. Aside from the rare original composition by a local playwright, Belfast audiences generally were content to watch the plays that were popular elsewhere, and the repertory varied little from those of Dublin or the other larger provincial cities, consisting predominately of tried-and-true stock plays, interspersed occasionally with new pieces that had recently been successful in Dublin and London. Strolling companies from Dublin or further abroad who paid short visits to Belfast tended to bring with them relatively large numbers of new pieces. In times when a settled company controlled the theatre for more extended periods the fare tended to be more standard and conservative.

In terms of the total number of performances of plays, the most popular playwright during this era in Belfast, both in comedy and tragedy, was William Shakespeare. Sixteen of his plays are known to have been performed, constituting about one-seventh of all recorded performances (ca. 114 nights). In Belfast his most-performed plays were *Romeo and Juliet* (23 nights), *Hamlet* (21 nights), and *Richard III* (14 nights).

Aside from Shakespeare's, only about 25 named tragedies were staged, representing about 140 performances or roughly 15% of the total and 16% of the total number of mainpieces. Not surprisingly, the bulk of the performances of non-Shakespearean tragedy were of works of the Restoration and early eighteenth century, such as Otway's *Venice Preserved* and *The Orphan*, Rowe's *The Fair Penitent* and *Jane Shore*, Philips's *The Distrest Mother*, Young's *The Revenge*, and Congreve's *The Mourning Bride*, although a few later writers of serious drama, such as Home (*Douglas*), Lillo (*The London Merchant*), Moore (*The Gamester*) and Murphy (*The Grecian Daughter*), enjoyed considerable success in Belfast, as they had in Dublin and London.

After mid-century, three-act comic operas became fairly popular: Bickerstaffe's *Lionel and Clarissa* was performed no fewer than fifteen times and his *Love in a Village* nearly as often. We have record of Colman's *Inkle and Yarico* being performed seven times, but it was almost certainly staged much more often. Gay's *The Beggar's Opera* (15 times) remained a perennial favorite, although during the century it was not the most frequently performed mainpiece in Belfast, as it was in London and Dublin.

Very popular forms of play in Belfast during this time were one- and two-act afterpieces that were termed, variously, ballad operas, musical entertainments, burlettas, or operettas. Chief among these, the most frequently performed play in Belfast during the eighteenth century, was the Coffey/Mottley ballad opera, *The Devil to Pay* (20 nights), followed closely by Kane O'Hara's burletta, *Midas* (16 nights). It seems likely that these pieces owed some of their popularity to the fact that both playwrights were Irishmen. Other popular musical afterpieces with Irish connections were the Bickerstaffe/Dibdin comic opera *The Padlock* (17 nights) and the Frances Brooke/William Shield collaboration, *Rosina* (12 nights). All of these plays had also enjoyed considerable success in Dublin and London.

Comedy was by far the most popular form of theatrical entertainment in Belfast, representing about 65% of the pieces staged, although no single mainpiece appears to have been wildly popular. Gay's *The Beggar's Opera* shared the honors with Cibber/Vanbrugh's *The Provoked Husband* as the most frequently performed comic mainpiece. A handful of other full-length comedies, new and old, received ten or more performances: Hoadly's *The Suspicious Husband* (13), Farquhar's *The Beaux' Stratagem* (14), Fielding's *The Miser* (13), Colman's *The Jealous Wife* (10). New and old full-length plays that had been very popular in Dublin and London also were performed in Belfast, but the surviving record indicates that they were performed fewer than ten times during the period: Murphy's *All in the Wrong* (7), Mrs. Cowley's *The Belle's Stratagem* (6), Mrs. Centlivre's *The Busy Body* (9), Garrick and Colman's *The Clandestine Marriage* (8), Steele's *The Conscious Lovers* (6), Farquhar's *The Constant Couple* (9), *The Inconstant* (5), and *The Recruiting Officer* (7), Cumberland's *The Fashionable Lover* (9) and *The West Indian* (9), Cibber's *Love Makes a Man* (6), and, surprisingly, Sheridan's *The Rivals* (9) and *The School for Scandal* (7) and Goldsmith's *She Stoops to Conquer* (8).

The bulk of the most frequently performed plays of this period were comic afterpieces, particularly farces. Chief among these are Murphy's *The Citizen*, Garrick's *The Lying Valet* and *Miss in Her Teens*, Townley's *High Life Below Stairs*, Fielding's *The Virgin Unmasked*, and the anonymous farce *The Ghost*. It should be remembered that the Belfast record contains record of over 65 unnamed "farces." In advertisements of this period the term "farce" was synonymous with "afterpiece," so there were obviously many more performances of the above afterpieces, and of others, than can now be ascertained.

It should perhaps not surprise us that a relatively small number of pantomimes were performed in Belfast (fewer than twenty) the most important of which were *Harlequin in Derry, Giant's Causeway, The Humours of Belfast, Poor Darty's Trip to Belfast,* and *Rambles Through Belfast.* As Clark has observed (1965, 290) these probably "presented little more than an amusing depiction of local settings and manners." Pantomimes were notoriously expensive to produce and required a troupe of specialist performers, machinists, and scene painters. Most of the pantomimes that were performed in Belfast were brought there by strolling companies, such as those of James Parker, George Dawson, and Thomas Ryder, all of whom wrote pantomimes and many of whose performers seem to have specialized in the form. On the other hand, Michael Atkins also probably wrote pantomimes for his resident company, and most of these are not known to have been performed again outside of Belfast.

Even if we include the anonymous pantomimes mentioned above, very few plays written by local playwrights were performed in Belfast. Those that had their debut performances in Belfast were Brownlow Forde's *The Miraculous Cure*, Mr. Eccles's, *The World*, Dr. Maryat's *Love in a Bog* and Dr. Bambridge's *The Guillotine; or, The Death of Louis XVI*. None of these was published or is known to have been performed outside of Belfast.

THE CALENDAR 1736–1800

1736–1737 through 1748–1749 SEASONS

Before 1750 the record of theatrical activity in Belfast is extremely fragmentary. From as early as 1730 Belfast possessed a theatre (antedated only by Dublin and Cork), called "The Vaults" (suggesting converted wine vaults), but the first recorded performance in Belfast took place on Friday, 17 July 1736, when members of Dublin's Smock Alley Theatre company visited The Vaults.

17 July 1736: Fri. *The Beaux' Stratagem.*
[Published in Belfast by James Magee in 1764 and 1767].

While it is probable that, in the interim, plays were staged in Belfast by strolling companies and by Dublin players, the next evidence of theatrical activity surfaces in 1741 when the Smock Alley Company again visited Belfast, possibly as a part of an established annual summer circuit of northern towns.

Spring or Summer, 1741: The Smock Alley Theatre players Elizabeth Furnival and Thomas Phillips are known to have performed in Belfast this season, but neither the names of the plays staged nor their roles in them has survived. The Smock Alley company's last Dublin performance this season took place on 30 May, so the Belfast performance presumably occurred after that date. Source: Clark 1965, 217

1749–1750 SEASON

The next surviving record of Belfast theatricals, and the first playbill found in *The Belfast Newsletter,* appeared in the issue for 2 January 1749/50 and is the only performance known to have taken place this season, but Belfast newspapers for the year 1750 are completely lacking.

Venue: The Vaults.
Company: Clark (1965, 218) suggests that the principals listed were "local professionals": Dougan [or Dugan] and Miss Quin are the only actors of

whom we have record. Clearly, more performances took place than the one of which we have record.

3   Jan. 1750 Wed. By permission of the worshipful Sovereign Belfast for the benefit of Mr. Dugan and Miss Quin. *The London Merchant.* Thorowgood–Dougan; Millwood–Miss Quin. The rest of the parts by young gentlemen who never appeared on a publick stage. [Published in Belfast by James Magee in 1764 and 1778]. With *Flora*. [Published in Belfast by James Magee in 1763]. With several entertainments of singing and dancing between the acts. A Prologue on the Occasion. To begin exactly at 6 o'clock. Source: 2 Jan. 1749/1750

1750–1751 SEASON

[The Belfast Theatre was dark].

1751–1752 SEASON

Venue: The Vaults.
Company: Playbills in Shaw Collection, Harvard University Library, indicate that this season a company of "Comedians from the Theatres of London and Dublin" were in Belfast, including, Brown; Bushby; Mr. and Mrs. Tobias Gemea; Guitar; Mr. and Mrs. James Love; Mr. and Mrs. William Lewis; Philip Lewis; Master Lewis; Phillipson; Master Sennet; Mr. and Mrs. Samuel Tyrer.

This company was under the management of **James Love**, an English "gentleman" actor and erstwhile law student. Born in London as James Dance, he first appeared on the London stage at some time before 1744 and acted occasionally in London and in the provinces, adopting the stage name of Love at some point before 1751. At about this time Love became involved in the management of strolling companies. This season in Belfast was evidently his first Irish venture. According to the *BD*, Love also performed during this time at Newry, and in 1752 "sold his Irish company" to William and Philip Lewis. Love made his first Dublin appearance at Smock Alley in 1754 and then returned to Scotland, ending his association with Ireland.

Love spent the remainder of his long career at the London theatres and managing companies in Scotland and in the British provinces. Love is perhaps best remembered for establishing the summer theatre at Richmond Green in 1766 which he managed until his death in 1777.

Mrs. Love was, according to the *BD*, "not the woman Dance had married in 1739 when he was enrolled at Lincoln's Inn" but perhaps a Mrs. L'Amour for whom Dance had abandoned his legal wife, children and name. In addition to performing in minor roles with Dance's strolling company, she acted in the English and Irish provinces with her "husband" before being engaged at Drury Lane in 1762. She was evidently a bad actress and performed only occasionally in London, although she appeared more regularly at Love's theatre in Richmond. She continued to act in minor roles even after Love's death and seems to have performed in London as late as 1790. She died in 1807.

The brothers **William** and **Philip Lewis** were the sons of a Welsh clergyman. Little is known about their early careers. Accompanying William in Belfast this year were his wife and their young son, who was later to become the famous actor "Gentleman" Lewis. In 1751 the brothers purchased the Newry company of actors from James Love. When William suddenly died shortly before 27 July 1753, his widow married the long-time Irish manager and actor William Dawson later that year. Philip then sold the Newry company and returned to England where for a time he had considerable success on the London stage. He returned to Ireland frequently and played in Dublin and other cities until as late as 1788.

Tobias Gemea is first recorded in Dublin in 1740 at Aungier Street Theatre, and he and his wife, Richabella, played at Smock Alley during the 1746–47 season during which the two acted secondary roles, usually in comedy. Gemea performed in Belfast during 1751–52, 1753, 1761, (April–July) 1770 and in Waterford and Kilkenny in the winter of 1773. In the 1765–66 Smock Alley season Gemea (or perhaps his son) is serving as prompter at Smock Alley but not acting. In the 1767–68 and 1770–71 seasons a Gemea was acting tertiary roles at Smock Alley, but this too may have been the son. Thereafter, Tobias Gemea disappears from the record.

Mrs. Gemea acted in Belfast 1751–52, 1753, 1758, 1759, 1761, and, perhaps, (April–July) 1770. She (but not her husband) is found in Dublin in 1758–59 and then in 1765–66.

The first recorded appearances of **Mr.** and **Mrs. Samuel Tyrer** took place in Belfast 1751, where they acted again in 1753, and in Tralee in 1756. Clark (1965, 375) errs in ascribing Tyrer's first Dublin performance to 1770 at Capel Street. In fact, he made his first appearance on 21 October 1765 at Smock Alley in the role of Peachum in *The Beggar's Opera*. Tyrer appeared at Capel Street through the 1771–72 and 1772–73 seasons after which he disappears from the record. His wife is not mentioned in the Dublin bills.

The rope dancer and equilibrist **William Guitar** is first noticed as a member of Madam German's (Garman) company of "celebrated Germans, Dutch, Italians, and French" equilibrists who leased Smock Alley theatre for a few weeks before the beginning of the 1742–43 season, although he probably had some experience performing in London before that time. Although the record is sketchy, he appeared in Dublin and in the Irish provinces sporadically but with considerable success until 1776.

The other performers listed in this season's playbills: **[Henry?] Brown**, **Bushby**, and **Master Sennet**, were evidently supernumeraries. Nothing is known about Bushby and Master Sennet. Brown may have been Henry Brown who was later associated with the Bath and Edinburgh theatres and who managed Smock Alley theatre for a time in the 1760s. Brown acted in Dublin and traveled to Newry in January, and then to Kilkenny and Cork. In September 1769 the record of his acting ends. He probably left Ireland, perhaps for the Scottish theatres, for in February 1770 the newspapers announced his death in Glasgow. See 1768–69 season.

Repertory, 1751–1752 Season

There were certainly many more performances this season than the two that survive.

Unspecified Monday night. *The Merry Wives of Windsor*. Falstaff–Love; Sir Hugh Evans–Lewis; Slender–Gemea; Ford–Phillipson; Page–Brown; Host–Tyrer; Fenton–Howard; Simple–Bushby; Rugby–Master Sennet; Robin–Master Lewis; Shallow–P. Lewis; Dr. Caius–Guitar; Anne Page–Mrs. Love; Mrs. Quickly–Mrs. Gemea; Mrs. Page–Mrs. Tyrer; Mrs. Ford–Mrs. Lewis. And *The Honest Yorkshireman*. Gaylove–Lewis; Sapscull–Tyrer; Muckworm–P. Lewis; Slango–Gemea; Blunder–Love; Servant–Bushby; Combrush–Mrs. Gemea; Arabella–Mrs. Love. No children or servants admitted without paying. No Gentleman will attempt to come behind the Curtain or into the Day Room this Night on any account whatever; the play being so extremely full of Business that but the presence of a single person behind the Scenes must greatly disconnect the Representation. [*The Honest Yorkshireman* was published in Belfast by James Magee in 1740, 1747 and 1758]. Source: undated Harvard playbill

December 1751

18 Wed.   *Jane Shore* and *The Virgin Unmasked*. Principal parts by Mr. and Mrs. Tobias Gemea, Mr. and Mrs. William Lewis, Mr. and Mrs. Love, and Mr. and Mrs. Tyrer. Source: undated Harvard playbill

1752–1753 SEASON

Venue: The Vaults. After 15 June the bills no longer refer to the theatre as "The Vaults" (until the name reappears as the principal venue six years later during the 1757–58 season). Since there is no record of any other theatre being built or used in the interim, it is here assumed that The Vaults continued in use throughout this period.

Company: Miss Dennisson; William Dawson; Mr. and Mrs. Tobias Gemea; Mrs. Layfield; Mr. and Mrs.William Lewis; Mr. and Mrs. James Love; Philip Lewis; Master Lewis; Maurice (from Theatre Royal, Dublin), Phillipson; Mr. and Mrs. John Sherriffe [often Sheriffe]; Mr. and Mrs. Tyrer.

James Love returned to Belfast with a strolling company comprised of several of the same actors who had accompanied him to Belfast the previous season.

For biographical sketches of **Mr.** and **Mrs. Gemea, Love, William** and **Phillip Lewis**, and **Tyrer** see the 1750–51 season.

This is the first record of **William Dawson**, the long-time Dublin and provincial actor and theatre manager. Late in 1753 William Dawson married the recently widowed Mrs. William Lewis, and he and the new **Mrs. Dawson** evidently spent the next six years as strollers in Ireland and in the British provinces. Clark finds them in Tralee in 1756 and Ballymena in 1759. Dawson made his Dublin debut, with his wife, who acted occasionally, and stepson (later the popular actor William "Gentleman" Lewis) in the 1760–61 Smock Alley season. That summer Dawson and a company billed as "his Majesty's Servants from the Theatres in Dublin" played in Belfast until September. With them was **Master Dawson**, probably their son, George, who was later to become a successful actor (for his biography see 1769–70 season). The Dawsons disappear for the 1762–63 and most of the 1763–64 seasons. Dawson and his son resurfacing only in mid-May 1764. Thereafter Dawson and Master Dawson (but not

Mrs. Dawson) performed in Dublin for the 1764–65 through the 1767–68 seasons. Clark finds Mrs. Dawson in Cork in August 1766.

The whereabouts of the Dawson family are not known during the 1768–69 season, but at the beginning of the 1769–70 season William Dawson began his managerial career when he leased the Capel Street theatre with Robert Mahon. It is possible that Dawson's wife had died when she disappears from the record in 1766, and Dawson may have remarried at about this time. Mrs. Dawson's name again appears in the Capel St. playbills, but now in younger women's roles.

The following season Dawson obtained a *de facto* monopoly of Dublin theatricals when Henry Mossop was arrested for debt and imprisoned in London while on a recruiting trip there. Dawson obtained the lease of Crow St. Theatre from Barry and moved his Capel St. company to the larger house in March 1771 where they remained until June 1773, when Barry demanded that the theatre be relinquished to his possession. At the time Barry complained in the press that Dawson owed him at least £1,000 in back rent and other considerations. Dawson is found at Belfast in July 1770 and in Cork that August. In 1772 he and his wife, who is found at Derry in early October 1771, acted in Derry in July and at Cork in October.

Dawson reopened Capel St. for the 1773–74 season, Master Dawson now being billed as Dawson, Jr. At the same time a Miss Dawson, probably a daughter, joined the company. Dawson and his son disappear from the record for the next two seasons, though Mrs. Dawson and her daughter performed regularly at SA, the mother in many principal roles. On 4 July 1776 Dawson was given a benefit at Crow St., billed as "his first appearance in this city these two years."

For the next twenty years Dawson was active in Ireland as actor and manager. At Crow St. in the 1780–81 season Dawson shared the management with Crawford and Owenson, and the following season, with Glenville, Hurst, Sparks and Owenson. In January 1780 Dawson evidently had a quarrel with Glenville which led to violence, Dawson geting the worst of the encounter. At the end of the 1780–81 season he was imprisoned for debt, but was released by the beginning of the next season. Mrs. Dawson is not listed in the Dublin bills from 1781. Perhaps she died.

At the beginning of the 1782–83 season the Dawson families parted, George and his wife preferring to engage with Daly at Smock Alley. But the Crow St. partnership was on its last legs and failed before the end of that season (the theatre was not used again until 1787). Dawson, Sr. then moved to Smock Alley for a time also. From the 1783–84 through the early1786–87 seasons Dawson father and son were active at Crow St. After George Dawson's death in early December 1786 William Dawson acted occasionally at Crow St., then moved to Smock Alley the following season. That season too a "Mrs. Dawson" appears regularly at Crow St. in younger women's roles. This is the widow of George Dawson, who continues to act at Crow St. and occasionally at Fishamble St. until her death on 21 April 1803 (see 1769–70 season for her biography).

By the end of the 1791–92 season, in addition to acting with and managing the Crow Street company, Dawson assumed management of the Newry theatre. In the following four seasons he performed less frequently. William Dawson died suddenly on the night of his Crow Street benefit on 22 December 1796, having spent 40 years on the Irish stage. That he was married around the time of his death is evinced by the fact that on the first anniversary of his death a benefit was given to his "Infant Daughter" with the aim of enabling her to be bound apprentice to a trade. A Miss Dawson (perhaps Dawsons's daughter or perhaps Mrs. George Dawson's) appeared occasionally at both Crow St. and Fishamble St. theatres from this time until the 1799–1800 season, when her name disappears from the record.

Mrs. Layfield (whom Clark identifies as Mrs. Robert Layfield, wife of the long-time Dublin actor-manager) seems to have made her acting debut with the United Company at Aungier Street Theatre in the 1743–44 season. She acted infrequently, however, until 1747, at Capel Street, which her husband Robert co-managed. She and her husband appeared at Smock Alley from the 1747–48 season through 1749–50, when she disappears from the record.

A **Mr. Maurice** played at Smock Alley for the 1750–51 through 1753–54 seasons, usually in secondary and tertiary roles. He always shared a benefit with one or two others. This season in Belfast he played more important roles and received two sole benefits after which he disappears from the record.

Aside from one notice at the theatre in Richmond, Surrey, in 1750, **John Sherriffe** seems to have spent his entire career in the provinces. He is next found in Belfast this summer with his wife. Thereafter Sherriffe went to Edinburgh (1754), Bath and Drogheda (1756) before returning to Belfast and Drogheda (1758), at which time he seems to have headed a strolling company based in Newry.

The Sherriffe's only joint Dublin appearances took place during the 1758–59 Smock Alley season. The *BD* is in error when it says that he was advertised as being from Bath. Nevertheless, the following season Sherriffe did act at Bath and remained there until his death in 1774.

Sometime in the winter or spring of 1753 John Sherriffe married the former Mrs. S. Crofts (d. 1778), who is known to have been with the York company about 1748 and with her first husband in Edinburgh in 1749. Mrs. Crofts, alone, made her Dublin debut at Smock Alley on 29 January 1753, but must have married John Sherriffe soon thereafter. The *BD* says that Mrs. Crofts "may have met her future husband, John Sherriffe" during their visit to Belfast in the summer of 1753, but it is clear from the Belfast notices where she is billed as "Mrs. Sherriffe" that they were already married by that time. Thereafter her movements parallel her husband's. She continued to act at the Bath theatre after John's death in 1774 until her own in 1778. Judging from the many leading roles played by each, the Sherriffes were more than competent actors, although no objective assessment of their merits has survived.

This is the only record of **Miss Dennisson**. There being no evidence that she acted, and it may be that she is mentioned in the bills only as the recipient of a benefit.

Repertory, 1753 Summer Season

This is the first season for which evidence of more than a handful of performances has survived. Since most of the playbills advertise benefits, when customarily the recipients and not the manager paid the advertising costs, it is reasonable to assume that other non-benefit plays were performed but not noticed in the newspapers. Considering that at the beginning of the summer performances were billed three times weekly but soon thereafter only one performance each week is advertised, it seems likely that one or two more performances took place each week than are recorded. Thus, assuming a thrice weekly schedule, it is possible that twice as many performances took place than are recorded.

Of interest is the relatively large number of mainpieces hailed as new (11), although most of these are in fact stock plays that were performed regularly, sometimes for decades, outside of Belfast, including *The Miser, Oroonoko,* and *The Mourning Bride.* This suggests that in earlier seasons, although the number of performances was certainly larger than the record indicates, the variety of plays performed in Belfast was probably quite limited. James

Love certainly catered to a demand for novelty in the repertory, and in fact, staged two plays, *The Earl of Essex* and *The Gamester*, that had premiered in London fairly recently. Interestingly, too, Rowe's *Tamerlane*, which since the Restoration had been a loyalist staple that was performed traditionally in Dublin and London on the anniversary of the Battle of the Boyne, was evidently not performed in Belfast before this season.

Total Performances: 23, of 20 different named mainpieces and 22 of 15 different named afterpieces.

    Shakespeare: 5.

    New Mainpieces: 11.

    Afterpieces: 7.

(For a key to repertory symbols see above, page 11)

Mainpieces: *As You Like It**; *The Careless Husband*■; *The Earl of Essex**(Jones); *The Fair Penitent*†(2); *The Gamester*(2)●; *Hamlet*†; *King Richard III*†; *The Miser**; *The Mourning Bride**; *Oroonoko**; *Othello*†; *The Revenge**; *Romeo and Juliet**□; *She Would and She Would Not**; *Sir Harry Wildair*†; *The Spanish Fryar**(2); *The Suspicious Husband*†; *Tamerlane**; *Twin Rivals*†; *Venice Preserved**.

Afterpieces: *The Anatomist* †(3); *The Cobbler of Preston**; *Damon and Phillida* †; *The Devil to Pay* †; *Flora*; *The Honest Yorkshireman*; *The King and the Miller of Mansfield* †; *Lethe* †; *The Lying Valet*†(2); *Miss in Her Teens* †(2); *The Mock Doctor*†; *Tom Thumb*† (2); Unspecified farce; *The Vintner in the Suds*†; *The Virgin Unmasked*; *The What D'Ye Call It* †(2).

Entr'acte singing: 1; dancing: 1.

Benefits (12): W. R. Chetwood; Dawson; Miss Dennisson; Gemea; Mrs. Gemea; Lewis; Widow Lewis and Master Lewis; Maurice (2); Phillipson; Sherriffe; Mrs. Sherriffe.

Summer Season, 1753

June 1753

4 Mon. The Company of Comedians lately come to this Town will begin on Monday next being the anniversary of the birthday of his Royal Highness the Prince of Wales with a Tragedy called *The Fair Penitent* and a farce called *Tom Thumb*. With Singing and Dancing as will be expressed in the Bills. Source: 1 June 1753

6 Wed. At the Vaults in Belfast. Never acted here. *The Mourning Bride.* Osmyn–Sherriffe; King–P. Lewis; Almeria–Mrs. Sherriffe. With a Farce called *Tom Thumb the Great.* Source: 5 June 1753

8 Fri. *The Suspicious Husband.* With *The Lying Valet.* [*The Lying Valet* was published in Belfast by James Magee in 1762 and 1781]. Source: 5 June 1753

15 Fri. Never acted here. *Venice Preserved.* Jaffier–Sherriffe; Renault–Gemea; Pierre–Lewis; Belvidera–Mrs. Sherriffe. Source: 15 June 1753

22 Fri. Never acted here. *Romeo and Juliet.* Romeo–Sherriffe; Friar Laurence–Maurice (from the Theatre Royal in Dublin); Juliet–Mrs. Sherriffe. As it was performed twenty Nights successively at the Theatres Royal in London with a Tomb-Scene and other Decorations. [*Romeo and Juliet* was published in Belfast by James Magee in 1767]. With a Farce called *The Vintner in the Suds.* Source: 22 June 1753

29 Fri. Never acted here. *The Spanish Fryar.* Torrismond–Sherriffe; Fryar–Tyrer; Gomez–Lewis; Elvira–Mrs. Gemea; Queen–Mrs. Sherriffe. With *The King and the Miller of Mansfield.* [*The King and the Miller of Mansfield* was published in Belfast by James Magee in 1747, 1750 and in 1764]. Source: 29 June 1753

July 1753

3 Tues. (Never acted in this Kingdom). *The Gamester.* Beverley–Sherriffe; Stukely–Maurice; Charlotte–Mrs. Lewis [i.e., Mrs. William (not Philip)]; Mrs. Beverley–Mrs. Sherriffe. With the original Prologue to be spoken by Lewis. With *The Honest Yorkshireman.* Source: 3 July 1753

6 Fri. By particular desire the second night. *The Gamester.* Cast as 3 July. With the original Prologue to be spoken by Lewis; Epilogue by Mrs. Sherriffe. With *Damon and Phillida.* [*Damon and Phillida* was published in Belfast by James Magee in 1753 and 1767]. Source: 6 July 1753

13 Fri. Benefit of Maurice. Never acted here. *Tamerlane.* Bajazet–Maurice; Tamerlane–Sherriffe; Arpasia–Mrs. Sherriffe. With a Dramatic Satire called *Lethe.* [*Lethe* was published in Belfast by James Magee in 1759]. Source: 13 July 1753

19 Thur. Benefit of Gemea. Never acted here. *Oroonoko.* Oroonoko–Sherriffe; Aboan–Maurice; Daniel–Gemea; Imoinda–Mrs.

Sherriffe; Charlotte Welldon–Mrs. Lewis; Widow Lackit–Mrs. Gemea. With *Flora* and several Entertainments between the Acts as expressed in the Bill. Source: 17 July 1753

23 Mon. Benefit of Miss Dennisson. Never acted here. *As You Like It.* Orlando–Sherriffe; Jacques–Maurice; Touchstone–Lewis; Rosalind–Mrs. Sherriffe; Celia–Mrs. Gemea. With a farce called *Miss in Her Teens.* [*Miss in Her Teens* was published in Belfast by James Magee in 1751, 1761, 1775]. Source: 20 July 1753

27 Fri. Benefit of Widow Lewis and her son. Never acted here. *The Earl of Essex.* Essex–Sherriffe; Southampton–Lewis; Burleigh–Maurice; Rutland–Mrs. Sherriffe; Nottingham–Mrs. Layfield; Queen Elizabeth–Mrs. Gemea. Written by Jones. [*The Earl of Essex* was published in Belfast by James Magee in 1778]. With *The What D'Ye Call It.* Source: 27 July 1753

August 1753

2 Thur. Benefit of Lewis. *Sir Harry Wildair.* Sir Harry Wildair–Sherriffe; Col. Standard–Maurice; Beau Clincher–Tyrer; Angelica–Mrs. Gemea; Lady Lurewell–Mrs. Sherriffe. With a farce and Entertainments as will be expressed in the Bills. Source: 31 July 1753

6 Mon. Benefit of Sherriffe. *Hamlet* and *The Anatomist.* Source: Lawrence "Annals," 8.

10 Fri. Benefit of Phillipson. *The Twin Rivals.* Younger Woudbe–Maurice; Capt. Trueman–Sherriffe; Teague–Tyrer; Constance–Mrs. Gemea; Aurelia–Mrs. Sherriffe; Mother Midnight–Mrs. Layfield. With a farce called *The Anatomist.* Phillipson was desired by several of his particular Benefactors to defer his Benefit Play till this Evening and he humbly hopes the kind Indulgence and favour of the town. Source: 10 Aug. 1753

14 Tues. Benefit of Dawson. *King Richard III.* Richard–Sherriffe; King Henry–Gemea; Duke of York–Master Lewis; Richmond–Maurice; Lady Ann–Mrs. Sherriffe; Queen–Mrs. Gemea. With a farce (never acted here) *The Cobbler of Preston.* [*The Cobbler of Preston* was published in Belfast by James Magee in 1751]. Source: 14 Aug. 1753

22 Wed. Benefit of Mrs. Gemea. Never acted here. *The Miser.* Lovegold–Gemea; Mariana–Mrs. Sherriffe; Lappit–Mrs. Gemea. With *The Lying Valet.* Source: 17 Aug. 1753

24 Fri.   Benefit of Mrs. Tyrer. *The Spanish Fryar* and *The Virgin Unmasked*. Source: Lawrence "Annals," 8.

28 Tues. Benefit of Master Lewis. Never acted here. *She Would and She Would Not*. Don Manuel–Lewis; Don Philip–Sherriffe; Don Octavio–Dawson; Trappanti–Gemea; Viletta–Mrs. Gemea; Hypolita–Mrs. Sherriffe. With the farce *The What D'Ye Call It*. After the play an address to the town spoke by Master Lewis. Source: 28 Aug. 1753 [not cited in Clark]

31 Fri.   Benefit of W. R. Chetwood. Never acted here. *The Revenge*. Zanga–Maurice; Don Alvarez–Lewis; Don Manuel–Gemea; Don Alonzo–Sherriffe; Leonora–Mrs. Sherriffe. [*The Revenge* was published in Belfast by James Magee in 1779]. By particular desire a farce called *The Anatomist*. Medicine–Maurice; Crispin–Sherriffe; Beatrice–Mrs. Sherriffe. Source: 31 Aug. 1753

September 1753

7   Fri.   Benefit Mrs. Sherriffe, the last this season. Not acted here these ten years. *The Careless Husband*. Lord Foppington–Sherriffe; Sir Charles–Maurice; Lady Easy–Mrs. Gemea; Lady Betty Modish–Mrs. Sherriffe. With *Miss in Her Teens*. Fribble–Sherriffe; Captain Flash–Maurice; Miss Biddy Bellair–Mrs. Sherriffe. Source: 7 Sept. 1753

11 Tues. The last time of playing here but once. *Othello*. Othello–Sherriffe; Cassio–Tyrer; Lodovico–Maurice; Iago–Lewis; Emilia–Mrs. Lewis; Desdemona–Mrs. Sherriffe. With *The Devil to Pay*. [*The Devil to Pay* was published in Belfast by James Magee in 1763 and 1768]. Source: 11 Sept. 1753

14 Fri.   By particular desire. Benefit Maurice. *The Fair Penitent*. Horatio–Maurice; Lothario–Gemea; Sciolto–Lewis; Lavinia–Mrs. Layfield; Calista–Mrs. Gemea. With the farce *The Mock Doctor*. [*The Mock Doctor* was published in Belfast by James Magee in 1752, 1763, and 1781]. Source: 14 Sept. 1753

1753–1754 SEASON

[The Belfast theatre was dark].

1754–1755 SEASON

Venue: The Vaults.
Company: Jo[seph?] Elrington; Mr. and Mrs. Richard Elrington (actor/manager); Master Elrington; Miss Fleming; Leech; Longfield; Mrs. Mozeen; Owen; Pitt; Mr. and Mrs. Henry Ward; White.

Richard Elrington was the son of Thomas Elrington, the long-time Smock Alley manager, and the nephew of Francis, Joseph, and Ralph Elrington. The Elrington family dominated the Dublin stage during the years between 1720 and 1745, and Richard began his own career in 1729 at Smock Alley acting in lilliputian roles which line he continued in until Thomas Sheridan assumed control of that theatre in 1745. Although his uncles Joseph and Ralph Elrington remained at Smock Alley for many years, Richard seems to have preferred to wander. In 1749 he is found with a strolling company in England; he returned to Dublin for a brief period in 1750; went to Covent Garden for the 1750–51 season; he was in Bath in 1751 and probably in Manchester for the 1753–54 season. He visited Dublin, briefly, at the beginning of the 1754–55 Smock Alley season, but traveled to Belfast this season where he, his "wife" Elizabeth, and a scratch company of former Smock Alley actors performed until March 1755. They made frequent visits to Lisburn to act, and after March probably concluded the season in Derry. Thereafter, Richard Elrington seems to have given up acting. *FDJ* 17 April 1770 reports that Richard Elrington died "lately" at Ballyboughbridge.

The identity of the **"Jo. Elrington"** who acted in Belfast with Richard Elrington's strolling company this season is unclear. He could not have been the Joseph Elrington who performed in Dublin at Smock Alley for the entire 1754–55 season, frequently on the same nights as his namesake was on stage in Belfast.

The long-time Smock Alley actor-manager Thomas Elrington (d. 1732) is known to have had a brother named Joseph, and an actor of that name died in 1715. Thomas Elrington's eldest son was also named Joseph (perhaps in memory of his uncle). The Joseph Elrington who first comes into the record at Smock Alley at the beginning of the 1731–32 season, would have been of about the right age to have been Thomas Elrington's son and was very popular in Dublin around 1749. This Joseph Elrington remained with the Smock Alley company playing a wide variety of mainly secondary roles through 1755, when his name disappears from the record. Biographers have always assumed that this was Thomas's brother, Joseph. However, the death notice of Joseph Elrington, "son of the late Thomas Elrington," appears in *FDJ* 6–8 Nov. 1755.

This Joseph Elrington shared a benefit with a "Master Elrington" at the end of the 1749–50 season. Perhaps the Jo Elrington who appeared in Belfast this season was Master Jo Elrington, a son or nephew of Joseph. What adds to the puzzle is the fact that all trace of the name Joseph Elrington disappears from the record after November 1755.

The *BD* errs in stating that the "Mr. Langfield" cited in W. J. Lawrence's notes as playing in Belfast and Lisburn in the winter of 1754–55 is the Dublin actor-manager, Robert Layfield. The Belfast playbills are clear in spelling the name **"Longfield**," and an actor of that name performed regularly in Dublin at this time. The first record of Longfield is in Dublin at Smock Alley in the 1751–52 season playing secondary and tertiary roles, usually older men. He is found again at Smock Alley in 1752–53, 1755–56 (when he was given an individual benefit), in 1758–59, and finally in the 1760–61 season. Longfield again visited Belfast with William Dawson's company during the summer season of 1761 but subsequently disappears from the record.

Mrs. [Mary?] Mozeen, fl. 1724–1773, was the daughter of the English singer Thomas Edwards. She was acting at Drury Lane in a lilliputian company by 1737, and continued there as a singer for several seasons, alternating performances at Covent Garden. Miss Edwards was engaged on a regular basis at Drury Lane for the 1745–46 season, when she met and married the singer Thomas Mozeen, and the couple performed at Drury Lane for the following two seasons until Sheridan engaged them at Smock Alley for the 1748–49 and 1749–50 seasons. It is clear from the bills that Mrs. Mozeen and not her husband was the attraction. When Thomas Mozeen returned to London at the beginning of the 1750–51 season, his wife did not accompany him. Evidently, they had decided to go their separate ways, for they are not known to have met again. Mrs. Mozeen spent most of the remainder of her career in Ireland. Mrs. Mozeen's *forte* was singing in such roles as Polly in *The Beggar's Opera*. She seldom undertook straight acting parts, and she appeared in tragedy even less frequently. Her last recorded role is that of Lucy in *The Beggar's Opera* in October 1773.

George Pitt danced at Smock Alley as early as the 1729–30 season, and his fragmentary record suggests that he remained in Dublin until the 1740–41 season. A "Master Pitt," presumably the son of George Pitt and perhaps named after him, made his stage debut at Aungier Street Theatre during the 1734–35 season. (The *BD* mistakenly attributes the father's performance at Violante's booth in 1730 to the son). The younger Pitt's career parallels that of his father until 1740–41, after which time it becomes difficult to separate the activities of the two. A Pitt continued to dance at Smock Alley during the 1742–43 and 1744–45 seasons (the *BD* errs in stating that Pitt's whereabouts for these seasons "cannot be traced." In fact, no record of him survives for the 1745–46 through 1747–48 seasons). A "Master" Pitt appeared at Capel Street during the 1746–47 season and "Mr. Pitt" appears at Smock Alley in the 1749–50 season, but confines his activities to acting. It may be that by this time Pitt, Sr. turned to acting, while the son continued to dance. A Pitt was appearing principally as a dancer at Smock Alley for the last time in the 1752–53 season. The Pitt who danced at Bath during the 1753–54 season may have been Pitt the younger. Thereafter the only surviving performance record of Pitt (presumably the younger) is his acting and dancing in Belfast this season.

Henry Ward, who flourished between 1738 and his death in 1758, is less well known than his wife, née Sarah Achurch, sometimes called Mrs. West Digges. Henry began his career around 1734 acting at the James Street and other minor London theatres. After spending a season as a member of the York company, where he met and married the popular actress Sarah Achurch, he played at Drury Lane, moving to Covent Garden when his wife was engaged there for the 1748–49 season, acting secondary roles.

Sometime in 1752 Sarah began her long relationship with the popular actor West Digges, although she and her husband acted together in Belfast this season and at Covent Garden the following year. After that season Henry Ward disappears from the record.

Sarah Achurch Ward began her career at York in the mid-1740s and acted in Edinburgh with her husband in 1745. She is credited with leading the effort to build the first Edinburgh professional theatre, and she, her husband and her long-time lover West Digges were members of the company when Edinburgh's Canongate Theatre opened in 1747.

After making her Covent Garden debut in the 1748–49 season, she moved to Drury Lane at the request of its manager, David Garrick, to replace the ailing Mrs. Cibber for the 1749–50 season and remained there through 1751–52. She was unsuccessful in establishing a theatre in Aberdeen during the summer of 1751. The following year she began her relationship with Digges, which was to last until their separation in 1758. She and Digges acted at Smock Alley for the 1752–53 season. Her Dublin debut was delayed until she had given birth to a daughter. When Digges fled Ireland to escape his creditors during the 1753–54 season, he left Sarah behind.

The following season Sarah Ward and her husband Henry were together acting in Belfast for the 1754–55 season. (Clark is certainly in error in ascribing these appearances to Mr. and Mrs. Thomas Ward). She and Digges (who assumed the management of the Canongate Theatre) were acting together in Edinburgh the following year. In December 1756 she appeared as the original Lady Randolph in Home's *Douglas*.

When Digges left Edinburgh, again one step ahead of his creditors, Sarah Ward traveled the English provinces with him, sometimes being billed as "Mrs. Digges." Henry Ward had died sometime in 1758. She and Digges returned to Smock Alley for the 1758–59 season, but in the summer of 1759 Digges's infidelities precipitated a final separation between the two.

Mrs. Ward returned to Covent Garden for the 1759–60 season and remained there for a further twelve seasons playing a "great number of capital roles," according to the *BD*. During the 1770–71 season she became seriously ill and died at the age of 44 in March 1771.

Sarah Ward is thought to have had at least nine children, two of whom became actors. Her daughter Margaretta Priscilla Ward (d.1793) married the actor Thomas Kniveton, who acted occasionally in Ireland (see Kniveton biography in Summer Season 1761), in September 1771.

[This is the only record of the acting of **Miss Fleming, Leech, Owen**, and **White**].

Repertory, 1754–55 Season

This is the first regular season for which a significant number of playbills has survived. It is probable that about 25 more performances took place than are recorded, assuming thrice weekly performances, as the early months of the calendar suggest, and taking into account the company's side trips to Lisburn and Derry. Richard Elrington's programs are very conventional, consisting of standard mainpieces and afterpieces with regular additional entr'acte entertainments of singing and dancing. Of the three pieces performed in Belfast for the first time, only one (*Harlequin Animated*) is genuinely new-written. Clark (1965, 220) thinks the 3 January performance of *Harlequin Amazed* was the first pantomime to be staged in

Belfast (the playbills show the proper title is *Harlequin Animated*). It is also interesting that Thomas Sheridan's long-popular farce, *The Brave Irishman*, had to wait until Sheridan had left Ireland for London to be performed in the North.

Total Performances: 27 of 22 different named mainpieces and 26 different named afterpieces.

Shakespeare: 4.

New mainpieces: 1.

New afterpieces: 2.

(For a key to repertory symbols see above, page 11)

Mainpieces: *The Beaux' Stratagem; The Beggar's Opera*†; *The Busy Body; The Conscious Lovers*†; *The Constant Couple*†; *The Country Lasses**; *The Double Dealer*†; *The Earl of Essex; The Fair Penitent; Hamlet; Jane Shore*(2); *Julius Caesar*†; *King Henry IV, Part One*†; *Love Makes a Man*†; *Oroonoko; The Orphan* †(3); *The Provoked Husband*†; *The Recruiting Officer*†; *Romeo and Juliet; The Suspicious Husband; Tamerlane*(2); *Venice Preserved.*

Afterpieces: *The Beggars' Wedding*†; *The Brave Irishman**; *A Cure for a Scold; Damon and Phillida*(3); *The Devil to Pay; Harlequin Animated**(2?); *The Intriguing Chambermaid*†; *Lethe*(2); *The Lottery*†; *Love for Love*†; *The Lying Valet; Miss in Her Teens*(5); *The Mock Doctor*(2); *The School Boy*†; *The Virgin Unmasked* (2); *The What D'Ye Call It.*

Entr'acte singing and dancing: 17.

Benefits (9): Jo Elrington; Mrs. Elrington; Miss Fleming; Longfield; Mrs. Mozeen; Owen; Pitt; the Poor; Mr. and Mrs. Ward.

November 1754

18 Mon. By a Company of Comedians. *The Fair Penitent.* Scialto–Longfield; Altamont–White; Horatio–Elrington; Lothario–Pitt; Rossano–Jo Elrington; Calista–Mrs. Elrington; Lavinia–Mrs. Mozeen; Lucilla–Mrs. Ward. With dancing by Pitt and a farce called *Damon and Phillida.* Damon–Mrs. Elrington; Arcas–Jo Elrington; Coridon–Longfield; Simon–Pitt; Mopsus–Elrington; Phillida–Mrs. Mozeen. The ladies and gentlemen may depend upon the curtain being drawn up punctually at seven o'clock. Source: 15 Nov. 1754

20 Wed. *The Busy Body.* Sir George–Elrington; Sir Jealous Traffick–Longfield; Sir Francis–Ward; Charles–White; Marplot–Pitt;

Whisper–Jo Elrington; Miranda–Mrs. Mozeen; Isabinda–Mrs. Elrington; Patch–Mrs. Ward. With dancing by Pitt and a farce called *The Mock Doctor.* Source: 18 Nov. 1754

22 Fri.   *Jane Shore.* Gloster–Elrington; Hastings–Pitt; Shore–Long-field; Bellmour–Jo Elrington; Catesby–White; Alicia–Mrs. Elrington; Jane Shore–Mrs. Mozeen. With dancing by Pitt and a farce called *Damon and Phillida.* Source: 22 Nov. 1754

25 Mon. *The Constant Couple.* Sir Harry Wildair–Pitt; Col. Standard–Longfield; Clincher Sr.–Elrington; Clincher Jr.–Jo Elrington; Alderman Smuggler–Ward; Vizard–White; Dicky–Leech; Lady Lurewell–Mrs. Elrington; Angelica–Mrs. Mozeen; Lady Darling–Mrs. Ward. With a farce called *Miss in Her Teens.* Source: 22 Nov. 1754

27 Wed. *The Orphan.* Acasto–Longfield; Castalio–Elrington; Polydore–White; Chamont–Pitt; Chaplain–Jo Elrington; Ernesto–Ward; Monimia–Mrs. Mozeen; Serina–Mrs. Elrington; Florella–Mrs. Ward. [*The Orphan* was published in Belfast by James Magee in 1767]. With *The Virgin Unmasked.* Source: 26 Nov. 1754

29 Fri.   *The Beggar's Opera.* Macheath–White; Peachum–Elrington; Lockit–Longfield; Filch–Pitt; Ben Budge–Ward; Nimming Ned–Jo Elrington; Watt Dreary–Leech; Polly–Mrs. Mozeen; Lucy–Mrs. Elrington; Mrs. Peachum–Mrs. Ward. [*The Beggar's Opera* was published in Belfast by James Magee in 1764]. In Act 3 a hornpipe by Pitt. To conclude with a country dance by the characters in the opera. With *Miss in Her Teens.* Source: 29 Nov. 1754

December 1754

6 Fri.   *The Recruiting Officer.* Justice Balance–Longfield; Capt. Plume–Pitt; Worthy–Jo Elrington; Kite–Elrington; Bullock–Ward; Silvia–Mrs. Elrington; Melinda–Mrs. Ward; Rose–Mrs. Mozeen. [*The Recruiting Officer* was published by James Magee in Belfast in 1773]. A song by Mrs. Mozeen. With dancing by Pitt and *The Virgin Unmasked.* Source: 6 Dec. 1754

11 Wed.   *Love Makes a Man.* Don Carlos–Longfield; Clodio–Pitt; Don Lewis–Elrington; Antonio–Owen; Charino–Ward; Governor–White; Sancho–Jo Elrington; Jaquez–Leech; Page–Master Elrington; Louisa–Mrs. Mozeen; Angelina–Mrs. Elrington; Elvina–Mrs. Ward. With dancing by Pitt and a farce called *The Devil to Pay.* Source: 10 Dec. 1754

13 Fri. *Tamerlane.* Tamerlane–Longfield; Bajazet–Elrington; Moneses–Pitt; Axalla–White; Omar–Owen; Dervise–Jo Elrington; Haly–Leech; Arpasia–Mrs. Mozeen; Selima–Mrs. Ward. With dancing by Pitt and *The Lying Valet.* Source: 13 Dec. 1754

17 Tues. *The Orphan.* Acasto–Longfield; Castalio–Elrington; Polydore–White; Chamont–Pitt; Chaplain–Jo Elrington; Ernesto–Ward; Page–Master Elrington; Monimia–Mrs. Mozeen; Serina–Mrs. Ward. With *Lethe.* Source: 17 Dec. 1754

January 1755

3 Fri. By desire. *The Conscious Lovers.* Young Bevil–White; Sealand–Longfield; Sir John Bevil–Jo Elrington; Myrtle–Owen; Tom–Pitt; Cimberton–Ward; Servant–Leech; Indiana–Mrs. Elrington; Mrs. Sealand–Mrs. Ward; Phillis–Mrs. Mozeen. With a Pantomime *Harlequin Animated; or, Fairy Friendship.* Source: 3 Jan. 1755

7 Tues. *Hamlet.* Hamlet–Elrington; Ghost–Pitt; King–Longfield; Horatio–Jo Elrington; Polonius–Owen; Osrick–White; Bernardo–Leech; Lucianus–Ward; Queen–Mrs. Ward; Ophelia–Mrs. Mozeen. With a Pantomime [probably *Harlequin Animated*] in which will be introduced the surprising escape of Harlequin into a quart bottle. Source: 7 Jan. 1755

10 Fri. Never performed here. *The Country Lasses.* Sir John English–Elrington; Modely–Pitt; Freehold–Longfield; Heartwell–White; Lurcher–Jo Elrington; Shacklefigure–Ward; Double Jugg–Owen; Sneak–Leech; Aura–Mrs. Elrington; Flora–Mrs. Mozeen. With dancing by Pitt and singing by Mrs. Mozeen and a farce called *Lethe.* Source: 10 Jan. 1755

17 Fri. *The Beaux' Stratagem.* Archer–Elrington; Aimwell–White; Bonniface–Longfield; Gibbet–Owen; Hounslow–Ward; Bagshot–Leech; Scrub–Pitt; Mrs. Sullen–Mrs. Mozeen; Dorinda–Miss Fleming; Cherry–Mrs. Elrington; Lady Bountiful–Mrs. Ward. With singing by Mrs. Mozeen and dancing by Pitt and *The Lottery.* Source: 17 Jan. 1755

18 Sat. *Jane Shore.* Gloster–Elrington; Lord Hastings–Pitt; Shore–Longfield; Bellmour–Jo Elrington; Catesby–White; Ratcliff–Owen; Jane Shore–Mrs. Mozeen; Alicia–Miss Fleming (first appearance on this stage). With dancing by Pitt and a farce (never acted here) called *The Brave Irishman.* [*The Brave Irishman* was published in Belfast by James Magee in 1761 and 1773]. Source: 17 Jan. 1755

24 Fri.   *The Suspicious Husband.* Ranger–Pitt; Strickland–Longfield; Frankly–White; Bellamy–Jo Elrington; Jack Meggot–Elrington; Tester–Ward; Buckle–Owen; Clarinda–Mrs. Mozeen; Jacintha–Mrs. Elrington; Mrs. Strickland–Miss Fleming; Lucette–Mrs. Ward. Singing by Mrs. Mozeen and a dance called *"The Drunken Peasant"* by Pitt. With *Miss in Her Teens.* Source: 21 Jan. 1755

27 Mon. Benefit   of   Pitt.   *Julius   Caesar.*   Brutus–Elrington; Cassius–Longfield; Anthony–Pitt; Casca–White; Caesar–Jo Elrington; Octavius–Owen; Artemidorus–Ward; Metellus Cimber–Mrs. Ward; Page–Mrs. Elrington; Cinna–Leech; Calphurnia–Miss Fleming; Portia–Mrs. Mozeen. With the following entertainments: a dance by Pitt in wooden shoes; a new Scotch dance; and *"Damon and Sylvia,"* a Dialogue by White and Mrs. Mozeen. With a farce called *The School Boy.* Source: 24 Jan. 1755

31 Fri.   *The Provoked Husband.* Lord Townly–Elrington; Manly–White; Sir Francis–Longfield; Count Basset–Owen; Squire Richard–Pitt; John Moody–Ward; Constable–Leech; James–Jo Elrington; Lady Townly–Mrs. Elrington; Lady Grace–Miss Fleming; Lady Wronghead–Mrs. Ward; Miss Jenny–Mrs. Mozeen. With singing and dancing as expressed in the bills and a farce called *The Devil to Pay.* Source: 28 Jan. 1755

February 1755

5   Wed.   *The Orphan.* With a farce called *The Mock Doctor.* Source: 4 Feb. 1755

7   Fri.   Benefit Mrs. Mozeen. *Venice Preserved.* Pierre–Elrington; Jaffier–Pitt; Priuli–Longfield; Bedamar–Jo Elrington; Spinosa–Owen; Theodore–White; Eliot–Leech; Belvidera–Mrs. Mozeen. With singing and dancing as expressed in the bills and *The Intriguing Chambermaid.* Source: 4 Feb. 1755

[The company performed in Lisburn on 19 and 22 February].

24 Mon. Benefit of Owen. *The Double Dealer.* Maskwell–Longfield; Lord Touchwood–Owen; Melefont–Elrington; Careless–White; Brisk–Pitt; Sir Paul Pliant–J. Elrington; Lord Froth–Ward; Lady Touchwood–Mrs. Ward; Lady Pliant–Mrs. Elrington; Lady Froth–Mrs. Mozeen; Cinthia–Miss Fleming. Singing by Mrs. Mozeen; Dancing by Pitt, particularly the dance called *"The Merry Old Woman, or, Pierrot in the Basket"* and an Epilogue on Everybody to be spoke by Somebody in the character of Nobody. With a farce called *The Beggars' Wedding.* Source: 21 Feb. 1755

[The company performed in Lisburn on 26 Feb]

28 Fri. Benefit of Ward and Mrs. Ward. *Romeo and Juliet.* Romeo–Elrington; Capulet–Longfield; Mercutio–Pitt; Friar Lawrence–Owen; Paris–White; Benvolio–Jo Elrington; Friar John–Ward; Apothecary–Leech; Juliet–Mrs. Elrington; Lady Capulet–Miss Fleming; Nurse–Mrs. Ward. With the funeral procession to the monument of the Capulets and a solemn dirge the vocal parts by Mrs. Mozeen, White, and others. In Act 1 will be performed the Masquerade Scene. The farce *The What D'Ye Call It.* Source: 25 Feb. 1755

[late February or early March 1755] Benefit of Mrs. Elrington. *Love for Love.* Valentine–Elrington; Sir Sampson–Longfield; Scandal–Jo Elrington; Tattle–White; Foresight–Ward; Jeremy–Owen; Ben (with a hornpipe in character)–Pitt; Angelica–Mrs. Mozeen; Mrs. Frail–Mrs. Ward; Mrs. Foresight–Miss Fleming. Mrs. Elrington begs leave to inform the gentlemen and ladies that for certain reasons she has put off the benefit to this Day se'nnight when tickets already given out will be taken. [Mrs. Elrington's benefit was originally scheduled for 14 February, but was then deferred until 28 February; apparently it was further deferred to a now unknown date]. With singing and dancing as expressed in the bills and a farce called *A Cure for a Scold.* Source: 11 Feb. 1755

March 1755

[On 1 March the company performed in Lisburn]

3 Mon. For the benefit of Jo Elrington, being the last time but one of performing in Belfast. *Oroonoko.* With *Damon and Phillida.* Singing by White and Mrs. Mozeen and dancing by Pitt. Source: 28 Feb. 1755

7 Fri. Benefit of Miss Fleming, being the last time of performing here. *The Earl of Essex.* Essex–Elrington; Southampton–Pitt; Burleigh–Longfield; Raleigh–White; Queen Elizabeth–Mrs. Elrington; Countess of Rutland–Mrs. Mozeen; Countess of Nottingham–Miss Fleming. With singing and dancing as expressed in the bills and *Miss in Her Teens.* Source: 4 Mar. 1755

14 Fri. Benefit of Longfield. *King Henry IV, Part One.* Hotspur–Elrington; Prince–Pitt; King Henry–White; Prince John–Mrs. Mozeen; Falstaff–Longfield. With an occasional prologue by Longfield and a humourous epilogue (representing the Count of Nassau) by Longfield in the character of Lord Chief Joker. *The Mock Doctor.* Source: 14 Mar. 1755

19 Wed. Benefit of the poor (being positively the last night of performing in this Town). *Tamerlane*. With *Miss in Her Teens*. Source: 18 Mar. 1755

[The company was advertised to perform in Derry on 24 March].

1755–1756 SEASON

During the summer of 1756 and well into the following winter Belfast was the scene of violent bread riots that brought business in the town to a virtual standstill. No professional performances took place this season. Clark does not notice the following amateur performance.

November 1755

20 Thur Benefit of the distressed, at the Market House, Belfast. *The Recruiting Officer.* Justice Ballance–Master Magee; Justice Scale–Master Ar. Macartney; Justice Scruple–Master Jo. Macartney; Worthy–Master Geo. Macartney; Capt. Plume–Master Forde; Brazen–Master Brooks; Serjeant Kite–Master Caddell; Bullock–Master Cha. Ward; Castor Pearmain–Master Ar. Macartney; Tho. Appletree–Master Walkinshaw; Melinda–Master Horace Smith; Silvia–Master Ralph Ward; Lucy–Master Thomas Lyons. Prologue on the glorious revolution by King William to be spoken by Master Forde. End Act 2 a dialogue song between Master Forde and Master Johnston; end Act 3 a mesologue on a namesake of Serjeant Kite's; end Act 4 a song by Master Forde. With a dialogue-epilogue between Serjeant Kite and his drum. After the play the *"Drunken Peasant"* after a new taste. The curtain to be drawn up precisely at half an hour after six o'clock. No admission behind the scenes. The profits to be given to the Clergy of the Church and the Meeting-houses to be disposed of at their discretion. Source: 18 Nov. 1755

1756–1757 SEASON

[The Belfast theatre was dark].

1757–1758 SEASON

Venue: The Vaults. Although none of the advertisements indicates the venue of performance this season, *BNL* 12 May 1758 prints an epilogue "as performed at the Vaults in Belfast" on 5 May 1758.

Company: Mr. and Mrs. [Francis?] Aickin; Bath; Miss Comerford; Mrs. Gemea; Mr. and Mrs. Hopkins; Samuel Johnson; O'Neill [sometimes O'Neal and O'Neil]; and Mr. and Mrs. Sherriffe (actor-manager).

John Sherriffe brought his company of strollers from Drogheda to the Vaults in Belfast in early February for a short season. See the 1753–54 season for biographical sketches of Mr. and Mrs. Sherriffe and the 1751–52 season of **Mrs. Gemea.**

Francis Aickin first enters the record as a member of the strolling company headed by Sherriffe that visited Belfast this season. According to the *BD* Francis made his Dublin debut at Smock Alley in secondary and tertiary roles in the 1756–57 season, but it also ascribes this debut to his brother James. No first names or initials appear in the playbills. The *BD* also finds Francis in Edinburgh in the summer of 1757 at the same time his brother was performing there. Again, it is not now possible to discriminate between the activities of the two brothers. Nevertheless, the Aickin who appeared with his wife in Belfast this season is probably Francis, who had married by this time, though his brother James evidently had not. We also can be fairly confident that the Aickin who acted in Dublin during the 1762–63 through 1764–65 seasons was Francis, although his wife is not mentioned in the bills. Judging from the roles each played during this period, it would seem that Francis tended to assume more singing parts than his brother, and it was probably Mr. and Mrs. Francis Aickin who were billed as being from the "Belfast Opera" when performing in Edinburgh in February 1762 (there is no record of any Aickin performing in Belfast after June 1758).

Francis Aickin (but not his wife, who disappears from the record) went to London's Drury Lane theatre in the spring of 1765 and remained there playing respectable parts until the end of the 1773–74 season, when Garrick dismissed him, allegedly for wearing his hat behind the scenes. Aickin moved to Covent Garden, again with considerable success, until he retired from acting at the beginning of the 1792–93 season.

The *BD* speculates that **Miss Rosetta Comerford** (later Mrs. Thomas Ryder) was the daughter or sister of Henry Comerford, the minor London actor who is not known to have acted in Ireland. She did not have a London career and is noticed only in passing in the *BD* in her husband's entry.

The fact that her first Dublin appearance, as a Captive in *The Constant Captives* in the 1751–52 Smock Alley season, attracted no special mention suggests perhaps that Miss Comerford had been appearing in supernumerary roles there for some time. Although her characters are not specified in the bills, she shared a benefit with several other actors at the end of the 1752–53 season. The following two seasons she appeared in a few minor named roles at Smock Alley. She disappears from the record for the 1755–56 through the 1756–57 seasons, but is found in Belfast with Sherriffe's strolling company this season, still billed as Miss Comerford and not Mrs. Ryder, as Clark asserts (1965, 373).

In the 1758–59 Smock Alley season she shared a benefit with the Mynitts, actors of some importance, and the following season she was acting minor roles in the Smock Alley company with the novice actor, Thomas Ryder, whom she married in the spring of 1760. Thereafter she acted for many years as Mrs. Ryder (see 1769–70 season for continued biographical sketch of Ryder).

William Hopkins (d. 1780) is best remembered as the longtime prompter at Garrick's Drury Lane theatre. He began his career on the stage acting in Edinburgh in the 1750–51 season, and the next year was at York, where he met his wife Elizabeth, née Barton, an actress whom he married in York in April 1753. Although the record is silent, the couple evidently continued at York for several seasons, and then they are found in Edinburgh in 1757. Mrs. Hopkins made her Dublin stage debut at Smock Alley on 8 December 1757 as Juliet, but the next day she was dismissed by Sheridan, who claimed that his stage was already "full." The couple spent the remainder of the season in the Irish provinces, first at Drogheda and then, in February and March 1758, in Belfast, as a part of Sherriffe's strolling company. Later that summer they traveled to Cork.

When Sheridan gave up the management of Smock Alley once and for all at the beginning of the 1758–59 season, Mrs. Hopkins returned to Dublin and increased her repertoire with several important roles, including Polly in *The Beggar's Opera*. When her husband became the Drury Lane prompter in 1761, Mrs. Hopkins began her long and distinguished Drury Lane career which spanned some 34 years. After her husband's death in 1780 Mrs. Hopkins continued to act until 1796. She died at Bath in October 1801.

Samuel Johnson, fl. 1752–1782. Citing Clark, the *BD* speculates that the Johnson who performed in Belfast on 24 May 1758 was the same Samuel Johnson who made his Dublin debut at Smock Alley in December 1759 and acted there for the remainder of the regular season. He is identified in the playbills of the two benefits he took that season as both "Samuel" and

"S." Johnson. Subsequently, Johnson "built up a circuit of provincial theatres in Wiltshire, Hampshire, and West Sussex," and, aside from a brief stint in London in the early 1770s, Johnson spent the remainder of his career in the English provinces as actor and manager.

Many O'Neills have been associated with the eighteenth-century Irish theatre, usually in minor capacities, and it is often difficult to distinguish between their activities. An **O'Neill** managed a strolling company that toured the Irish provinces from as early as 1757–58 until perhaps as late as 1795. Clark identifies this person as John "Shane" O'Neill; however, this seems unlikely. More probably, the Mr. O'Neill who is found in Belfast this season and again in 1765–66 and also in Cavan in 1768 is a different person from the John "Shane" O'Neill who is first documented at Capel Street in 1783, although they may have been related. See the 1782–83 season for the biography of John "Shane" O'Neill.

This season in Belfast is the only record of **Mr. Bath**.

Repertory, February–June 1758

The performance record for the eighteen weeks that Sherriffe's Drogheda Company spent in Belfast is remarkably complete and suggests that the manager made a concerted effort to bring novel entertainment to the audiences there. In addition to the favorite Shakespeare plays *King Richard III* and *Romeo and Juliet*, he performed *King Henry V* and *The Tempest*, two pieces that saw the stage much less frequently, the latter because of the extraordinary expense of staging it. More importantly, Sherriffe brought out two entirely new pieces by the Scottish playwright, the Rev. John Home, in less than a year after their stage premieres, including the very popular *Douglas*. Home's *Agis* is one of the few mainpieces performed in Belfast that was never performed in Dublin. The five new afterpieces, particularly *The Oracle*, seem to have attracted large audiences and were also expensive to stage.

The fact that the playbills provide such detailed programs, stressing, in addition to relatively elaborate main and afterpieces and entr'acte entertainments, processions, prologues and epilogues, strongly suggests increasing sophistication of taste on the part of the Belfast audiences.

Total Performances: 32 of 27 different named mainpieces and 28 performances of 18 different named afterpieces.
Shakespeare: 6.
New mainpieces: 2

New afterpieces: 5

(For a key to repertory symbols see above, page 11)

Mainpieces: *Agis**; *Barbarossa*†; *The Beggar's Opera*(2); *A Bold Stroke for a Wife* †; *The Conscious Lovers; The Constant Couple; The Distrest Mother* †; *Douglas** (3); *The Earl of Essex; The Fair Penitent; The Foundling* †; *Hamlet; The Inconstant*†; *King Henry V* †; *King Richard III; The London Merchant; The Merchant of Venice*†; *The Mourning Bride; The Orphan; The Provoked Husband; The Recruiting Officer; The Revenge; Romeo and Juliet*(2); *The Spanish Fryar; The Suspicious Husband*(2); *The Tempest* †; *Theodosius* †.

Afterpieces: *The Anatomist; The Apprentice**; *The Author**; *The Brave Irishman*(2); *Catherine and Petruchio*†(2); *Damon and Phillida; The Devil to Pay*(2); *Florizel and Perdita**(2); *The Intriguing Chambermaid; The King and the Miller of Mansfield; Lethe; The Lottery; The Lying Valet*(2); *Miss in Her Teens; The Mock Doctor; The Oracle**(3); *The Reprisal**(3); *The Virgin Unmasked*(2);

Entr'acte singing and dancing: 2

Benefits: 7: Aickin; Mrs. Aickin; Mr. and Mrs. Aickin; Baker; Miss Comerford; Sherriffe; Mrs. Sherriffe.

February 1758

6 Mon. By the Drogheda company of comedians. *The Inconstant.* Young Mirabel–Aickin; Capt. Duretete–Sherriffe; Bisarre–Mrs. Hopkins; Oriana–Mrs. Sherriffe. With a farce called *The Virgin Unmasked.* Miss Lucy–Mrs. Sherriffe. To begin at 6 o'clock. Source: 3 Feb. 1758

8 Wed. *The Fair Penitent.* Horatio–Aickin; Lothario–Sherriffe; Lavinia–Mrs. Sherriffe; Calista–Mrs. Hopkins. With a farce called *The Brave Irishman.* O'Blunder–O'Neal. [Clark (1965, 221) errs in ascribing this performance to 7 Feb.]. Source: 7 Feb. 1758

10 Fri. *The Recruiting Officer.* Capt. Plume–Aickin; Capt. Brazen–Sherriffe; Melinda–Mrs. Hopkins; Sylvia–Miss Comerford. With a farce called *The Mock Doctor.* Mock Doctor–O'Neal; Dorcas–Miss Comerford. Source: 10 Feb. 1758

13 Mon. *King Richard III.* Richard–Sherriffe; King Henry–Hopkins; Earl of Richmond–Aickin; Lady Anne–Mrs. Hopkins; Queen Elizabeth–Mrs. Sherriffe. With a ballad farce called *Damon and Phillida.* Source: 10 Feb. 1758

15 Wed. *The Provoked Husband.* Lord Townly–Aickin; Count Basset–Sherriffe; Sir Francis Wronghead–O'Neal; Lady Townly–Mrs. Sherriffe. With a farce never acted here called [*The Sheep Shearing; or,*] *Florizel and Perdita.* Autolicus–Mrs. Hopkins. The new tragedy of *Douglas* is now in rehearsal and will be performed some time next week. Source: 14 Feb. 1758

21 Tues. *Douglas.* Young Norval–Aickin; Old Norval–Sherriffe; Anna–Mrs. Sherriffe; Lady Randolph–Mrs. Hopkins. [Published in Belfast by James Magee in 1757, 1758 and 1766]. With the original prologue and epilogue and a ballad farce called *The Intriguing Chambermaid.* Drunken Colonel–Sherriffe; Lettice–Miss Comerford. Source: 16 Feb. 1758

24 Fri. *A Bold Stroke for a Wife.* Col. Fainwell–Sherriffe; Sarah Prim–Mrs. Gemea; Anne Lovely–Miss Comerford. [Published in Belfast by James Magee in 1760]. With a farce called *The Brave Irishman.* Source: 24 Feb. 1758

27 Mon. *The Spanish Fryar.* With a new farce called *The Oracle.* Source: 24 Feb. 1758

29 Wed. *Barbarossa.* Achmet–Sherriffe; Barbarossa–Bath; Irene–Mrs. Hopkins; Zaphira–Mrs. Sherriffe. With a farce acted here but once called [*The Sheep Shearing; or,*] *Florizel and Perdita.* Florizel–Aickin; Autolicus–Sherriffe; Perdita–Mrs. Hopkins. Source: 28 Feb. 1758

March 1758

8 Wed. *The Beggar's Opera.* Macheath–Bath; Lucy–Miss Comerford; Polly–Mrs. Hopkins. And *Miss in Her Teens.* Fribble–Gemea; Miss Biddy–Mrs. Aickin. Source: Lawrence, "Annals."

15 Wed. *Romeo and Juliet.* Romeo–Sherriffe; Mercutio–Aickin; Juliet–Mrs. Sherriffe. With a grand masquerade scene and dance as also a solemn dirge and funeral procession of Juliet to the monument of the Capulets. With *The Lottery.* Lady Lace–Miss Comerford. Source: 14 Mar. 1758

17 Fri. *The Suspicious Husband.* Ranger–Sherriffe; Clarinda–Mrs. Hopkins. [*The Way of the World* originally announced]. To conclude with a country dance and a farce called *The Devil to Pay.* Nell–Mrs. Sherriffe. Source: 17 Mar. 1758

20 Mon. *Romeo and Juliet.* With a masquerade scene and dance also a solemn dirge and funeral procession of Juliet to the monument of the Capulets. Last time of playing till Easter Monday. Source: 17 Mar. 1758

27 Mon. *The Beggar's Opera.* Macheath–Bath; Mat o' th' Mint–Sherriffe; Lucy–Miss Comerford; Polly–Mrs. Hopkins. To conclude with a country dance by the characters of the opera and a farce *The Anatomist.* Source: 24 Mar. 1758

31 Fri. By particular desire. *The Suspicious Husband.* Ranger–Sherriffe; Frankly–Aickin; Strickland–Hopkins; Mrs. Strickland–Mrs. Sherriffe; Clarinda–Mrs. Hopkins. With *The Devil to Pay.* Source: 31 Mar. 1758

April 1758

3 Mon. Second night. *King Henry V.* Source: 31 Mar. 1758

5 Wed. *Hamlet.* Hamlet–Sherriffe; Ophelia–Miss Comerford. And *The Oracle.* Source: Lawrence, "Annals," 10

7 Fri. *The Conscious Lovers.* Bevil Jr.–Aickin; Tom–Sherriffe; Phillis–Mrs. Sherriffe; Indiana–Mrs. Hopkins. With a farce called *Catherine and Petruchio.* Source: 7 Apr. 1758

10 Mon. *Theodosius.* Varannes–Sherriffe. With a grand procession according to the manner of the ancient Romish church with a new altar piece for the occasion. Source: 7 Apr. 1758

12 Wed. *Douglas.* Positively the last time of performing it. With a new farce called *The Reprisal.* Source: 11 Apr. 1758

14 Fri. *Agis.* Agis–Sherriffe; Lysander–Aickin; Agistrata–Mrs. Sherriffe; Sandane–Miss Comerford; Euanthe–Mrs. Hopkins. [Published in Belfast by James Magee this year.] With a farce called *Lethe.* Source: 14 Apr. 1758

19 Wed. *The Merchant of Venice.* Shylock–Sherriffe; Antonio–Hopkins; Bassanio–Aickin; Nerissa–Miss Comerford; Portia–Mrs. Sherriffe. With *The Reprisal.* Source: 18 Apr. 1758

21 Fri. *The Distrest Mother.* Orestes–Sherriffe; Pyrrhus–Aickin; Hermione–Mrs. Hopkins; Andromache–Mrs. Sherriffe. Translated from the French of Racine by Philips. The original epilogue to be spoken by Mrs. Sherriffe. With *The King and the Miller of Mansfield.* King–Sherriffe; Joe (with a song in character)–Bath; Peggy–Mrs. Aickin. Source: 21 Apr. 1758

24 Mon. Never acted here. *The Tempest; or, The Enchanted Island.* As this play is got up in a proper manner with a set of new scenes and all decorations as represented in London and Dublin it has been attended with a great expense and trouble and doubt not it will give general satisfaction. It's therefore hoped the town will give it proper encouragement. Source: 21 Apr. 1758

28 Fri. *The Revenge.* Zanga–Sherriffe; Don Carlos–Aickin; Leonora–Mrs. Hopkins. To which by desire will be added *The Reprisal.* Champignon–Baker; Ben Block–Sherriffe; Miss Harriet–Mrs. Aickin. The farce to conclude with a proper song by Bath. Source: 28 Apr. 1758

May 1758

3 Wed. Benefit of Sherriffe. *The Mourning Bride.* Osmyn–Sherriffe; Zara–Mrs. Sherriffe; Almeria–Mrs. Hopkins. And by desire a farce called *Catherine and Petruchio.* Source: 2 May 1758

5 Fri. Benefit of Aickin. *The Earl of Essex.* Essex–Sherriffe; Southampton–Aickin; Rutland–Mrs. Hopkins; Queen Elizabeth–Mrs. Sherriffe. With singing between the acts and a farce of two acts called *The Lying Valet.* Sharp–Aickin; Kitty Pry–Mrs. Sherriffe. [*BNL* 12 May 1758 prints the epilogue spoken by Aickin in the character of Sharp as performed "at the Vaults in Belfast" on this date]. Source: 5 May 1758

12 Fri. Benefit of Baker. *The Orphan.* Castalio–Aickin; Polydore–Baker; Chamont–Sherriffe; Monimia–Mrs. Hopkins. By desire. New prologue written and spoken by Baker in the character of a Master Mason. With a farce of two acts never performed here called *The Author.* Cadwallader (after the manner of the original)–Baker; Young Cape–Aickin; Mrs. Cadwallader (after the original)–Mrs. Hopkins. With the original prologue to be spoken by Baker; epilogue by Aickin. Source: 12 May 1758

19 Fri. Benefit of Miss Comerford. *The Foundling.* Young Belmont–Sherriffe; Faddle–Baker; Sir Charles Raymond–Aickin; Rosetta–Miss Comerford; Fidelia–Mrs. Sherriffe. With singing between the acts. With a new farce called *The Oracle.* Oberon–Aickin; Fairy Queen–Mrs. Sherriffe; Cinthia (with original song and epilogue)–Mrs. Hopkins. Source: 19 May 1758

24 Wed. Benefit of Mrs. Sherriffe. *The Constant Couple.* Sir Harry Wildair (by desire)–Mrs. Sherriffe (first time in character); Col. Standard–Aickin; Beau Clincher–Sherriffe; Lady Lurewell–Mrs. Hopkins. With a new farce called *The Apprentice.* Dick–Johnson (first appearance on this stage); Charlotte–Mrs. Sherriffe. [Published in Belfast by James Magee in 1773]. Source: 23 May 1758

26 Fri.   Benefit of Mrs. Aickin. *The Provoked Husband.* Lord Townly–Aickin; Manly–Baker; Count Basset–Sherriffe; Sir Francis Wronghead–Hopkins. With *The Lying Valet.* Sharp–Aickin; Melissa–Miss Comerford; Kitty Pry–Mrs. Sherriffe. With a new epilogue in the character of a strolling player written by Baker and to be spoken by Aickin. Source: 26 May 1758

June 1758

2 Fri.   *Douglas.* Young Norval–Aickin; Old Norval–Sherriffe; Lady Randolph–Mrs. Hopkins. With *Damon and Phillida.* Damon–Bath; Phillida–Mrs. Aickin. Source: 2 June 1758

12 Mon. Benefit of Mr. and Mrs. Aickin. *The London Merchant.* Barnwell–Aickin;   Trueman–Sherriffe;   Millwood–Mrs.   Sherriffe; Maria–Mrs. Hopkins. With *The Virgin Unmasked.* Source: 9 June 1758

[The company then went to Newry, Clark (1965, 222)]

1758–1759 SEASON
[The Belfast theatre was dark].

1759–1760 SEASON
[The Belfast theatre was dark].

1760–1761 SEASON
[The Belfast theatre was dark until the summer].

SUMMER SEASON 1761
Venue: The Vaults. Because virtually every advertisement for this summer season indicates the venue as "the Vaults" that information has not been repeated in the entries below.
Company: A scratch company of Dublin actors, including the following, played in Belfast from July to early September. They were frequently billed as "his Majesty's Servants from the Theatres in Dublin": Banford; Blackler

[sometimes spelled Blacker]; Carthy; Mr. and Mrs. William Dawson; Master Dawson; Miss Dillon; Thomas Kniveton; Master Lewis; Longfield; Mahon [sometimes McMahon]; Manwaring; Reed; Isaac Sparks; Mrs. Trevillian; Mr. and Mrs. Howard Usher; Vernel [often spelled Vernal]; Mrs. Willis.

William Dawson (see 1752–53 season for biography) had matured considerably as performer and manager between this and his first Belfast appearance in 1751. He led a strolling company in the Irish provinces for a time and had made his Smock Alley debut in the 1760–61 season bringing several of that company, including his wife and stepson, with him to Belfast this summer.

For a biographical sketch of **Longfield** see the 1754–55 season.

The **Miss Dillon** who made her Dublin debut at Smock Alley in April 1761 and acted there that season in a handful of tertiary roles is probably the same Miss Dillon who appeared in secondary parts with Dawson's strolling company in Belfast this summer. She disappears from the record thereafter.

The *BD* observes that **Thomas Kniveton** "spent most of his 16 years on the stage as a provincial actor." He first surfaces in Edinburgh in the summer of 1757 playing tertiary roles. He evidently joined the strolling company that was touring the north of Ireland in the autumn of 1759, for Clark finds him in Ballymena in September and in Coleraine in December of that year. Shortly thereafter Kniveton made his Dublin debut at Smock Alley on 5 January 1761, playing secondary and tertiary roles with Mossop's company where he remained for the next two seasons. During the summer of 1761 Kniveton joined of William Dawson's strolling company that visited Belfast.

At the end of the 1762–63 season, Kniveton traveled to England and comes into the record next, spending his time between 1766 and 1769 mainly in Manchester and in York. Kniveton began his brief London career at Covent Garden during the 1769–70 season, remaining there for that and the following three seasons. He is said to have received "great applause" in several of the primary roles he performed there. At the beginning of the 1773–74 season Kniveton left Covent Garden to join the Liverpool theatre, where he had become joint manager. Shortly thereafter, Kniveton died (in August 1775) "in excruciating agonies," according to his friend Tate Wilkinson, evidently as the result of the infection of an amputated leg.

During the 1760–61 season a **Mahon**, Mahon, Jr., and McMahon are all billed at Smock Alley in Dublin. In the cast Mahon is generally listed as playing secondary roles as well as singing and dancing, with the perhaps significant exception of the role of Macheath. Mahon, Jr. (presumably Robert Mahon and not a fourth Mahon) also dances and takes a few supernumerary roles. The actor billed as "McMahon" appears only once, and then as a supernumerary. But, the Mahon who acted this summer in Belfast is probably not Robert Mahon, as Clark and the *BD* believe, but his elder brother Gilbert, or less likely, an older man, T. Mahon.

The identity of the **Manwaring** who acted tertiary roles with William Dawson's strolling company in Belfast this summer and again in the 1765–66 season is unknown, but he may have been another brother, or perhaps, a son, of one of the Manwaring [often Mainwaring] brothers, Bartholomew and William, long-time Dublin musicians, who had retired from performance by this time. Our Manwaring evidently did not perform in Dublin or London for no record of him survives in either place.

It is unlikely that the **Reed** who acted in Dublin at Smock Alley and Aungier Street Theatre between 1733–34 and 1737–38 is the same man who was performing in the line of young men at Smock Alley in 1758–59, 1759–60, 1760–61, 1761–62, 1762–63, in secondary and tertiary roles. It is probably this Mr. Reed who was with the strolling company that William Dawson brought to Belfast in the summer of 1761.

Isaac Sparks (1719–1776), Ireland's premier comedian in the mid-eighteenth century, was born in Dublin on 16 September 1719 in College Street. Sparks probably made his stage debut in Dublin with Madam Violante's lilliputian company in the autumn of 1731. Robert Hitchcock (1788–94 1: 49) says that "Master Isaac Sparks" played Peachum to Peg Woffington's Polly in this very popular production of *The Beggar's Opera*. He soon graduated to more mature roles in the comic and singing line and from 1734–35 through 1745–46 performed (often with his elder brother Luke) at Rainsford Street, Smock Alley, and Aungier Street theatres. He accompanied the Smock Alley company on its travels to Cork and Limerick during many summers.

Sparks made his London debut at Drury Lane in September 1745 and remained there until the end of the 1747–48 season, when he returned to Dublin. Sparks remained in Dublin for most of his long career. He was at Smock Alley from 1748–49 through 1757–58, Crow Street 1758–59 and 1759–60, back at Smock Alley in 1760–61 and 1761–62. In the summer of

1761 Sparks was with the strolling company led to Belfast by William Dawson. Thereafter, Sparks traveled in provincial England acting in Shrewsbury, Bridgnorth, and Chester. He is found at Drury Lane at the beginning of the 1769–70 season where he remained through the 1770–71 season. Isaac and his son, Richard, returned to Dublin and Crow Street in the summer of 1771, after which Isaac Sparks evidently retired from the stage. He died on 21 April 1776.

Howard Usher, according to the *BD*, had a career on the London stage that spanned 60 years. He made his stage debut at Drury Lane in 1739–40 and remained there until the 1749–50 season, when he moved to Covent Garden for four seasons. He came back to Drury Lane at the beginning of the 1754–55 season and acted there for another four years. Usher made his Dublin debut at Smock Alley on 16 November 1758. With him was his wife (date of marriage unknown), the former Miss Phillips, a member of the Phillips family of actors, and sister of Grace and Maria Phillips, all of whom were performing in Dublin that season and had performed in Dublin previously.

The Ushers whereabouts is unknown for the 1759–60 season, but they were acting again at Smock Alley with Mossop's company for the entire 1760–61 season. That summer they joined Dawson's strolling company in Belfast. The Ushers appeared sporadically in Dublin from 1762 through the 1766–67 seasons.

The Ushers then disappear from the record until Mrs. Usher makes her London debut at Drury Lane in May 1772. Evidently, she was unsuccessful, for she never again appeared in London, although she continued to acted in the provinces, in York in 1773–74 and again in 1783, after which the record is largely silent. The *BD* thinks that she "probably died before her husband." Usher was again engaged at Drury Lane for the 1774–75 season, but thereafter he enters and disappears from the record for several seasons, until he joined the Haymarket company in the summer of 1778. There he was to remain for the last 21 years of his working life. His final recorded performance took place in September 1799 and he died in April 1802.

John Vernel (1741–70) is not known to have had a London or provincial English career. Advertised as his "first appearance," Vernal evidently made his stage debut in Dublin in March 1760 when he recited the favorite monologue "Bucks Have at Ye All." He repeated this piece many times in the seasons that followed, and performed in a wide variety of tertiary, and, increasingly, secondary characters. Vernal was with the strolling company that William Dawson took to Belfast in the summer of 1761, and he also acted in Cork with the touring Smock Alley company in the autumns of 1763, 1764, 1765, 1766, 1768 and 1769. A promising and versatile actor, Vernel remained in Dublin at Smock Alley until January 1770, when he died at the age of 29 after a short illness, leaving a pregnant wife and three children.

Beginning in October 1758 a **Mrs. Willis** is found at Crow Street acting in tertiary roles. She also performed in Belfast with Dawson's strolling company in the summer of 1761 and in Cork the following spring. She continued in Dublin in much the same capacity through the 1765–66 season, after which she disappears from the Irish record. The *BD* thinks that this may be the same Mrs. Willis who made her stage debut at the Haymarket Theatre in January 1758 and acted there during that season. She may have returned to the Haymarket Theatre for a single performance at the beginning of the 1771–72 season.

This is the only evidence of theatrical activity for **Banford** (who is not listed in Clark).

Clark includes in his appendix of actors a "Mr. Trevillian" whom he believes to have been active in Belfast this summer. One playbill, indeed, does list "Mr. **Trevillian**" singing between the acts, but this is clearly a compositor's error, and should read "Mrs. Trevillian." No other evidence for "Mr. Trevillian" survives, nor is Mrs. Trevillian known to have performed anywhere else before or after this season.

Repertory, Summer 1761

Dawson produced little that was novel this summer. Most of the plays performed were stock pieces, the only exceptions being Dodsley's *Cleone*, which had its Irish premiere the previous January at Smock Alley, *High Life Below Stairs*, a very successful play at Smock Alley for the previous two seasons, and *The Wapping Landlady*, a stock piece at Smock Alley, but evidently never performed in Belfast.

Total Performances: 20 of 17 different plays; 19 of 10 different named afterpieces.
    Shakespeare: 5.
    New Mainpieces: 1.
    New Afterpieces: 2.

(For a key to repertory symbols see above, page 11)

Mainpieces: *The Beaux' Stratagem; The Beggar's Opera; The Careless Husband; Cato†; Cleone*□; The Conscious Lovers; Douglas*(2); *Hamlet; King Henry IV, Part One; King Richard III; Love Makes a Man; Oroonoko; Othello*(2); *The Provoked Husband*(2); *Romeo and Juliet; She Would and She Would Not; The Twin Rivals.*

Afterpieces: *The Brave Irishman*(4); *Catherine and Petruchio; Damon and Phillida; Flora*(2); *High Life Below Stairs**(2); *The Honest Yorkshireman; Lethe; The Lying Valet;* Unspecified farce(2); *The Vintner Tricked†; The Virgin Unmasked; The Wapping Landlady**(2).

Entr'acte singing and dancing: 4

Benefits (10): Dawson; Mrs. Dawson and Master Lewis; Kniveton; Longfield; McMahon; Mrs. Trevillian(2); Mrs. Usher(2); Mrs. Willis.

July 1761

1 Wed. Yesterday [Monday, 29 June] arrived in Town a Company of comedians from the Theatres in Dublin who intend to perform here for one month only. Their first play will be *The [Beaux'] Stratagem.* Aimwell–Kniveton; Archer–Usher; Sullen–Mahon; Freeman–Vernel; Foigard–Sparks; Gibbet–Reed; Hounslow–Blackler; Bagshot–Banford; Boniface–Longfield; Scrub–Dawson; Lady Bountiful–Mrs. Dawson; Dorinda–Mrs. Trevillian; Mrs. Sullen–Mrs. Usher; Gipsy–Miss Dillon; Cherry–Mrs. Willis. With a farce. Source: 30 June 1761

3 Fri. At the Vaults. *King Henry IV, Part One.* Falstaff–Sparks. With *The Lying Valet.* Source: 30 June 1761

8 Wed. *Othello.* Duke–Sparks; Brabantio–Longfield; Gratiano–Mahon; Lodovico–Vernel; Othello–Usher; Cassio–Dawson; Iago–Kniveton; Roderigo–Reed; Montano–Blackler; Desdemona–Mrs. Trevillian; Amelia–Mrs. Dawson. With *The Brave Irishman.* O'Blunder–Sparks. Source: 8 July 1761

9 Thurs. *The Beggar's Opera.* Source: 8 July 1761

10 Fri. *Hamlet.* King–Longfield; Hamlet–Kniveton; Polonius–Dawson; Horatio–Usher; Rosencrans–McMahon; Guildenstern–Blackler; Osrick–Master Lewis [WilliamT., age15]; Marcellus–Vernel; Francisco–Manwaring; Ghost–Reed; Priest–Carthy; Gravedigger–Sparks;

Queen–Mrs. Usher; Ophelia–Mrs. Trevillian; Player Queen–Mrs. Willis. With *The Brave Irishman.* O'Blunder–Sparks. Source: 10 July 1761

15 Wed.   By his Majesty's Servants from the Theatres in Dublin. *Othello.* Duke–Sparks;   Brabantio–Longfield;   Gratiano–McMahon; Lodovico–Vernel;   Othello–Usher;   Cassio–Dawson;   Iago–Reed; Roderigo–Kniveton;   Montano–Blackler;   Senator–Manwaring; Senator–Banford; Senator–Carthy; Desdemona–Mrs. Usher; Emilia–Mrs. Dawson. With a farce as will be expressed in the Bills. Source: 14 July 1761

17 Fri.   At the particular Request of several Ladies and Gentlemen. *The Provoked   Husband.*   Lord   Townly–Usher;   Manly–Kniveton;   Sir Francis–Dawson; Squire Richard–Master Lewis; John Moody–Sparks; Count   Basset–Reed;   Poundage–Longfield;   Constable–McMahon; James–Blackler; Lady Townly–Mrs. Usher; Lady Grace–Mrs. Trevillian; Lady Wronghead–Mrs. Dawson; Miss Jenny–Mrs. Willis; Myrtilla–Miss Dillon. With a farce called *The Brave Irishman.* O'Blunder–Sparks. Source: 17 July 1761

22 Wed. *Douglas.* Lord Randolph–Longfield; Young Norval–Usher; Norval–Kniveton;   Glenalvon–Dawson;   Officer–McMahon; Servant–Vernel; Lady Randolph–Mrs. Usher; Anna–Mrs. Trevillian. The Characters dressed after the manner of the Ancient Scots. With a farce never performed here called *High Life Below Stairs.* [*High Life Below Stairs* was published in Belfast by James Magee in 1760 and 1767]. Source: 21 July 1761

24 Fri.   *The Twin Rivals.* Woudbe–Usher; Young Woudbe–Kniveton; Capt.   Trueman–Reed;   Richmore–Vernel;   Subtleman–Dawson; Balderdash–Longfield;   Clear   Account–McMahon;   Poet–Banford; Constable–Blackler; Page–Master Lewis; Teague (with a song in Character)–Sparks; Constance–Mrs. Trevillian; Aurelia–Mrs. Usher; Mrs. Midnight–Mrs. Dawson; Steward's Wife–Miss Dillon. With a farce called *High Life Below Stairs.* Source: 24 July 1761

29 Wed.   Benefit of Longfield. *King Richard III.* King Henry–Dawson; Prince   Edward–Mrs. Willis;   York–Master Lewis;   Richard–Usher; Buckingham–Reed; Stanley–Longfield; Lieutenant–Vernel; Blunt–Blackler; Oxford–Manwaring;   Ratcliff–McMahon;   Lord   Mayor–Sparks; Richmond–Kniveton; Queen–Mrs. Usher; Lady Anne–Mrs. Trevillian; Duchess of York–Mrs. Dawson. With *Flora.* Source: 28 July 1761

31 Fri. *Douglas*. Douglas–Usher; Lady Randolph–Mrs. Usher. With *The Vintner Tricked*. Mixum–Sparks; Vizard–Dawson; Mrs. Mixum–Mrs. Dawson. [Published in Belfast by James Magee in 1753, 1766, and 1786]. Source: 31 July 1761

August 1761

3 Mon. Benefit of Mrs. Dawson and Master Lewis. *The Conscious Lovers*. With a farce never performed here called *The Wapping Landlady*. Patrick O'Monaghan–Sparks. Source: 31 July 1761

5 Wed. For the benefit of Mrs. Usher. Never acted here before. *The Careless Husband*. Sir Charles–Usher; Lord Foppington–Reed; Lord Morelove–Kniveton; Lady Betty Modish–Mrs. Usher; Lady Easy–Mrs. Trevillian; Lady Graveairs–Miss Dillon; Edging–Mrs. Willis. With a farce called *Lethe*. Source: 4 Aug. 1761

7 Fri. Benefit of Kniveton. *Oroonoko*. Oroonoko–Kniveton; Aboan–Reed; Governor–Blackler; Blandford–Vernel; Captain Driver–Sparks; Stanmore–McMahon; Jack Stanmore–Henry; Hotman–Carthy; Daniel–Dawson; Printer–Banford; Printer–Manwaring; Imoinda–Mrs. Usher; Widow Lackit–Mrs. Dawson; Charlotte Weldon–Mrs. Trevillian; Lucy Weldon–Mrs. Willis. With singing between acts by Mr. [almost certainly a compositor's error for "Mrs." Trevillian. With *The Wapping Landlady*. Patrick O'Monaghan–Sparks. Source: 7 Aug. 1761

12 Wed. Benefit of Mrs. Willis. *She Would and She Would Not*. Don Manuel–Sparks; Don Octavio–Reed; Trappanti–Dawson; Don Philip–Usher. With *Damon and Phillida*. Source: 11 Aug. 1761

14 Fri. Benefit of Dawson. *Love Makes a Man*. Don Lewis–Sparks; Carlos–Usher; Don Duarte–Kniveton; Sancho–Dawson; Governor–Vernel; Charino–McMahon; Antonio–Carthy; Lawyer–Blackler; Priest–Banford; Page–Master Lewis; Credio–Reed; Louisa–Mrs. Usher; Elvira–Mrs. Willis; Angelina–Mrs. Trevillian; Honoria–Mrs. Dawson. End Act 2 a Cantata called *"The Wheel Barrow"* by Mrs. Trevillian; end Act 4 a Song called *"Young Dorillas"* by the same; end of the Play an Epilogue called *"Bucks have at ye All"* by Dawson. And by Desire *The Brave Irishman*. O'Blunder–Sparks. Being the last time of performing it. The Company will perform but two Nights in Town. Source: 14 Aug. 1761

24 Mon. Never acted here before. For the Benefit of McMahon. *Cleone.* Sifroy–Usher; Glanville–Kniveton; Beaufort Jr.–Reed; Paulet–McMahon; Old Beaufort–Vernel; Ragozin–Blackler; Young Sifroy–Master Dawson (first appearance on any stage); Isabell–Mrs. Dawson; Cleone–Mrs. Usher. As it was performed at the Theatre Royal in Covent Garden seventeen Nights successively. [*Cleone* was published in Belfast in 1759 by James Magee]. With a farce called *Catherine and Petruchio.* Grumio–Sparks; Petruchio–Usher; Catherine–Mrs. Usher. Source: 21 Aug. 1761

26 Wed. Benefit of Mrs. Trevillian. *Romeo and Juliet.* Romeo–Usher; Mercutio–Reed; Fryar Lawrence–Kniveton; Capulet–McMahon; Montague–Carthy; Tibalt–Vernel; Benvolio–Blackler; Paris–Henry; Peter–Master Lewis; Fryar John–Banford; Abram–Manwaring; Juliet–Mrs. Usher; Lady Capulet–Mrs. Trevillian; Nurse–Mrs. Dawson. In Act 2 a Grand Masquerade Scene. With the grand Funeral Procession of Juliet to the monument of the Capulets accompanied with a Solemn Dirge set to Music by Signior Pasqualli. With Singing between the Acts by Mrs. Trevillian. With a farce called *The Virgin Unmasked.* Source: 25 Aug. 1761

28 Fri. Benefit of Mrs. Trevillian. *The Provoked Husband.* Lord Townly–Usher; Manly–Kniveton; Sir Francis–Dawson; Squire Richard–Master Lewis; John Moody–Sparks; Count Basset–Reed; Poundage–Carthy; Constable–McMahon; James–Blackler; Lady Townly–Mrs. Usher; Lady Grace–Mrs. Trevillian; Lady Wronghead–Mrs. Dawson; Miss Jenny–Mrs. Willis; Myrtilla–Miss Dillon. With *Flora.* Young Hob–Sparks; Friendly–Usher; Dick–Dawson; Flora–Mrs. Trevillian. Source: 28 Aug. 1761

September 1761

4 Fri. Benefit Mrs. Usher. Being positively the last Night of the Company's performing in Town. *Cato.* Cato–Usher; Syphax–Sparks; Juba–Mrs. Dawson [*sic.*]; Sempronius–Kniveton; Portius–Dawson; Marcus–Vernel; Lucius–McMahon; Decius–Carthy; Conspirator–Banford; Conspirator–Blackler; Conspirator–Manwaring; Lucia (with original Epilogue)–Mrs. Usher; Marcia–Mrs. Trevillian. [*Cato* was published in Belfast by James Magee in 1764 and 1772]. With Singing between the Acts by Mrs. Trevillian. With *The Honest Yorkshireman.* Source: 4 Sept. 1761

1761–1762 SEASON

[The Belfast theatre was dark].

1762–1763 SEASON

Venue: The Vaults.

Company: Mr. and Mrs. Bloomer; Coghlan [or Coughlan or McCoghlan]; Dougan [or Dugan]; Mr. and Mrs. Hinde; Miss Hinde; Master Hinde; Mr. and Mrs. Parks; Mr. and Mrs. Remington; Saucadau (dancer).

It is not now possible to determine who was at the head of the company of strollers (if in fact they were strollers and not local amateurs) who performed in Belfast this season. Since this is the first and last record of acting for virtually all of the company, perhaps the manager was **Edward Hinde**, the only member of the troupe who evinces any theatrical experience.

The **Hinde** family, consisting of Mr. and Mrs. Hinde, Master and Miss Hinde, who acted with the strolling company that performed in Belfast this season, had evidently been strollers for some time prior to this engagement. At the end of the company's visit to Belfast, Edward Hinde published the following notice, attached to the playbill for his benefit performance:

> "For the Benefit of Hinde to enable him to become a Residencer in the Town.
> . . . To the worthy inhabitants of the Town of Belfast. A conscientiousness of declining Years and an ardent Desire (for the better Education of my Children) to settle my Family in some agreeable Place has induced me to pitch upon the Town of Belfast and to throw myself upon that good Nature so visibly the Characteristic of the Place by a Residence in a Public Way. But as means are necessary at the beginning for such a Purpose the Favour and Approbation of the Town shown in their kind Encouragement of the above-mentioned Play will enable me to pursue the Plan in Consequence of which the best Returns of Thanks and Gratitude attended with all the Care probity and good Usage which are the Expectations of the Public shall daily be given. This may be the happy Means of a whole Family's enjoying the Comfort of an agreeable Retirement and putting my Children in a Way most profitable for themselves and advantageous for the Community and productive of the sincerest Acknowledgments from Gentlemen and Ladies your most obedient humble Servant [signed] Edward Hinde."

Whether Edward Hinde actually settled in Belfast is not known. Hinde may have been related to the long-time Smock Alley actors Mr. and Mrs. Samuel Hinde. Sybil Rosenfeld finds a Mr. and Mrs. Hinde acting with the Norwich players in 1752 and 1753, when a Miss Hinde, who played Tom Thumb, was advertised as being five years old. However, bills for this company in 1754 and 1755 clearly identify this Hinde as William. Master

Hinde, again, aged five years, was playing Tom Thumb in February 1756 with the Norwich company.

To complicate matters, another Hinde was acting in the Norwich company in 1756, at the same time as William Hinde and his family. This, the *BD* suggests, was Edward.

The only record of **Mr.** and **Mrs. Parks** performing is for this season in Belfast. Interestingly, considering Mr. Parks's later obscurity, he played several major parts during this season, including Macheath. Mrs. Parks played mainly secondary roles in Belfast. During the 1765–66 season a Mrs. Parks, probably the same women, is recorded as having acted twice at Smock Alley in the minor part of Mrs. Coaxer in *The Beggar's Opera.*

This is the first notice of the careers of **Mr.** and **Mrs. Remington**. Subsequent to this visit to Belfast, Remington made his Dublin debut at Smock Alley playing tertiary roles in the 1764–65 season, but without his wife. He remained at Smock Alley for the 1765–66 season, disappears for a season, then is found at Smock Alley again, briefly, for the 1766–67 season. In the 1768–69 and 1770–71 Crow Street seasons he is playing secondary characters, and a "Master Remington," probably his son, is mentioned in the same bills.

When Remington reappears at Crow Street in the 1776–77 season it is billed as his "first appearance in Dublin these six years." Master Remington (who received a sole benefit) is in the Crow Street bills, but Mrs. Remington is not mentioned until the opening night of the Fishamble Street theatre on 22 January 1777. Thereafter she played at the rival theatre while her son and husband acted at Crow Street.

Remington and son performed regularly from the beginning of the 1777–78 season, although Mrs. Remington played only after January. The three Remingtons are seldom absent from the Crow Street bills in the 1778–79 season, but they disappear from the Dublin record thereafter. Clark has conflated the events of Remington's son's career with those of the father.

Clark places Remington at Waterford in 1766, at Kilkenny in 1767, 1768, 1770 (with his wife), 1779, and 1781. His presence there is doubtless as a part of the regular summer tour to those theatres by the Crow Street company. The *PRFJ* 8 Feb. 1783 announces the death of James Remington, comedian, at Kilkenny.

This season in Belfast is the only record of theatrical activity for the **Mr.** and **Mrs. Bloomer** who both played primary and secondary roles, and for

Coghlan who acted mainly secondary parts. **Saucadau** was probably a visiting French dancer, but the record is otherwise silent as to his existence. This may be the same actor named **Dougan** who performed in Belfast briefly in the 1749–50 season.

Admission Prices: Pit 2s. 2d., Gallery 1s. 1d. This is the first season in which admission prices are specified in Belfast. Although it is nowhere explicitly stated, the universal practice in Ireland was to charge in British shillings and pence. A slight increase in price was made if Irish money was proffered.

Curtain time: Doors to be opened at 6 and to begin at 7 o'clock.

Repertory, January–April 1763

Judging from the small number of plays performed, the strollers gave the Belfast audience only stock pieces.

Total mainpiece performances: 14 of 11 different mainpieces; 12 of 9 different named afterpieces.
  Shakespeare: 2.
  New Mainpieces: 0.
  New Afterpieces: 0.

(For a key to repertory symbols see above, page 11)

Mainpieces: *The Beggar's Opera* (2); *A Bold Stroke for a Wife*; *The Busy Body* (2); *The Distrest Mother*; *Douglas*; *The Fair Penitent*; *King Richard III*; *The Miser*; *The Provoked Husband* (2); *Romeo and Juliet*; *The Spanish Fryar*.

Afterpieces: *The Cobbler of Preston*; *The Contrivances*†; *The Devil to Pay* (2); *High Life Below Stairs* (2); *The King and the Miller of Mansfield*; *The Lying Valet*; *Miss in Her Teens*; *The Oracle*; *The Virgin Unmasked* (2).

Entr'acte singing and dancing: 8. The bills often print the names of the dances offered, suggesting that Saucadau and his troupe were an important attraction.

Benefits (8): Mr. and Mrs. Bloomer; Dougan and McCoghlan; Hinde(2); Master and Miss Hinde; the Poor; Remington and Parks; Mr. and Mrs. Remington.

January 1763

14 Fri. *The Fair Penitent.* Sciolto–Parks; Rossano–Coghlan; Lothario–Bloomer; Lucilia–Mrs. Remington; Lavinia–Mrs. Hinde; Calista–Mrs. Bloomer. With Dancing by M. Saucadau and a farce called *The Virgin Unmasked.* Pit 2s. 2d., Gallery 1s. 1d. Doors to be opened at 6 and to begin at 7 o'clock. [Clark (1964, 223) identifies this as the first performance this season, but there is no evidence to preclude earlier performances. The fact that the advertisement announces the play with so little fanfare may suggest that the season was already well under way. This is, however, the first mention of admission prices in the Belfast theatre. That admission prices are listed for only a pit and a gallery strongly suggests that The Vaults contained no box seats or second gallery]. Source: 14 Jan. 1763

19 Wed. *Douglas.* Douglas–Remington; Lord Randolph–Bloomer; Lady Randolph–Mrs. Remington. With *The Devil to Pay*. Source: 18 Jan. 1763

21 Fri. *The Provoked Husband.* Lord Townly–Hinde; Manly–Remington; Sir Francis Wronghead–Dougan; John Moody–Bloomer; Squire Richard–Master Hinde; Count Basset–Parks; Myrtilla–Mrs. Remington; Miss Jenny–Miss Hinde; Miss Wronghead–Mrs. Hinde; Lady Grace–Mrs. Parks; Lady Townly–Mrs. Bloomer. With a grand *"Statue Dance"* by Saucadau and others. With a farce called *The Oracle*. Oberon–Master Hinde; Cynthia–Miss Hinde; Fairy Queen–Mrs. Remington. Source: 21 Jan. 1763

26 Wed. *The Busy Body.* With *The Virgin Unmasked.* Source: 25 Jan. 1763

28 Fri. *The Beggar's Opera.* Macheath–Parks. With dancing between the acts and *High Life Below Stairs.* Source: 28 Jan. 1763

February 1763

15 Tues. Benefit of Dougan and McCoghlan. *The Beggar's Opera.* Macheath–Parks; Peachum–Hinde; Lockit–Remington; Filch–Coghlan; Mat o' th' Mint–Bloomer; Budge–Dougan; Polly–Mrs. Remington; Lucy–Mrs. Bloomer; Jenny–Mrs. Parks; Mrs. Coaxer–Miss Hinde; Mrs. Peachum and Diane Trapes–Mrs. Hinde. At the end of Act 1 *"The Drunken Man"* by Dougan. Act 2 a new Dance by M. Saucadau. After the Play will be presented a *"Pierrot Dance."* Pierrot–Saucadau; Pierrette–Coghlan. With *Miss in Her Teens.* Fribble–Parks; Capt. Flash–Remington; Miss Biddy Bellair–Mrs. Remington. Source: 15 Feb. 1763

23 Wed. Benefit of Mr. and Mrs. Remington. *The Miser.* Lovegold–Dougan; Frederick–Remington; James–Coghlan; Ramillie–Parks; Lappit–Mrs. Hinde; Weedle–Mrs. Remington; Mrs. Wisely–Mrs. Parks; Harriet–Mrs. Hinde; Marianne–Mrs. Bloomer. With singing and dancing between the Acts: end of Act 2, *"If Love's a Sweet Passion"* by Mrs. Remington; end of Act 3, *"A Grand Dance"* by Saucadau; Act 4, *"Liberty"* by Mrs. Remington; after the Play an *"Epilogue on Somebody in the Character of Nobody"* by Remington. With *The Lying Valet.* Sharp–Remington; Kitty–Mrs. Remington. Source: 18 Feb. 1763

28 Mon. Benefit of Hinde. *King Richard III.* King Richard–Hinde; King Henry–Bloomer; Buckingham–Parks; Lord Stanley–Coghlan; Norfolk–Dougan; Richmond–Remington; Prince Edward–Miss Hinde; Duke of York–Master Hinde; Queen Elizabeth–Mrs. Hinde; Lady Ann–Mrs. Bloomer; Duchess of York–Mrs. Parks. With several entertainments of singing and dancing, particularly in Act 2 a song by Mrs. Hinde. Act 4 *"Liberty"* Mrs. Remington. Act 5 a new *"Grand Dance"* by Saucadau, Coghlan, and Miss Hinde. With *High Life Below Stairs.* Source: 25 Feb. 1763

March 1763

3 Thurs. *A Bold Stroke for a Wife.* Col. Fainwell–Remington; Sir Philip Modelove–Hinde; Periwinkle–Dougan; Tradelove–Coghlan; Obadiah Prim–Parks; Sackbut–Bloomer; Sarah Prim–Mrs. Hinde; Betty–Mrs. Parks; Anne Lovely–Mrs. Bloomer. By Desire a Prologue (in the Character of a Master Mason) by Parks and an Epilogue in the Character of a Mason's Wife by Mrs. Parks. The original Masons' Songs and Choruses and dancing between the Acts by Saucadau. With a farce called *The Cobbler of Preston.* [This is the first recorded Masonic entertainment to be presented in Belfast]. Source: 1 Mar. 1763

9 Wed. Benefit of Bloomer and Mrs. Bloomer. *The Distrest Mother.* Pyrrhus–Hinde; Orestes–Remington; Pylades–Hinde; Hermione–Mrs. Bloomer. With Dancing by M. Saucadau. Act 2 *"The Life of a Belle"* by Mrs. Hinde. After the Play a humorous Epilogue in Boy's Cloths by Mrs. Bloomer. With *The King and the Miller of Mansfield.* King–Hinde; Miller–Dougan; Peggy–Miss Hinde. Source: 8 Mar. 1763

14 Mon. Benefit of Master Hinde and Miss Hinde. *The Spanish Fryar.* Torrismond–Parks; Bertram–Bloomer; Lorenzo–Remington; Fryar Dominick–Hinde; Gomez–Dougan; Alphonso–Coghlan; Queen Leonora–Mrs. Hinde; Teresa–Mrs. Remington; Elvira–Mrs. Bloomer.

With Singing and Dancing: Act 1 *"The Judgment of Paris"* by Mrs. Hinde. Act 2 a Dance. Act 3 *"Cymon and Iphigenia"* by Mrs. Remington. Act 5 *"A Grand Ballet Dance"* by Saucadau, Coghlan, and Miss Hinde. With *The Contrivances.* The whole to conclude with an Epilogue by Miss Hinde. Source: 11 Mar. 1763

25 Fri.   Benefit of the Poor. *The Busy Body.* The Town of Belfast having always and with great Justice sustained the amiable Character of being remarkably charitable to the Poor in Times of Publick Distress. It is therefore hoped that as Provisions are now dear this Benefit will be considerable and that those well disposed Persons who cannot come themselves will take Tickets to give away in order to increase the Charity. Source: 25 Mar. 1763

29 Tues. Benefit of Remington and Parks. *Romeo and Juliet.* Romeo–Remington; Fryar Laurence–Bloomer; Mercutio–Parks; Juliet–Mrs. Bloomer. With a solemn Dirge and a funeral Procession of Juliet to the Monument of the Capulets, the vocal Parts by Miss Hinde, Mrs. Remington, Mrs. Parks. With *The Devil to Pay.* Source: 29 Mar. 1763

April 1763

4 Mon.   For the Benefit of Hinde to enable him to become a Residencer in the Town. *The Provoked Husband.* [See Hinde biographical sketch above for text of his address to the town]. Source: 1 Apr. 1763

1763–1764 SEASON

[The Belfast theatre was dark].

1764–1765 SEASON

[The Belfast theatre was dark].

1765–1766 SEASON

Venue: The Vaults. The last season they were used for theatrical productions. Since virtually every playbill for this season indicates the venue as "the Vaults" this note has not been repeated in the citations below.

Company: Allen [not Allis, as Clark indicates]; Mr. and Mrs. Francis Berry; Francis Blissett; Mr. and Mrs. Alexander Fisher; Master [P.] Fisher; Mr. and Mrs. Richard Knipe; Miss Knipe; Manwaring; O'Neill.

The Belfast company this season was probably under the management of **Richard William Knipe.** According to his obituary notice in the *Newry Chronicle* (25 March 1779) Knipe had studied law and been admitted to the King's Bench in London, but "about thirty years ago" (i.e., around 1749) abandoned the law for the stage. The Knipes had probably been acting for some time before they are first noticed, with the Norwich company in November 1752, playing some leading roles, such as Oroonoko and Lucy Welldon, and later Archer and Cherry in *The Beaux' Stratagem*. They were still with the Norwich company in 1753 although their whereabouts for the following four seasons are unknown.

The Knipes made their Dublin debut at Crow Street in the 1758–59 season when they both played various minor roles. They continued there in the same capacity during the 1759–60, 1760–61, and 1761–62 seasons. They were numbered among the company that visited Cork in the summers and early autumn of 1760, 1761, and 1762 and Wexford in June of 1764. It was while visiting Wexford that Knipe's farce, *The Wexford Wife; or, The True-Born Irishwoman*, had its premiere (it is not known to have been performed elsewhere or to have been published).

During the 1765–66 season Knipe evidently organized his own strolling company and performed in Belfast from 7 October 1765 until the following March. With them was a Miss Knipe (later Mrs. Andrew Cherry) who sang with her parents. Mrs. Knipe seems to have been a good singer and many of the plays performed in Belfast required that talent. Knipe may have written the two-act ballad farce entitled *The Humours of Belfast* that was performed for his wife's benefit in 1766. The Knipes don't appear in the Dublin bills again until the 1767–68 season, although they were probably members of a touring company. They certainly acted in Cork (1760, 1762, and 1764) and in Wexford in 1764.

Back at Crow Street the Knipes returned to their accustomed places as serviceable secondary actors. Miss Knipe played the Duke of York in *King Richard III* in May 1768. The Knipes probably took to the road again for the 1769–70 season for there is no record of them in Dublin. Mrs. Knipe, but not her husband, returned to Dublin for a final season in 1769–70. Clark finds both Mr. and Mrs. Knipe in Cork in 1767, in Belfast in 1774 (he places Richard Knipe in Belfast at this time, but I can find no record of him during this season), and in Newry in 1779. By 1769 Knipe had become an important member of Michael Atkins's company, but his career ended when on 24 March 1779 he died suddenly and penniless "after a short illness." Thereafter, his wife evidently left the stage, for there is no record of any further activity. For their daughter's later activities see below under **Mrs. Andrew Cherry** in the 1782–83 season.

The only record of **Francis Berry**, besides the two performances given by both him and his wife in Belfast this season, is a benefit in January 1771, again in Belfast, this time with Parker's troupe, but there is no record of his having acted that season.

The *BD* says that **Blissett** was born in Berkshire and made his London debut in the English provinces, at Shepton Mallet, at some date before he made his Smock Alley debut in the 1763–64 season in tertiary roles. Thereafter Blissett may have joined a strolling company in the Irish provinces for he is not again listed as having acted in Dublin. Neither Clark nor *BD* has noted that Blissett spent the 1765–66 season in Belfast, where he received two sole benefits, but none of his roles has survived. From Belfast Blissett traveled to Scotland where he performed both in Dundee and in Edinburgh in 1767. For the next nine years Blissett toured in the north of England until he established himself at the Theatre Royal, Bristol, around 1776. He remained there as a popular mainstay of the company until 1797–98.

The *BD* observes that Blissett "would have been a leading actor in London" but "he had a superstitious dread of playing an engagement in the metropolis," although he was lured to the Haymarket Theatre for a short time in 1776 and he returned there each summer through 1781. Blissett is said to have excelled "in acting Midas, and all characters in which are painted the avarice, decrepitude, or folly of old age." He seems to have retired from the stage near the end of the century, although he re-appears at the Haymarket Theatre in the spring of 1803. He died in Bath in 1824.

Alexander Fisher, the Irish-born provincial actor and manager, first comes to notice as a member of the Smock Alley company in the 1758–59 season when he acted with his son. The two continued at Smock Alley through 1759–60. Thereafter, Fisher may have joined an itinerant company, although the record is silent until he is found with a strolling company that visited Lurgan and Belfast for the 1765–66 season. It is possible that Fisher was managing this strolling company.

His son, whose first initial is cited as "P." in a Belfast playbill printed when his family and he performed there for the 1765–66 season (overlooked by

Clark), made his Dublin debut in 1758 at Crow Street in the title role in *The Life and Death of Tom Thumb the Great*, billed as "his first appearance in this Kingdom." Fisher is best known for his direction of the itinerant company which, after traveling to France, Flanders, and Denmark, established a theatre in 1771 at the St. Petersburg court of Empress Catherine of Russia and remained there for some time.

The young Fisher and his mother had brief careers in London, although Alexander Fisher does not seem to have acted there. They made their London debuts at the Haymarket Theatre in April 1776 in *Isabella*. Contemporary accounts say she is of Irish birth. As late as September 1782 she is acting at the Haymarket Theatre after which she disappears from the record.

This is the only record of **Allen's** acting.

For biographical sketch of **Manwaring** see Summer Season 1761.

For biographical sketch of **O'Neill** see 1757–58 season

House charges: The charity benefit for reduced housekeepers on 9 December 1765 produced total receipts of £49. 16s. with net receipts to the charity of £35. 4s. 5d., suggesting that house charges at the theatre during this time were about £15.

Repertory, 1765–66 Season

This company of strollers depended heavily on stock pieces, although one new mainpiece and three new afterpieces were staged. The fact that most of the new plays were musical entertainments requiring competent singers suggests that Knipe's company excelled in that area. Bickerstaffe's very popular comic opera, *Love in a Village*, probably received its Belfast premiere this season, at the command of the Countess of Donegall, two years after its first staging in Dublin. The new afterpieces were *Polly Honeycombe*, long a Dublin favorite, *The Wanton Wife* and *The Humours of Belfast*. This two-act ballad farce seems to have been written by Knipe especially for his wife's benefit in Belfast, for no other record of it exists.

Total Performances: 40, of 24 different mainpieces and 40 of 21 different named afterpieces.
   Shakespeare: 5.
   New Mainpieces: 1.

New Afterpieces: 3.

(For a key to repertory symbols see above, page 11)

Mainpieces: *The Beggar's Opera; A Bold Stroke for a Wife; The Busy Body; The Constant Couple; The Distrest Mother*(2); *Douglas*(2); *The Earl of Essex; The Fair Penitent; Hamlet; The Inconstant; King Richard III*(3); *Love in a Village**(4); *Macbeth*†(2); *Oroonoko*(2); *The Orphan*(2); *Othello*(2); *The Provoked Husband*(2); *The Recruiting Officer; The Revenge*(3); *Romeo and Juliet*(2); *The Suspicious Husband; Tamerlane; Theodosius; Venice Preserved*(2).

Afterpieces: *The Adventures of Half an Hour; The Anatomist(2); Chrononhotonthologos* (3); *The Cheats of Scapin*†; *The Citizen*†(4); *The Contrivances*(3); *Damon and Phillida; The Devil to Pay*(2); *High Life Below Stairs*(2); *The Honest Yorkshireman; The Humours of Belfast *Θ; The King and the Miller of Mansfield; The Mayor of Garratt*†; *Miss in Her Teens(2); The Mock Doctor; The Old Maid*†(3); *Polly Honeycombe*; The Vintner Tricked* (2); *The Virgin Unmasked* (4); *The Wanton Wife **(3); *What We Must All Come To*†.

Entr'acte Singing and Dancing: None listed

Benefits (11): Berry; Blissett (2); Fisher; Mrs. Fisher; Knipe; Mrs. Knipe; Miss Knipe; Manwaring; O'Neill; Reduced Housekeepers.

October 1765

7 Mon. At the Vaults. *Othello*. Othello–Knipe; Brabantio–Berry; Cassio–O'Neill; Duke–Manwaring; Roderigo–Master Fisher; Montano–Allen; Iago–Fisher; Emilia–Mrs. Berry; Desdemona–Mrs. Knipe. With *High Life Below Stairs*. Source: 4 Oct. 1765

9 Wed. By Command of the Countess of Donegall. *Love in a Village*. With *Miss in Her Teens*. Source: 8 Oct. 1765

11 Fri. *Theodosius* and *The Citizen*. Source: 11 Oct. 1765

16 Wed. *The Provoked Husband*. With *The Honest Yorkshireman*. Source: 15 Oct. 1765

18 Fri. *The Distrest Mother*. Pyrrhus–Knipe; Orestes–Fisher; Hermione–Mrs. Fisher; Andromache–Mrs. Berry. With a farce called *The Devil to Pay*. Jobson–Berry; Nell (songs in Character)–Mrs. Knipe. Source: 18 Oct. 1765

23 Wed. *Oroonoko.* Oroonoko–Knipe; Aboan–Fisher; Charlotte Weldon–Mrs. Knipe; Imoinda–Mrs. Fisher. With *The Virgin Unmasked.* Source: 22 Oct. 1765

25 Fri. Second Night. By particular desire of several Ladies and Gentlemen. *The Distrest Mother.* Third Night. *The Citizen.* Source: 25 Oct. 1765

30 Wed. *The Suspicious Husband.* With *The Mock Doctor.* Source: 29 Oct. 1765

November 1765

1 Fri. *King Richard III.* With *The Vintner Tricked.* Source: 1 Nov. 1765

6 Wed. *Douglas.* With a farce never performed here called *The Wanton Wife.* Source: 5 Nov. 1765

8 Fri. *Love in a Village.* With a farce called *Chrononhotonthologos.* Source: 8 Nov. 1765

13 Wed. *The Recruiting Officer.* With a farce called *Damon and Phillida.* Source: 12 Nov. 1765

15 Fri. By Desire. *The Beggar's Opera.* With a farce called *The Wanton Wife.* Source: 15 Nov. 1765

19 Wed. By desire. Second Night. *Tamerlane.* By desire. Fourth Night *The Citizen.* Source: 19 Nov. 1765

22 Fri. *Venice Preserved.* With *The King and the Miller of Mansfield.* Source: 22 Nov. 1765

27 Wed. *The Busy Body.* With *The Contrivances.* Source: 26 Nov. 1765

29 Fri. By particular Desire of several Ladies and Gentlemen. *Othello.* With *High Life Below Stairs.* Source: 29 Nov. 1765

December 1765

2 Mon. *The Orphan* and *The Old Maid.* [Published in Belfast by James Magee in 1769]. Source: 29 Nov. 1765

4 Wed. *The Fair Penitent* and *The Vintner Tricked.* Source: 3 Dec. 1765

[No performance 6 December 1765].

9 Mon. Benefit of Reduced House-Keepers. *Douglas.* With *The Devil to Pay.* The Produce arising from this Play will be laid out in Coals to be bought on the best Terms and delivered out to reduced House-Keepers. Ladies and Gentlemen who patronize this Charity and dispose of ten Tickets or more to have the Nomination of Objects for the distribution to the Value of the Tickets they respectively take. Tickets 2s. 2d. each. The Company of Comedians have declined performing on Friday the 6th Instant that there may be sufficient time to carry this laudable Scheme into Execution. The Tragedy of *Macbeth* is now in rehearsal and will soon be performed; no methods will be left untried to render the Performance as complete as possible. [A prologue on the occasion written by Knipe and disbursement of proceeds (total receipts £49. 16s.) may be found in 13 December 1765]. Source: 6 Dec. 1765

11 Wed. *A Bold Stroke for a Wife.* With (by Desire) *The Old Maid.* Source: 10 Dec. 1765

13 Fri. *The Revenge.* With *The Wanton Wife.* Source: 13 Dec. 1765

18 Wed. Second Night. By particular Desire of several Ladies and Gentlemen. *The Revenge.* Third Night. With, by desire, a Farce called *The Old Maid.* Source: 17 Dec. 1765

20 Fri. The last Time of the Company's performing till after Christmas. *Romeo and Juliet.* With a farce called *The Virgin Unmasked.* Source: 20 Dec. 1765

27 Fri. *Macbeth.* With a farce called *Miss in Her Teens.* Source: 27 Dec. 1765

January 1766

1 Wed. By Desire. *The Provoked Husband.* With, by Desire, fifth Night, a Farce called *The Citizen.* Source: 31 Dec. 1765

3 Fri. By Desire. *Love in a Village.* With, by Desire, a Farce called *The Contrivances.* Source: 3 Jan. 1766

8 Wed. Second Night. By particular Desire of Several Ladies and Gentleman. *Macbeth.* With *Chrononhotonthologos.* Source: 7 Jan. 1766

10 Fri.   Second Night. By particular Desire of Several Ladies and Gentlemen. *The Earl of Essex.* With *The Virgin Unmasked.* Source: 10 Jan. 1766

15 Wed.   Third Night. By particular Desire of Several Ladies and Gentlemen. *The Revenge.* With *Chrononhotonthologos.* Source: 14 Jan. 1766

20 Mon.   Benefit of Knipe. *Oroonoko.* With Singing by Mrs. Knipe and Miss Knipe and a farce called *The Anatomist.* Source: 17 Jan. 1766

27 Mon.   Benefit of O'Neill. *The Constant Couple.* With *The Cheats of Scapin.* The Play intended for this Evening is obliged to be put off on Account of Knipe's hoarseness which is to be much increased as to render him unable to perform. Source: 24 Jan. 1766

29 Wed.   Benefit of Blissett. *Love in a Village.* With a farce called *The Adventures of Half an Hour.* Source: 28 Jan. 1766

31 Fri.   Benefit of Fisher. *King Richard III.* With a farce called *Polly Honeycombe.* Source: 31 Jan. 1766

February 1766

5   Wed.   Benefit of Miss Knipe. By particular Desire of several Ladies and Gentlemen. *The Orphan.* With a farce called *The Anatomist.* Source: 4 Feb. 1766

7   Fri.   Benefit of Blissett [second]. By particular desire of several ladies and gentlemen. *King Richard III.* With a farce called *The Contrivances.* Source: 7 Feb. 1766

19 Wed.   Benefit of Mrs. Fisher. *Venice Preserved.* With *The Virgin Unmasked.* The company of comedians beg leave to inform the public that they will not perform till Wednesday next as they are determined on all occasions to shew a ready obedience to the law and customs of this town and particularly on this and such like solemn occasions [i.e., the first week of Lent]. And as they will perform very few nights more they embrace this opportunity to return the public their sincere and humble acknowledgments for the many favours they have been indulged with. Source: 18 Feb. 1766

21 Fri.   Benefit of Mainwaring. *Romeo and Juliet.* With *The Mayor of Garratt.* With variety of entertainments. Source: 21 Feb. 1766

28 Fri.   Positively the last night but two. Benefit of Mrs. Knipe. *Hamlet.* Hamlet–Knipe. With variety of the most celebrated songs now in vogue never sung on this stage before by Mrs. Knipe. With a new ballad farce of two acts never performed before in any place called *The Humours of Belfast.* With an occasional prologue written by a gentleman of this place to be spoken by the author and his wife. Knipe takes this opportunity to return his hearty thanks to several gentlemen and ladies who proposed his taking a second night as he had the worst benefit in the whole company which he humbly begs leave to decline and intreats their protection for Mrs. Knipe's night which he will ever remember with the highest sense of gratitude. Source: 25 Feb. 1766

March 1766

10 Mon.   Positively the last night of performing. Benefit of Berry. *The Inconstant.* With by particular desire a farce called *What We Must All Come To.* Source: 7 Mar. 1766

1766–1767 SEASON

[The Belfast theatre was dark].

1767–1768 SEASON

[The Belfast theatre was dark].

1768–1769 SEASON

Venue: The theatre known as James Parker's "New Theatre in Mill Street" and, more commonly, "the Theatre, Millgate." Not to be confused with Thomas Ryder's "new Theatre in Mill Gate," which opened in 1770. **Company**: "Comedians from the Theatres Royal of London, Dublin, and Edinburgh": Michael Atkins; Bullock; Mr. and Mrs. Brown; Mr. and Mrs. Thomas (Elizabeth) Farrell; Michael Fullam; Myrton Hamilton; Jackson; Mrs. Maxwell; Mrs. Mozeen; James Parker (actor-manager); Mr. and Mrs. Pye; Master Pye; Mr. and Mrs. Joseph Waker; Mrs. Wright.

This superior strolling company was headed by **James Parker.** The identity of the actor named Parker who made his "first appearance in the character" of Ben in *Love for Love* at Capel Street on 10 February 1747 is uncertain but he may be identified as James Parker. It is perhaps he who acted in Tralee in the spring of 1756. The first definite evidence identifying James Parker are the playbills advertising the company of "Comedians from the Theatres Royal of London, Dublin, and Edinburgh" that acted in Belfast this season (and later this year in Newry and Kilkenny).

Clark (1965, 226) speculates that at some time before the beginning of the 1768–69 Belfast season, Parker "fixed up a small unpretentious theatre" in Mill Street, and at about the same time Parker built a new theatre in High Street, Newry, which the company also used. Evidently, Parker continued to lead his strolling company in the Irish provinces during the 1769–70 and 1770–71 seasons, but the record is silent.

Parker returned to Belfast in the summer of 1771, and the preseason playbills announced that "the Theatre in Mill Street is repairing," a statement that throws no light upon whether he used the old playhouse he had abandoned in 1769 or took over Ryder's new theatre (*BNL* 16 July 1771). Parker and his company acted in the Mill Gate theatre from November 1771 through January 1772, when his association with Belfast theatricals ends. In 1776 Parker evidently accompanied the Smock Alley company to Kilkenny, but the record is otherwise silent. *PRFJ* 7 April 1778 announces the death in Temple Lane (Dublin) of James Parker, comedian.

Michael Atkins, c. 1747–1812, was the most important person in the history of the Belfast theatre in the eighteenth century. Atkins was the son of Michael Atkins, a minor Drury Lane actor and singer. The younger Atkins was born ca. 1747, presumably in London, and it was probably in London that he made his stage debut, although details are lacking. He first appears in the record in 1759, at Drury Lane, in an all-juvenile production. He and a sister may have acted in Bristol in the summers of 1761 and 1762.

The *BD* places Atkins in Kilkenny in the winter and spring of 1761, although Clark does not list these performances (the *BD* has confused several details of the record of Atkins). By the time he made what seems to have been his Dublin debut in December 1762, Atkins was already a fairly substantial performer and displayed versatility also as a painter, machinist and harlequin. On 3 December 1761, the opening night of Smock Alley, he played the main role in a piece of his own composition (music by Claget) titled *Harlequin's Funeral; or, Sir Sawney Outwitted*, which was liked and brought some money.

Atkins disappears from view until this season, when, in addition to playing in Belfast, he also is found acting in Newry, and Kilkenny, playing primary

(Romeo; Richard III) and secondary roles and dancing. He probably stayed with Parker's company, although the record is again silent until the summer of 1771, when, according to the *BD*, he sang at Dublin's Ranelagh Gardens in burlettas. Later that summer and through January 1772, Atkins is found with Parker's company in Belfast. That season, in addition to singing, dancing and acting in several primary roles, he painted "proper scenes, particularly, the library, moonlight, garden" in *Lionel and Clarissa* and also composed new music for the premiere of a piece written by Dr. Maryat called *Love in a Bog* (the *BD* errs in stating that "the title has been forgotten").

At about this time James Parker relinquished control of his company to Michael Atkins, and thus began Atkins long management of the Belfast theatre. After leaving the theatre dark for the 1772–73 season, Atkins reopened it on 6 September 1773 for a season of six months. Thereafter, Atkins brought his company to Belfast in alternate seasons (1775–76, 1777–78), performing in the new theatre he had built in Derry in the intervening years.

Atkins married the actress Catherine Hutton of Belfast in that city in 1771. She made her Belfast debut on 8 September 1773 as Clarissa in *Lionel and Clarissa*. Few of her roles survive, but her record parallels that of her husband until she evidently retired from the stage in 1798. She died in 1808 at the age of 58.

Late in the 1777–78 season Atkins apparently had a row with members of his company, and he withdrew from it for a season, preferring instead to act with Ryder's Smock Alley company, then visiting Cork. Atkins was soon back in Belfast, however, and beginning with the 1780–81 season Atkins managed the theatre company that played there and in Derry without interruption until the end of the century. Atkins was responsible for building two new theatres in Belfast: Rosemary Lane Theatre (1784) and Arthur Street (1792).

If Belfast can be said to have had a "resident" theatre company during this era it must be identified with the seasons between 1780–81 and 1784–85 when Atkins's company performed in Belfast for extended periods each year making short visits only to Lisburn. After 1784–85 Atkins went back to his former custom of alternating the venue of his company between Belfast and Derry (1785–86; 1787–88; 1789–90; 1793–94).

The civil unrest associated with the 1798 rebellion seriously affected Atkins's finances, but after three years interruption (1796–97 through 1798–99) Atkins reopened Arthur Street theatre in December of 1799 and continued to manage the theatre until he relinquished the management in 1805. He continued to act in Belfast almost until his death on 15 April 1812.

Henry Brown, according to the *BD*, was acting in Bath as early as 1751–52 at the playhouse known as "Mr. Browne's Theatre." When he made what was probably his first London appearance, at Drury Lane in February 1753, he was billed as being "from Bath and Ireland," implying that he had acted in Ireland sometime previous to that date. Perhaps, as was suggested above, he was the Brown who is found in Belfast in the winter of 1750–51.

After a brief sojourn in Chester, Brown returned to Bath were he remained until making his Dublin debut at Smock Alley on 1 December 1757 in his most famous role, the Copper Captain, in *Rule a Wife*. Brown was then billed as "from Bath, his first appearance in this Kingdom." George Faulkner, the Dublin printer, in a letter to Samuel Derrick dated 16 November 1758, observes that "We have got one Brown, who is a most surprising Comedian and hath played the Copper Captain in *Rule a Wife and Have a Wife*, several Times to very crowded Audiences to their entire Satisfaction" (cited in *BD*).

At the end of April in the 1757–58 season Thomas Sheridan gave up the management of the Smock Alley theatre and was succeeded by Brown who helped the company limp through to the end of a generally unsuccessful season. The 1758–59 season also opened at Smock Alley under Brown's direction. This season was more successful that the previous due in part to the fact that Brown had convinced Mrs. Abington to break her articles with Drury Lane and to accept his offer to appear in Dublin. They had known one another in Bath in 1757. That summer Brown took the company to Cork.

According to Tate Wilkinson (1790, 156) who was acting in Dublin during the 1759–60 season, Brown had been "in much esteem as an actor and a gentleman at Bath and Edinburgh—once attempted Richard at Drury Lane, but was barely permitted to finish the part—He had been in the army, and was well known by most of the officers; was a most pleasing well-behaved companion, was very indolent, a second Digges for extravagance, was much in debt in England and in Dublin, and it was immaterial to him if he failed as manager, for he could not be poorer." 1760–61 went off with reasonable success but 1761–62 found Brown in considerable financial distress, despite the fact that the Barry-Woodward partnership at Crow Street was fast unraveling. Brown evidently transferred the management at Smock Alley to Henry Mossop. His whereabouts during the 1763–64 season are not known.

On 20 December 1764 Henry Brown made his first appearance at Crow Street under Barry his former rival. Brown's stature at this time is suggested by the fact that he was advertised as performing a limited engagement of six nights, although in the event he continued his engagement through the 1765–66, 1766–67, and 1767–68 seasons. Brown visited Cork in the autumn of 1765 and 1766 and Belfast in August of 1768.

Some confusion arises with Brown's whereabouts during the 1767–68 season. A Mr. Brown is engaged for six performances at Crow Street early in the season, and his engagement is renewed until late January. Judging from the roles that he is advertised to play (Copper Captain, Benedict) this was probably Henry Brown. Then there is a hiatus, and in May a Mr. Brown, announced as just arrived from England, his "first appearance this season" arrives at Crow Street and appears in many of the same roles. We must assume that Henry Brown had traveled to England (but not to London) for a few months and then returned to Dublin. The reference to his "first appearance this season" must refer to the summer season.

To further complicate matters, a Brown acted in minor roles at Crow Street in March and April 1768 during the period when Henry Brown was evidently abroad. This is probably the Brown who acted in more tertiary roles at Crow Street during the 1768–69 and 1769–70 seasons.

Henry Brown evidently left Dublin traveling to Newry in January, Kilkenny in June, and Cork in September 1769. There the record of his acting ends. He probably left Ireland, perhaps for the Scottish theatres. However, in February 1770 the newspapers announced his death in Glasgow. Henry Brown married the actress Elizabeth Slack not long before his death. When she appeared in Dublin for the 1770–71 season the bills read: "Mrs. Brown, late Miss Slack, is arrived from England and is to perform this season at Smock Alley."

According to the *BD*, Elizabeth Slack made her stage debut at Drury Lane in November 1764 and she acted and sang there, at Covent Garden and at the new Richmond Theatre through 1765 before coming to Dublin. The preliminary bills for her Smock Alley debut on 6 December 1765 read: "Yesterday [25 November] Miss Slack a celebrated Actress from the Theatre Royal, Drury Lane arrived here from England; and we hear she is engaged to perform at the Theatre in Smock Alley." Henry Brown was in the same company, and they probably first met at that time. Miss Slack went over to the Crow Street company for the 1766–67 season and traveled to Cork with the company that summer. Evidently, Miss Slack was not paid her salary while in Cork, for a year later the newspapers announce that her singing teacher, Mr. Bates, sued Spranger Barry "for a Large Sum of Money due to him from the Defendant for the performances of Miss Slack, the Plaintiff's Apprentice, in the Theatre at Cork. After a short Hearing, a Verdict was given in Favour of the Plaintiff" (*FDJ* 1–3 Dec. 1768).

Miss Slack was evidently back in Britain during the 1767–68 and 1769–70 seasons although the record is silent. At some time before February 1770 she married Henry Brown who died shortly thereafter. Billed as Mrs. Brown, "the late Miss Slack, her first appearance here these five years" the actress returned to Dublin for the 1770–71 season playing primary roles and singing. Interestingly, the *HM* April 1771 announces: "This night [16 March 1771], at the fourth performance of *Cymon*, Mrs. Brown, who did the part of the Virgin Silvia, took her labour on the stage in the third act, and was safely delivered during the fourth."

After this season Mrs. Henry Brown disappears from the record for a time, but she returned to Dublin for the 1772–73 Capel Street season ("first appearance in Dublin in three years"), moving to Smock Alley after Capel Street closed. She continued to act at Smock Alley through the 1775–76 season. Her whereabouts are not known for the intervening seasons, but she is found performing in Dublin again in the 1778–79 season, for the first time at Crow Street, but remained in Dublin only through that season (the *BD* errs in saying her last Dublin appearance was in 1777). Thereafter, she disappears from the record.

The only theatrical records for the actor named **Bullock** are that for this Belfast season, performing secondary roles, such at Friar Lawrence in *Romeo and Juliet*, and again with Parker's company in Kilkenny in June of 1769. Thereafter he disappears from the record.

A **Mr.** and **Mrs. Farrell** were acting in secondary roles at Capel Street during the 1747–48 season. It is possible that these were the same Farrells who performed regularly at Smock Alley in 1757–58 (Mrs. Farrell only, in the line of older women) and 1758–59 (both Mr. and Mrs. Farrell). However, it is much less probable that the early Farrells can be identified with the performers Clark calls Mr. and Mrs. Thomas Farrell, who were principally provincial performers. Clark finds them often in Belfast: in the 1768–69 season (and also in Cavan, Newry and Kilkenny at various times during that season), and in the 1770–71, 1771–72, 1773–74 and 1778–78 seasons. It was probably Thomas Farrell also who acted (without his wife) in supernumerary roles at Crow Street in the 1765–66 and 1769–70 seasons and in the 1768–69 (with Mrs. Farrell). The *BD* speculates that the Mr. Farrell who performed with Foote's summer company at the Haymarket Theatre from 1769–1772 may have been Thomas Farrell.

Evidently, the Farrells had more than one daughter active on the Belfast stage. The **Miss Farrell** who was present with her parents in Belfast during the 1771–72, 1773–74 (as one of the "Misses Farrell"), 1778–79 seasons and alone during the 1779–80 season, and also for one night at Smock Alley in the 1782–83 season was Miss L. Farrell, the only daughter who sought to make a career of acting.

The details relating to **Mr.** and **Mrs. Michael Fullam** found in Clark (1965, 358) and in *BD* are often inaccurate. The earliest record we have of the activities of any Fullam (sometimes spelled "Fulham") in Ireland is during the 1767–68 Crow Street season, playing mainly young men's tertiary roles. The appearance in December 1768 in Belfast of a Mr. Fullam, billed as "his first appearance on this stage," suggests at the least that this Fullam, whom Clark identifies as Michael, had previously acted elsewhere. A Mrs. Fullam is listed in the bills for the same season, once, as a supernumerary at Crow Street in May 1768 and again in the 1768–69 season.

Clark, erroneously, finds a Mrs. Fullam acting in Belfast on 23 August 1768 and 20 January 1769; her name is not listed in any Belfast playbill, either on those dates or any other of that season. Mr. and Mrs. Fullam certainly acted in Newry and Kilkenny later in 1769.

The *BD* distinguishes between the Fullam acting in the late 1760s and Michael Fullam, who was to become manager of Crow Street in the early nineteenth century, based upon the questionable assertion of W. J. Lawrence that Michael Fullam was born in 1758. According to the *BD*, the activities of the Fullams prior to 1780 are those of Michael's "mother and father." However, a brief biographical sketch and portrait of Michael Fullam, "Deputy Manager of the Theatre Royal, Crow Street," may be found in *HM* May 1804 and suggests otherwise. Its details are few, saying only that Michael Fullam was born in Dublin in the parish of St. Catherine. Fullam lost his parents at an early age and was raised by his grandfather until he, too, died when Fullam was 17. Thomas Ryder befriended him and he made his debut in Waterford. Fullam later acted in England.

However, there is nothing incompatible about Michael Fullam's performing in both 1767 and 1771, if we assume that Lawrence was wrong in assigning

Fullam's birth date. The Fullam who played Fulmer in the Crow Street 18 November 1771 production of *The West Indian* and who appeared regularly during the 1774–75 season in younger men's roles is probably Michael Fullam. Mrs. Fullam also acted regularly, in younger women's roles, during the 1774–75 season. The Fullams are also found acting in the provinces: in Derry (1771) and Kilkenny (1772–73).

After the 1774–75 season the whereabouts of the Fullams is uncertain for some years. They may have acted in Birmingham in 1779 and in Exeter in the 1780s. Michael Fullam played at Brighton in July 1790 and again the following summer.

When Fullam next appears in Ireland, briefly, at Crow Street on 11 November 1791, he is billed as being "from the Theatre Royal, Edinburgh, his first appearance on this stage" (facts overlooked by *BD*). Although he is not known to have acted in Dublin again until 1797–98, Fullam is found in Kilkenny in the autumns of 1792, 1793 (as manager), 1795,1796, and 1799; in Waterford in 1792 and 1793; and in Limerick in 1799 and 1800. Mr. and Mrs. Fullam performed in Belfast again from 3–10 February 1800. The playbills state that "Jones, manager of the Theatre-Royal Dublin, with that liberality which has always distinguished him as a leader of taste in the Metropolis having consented to give Fullam a week's absence."

When the new Fishamble Street theatre opened on 1 December 1797 Fullam is playing primary roles there ("his first appearance on this stage"), and he transferred to Crow Street in the same capacity when Fishamble Street closed in late January. He continued there through 1799–1800. Mrs. Fullam acted in the English provinces during the last decade of the eighteenth century: in Brighton (1791), Plymouth (1792), and Norwich between 1793 and 1796.

The Crow Street bills for 1 November 1801 state that it is Fullam's "first appearance these two years." He was to remain at Crow Street for the remainder of that theatre's existence. Mrs. Fullam made her first appearance on the Crow Street stage the same season, on 19 May 1801. Thereafter she performed infrequently, usually only once a season for her husband's benefit (e.g., 19 May 1803).

By the 1803–04 season Fullam had been appointed "deputy manager" of the Crow Street theatre by Frederick Jones. For a memoir and portrait of Fullam see *HM* for May 1804: "The manner in which he conducts himself, in the situation he fills, of deputy manager, has gained him the universal good-will of his brother performers, and fully justifies the opinion Mr. Jones formed of him, when he appointed him to that office, on Mr. Holman's quitting this Kingdom."

Fullam continued to act at Crow Street until it closed in 1820 and then moved with the company to the temporary Theatre Royal in the Rotunda while the new Hawkins's Street Theatre was under construction. He probably performed there regularly also. Michael Fullam died in January 1826 in Dublin.

Myrton Hamilton was evidently the youngest of a family of actors that included his father, his mother and two brothers, James and William, who were active in London in the 1730s. Amazingly, considering his long and relatively distinguished career on the Irish stage, Myrton Hamilton did not perform in London and is therefore not included in the *BD*.

The Hamilton who was performing at Cork with the Crow Street company in 1756 and then again the summers of 1760 through 1765 was very probably William, who was at that time a regular member of the Crow Street company, and not Myrton, as Clark indicates (1965, 360). On the other hand, the Hamilton found in Belfast and Newry from 1768 and for many seasons until 1783 is almost certainly Myrton (his brother William is known to have been acting in London for much of that time, except for a brief period in Belfast in the autumn of 1779).

At the end of the 1778–79 season, the direction of the Belfast theatre passed for a time into the hands of Myrton Hamilton, who moved the company to the new Ann Street theatre. Hamilton and his company continued to use the Ann Street venue for the 1778–79 and 1779–80 seasons. The following season, however, Hamilton left Belfast and was engaged at Dublin's Smock Alley theatre, where he played secondary and tertiary parts.

At the end of the 1780–81 season, Hamilton evidently organized a strolling company that toured the northern Irish provinces through the summer of 1783. In June of that year Hamilton was challenging Atkins again for the direction of Belfast stage, and there was a struggle for possession of the theatre. He proposed to enlarge the Ann Street theatre but was unable to attract the subscription money he needed and gave up the idea. Clark suggests that Myrton Hamilton went to England after this (1965, 246), but I am unable to find any evidence confirming the assertion.

The name of Hamilton disappears from the Dublin record again for several years until 22 December 1784 when at Fishamble Street a Hamilton played

Papillion in *The Lyar* and the performance is billed as his "first appearance in this city these eight years." In later bills that season two actors named Hamilton are listed: one is designated as "M. Hamilton," the other simply as "Hamilton." The former was almost certainly Myrton Hamilton, the latter possibly his elder brother William. There is no further record of Myrton Hamilton after the 1784–85 season.

John Jackson (1730–1806) was born in Berkshire in 1730 and educated for the clergy. His heart was on the stage, however, and he made his stage debut in Edinburgh in 1762. Thinking the competition for roles in Edinburgh too stiff at that time, Jackson went to London and made his Drury Lane debut in October and met with some success. He remained at Drury Lane for several seasons, acting in the summers at the new Richmond theatre. The *BD* errs in saying that Jackson went to Dublin after the summer of 1765; no Jackson is listed there during the 1765–67 season, although a Mr. Jackson first appears in Dublin at Smock Alley during the 1766–67 season playing mainly secondary roles. The identity of this Jackson is difficult to determine with certainly because, as we shall see, later playbills clearly state that John Jackson made "his first appearance in this kingdom," in May 1771. (The actor Thomas Jackson made his Irish debut in 1772). It is probably John Jackson who was with the company of "Comedians from the Theatres Royal of London, Dublin, and Edinburgh" in Belfast this season.

John Jackson visited Dublin in the spring of 1771. Mrs. John Jackson (billed as from Theatre Royal, Edinburgh "formerly Miss Brown, her first appearance on this stage these five years)," is found at Crow Street performing in *The Beggar's Opera* on 6 May 1771. John played Oroonoko two days later and is billed also as "from the Theatre Royal, Edinburgh," but the advertisement stresses that this is "his first appearance in this kingdom."

For the 1771–72 season the Jacksons moved to Smock Alley and acted with Mossop's company. When Mrs. Brown made her first Smock Alley appearance that season (on 15 November 1771) it was said to be "her first appearance on this stage these four years." They continued at Smock Alley for the 1772–73 season. Thomas Jackson was also acting at Smock Alley this season and it is possible that some of his roles have become confused with John Jackson's.

The John Jacksons moved to Capel Street during the 1773–74 season and on 2 December 1773 a play entitled *Eldred; or, The British Freeholder* written by John Jackson was performed for the first time. The Jacksons left Dublin at the end of that season and traveled to York and Liverpool in late 1774.

The following summer Mr. and Mrs. Jackson acted at the Haymarket Theatre, and his wife continued on in London for several years. John, however, returned to the life of a stroller, playing at Birmingham (summers 1775 and 1776), Bristol (1776 and 1777) and Edinburgh (1776–77).

The Jacksons returned to Dublin in the winter of 1777 (billed as their first appearance in three years). On 13 January 1777 at Crow Street Jackson's second play *Gerilda; or, The Siege of Harlech* received its premiere performance. This tragedy was later performed in London as *The British Heroine*. A Dublin critic stated that it was "performed to a brilliant and crowded audience with very great applause."

In May 1780 John Jackson took over the management of the Alston Street Theatre in Glasgow, in partnership with a Mr. Mills and the actor John Bland. This theatre and all its contents was burned down shortly thereafter by anti-theatre fanatics, but Jackson resolved to build another theatre on the outskirts of the city in Dunlop Street, which opened in January 1782. By the end of the decade Jackson had an interest in virtually every theatre in Scotland, including those in Edinburgh, Aberdeen, and Dundee. Jackson continued to act in Ireland and the provinces during this period. The Jackson found at Crow Street during the 1783–84 season may have been John.

By 1790, however, Jackson was in financial difficulty and was forced to auction the theatres in Glasgow and Edinburgh in 1791. Stephen Kemble, the Newcastle manager, got the leases after a long and rancorous legal battle. Meanwhile the Jacksons performed at Crow Street in the 1795–96 season and later in the English provinces. In 1800 Jackson raised the money to buy back the Edinburgh and Glasgow theatres, selling a half-interest to Francis Aickin, the Liverpool manager. Jackson sold his interest in the theatres to Anthony Rock in 1806. He died on 4 December 1806 at the age of 76.

In addition to three plays (his *Sir William Wallace, of Ellerslie; or, The Siege of Dumbarton Castle* was unsuccessful and not performed outside of Glasgow), John Jackson also published (1792) a *History of the Scottish Stage, from its first establishment to the present time*." Jackson evidently had meager talent as an actor, but was much more successful as a manager and entrepreneur. His tenacity in establishing a theatre in Glasgow against powerful forces of resistance establish his claim to be the father of the Glasgow stage.

Mrs. Maxwell first comes to our attention at Crow Street in the 1758–59 season, playing as a supernumerary. She was seldom to rise about that level in any company. The following six seasons she is found at Crow Street in tertiary roles and dancing, and she was with the Crow Street company when it visited Cork in the autumns of 1762 and 1763. Mrs. Maxwell abandoned Dublin for a time after the 1767–68 season, joining James Parker's strolling company that played in Belfast for this season. She remained with Parker's company, which visited Newry and Kilkenny in the winter of 1769, and returned to Belfast for the 1770–71 season.

Mrs. Maxwell reappears in Dublin at the beginning of the 1770–71 Capel Street season, transferring to Crow Street by the end of the season after Capel Street closed. She remained at Crow Street for the following season, visiting Derry in the summer of 1772, but again moved to Capel Street when it reopened at the beginning of the 1773–74 season. For the first time in her career Mrs. Maxwell is found at Smock Alley during the 1774–75 season. She acted there the following season but moved, once again, to Crow Street for 1775–76. She was to remain at Crow Street (she was with the touring company that visited Cork in the summer of 1779) until she disappears from the record at the end of the 1782–83 season, having spend nearly 25 years on the Dublin stage.

For a biographical sketch of **Mrs. Mary Mozeen** see the 1754–55 season.

According to the *BD* **Mrs. Pye** was the first wife of the Irish actor and flutist **Mr. Pye** (fl. 1753–1791). Pye is not known to have performed in either London or Dublin, his career having been confined to provincial Irish companies acting in secondary and tertiary roles. He and his wife were acting together in Belfast this season (also in Newry and Kilkenny) and again in the 1770–71 season. In later years he visited Belfast again (summer 1773; 1776–77; 1779–80; 1788–89; and 1790–91). He also is found in Derry in 1774 and in 1790–91.

Mrs. Pye is first noticed in Dublin at Smock Alley during the 1753–54 season playing tertiary and (occasionally) secondary roles and singing. She traveled with the Smock Alley company on its summer tour of the provinces, playing in Cork in the summers of 1757 and 1758. Mrs. Pye remained at Smock Alley through the 1758–59 season, and she finished her Dublin career at Crow Street in 1759–60, her roles gradually increasing in importance. Her *forte* was singing, and she seems to have been a particularly successful Lucy in *The Beggar's Opera*.

Thereafter mention of the Pyes is rare: they are found in Manchester (1760–61), and she made her Edinburgh debut in 1763. Mrs. Pye was a member of James Parker's company of "Comedians from the Theatres Royal of London, Dublin, and Edinburgh" that visited Belfast during the 1768–69 season, later visiting Newry and Kilkenny and Belfast in 1771. Mrs. Pye is found with Parker's company in Belfast again in the winter of 1774. The last mention of Mrs. Pye in the bills occurs in the *BNL* 12–15 April 1774, which announces the death in Belfast of the "comedian" Mrs. Pye, "after a tedious illness."

The **Master Pye** who also acted at Smock Alley in the 1753–54 and 1755–56 season is probably the Pye's son, and it may have been he who accompanied his parents to Belfast this season.

Joseph Waker first comes to notice during the 1759–60 season at Smock Alley, but the fact that he played primary and secondary roles in farces and comedies at that time and was given an individual benefit strongly suggests that he had been on the stage for some time. Perhaps Joseph is the Waker whom Sybil Rosenfeld finds acting in York in 1748. Waker's whereabouts are unknown for the 1760–61 season, but he is again at Smock Alley the next season joined by **Mrs. Waker**. Waker remained at Smock Alley through the 1767–68 season. His wife is not found in the bills from 1760–61 until the 1766–67 season, and she disappears from the Dublin record entirely thereafter.

Mr. and Mrs. Waker were with James Parker's strolling company when they visited Belfast this season, and they continued with it for the following year, performing in Newry and Kilkenny (June–August 1769). When Waker reappears in Dublin at Crow Street at the beginning of the 1771–72 season it is billed as his "first appearance in this kingdom these 4 years." Later that season, at Smock Alley, for his own benefit Waker presented his "Comic Lecture on Noses," in which will be given a description of the noses of some certain personages known well in the world of gallantry and taste. W. J. Lawrence ("Annals", 26) observes that "Waker was disfigured with two bladder-like excrescences pendent from his nostrils, thus all this was in shocking bad taste." That summer he acted in Derry with Parker's company.

Waker disappears from the Dublin record after the 1772–73 season. Both he and his wife acted in Belfast in Michael Atkins's first company in the summer of 1773. After that, Mrs. Waker disappears from the record entirely. Waker continued to perform in the Irish provinces and is found in Kilkenny in January 1778, in Waterford in 1781, and perhaps in Mallow in 1782. Thereafter we lose track of him.

The first record we have of **Mrs. Wright** (fl. 1768–1769) is in Belfast with James Parker's company this season. She spent the following season at Crow Street billed as "her first appearance on this stage," suggesting that she had been active in the theatre for some time previous to this season. She traveled with the company to Kilkenny in the summer of 1769. Mrs. Wright seems to have excelled in the line of older women. The *BD* says that later that year "Mrs. Wright was imported from Ireland apparently specifically to play the Queen (Elizabeth) in *Richard III*, presented at the benefit arranged for the ill Thomas Weston at the Haymarket Theatre on 19 September 1769. The *BD* errs in finding Mrs. Wright at Smock Alley during the 1770–71 season. A Mr. Wright, however, did act there during that time. They may have been related.

Repertory, 1768–69 Season

James Parker offered little new in the way of mainpieces during this short visit to Belfast. Colman's *The Jealous Wife* had been a popular London and Dublin staple since 1761. Of the four new afterpieces O'Hara's three-act burletta, *Midas*, had been immensely popular in Dublin since January 1762, and Bickerstaffe's *The Absent Man* since 1764; neither of the two new pantomimes seem to have been performed again outside of Belfast, despite the claim in the *BNL* that *The Escape* had come from Sadler's Wells. The interlude of *Harlequin in the Shades* would seem to be the first such piece performed in Belfast.

Total performances: 33 of 26 named mainpieces and 31 of 18 named afterpieces.
New mainpieces: 1.
New afterpieces: 4.
Shakespeare: 3.

(For a key to repertory symbols see above, page 11)

Mainpieces: *The Beaux' Stratagem*(2); *The Beggar's Opera*; *The Careless Husband*; *The Clandestine Marriage*†(2); *The Conscious Lovers*; *The Distrest Mother*; *The Earl of Essex*; *The Fair Penitent*; *False Delicacy*†; *The Gentle Shepherd*†; *Hamlet*; *The Jealous Wife**(2); *King Richard III*; *The Maid of the Mill*†; *The Miser*; *The Mourning Bride* (2); *The Orphan*; *The Provoked Husband*; *The Recruiting Officer*; *The Rival Queens*†; *Romeo and Juliet*; *The Spanish Fryar*; *The Suspicious Husband*; *Tamerlane*; *Tunbridge Walks*†; Unspecified play(2); *Venice Preserved*.

Afterpieces: *The Absent Man**; *Catherine and Petruchio* (2); *The Citizen*; *The Contrivances*; *The Deuce is in Him*†; *The Devil to Pay*; *The Escape**; *The Fashionable*

Wife†; *The Genii*; The Ghost*†; *The Honest Yorkshireman; The Judgment of Paris; The King and the Miller of Mansfield; The Lying Valet; Midas** (6); *The Mock Doctor; Thomas and Sally*†; Unspecified farce(6); *Wrangling Lovers*†(2).

Interlude: *Harlequin in the Shades**□

Entr'acte singing and dancing: None listed.

Benefits (4): Mr. and Mrs. Farrell; Hamilton; Mrs. Mozeen; the Poor.

Admission Price: Evidently admission to both pit and gallery was 2s. 2d.

August 1768

23 Tues. By Command of the Right Hon. Countess of Donegall at the New Theatre in Mill Street by Comedians from the Theatres Royal London, Dublin, and Edinburgh. *The Beggar's Opera.* Macheath–Parker; Peachum–Waker; Lockit–Bullock; Mat o' th' Mint–Pye; Filch–Hamilton; Ben Budge–Jackson; Wat Dreary–Brown; Drawer–Master Pye; Polly–Mrs. Mozeen; Lucy and Mrs. Peachum–Mrs. Pye; Mrs. Slammakin–Mrs. Maxwell; Jenny–Mrs. Farrell; Diana Trapes–Mrs. Wright; Dolly Trull–Mrs. Waker. With *The King and the Miller of Mansfield.* King–Atkins; Miller–Waker; Madge–Mrs. Farrell; Kate–Mrs. Pye; Peggy–Mrs. Maxwell. To begin at seven o'clock. No person whatever can be admitted behind the scenes. Source: 23 Aug. 1768

26 Fri. At the Theatre, Mill Gate. *The Conscious Lovers.* Young Bevil–Atkins; Sealand–Waker; Myrtle–Pye; Cimberton–Hamilton; Sir John Bevil–Bullock; Daniel–Master Pye; Tom–Parker; Indiana–Mrs. Mozeen; Lucinda–Mrs. Maxwell; Mrs. Sealand–Mrs. Farrell; Isabella–Mrs. Waker; Phillis–Mrs. Pye. With *The Devil to Pay.* Sir John Loverule–Pye; Jobson–Waker; Butler–Hamilton; Conjurer–Bullock; Cook–Jackson; Coachman–Brown; Lady Loverule–Mrs. Maxwell; Lucy–Mrs. Farrell; Lettice–Mrs. Wright; Nell–Mrs. Pye. The days of playing are Monday, Wednesday and Friday. The Company's stay in town is very short. Source: 26 Aug. 1768

September 1768

2 Fri. *Romeo and Juliet.* Romeo–Atkins; Capulet–Waker; Fryar Lawrence–Bullock; Benvolio–Pye; Paris–Mrs. Maxwell; Montague–Hamilton; Prince–Mrs. Farrell; Fryar John–Jackson; Peter–Master Pye; Mercutio–Parker; Juliet–Mrs. Mozeen; Lady Capulet–Mrs. Waker; Nurse–Mrs. Pye. With *The Fashionable Wife.* Barnaby

Brittle–Hamilton; Lovemore–Pye; Sir Peter Pride–Bullock; Jeremy–Master Pye; Clodpole–Parker; Mrs. Brittle–Mrs. Pye; Lady Pride–Mrs. Farrell; Damaris–Mrs. Maxwell. [Later in the century a popular adaptation of this play was performed as *Barnaby Brittle*. See below]. Source: 2 Sept. 1768

7 Wed. *King Richard III.* Richard–Atkins; King Henry–Waker; Prince Edward–Mrs. Mozeen; Duke of York–Master Pye; Richmond–Pye; Stanley–Bullock; Catesby–Hamilton; Buckingham–Parker; Queen–Mrs. Pye; Duchess of York–Mrs. Waker; Lady Ann–Mrs. Maxwell. With a Musical Entertainment called *Thomas and Sally*. [*Thomas and Sally* was printed in Belfast by James Magee in 1767]. Source: 6 Sept. 1768

14 Wed. *The Clandestine Marriage.* Sterling–Parker; Sir John Melvil–Atkins; Mrs. Heidelberg–Mrs. Pye; Miss Sterling–Mrs. Mozeen. With *The Lying Valet.* Shark–Hamilton; Kitty–Mrs. Pye; Melissa–Mrs. Maxwell. Source: 13 Sept. 1768

21 Wed. *The [Beaux'] Stratagem.* With an English Burletta called *The Judgment of Midas.* Jupiter–Bullock; Apollo–Pye; Cupid–Master Pye; Juno–Mrs. Maxwell; Midas–Hamilton; Sileno–Parker; Damaetas–Atkins; Nisa–Mrs. Mozeen; Daphne–Mrs. Pye; Shepherds–Jackson and Brown; Shepherdesses–Mrs. Farrell and Mrs. Wright. [The *dramatis personae* suggests that this piece is the same as O'Hara's *Midas*]. Source: 20 Sept. 1768

23 Fri. *Hamlet.* With *Midas.* Source: 23 Sept. 1768

26 Mon. *The Maid of the Mill.* [Published by James Magee in Belfast in 1765]. With a farce as will be expressed in the Bills. Source: 23 Sept. 1768

28 Wed. *The Recruiting Officer.* Captain Plume–Atkins; Capt. Brazen–Parker; Worthy–Hamilton; Sylvia–Mrs. Maxwell; Rose–Mrs. Pye; Melinda–Mrs. Mozeen. With *Catherine and Petruchio.* Source: 27 Sept. 1768

30 Fri. *The Clandestine Marriage.* With *Midas.* Source: 30 Sept. 1768

October 1768

3 Mon. *The Orphan.* With a farce as will be expressed in the Bills. Source: 30 Sept. 1768

7 Fri. *The Distrest Mother.* With a farce called *The Deuce is in Him.* Source: 7 Oct. 1768

10 Mon. *The Suspicious Husband.* With *The Devil to Pay* Source: 7 Oct. 1768

14 Fri.   *The Suspicious Husband.* With *Midas.* Source: 14 Oct. 1768

17 Mon.   *The Fair Penitent.* With a farce as will be expressed in the Bills. One night last week a piece of money was taken at the door of the Theatre of much more value than the price of admittance. Whoever it belongs to may have it restored by applying to Parker. Source: 14 Oct. 1768

21 Fri.   *The Earl of Essex.* With *The Ghost.* Last night of performing till Monday the 31st. Source: 21 Oct. 1768

31 Mon.   Benefit of the Poor. *False Delicacy.* With a farce as will be expressed in the Bills. Source: 21 Oct. 1768

November 1768

5   Sat.   By desire of the gentlemen of the Musical Society. *Tamerlane.* With the English burletta *Midas.* Source: 4 Nov. 1768

11 Fri.   *Tunbridge Walks.*   Woodcock–Parker;   Reynold–Atkins; Maiden–Mrs. Mozeen; Hillaria–Mrs. Pye; Belinda–Mrs. Maxwell. With a Pantomime called *The Genii; or, Harlequin Restored.* Being the last time of performing it this Season. Source: 11 Nov. 1768

14 Mon.   *The Mourning Bride* and *The Wrangling Lovers.* Source: 11 Nov. 1768

16 Wed.   *The Mourning Bride.*   Osmyn–Atkins;   Gonsalez–Parker; Almeria–Mrs. Pye; Zara–Mrs. Maxwell. With a farce called *The Wrangling Lovers.* Source: 15 Nov. 1768

18 Fri.   *The Spanish Fryar.* Torrismond–Gentleman who never appeared on   any   Stage;   Colonel–Atkins;   Gomez–Hamilton;   Fryar–Parker; Queen–Mrs. Mozeen; Teresa–Mrs. Maxwell; Elvira–Mrs. Pye. With (for the last time) *Midas.* Source: 18 Nov. 1768

21 Mon.   Never performed here. *The Jealous Wife.* With a Farce as will be expressed in the Bills. Source: 18 Nov. 1768

23 Wed.   *The Rival Queens.* The bower of Semaramis with new Trophies, Standards, Banners, etc., painted for the Occasion. [*The Rival Queens* was published in Belfast by James Magee in 1776]. Source: Clark 1965, 227.

25 Fri.   *The Gentle Shepherd.* [Published in Belfast by and for Samuel Wilson and James Magee, 1743 and by James Magee in 1755, 1765, and

1782]. With *Catherine and Petruchio*. After the Farce the celebrated interlude called *Harlequin in the Shades* as performed at the Theatres of London with universal applause. Source: 25 Nov. 1768

28 Mon. Unspecified "play" and "farce." Other details of program unavailable. Source: 25 Nov. 1768

30 Wed. Unspecified "play." With *The Citizen*. Citizen–Parker; Old Philpot–Hamilton; Young Wilding–Atkins; Sir Jasper–Bullock; Beaufort–Pye; Quilldrive–Jackson; Maria–Mrs. Pye; Corinna–Mrs. Maxwell. Source: 29 Nov. 1768

December 1768

2 Fri. *Venice Preserved*. Jaffier–Fullam (first appearance on this Stage). With *The Honest Yorkshireman*. Source: 29 Nov. 1768

23 Fri. *The Jealous Wife*. After the Play a Highland dance by Farrell. With *The Mock Doctor*. Admittance 2s. 2d. [Same price for pit and gallery]. Source: 30 Dec. 1768

30 Fri. Benefit Hamilton. *The Miser*. With a song by Mrs. Mozeen and a hornpipe by Atkins. After the play a humorous Epilogue in the Character of an old Poet by Hamilton. With *The Contrivances*. Source: 30 Dec. 1768

January 1769

6 Fri. Benefit of Mr. and Mrs. Farrell who failed in their former attempts. Not acted here these several years. *The Careless Husband* with the following entertainments between the acts: a Highland dance and a comick dance called *"The Dusty Miller"* by Farrell; an epilogue to be spoke by a Free Mason wife. With a new pantomime entertainment never performed here called *The Escape; or, Harlequin Victorious*. With proper scenery, deceptions and every necessary decoration as it was performed at Sadler's Wells, London with universal applause. In which will be introduced the celebrated scene of *The Flying Taylor* taken from *Harlequin Sorcerer* to conclude with a dance by the characters. Source: 6 Jan. 1769

13 Fri. By particular desire. Benefit of Mrs. Mozeen. *The Provoked Husband*. With a comedy of two acts never performed here called *The Absent Man*. Source: 13 Jan. 1769

20 Fri. Benefit of the Poor. *The Beaux' Stratagem*. To which will be added *Midas*. Pit and gallery doors will be opened. The Sovereign will attend to receive the tickets. Source: 20 Jan. 1769

1769–1770 SEASON

Venue: Thomas Ryder's "New Theatre" in Mill Gate.
Company: Mrs. and Miss Bridges; Cannen; Master George Dawson; Duffy; Miss Eaton; James Fotteral; Mr. and Mrs. Tobias Gemea; Miss Gemea; Geoghegan (machinist); Miss Hern; Mr. and Mrs. Logan; Mrs. Maxwell; McCarthy [sometimes spelled Carthy]; Nugent; John O'Keeffe [at this time usually spelled Keefe or Keeffe]; John Linegar Owens, Sr.; [Preswick] Ryder, Sr. (officekeeper); Mr. and Mrs. Thomas Ryder; Mr. and Mrs. Samuel Ryder; James Beatty Stewart; Samuel Whitmore (scene painter); Miss Whitmore (or Whitemore); Wilson.

This company was brought to Belfast by **Thomas Ryder** (1735–1791). Ryder was the son of **Preswick Ryder**, Dublin printer and provincial actor, and the provincial actress Sarah Darby. The young Thomas Ryder (and his brother **Samuel Ryder,** 1738–1771) took to the stage in the English and Scottish provinces, acting under the name of Darby from at least as early as 1757, when their father had been forced to flee Dublin for printing political libels. Clearly, the Ryder family of actors continued to travel long after Thomas made his Dublin acting debut at Smock Alley on 7 December 1757, appearing in a few primary characters, such as Romeo, but mainly in secondary parts, usually young men. He remained at Smock Alley for the 1758–59 and 1759–60 and married the actress Rosetta Comerford during the latter season. Mrs. Ryder occasionally acted opposite him thereafter.

The *BD* errs in finding Mr. and Mrs. Ryder in Dublin during the 1760–61 season when there is no record of their having acted anywhere. However, the Ryders were back at Smock Alley for the 1761–62 through 1763–64 seasons, playing a wide variety of roles. Mrs. Ryder appears less frequently during this time, and is not recorded at all for the 1762–63 season, and then, after 1763–64, not again until 1770–71, which appears to have been her last season of acting.

By the early 1760s Ryder had become a moderately popular actor and remained at Smock Alley for the 1764–65 through the 1766–67 seasons. In the summer of 1765 he is found in Drogheda where he is credited with having written and performed "a humourous cantata" called *The Gates of Calais.*

During the 1765–66 season Ryder evidently made his first attempt at play writing. In May 1766 the Dublin newspapers announce the publication of

Friendship a la Mode, "A new Farce never yet performed. Taken from Sir John Vanbrugh's *False Friend.*"

At the end of the 1766–67 season Ryder decided to strike out on his own. Barry relinquished management of Crow Street at the end of that season, and Mossop acquired the lease at Crow Street, thereby obtaining a virtual monopoly of Dublin theatricals. Seeing the Dublin theatre manager so firmly ensconced, and his own chances of becoming a Dublin manager increasingly remote, Ryder took to the provincial towns with a strolling company for the next three seasons. Between October 1767 and 1769 Ryder (and occasionally his wife) appeared in Waterford, Kilkenny Sligo, Galway and Derry.

Ryder spied an opportunity when James Parker's company left Belfast in 1769. The company performed in Belfast for fifteen weeks, then Ryder closed his theatre on 15 August 1770 and returned to Dublin for the regular Smock Alley season after a hiatus of three years. The topical pantomime *Harlequin with Thurot; or, The Taking of Carrickfergus,* which was performed in Belfast at this time, may have been written by Ryder. Ryder acted with Mossop at Smock Alley in the 1770–71 season and when Mossop went to London at the end of that season and was arrested for debt, Ryder assumed the management of Smock Alley. He remained there as actor-manager from the 1771–72 through the 1780–81 season, when he gave up the management of Smock Alley to Richard Daly.

Ryder acted for Daly through the 1785–86 season and then traveled to England where he made his London debut at Covent Garden on 25 October 1786. He remained at Covent Garden for the following four and a half winter seasons, returning to Crow Street with his daughters for a brief visit in 1788. In November 1790 he evidently took over the management of the Edinburgh theatre, but meeting with little success there, he returned to Ireland and is found in the spring of 1791 in Belfast with his daughters. Ryder was evidently ill at this time, and after his Belfast engagement he traveled to Dublin where he died on 26 November 1791 and was buried in the Drumcondra churchyard.

Mrs. Thomas Ryder, née Rosetta Comerford, was the daughter or sister of Henry Comerford, the minor London actor who is not known to have acted in Ireland. She did not have a London career and is noticed only in passing in the *BD.* The fact that her first Dublin appearance, in the 1751–52 Smock Alley season, attracted no special mention suggests perhaps that Miss Comerford had been appearing in supernumerary roles there for some time. Although no named roles for her appear in the bills, she remained at Smock Alley through 1754–55 appearing in a few minor named roles . She disappears from the record for the 1755–56 through the 1756–57 seasons, but is found in Belfast with Sherriffe's strolling company in the spring of 1758 (still billed as Miss Comerford and not Mrs. Ryder, as Clark asserts (1965, 373).

In the 1758–59 Smock Alley season she was again acting minor roles in the Smock Alley company where she met the novice actor, Thomas Ryder, whom she married in the spring of 1760. Thereafter she acted regularly under that name until 1770–71, which appears to have been her last season on the stage.

At Crow Street on 1 December 1760 a "Young Gentlewoman" made her "second appearance on any stage" singing the character of Polly in *The Beggar's Opera*. The date of her stage debut is not known, but judging from the wide variety of ingenue roles she played this season, **Mrs. Bridges** possessed considerable talent. We learn her identity from later playbills.

Her efforts, particularly as a singer, met with such success that her engagement was extended through the 1760–61 season, and she was given a sole benefit. Mr. Bridges is not known to have acted but may have been serving as treasurer to the theatre. That summer Mrs. Bridges joined the company on its annual visit to Cork.

Mrs. Bridges remained at Crow Street for the following season and had the same success, again receiving a sole benefit. She is absent from the Dublin bills during the 1762–63 season. In the 1763–64 summer season Mrs. Bridges is found singing and acting at Smock Alley theatre in many of the same roles she had performed previously. Thereafter, Mrs. Bridges disappears from the record for a time. She is found in Kilkenny in the spring of 1768.

In the 1770–71 Smock Alley season Mrs. Bridges is again singing Lucy in *The Beggar's Opera* and similar roles. With her, acting children's roles, is a Miss Bridges, presumably her daughter. Mrs. and Miss Bridges appeared as an entr'acte singer with Ryder's company when it visited Belfast this season. She remained with the Smock Alley company through the 1773–74 season, her star being then on the wane. Miss Bridges continued to act in Dublin for the 1773–74 and 1774–75 seasons. Thereafter the Bridges evidently performed with provincial strolling companies: they last appear in the record in 1792–93 when they are found with John Davison's company in Kilkenny, Waterford and Wexford.

This is the only record of the actor named **Cannen.**

It is probable that the Mr. Dawson who played a Guard in *Barbarossa* and a French Soldier in *Harlequin with Thurot* in Belfast in July of this season was William Dawson, later the Dublin and provincial actor and manager (see 1752–53 season for biography). It is virtually certain that the "Master Dawson" also present in Belfast at this time is William Dawson's son, **George Dawson**. George Dawson, who is billed as having made "his first appearance on any stage" in Belfast on 24 August 1761 when his father took a strolling company to Belfast, made his Dublin debut on 28 December of that year. At the time his father and his mother were acting in secondary and tertiary roles at Smock Alley. The Dawson family's whereabouts are unknown for the 1762–63 season, but Dawson and Master Dawson were again with the Smock Alley company in the summer of 1764, and Master Dawson continued there acting occasionally for the 1764–65, 1765–66, and 1767–68 seasons. The Dawsons were with the Smock Alley company on its summer tours of Cork in 1766 and Limerick in 1767. Evidently, Dawson father and son performed in Belfast for the summer of 1770, then the three Dawsons played at Capel Street, with the stepson William Lewis as the main attraction, for the bulk of the 1770–71 season. Dawson, Sr. obtained a *de facto* monopoly on Dublin theatricals when Mossop was arrested for debt while on a recruiting visit to London in 1772, but Spranger Barry returned to Dublin the following season and threatened to have Dawson himself arrested for debt. The family retreated to Limerick and Cork taking most of the company with it. For the 1773–74 season William Dawson reopened the Capel Street theatre and he and his company acted there, George now being billed as "Dawson, Jr." Dawson had reached an accommodation with Ryder, for at the beginning of the 1776–77 season he is again acting at Crow Street theatre and the company now includes his wife and son, who is now billed variously as "Dawson, Jr." and "George Dawson."

At some point George Dawson had married, for a "Mrs. G. Dawson" begins to appear regularly in the playbills after 4 December 1776. The fact that this first record of her performing finds her acting a secondary role and that no notice is taken of this, her first documented performance, suggests strongly that she was already known to Dublin audiences. The entire Dawson family continued at Crow Street from the 1777–78 season (when Miss Dawson's name appears frequently in the bills) through1781–82. By the 1779–80 season Mr. and Mrs. George Dawson were important enough in the company that they took a joint benefit. During the 1782–83 season William Dawson and several other members of the company leased Crow Street but George and his wife then moved to Smock Alley. This is the last season that the younger Dawson and his wife are known to have performed together.

Bills of this period indicate that George Dawson excelled as a Harlequin and acrobat. The fact that he took the part of Harlequin in several pantomimes written by Messink may suggest some association with him, and Dawson may have learned his craft under Messink. George Dawson also may have written several pantomimes, which were performed only in Ireland: *Harlequin Foundling* (Smock Alley, 1783); *Harlequin's Animation* (Smock Alley, 1783); and *The Medley; or, Harlequin Manufacturer* (Smock Alley, 1784).

George Dawson, but not his wife, remained at Smock Alley for the 1783–84 through 1785–86 seasons. He also performed at Newry in June 1784 and in Cork and Limerick in the early autumn of 1785 and the next autumn with the Smock Alley company in Waterford, Cork and Limerick. Mrs. George Dawson, but not her husband, acted in Belfast in the winter of 1784–85.

George began the 1786–87 season at Smock Alley, but he evidently became ill. The last record of his performing is on 4 December 1786. *FDJ* 20–22 Feb. 1787 announced: "Sunday [18 February] at noon the remains of Mr. George Dawson late of the Theatre Royal, comedian, were carried in funeral pomp through this city, attended by the Company of Goldsmiths Volunteers of this city, of which he was a member, to the burial ground in Drumcondra. Several coaches followed the procession, particularly that of Mr. Daly, the manager, in which he sat with other gentlemen; almost every one who saw the melancholy file dropt a tear to the memory of a man by his comic talents so often filled the mind with the most agreeable sensations, unbent the rigid bow of care, wreathed the smile, and raised the laugh. 'Alas, poor Yorick'."

After her husband's death Mrs. George Dawson continued on the Dublin stage until her death. With the exception of the 1791–92 season, she acted at Crow St. from 1787–88 though 1792–93 and then from 1798–99 until 1803. She is found at Frederick Jones's Fishamble St. Theatre when it opened in 1793–94 and later in 1797–98 (as was a Miss Dawson, perhaps her daughter or perhaps William Dawson's).

Mrs. Dawson was also occasionally active in the provincial theatres, receiving a sympathy benefit in Belfast in March 1787, but it is not clear if she acted that night or was even present in the city. Mrs. Dawson is found in Limerick and Cork in the autumn of 1788. She shared a benefit with Andrew Cherry at Smock Alley on 26 May 1789, but evidently did not act that season. She performed in Waterford in October 1789, in Cork in September 1790 and in October 1791, and, finally, in Galway in the summer and fall of 1793.

Mrs. Dawson, "Widow of the late George Dawson," appeared on stage for the last time in December 1802 and died on 21 April 1803 after an illness which lasted several months.

The **Duffy** who was active on the Irish stage between 1768 and 1773 was not Peter Duffey, the Dublin hatter, as Clark and the *BD* report, but another Duffy whose first name is unknown. Duffy is first found in Dublin at Smock Alley during the 1766–67 season playing tertiary roles, suggesting that he had some stage experience prior to this time. Duffy is next found in the Irish provinces, in Kilkenny in the spring of 1768 and then with Ryder's strolling company in Belfast in the spring of 1770 and later that year in Kilkenny. After a brief period in Waterford in October 1771, Duffy's name appears regularly in the Smock Alley playbills in the 1771–72 and 1772–73 seasons. A Duffy performed in Kilkenny in the winter of 1778 but disappears from the record thereafter.

Miss Eaton first appears on the record in the 1766–67 Smock Alley season, acting mainly secondary and tertiary roles, chambermaids and the like. She then evidently joined Ryder's strolling company, for she is found acting similar roles at Belfast in the spring of 1770 and again at Kilkenny the following autumn and winter. Thereafter, she disappears from the record.

The *BD* does not record the fact that the first notice of **James Fotteral's** stage activity is at Crow Street during the 1768–69 season, when he played tertiary roles. Since this notice makes no mention of its being his first appearance, we can assume that he had been acting for some time previous to this season. Fotteral spent most of the 1769–70 and 1770–71 seasons at Crow Street, acting at Cork in the autumn of 1769 and at Belfast with Ryder's company in the spring and summers of 1770 and later at Kilkenny in the autumn of 1770.

Fotteral's whereabouts are unknown for the 1771–72 season, but he is acting again in Belfast in the autumn of 1771 and he remained there through January 1772. Fotteral played regularly at Crow Street during the 1773–74 and 1774–75, going with the company to Cork in the summer of 1775. He began the 1775–76 at Smock Alley, but soon moved to Crow Street where he finished the season.

Fotteral probably was traveling in the English provinces during the 1776–77 season but the record is silent. He made his London debut at the Haymarket Theatre on 29 August 1777 billed as "A Gentleman from the Theatre Royal Dublin, his first appearance" in London. His London performances evidently did not impress for he returned to the provinces, acting in Derby (October 1777–January 1778).

Fotteral was back at Crow Street in the spring and summer of 1779 and for all of the 1779–80 and 1780–81 seasons. During the latter season a reviewer of Sophia Lee's new play, *The Chapter of Accidents*, first performed at Crow Street on 27 November 1780, remarked: "Mr. Fotteral met with deserved applause in Lord Glenmore; indeed this actor has justly established a reputation in his performances of elderly characters." He traveled to Cork with the Crow Street company in the summer of 1781.

Fotteral moved to Smock Alley for the 1781–82 and 1782–83 seasons, acting in Cork with them in the autumn of 1783. His whereabouts are not known for the 1783–84 season, but he may have been acting in the provinces. He is found again acting regularly at Smock Alley during the 1784–85 season, where, on 13 May 1785 he received a sole benefit. He is also known to have acted in Limerick, Derry, Newry, Dundalk, Galway, and Sligo.

Fotteral continued at Smock Alley for the 1785–86 season and is acting in Belfast in the spring of 1787, but then seems to have moved to Wales. He is found in Abergavenny in July 1793 and again at Swansea in October 1795.

The *BD* overlooks the Crow Street performance on 6 June 1797 when Fotteral is listed as playing Sir Peter Teazle in *The School for Scandal*, "his first appearance these eleven years." After this single performance, Fotteral disappears from the acting record. He was evidently still alive in 1805 when *The Thespian Dictionary* (1805) mentions him.

For biographies of **Mr.** and **Mrs. Tobias Gemea** see 1751–52 season. Mrs. Gemea shared a benefit this season but she is not known to have acted.

Neither *BD* nor Lacy mentions **Geoghegan's** scene-painting, which seems to have been confined to the Irish provincial theatres. Geoghegan was attached to Ryder's strolling company that was active between 1767 and 1770 and is found in Kilkenny in the autumn of 1767 and 1770 and in Belfast for the spring and summer of 1770. A Geoghegan is also found in

Newry as late as July 1792. Geoghegan evidently collaborated with **Samuel Whitmore**, the scene painter and actor, designing and "executing" the machinery that complemented Whitmore's scenes (see below for Whitmore biography).

Clark also cites a **Mrs. Whitmore** as performing on 5 July (1965, 377), but I am unable to find any record of a performance on that date or of any performer by that name. A Miss Whitmore (or Whitemore) performed in Belfast twice this season (on 9 May and 11 August) and perhaps she is the same person who acted in Kilkenny during the 1770–71 season.

Miss Hern (sometimes Herne) may have made her stage debut at Smock Alley during the 1764–65 season. She received a sole benefit there on 14 May 1765 acting the primary role of Monimia in *The Orphan*, but that is the only record of her having performed that season. She appeared regularly at Smock Alley the following two seasons, almost always in primary or secondary characters and is found with the Smock Alley touring company in Cork and Kilkenny during the 1766–67 season and at Kilkenny in the winter of 1768.

She was with Ryder's company in Belfast in the spring and summer of 1770 but returned to Smock Alley for the 1770–71 season. She began the 1771–72 season at Derry in October, but finished the season, again, at Smock Alley, after which she disappears from the record. Judging from the roles she played, Miss Hern was a very serviceable actress, mainly in serious roles, and had a fairly large repertoire.

Mr. Logan is first found acting at Smock Alley in supernumerary roles in the 1764–65 season. The following season both Logan and a Mrs. Logan, presumably his wife, are acting in minor roles at the same theatre, and the couple is listed again in the Smock Alley playbills during 1766–67. **Mrs. Logan**, but not her husband, is listed with the Cork company in the autumn of 1766. Both Logans evidently spent the 1767–68 with a strolling company and are found in Kilkenny in the winter and spring.

Logan, but not his wife, is with the Crow Street company, again in minor roles, during the 1768–69 season. Both Logans acted with Ryder's strollers in Belfast during the spring and summer of 1770 and visited Kilkenny again in the autumn of 1770. The 1770–71 season finds Mrs. Logan without her husband acting at Capel Street. With her, billed as a "Young Gentlewoman, a pupil of Mahon, her first appearance on any stage," is probably a daughter, (not Maria, b. 1770, for whom see below).

Both Mr. and Mrs. Logan acted at Crow Street during the 1771–72 season and at Smock Alley in 1772–73 in roles that seldom rise above the tertiary. Logan is sometimes listed among the dancers during this period. The Logans were in Cork in the autumn of 1773 and are again found among the Smock Alley company during the 1774–75 season, after which Mr. Logan's name disappears from the bills for several years.

Mrs. Logan continued to act in Dublin (Smock Alley 1775–76; Crow Street 1776–77). Mrs. Logan's roles increase in importance during 1777–78 Crow Street season, and her husband reappears for a season, acting as a supernumerary. Mrs. Logan's line for the next three Crow Street seasons is that of serving women and dowagers. She is found in Cork with the Crow Street company during the autumns of 1776, 1779 and 1780.

The last record we have of Mrs. Logan is during 1782–83 when she acted and sang at Capel Street. However, she was probably with her daughter, Maria, when that "Very Young Lady" made her Haymarket debut on 18 June 1783. (Maria, later Mrs. Gibbs and later still the second Mrs. George Colman, the younger, did not perform in Ireland).

See 1768–69 season for a biography of **Mrs. Maxwell.**

Clark believes that the Carthy who acted in Belfast during the 1761 summer season is the same man found with Ryder's strolling company in Kilkenny (1768 and 1769) and in Belfast this season, listed (usually) under the name **McCarthy**. However, it seems more likely that the McCarthy who was with Ryder's company in Kilkenny and Belfast is a different actor, if only because Carthy played mainly older men and secondary roles, while McCarthy (the actor is usually billed as such, and only infrequently as Carthy) played only a few tertiary but mainly supernumerary roles and these mainly as young men in pantomimes. Nothing else is known about his career.

This is the only record of the actor named **Nugent.**

John O'Keeffe, playwright and actor, (in his earliest notices his name is usually spelled Keefe, or, occasionally, Keeffe), made his stage and play writing debut at Smock Alley on 17 January 1767 acting a principal character in his own two-act farce *The She Gallant* billed as "a young gentleman." In his *Recollections* O'Keeffe says he wrote this play when he was sixteen. He would have been a few months short of being twenty years old at this time. O'Keeffe is known to have acted in a few other roles that season.

Using his own name, O'Keeffe played tertiary roles at Crow Street during the 1767–68 season. For the next two seasons O'Keeffe is found among the company of actors Thomas Ryder was leading in the Irish provinces. He acted in Limerick and Drogheda during 1768–69 and in Belfast and Kilkenny (autumn 1770).

O'Keeffe spent the latter part of the 1770–71 season at Capel Street playing and singing a wide variety of young man's roles, including Jessamy in *Lionel and Clarissa*. The *HM* of April 1771 prints a "Scale of Merit" comparing the casts of the Smock Alley and Capel Street companies staging of *Cymon*. O'Keeffe's Linco is judged much inferior to Wilder's at Smock Alley. When, on 22 March 1771, Capel Street was closed, the company moved to Crow Street and O'Keeffe accompanied them. He continued there for many seasons in increasingly more important roles. By 1772 he had found his *forte* in the line of mischievous servants, bumpkins and clodpoles, particularly clownish Irishmen (e.g., Fitzmungrel in *The True Born Irishman* and Paddy Kearney in the pantomime *Harlequin in Ireland*). Prior to the Dublin theatre's opening in the autumns of 1771 through 1780 O'Keeffe is found with the touring Crow Street company in both Limerick and Cork.

On 29 January 1773 Crow Street staged *A View of Stephen's Green* "a new comic interlude never yet performed" written by O'Keeffe with the author in the role of Doderidge "the poet and the player." This piece is evidently O'Keeffe's attempt to capitalize on the scurrilous newspaper series of the same title which had been appearing for some time in *The Public Monitor*. O'Keeffe joined the Crow Street company in Derry 1771–1772, and Cork (autumn 1773)

O'Keeffe was with Ryder's Smock Alley company in the 1773–74 season where he played the original Tony Lumpkin in *She Stoops to Conquer* with so much success that toward the end of the season he brought out his own *Tony Lumpkin in Town*, "a comedy in two acts," which premiered on 13 April 1774. In March 1776 the piece, billed now as a comical interlude, was advertised at Smock Alley as *Tony Lumpkin's Frolicks through Dublin*. "It will for that night only, be performed, with humorous characters and adventures, whimsical descriptions, the Mishap, or Bet Bouncer in the Sedan, the complete Female Maccaroni, the Breakfast, the Rotunda, public buildings, streets, taverns, theatres, etc."

At the beginning of the 1774–75 season O'Keeffe seems to have insisted on the standardizing of the spelling of his name to its now accepted form. While in Limerick, on 1 October 1774, he married Mary Heaphy, the elder daughter of the actor-manager Tottenham Heaphy and his wife.

The Stewart whose name first appears in the Crow Street playbills of the 1762–63 season may have been **James Beatty Stewart**. That season he played a variety of tertiary roles but the name disappears from the bills for several seasons after that. Clark (1965, 374) finds James Beatty Stewart at Kilkenny during the winter of 1767–68 and again in June 1769 with James Parker's company. During the 1769–70 season the name Stewart appears twice in Dublin bills, at Crow Street, in the same supernumerary role. Stewart spent the spring and summer of 1770 with Ryder's strolling company at the new Mill Gate Theatre in Belfast and remained with that troupe (which now included Mrs. Stewart) when it visited Kilkenny in the autumn.

During this time Stewart's roles seldom rose to the secondary level, but he seems to have attracted applause reciting various comic monologues, in particular, *The Picture of a Playhouse; or, Bucks Have At Ye All* ("with alterations and additions as spoken originally by King"). Whatever his popularity, Stewart was clearly having financial troubles by December 1770 when he took a second Kilkenny benefit, the first having been insufficient to discharge "the several debts contracted here. . . ."

During the 1771–72 and 1772–73 season Stewart is again acting at Crow Street, again mainly in tertiary roles. The latter season his wife first appears at Crow Street in a few supernumerary parts. Stewart spent the 1773–74 season at Capel Street, where he enacted more important roles than previously and took as his benefit play the title role in *Othello*. He is absent from the Dublin bills during the regular 1774–75 season, but is acting at Crow Street again during the summer.

Stewart transferred to Smock Alley for the 1775–76 season, but it is clear that by that time he was fairly advanced in mental illness. He was back at Crow Street for the 1776–77 season, usually playing secondary and tertiary roles, and again playing Othello for his sole benefit. He continued at Crow Street at much the same level for the 1777–78 and 1778–79 seasons. During the performance of *The Devil to Pay* on 3 February 1779 Stewart made an exhibition of himself. Years later, *The Theatric Magazine* (1806) reported that this night "Mad Stewart," (as he had come to be called) playing the Enchanter, received an uproarious reception when he came on stage and waved his wand. As the audience would not stop laughing Stewart sought to break the charm of his wand by relating the Fable of the Frogs (meant to make the audience feel guilty for ridiculing him) but the fable had the opposite effect. Ryder later broke the wand into pieces and distributed it among the actors in the company "whose abilities in the dramatic line have not yet been able to procure any applause from the Dublin audience." That season, for the first time, Stewart played Lear for his benefit.

Stewart continued to act regularly at Crow Street in tertiary roles through the 1781–82 season when the name disappears from the record for nearly a decade. The Master Stewart who played Fleance in *Macbeth* on 8 March 1782 and again the following season (when Stewart's name disappears from the bills) is probably his son, James R. Stewart. The Stewart who was with Atkins's Belfast company and who played the Ghost in *Hamlet* on 8 November 1790 may have been James Beatty Stewart; the role was one he had performed many times in Dublin.

On 29 December 1790 in Belfast a benefit was advertised for "Stewart and his son young Stewart." The program was *The Merchant of Venice* and *Midas* between the acts were recited *"Bucks Have at Ye All "* by young Stewart and *"British Loyalty"* by Stewart. Thereafter, Stewart disappears from the record.

Samuel Whitmore, probably the most successful Irish scene painter of the last half of the eighteenth and the first quarter of the nineteenth centuries, first comes to notice at Smock Alley, painting scenery for Tenducci's production of *The Revenge of Arthridates* in December 1765. Thereafter, as the *BD* states, his record "has many gaps and uncertainties." The surviving record of Whitmore's scenes may be found in Lacy (1990, 648–49) and *BD*. (Only scenes not listed in those sources will be noticed here.)

Whitmore is next found with Ryder's strolling company in Belfast and Kilkenny in the autumn of 1770. Of interest is the scenery prepared in association with the machinist, Geoghegan. At Dublin's Ranelagh Gardens on 4, 6, 11, June 1771 Whitmore is credited with a series of "Transparent emblematic paintings" for a "Grand Scenico-Pastoral entertainment" in honor of the King's birthday.

After spending the autumn of 1773 in Kilkenny with Forde's company, Whitmore is found at Smock Alley in association with the scene-painter William Jolly. At the beginning of the 1775–76 season Whitmore painted "new scenery" for the Smock Alley production of *The Rival Candidates*, a "new comic opera by Bate Dudley," and later that season for *Harlequin from the Moon* of which it was reported that "particular attention . . . has been paid to striking contrastic changes, pleasing perspectives, and elegant objects in scenery."

The following season Whitmore is billed as having painted new scenery for the 20 March 1777 Crow Street production of *The Governess*. On 28 December 1778 Whitmore, Bamford, and Jolly are listed as the scene painters of the new pantomime, *The Enchanters,* and later that season, again with Bamford and Jolly, for the new scenery for the Crow Street revival of *King Arthur; or, The British Worthy*.

The first record of Whitmore as an actor is in an unspecified character in the afterpiece *The Flitch of Bacon* at Crow Street on 2 December 1779. Later that season the *FDJ* 14–16 Dec. 1779 reports: "The pantomime entertainment called *The Elopement; or, A Trip to the Dargle,* (entirely new) has been these two years preparing at very considerable expence, and will be performed in the course of the next week. The scenery, which surpasses any thing exhibited in this kingdom, is entirely new, painted by Messrs. Bamford, Whitmore, and Jolly. The machinery by Hamilton. In which will be introduced several well-known views, particularly the bay of Dublin at sun-rise; the Royal Charter School on the Strand; Fortick's Grove, with the mill at work; Cockle ware-house at Ballybough Bridge; an inside view of the Bird-house in Capel street, which changes to a chymist's shop; a representation of a country village with a cabin on fire; a view of the Dargle, waterfall, etc."

On 25 April 1780 Whitmore was probably also responsible for the "representation of the *Grand Monarque,* as brought in prize by *The Sturdy Beggar* privateer" which was a principal attraction in the new patriotic farcical spectacle *The Liverpool Prize; or, The British Flag Triumphant*. Whitmore also played the part of a Sailor in the piece.

On 19 February 1781 "Whitmore, [John James] Barralet and others" are credited with painting scenery for the Crow Street production of the new pantomime *The Touchstone; or, Harlequin Traveller*. Although playbills are not specific, it is likely that Whitmore created the "new" scenery for the Crow Street pantomime *The Duchess of Brabant; or, Virtue Triumphant* which premiered on 3 February 1783 in which he played a minor role. Whitmore may also have assisted Jolly with the scenery for the first production of *Gibraltar* at Capel Street on 18 December 1783, although he is only known to have acted that night and on a few other occasions that season, always in supernumerary roles.

Thereafter, Whitmore disappears from the record for a time. It may have been he and his wife who are said to have been acting in Dover in 1785 and in France in 1785. He was certainly acting and painting scenery at Cheltenham at the Theatre Royal in 1788 and in Gloucester in 1789.

During the autumn and winter of 1791–82 a Whitmore is found in the Irish provinces: at Waterford, Derry, and Ennis. However, as the *BD* observes, from this point it becomes difficult to distinguish the mentions of Samuel Whitmore from those of his brothers, James and John, who also painted scenery.

In the 1790s a Whitmore is noticed regularly in the bills of Astley's Amphitheatres in London and Dublin as an actor, singer, and dancer. This was probably one of the brothers and not Samuel. It is equally difficult to discriminate between the activities of the brothers who were active in Edinburgh, Newcastle, and at Covent Garden from 1797 through 1800.

The last Irish record of a Whitmore is during the 1819–20 season. The 19 June 1820 production of *The Belle's Stratagem* at the temporary theatre royal at the Rotunda contains the notice: "The scenery painted by Grieve, T. Grieve, W. Grieve, Henderson, and Whitmore." It is possible that this scenery was imported from Covent Garden and that neither Whitmore nor the other scene painters were present in Dublin at this time. Finally, Whitmore and the others are also credited with having painted the new scenery for the Rotunda premiere of *Henri Quatre; or, Paris in the Olden Times* on 3 July 1820, specifically in "Act 2 Henri's tent and encampment by Whitmore."

"S. Whitmore" certainly is credited with having painted the scenery at the Haymarket Theatre in the summer of 1801 and a scene painter named Whitmore is found in the bills for the Circus Royal, London, at Edinburgh, Bristol, Brighton, and at Covent Garden as late as 1820. Again, it is not often possible to determine if Samuel is the sole scene painter in these instances, although he is definitely responsible for some of these works.

Richard Wilson was one of the most serviceable low comedians of the English and Scottish stages in the last quarter of the eighteenth century. He created many original roles at both the Haymarket and Covent Garden theatres and only his frequent illnesses and constant financial woes prevented him from becoming one of the most popular actors of his age.

His early connection with Ireland is tenuous. Wilson began his acting career around 1766, when he is found in the north of England and Scotland and at Leeds in 1767. The fact that he was active in the north at this time leads the *BD* to say that Richard Wilson was possibly the Wilson who acted in Ireland, at Carrickfergus in October 1768 and in Belfast in the summer of 1770.

A "Mr. Wilson" played the minor role of the Drawer in the 5 December 1763 Crow Street production of *Mercury Harlequin in Ireland; or, The Rape of Colombine*; however, when Richard Wilson is first definitely known to have performed in Dublin, during the 1786–87 season, his bills read: "from the Theatre Royal, Covent Garden, his first appearance in this city."

Richard Wilson visited Dublin again, near the end of his life, when on 4 November 1795, billed as "from the Theatre Royal, Covent Garden," he played Lovegold in *The Miser* at Crow Street as well as other roles, leaving in early December. This visit is not noticed in the *BD*. When Wilson returned to London he was soon arrested for debt and he died in debtor's prison on 14 June 1796.

Repertory, May–August 1770 Season

The three mainpieces performed for the "first time here" were all stock plays in Dublin and London. However, Ryder's presentation of no fewer than six new afterpieces in Belfast is significant because of their emphasis on contemporary Irish subject-matter, landscape, and music. The afterpieces often featured the popular stage Irishman and playwright John O'Keeffe. The Irish playwright Isaac Bickerstaffe's very popular comic opera *The Padlock* was performed in Belfast for the first time, and Ryder's own farce *The Connaught Wife* had received its stage premiere at Smock Alley in 1767. O'Keeffe's frequent singing of Scottish songs and the staging of the Scottish pantomime *A Trip to Scotland* (performed in February at Crow Street) certainly suggest an attempt by the company to play upon the Belfast-Scotland connection. The three new pantomimes *(The Giant's Causeway, Harlequin in Derry,* and *Harlequin with Thurot)* all had direct relevance to the north of Ireland, and only John O'Keeffe's *The Giant's Causeway* was performed anywhere besides Belfast (Dublin, February. 1763; Kilkenny October. 1770). *Harlequin in Derry* was almost certainly O'Keeffe's earlier *Harlequin in Waterford; or, The Dutchman Outwitted*, adapted to local circumstances. *Harlequin with Thurot*, probably written by Ryder, was a clear attempt to play on the patriotism of northern audiences by referring to the French invasion attempt in 1760 that was repulsed by volunteers from Belfast. The pantomimes required elaborate scenery and machinery, and these were supplied by the company's permanent scene painter and machinist Whitmore and Geoghegan.

It may be that the pervasively patriotic tone of this season's repertory is in some way associated with recent "Hearts of Steel" riots in the northern countryside occasioned by evictions resulting from the re-leasing of property and fines levied by the Earl of Donegall and other landowners. It is hardly a coincidence that at the end of the season O'Keeffe dedicated a monologue to the Countess of Donegall. The Belfast theatre was to remain dark the next season and be frequently disrupted for months thereafter as an indirect result of such riots.

Total Performances: 40, of 36 different named mainpieces; 35 of 29 different named afterpieces.
    Shakespeare: 3.
    New Mainpieces: 5.
    New Afterpieces: 8.

(For a key to repertory symbols see above, page 11)

Mainpieces: *All in the Wrong*†; *Barbarossa; The Beaux' Stratagem; The Beggar's Opera*(2); *Cato; The Clandestine Marriage; Comus*†; *The Conscious Lovers; The Constant Couple; The Countess of Salisbury*†; *Douglas; Every Man in His Humour**; *The Fair Penitent; The Foundling; Hamlet* (2); *Jane Shore; The Jovial Crew**; *King Lear*†; *Love for Love; Love in a Village* (2); *Love Makes a Man; The Maid of the Mill; The Merchant of Venice; The Miser; The Mourning Bride; The Orphan; Polly Honeycombe; The Revenge* (2); *The Rival Queens; Romeo and Juliet; Rule a Wife and Have a Wife**; *The Siege of Damascus**; *The Suspicious Husband; Theodosius;* Unspecified mainpiece; *Venice Preserved; The Wonder**.

Afterpieces: *Catherine and Petruchio; The Cheats of Scapin; Chrononhotonthologos; The Citizen; The Connaught Wife**; *The Contrivances; Florizel and Perdita; The Ghost; The Giant's Causeway**(3); *Harlequin in Derry**(2); *Harlequin with Thurot**; *The Honest Yorkshireman; The Intriguing Chambermaid; The King and the Miller of Mansfield; The Lottery; The Lying Valet; The Mayor of Garratt; Midas; Miss in Her Teens; The Mock Doctor; The Orators**; *The Padlock**(3); *The Reprisal*(2); *Tom Thumb the Great; A Trip to Scotland**; *The Vintner Tricked; The Way to Keep Him**; *The What D'Ye Call It* ⏩; *The Wrangling Lovers.*

Interludes: *Colin's Welcome**(2); *The Disappointment** (2); *Lady Pentweazle of Blowbladder Street**(2); *Linco's Travels* ⏺(2); *Mrs. Cole the Methodist**.

Entr'acte singing: 12; dancing 1

Admission: Pit 2s. 2d., Gallery 1s. 1d.

Curtain time: 7 o'clock.

Benefits (20): Anderson (carpenter); Mrs. Bridges; Mrs. and Miss Bridges; Duffy; Fotteral; Gemea; Mrs. and Miss Gemea; Geoghegan (machinist); Miss Hern; O'Keeffe; Owens(2); P. Ryder, Sr.; S. Ryder; S. Ryder and Fotteral; T. Ryder(2); Mrs. Ryder; Stewart; Wilson.

April 1770

30 Mon. By Permission of the Worshipful Stephen Haven, Sovereign of Belfast. At Ryder's New Theatre in Mill Gate. *The Suspicious Husband.* Ranger–Ryder; Frankly–O'Keeffe; Jack Maggot–Duffy; Bellamy–Gemea; Tester–S. Ryder; Buckle–Carthy; Simon–Logan; Strictland–Fotteral; Jacintha–Miss Hern; Mrs. Strictland–Mrs. Bridges; Lucetta–Mrs. Logan; Milliner–Miss Gemea; Maid–Miss Eaton; Landlady–Mrs. Maxwell; Clarinda–Mrs. Ryder. With a farce called *The Mock Doctor.* Mock Doctor–Ryder. Pit 2s. 2d., Gallery 1s. 1d. No person will be admitted behind the scenes or to a rehearsal. Ryder hopes so necessary a regulation will not give offence as his sole motive for it is to exhibit all his plays with the utmost propriety and decorum. Places cannot be kept in the pit nor servants admitted without payment. To begin exactly at seven o'clock. Source: 24 Apr. 1770

May 1770

2 Wed. *Romeo and Juliet.* Romeo–Ryder. With a farce called *The Ghost.* Source: 24 Apr. 1770

4 Fri. *Love in a Village.* Young Meadows–Ryder. With a farce called *The Cheats of Scapin.* Scapin–Ryder. Source: 4 May 1770

9 Wed. *The Countess of Salisbury.* Lord Salisbury–Ryder; Countess of Salisbury–Mrs. Ryder. [Published in Belfast by James Magee in 1771]. Between the play and the farce a song *"The De'el take the wars that has hurried Willy frae me"* by O'Keeffe. With a pantomime entertainment called *Harlequin in Derry; or, The Dutchman Outwitted.* Harlequin–Logan; Dutchman–Stewart; Monsieur Frislecankee–Duffy; Conjurer–Ryder; Dundspate Dismal–O'Keeffe; Scaramouch–S. Ryder; Country Lad–Gemea; Country Lad–Carthy; Country Lad–Nugent; Country Lass–Mrs. Maxwell; Country Lass–Miss Whitmore; Country Lass–Miss Eaton; Country Lass–Miss Gemea; Country Lass–Mrs. Logan; Colombine–Miss Hern. With new scenes and machinery particularly an elegant view of the city of Derry, the paintings by Whitmore, the machinery by Geoghegan. N.B. Ryder was under the disagreeable necessity of putting off the exhibition of the above tragedy [originally advertised for 7 May] and entertainment on account of the machinery of the pantomime not being entirely ready. Source: 8 May 1770

10 Thur. *The Clandestine Marriage* and *Midas.* Source: 8 May 1770

16 Wed. Never acted here. *The Siege of Damascus.* Caled–Ryder. With a new comic opera in two acts never performed here called *The Padlock.* With all the original music as performed with great applause in London and Dublin. Written by the author of *Love in a Village.* With a new scene representing Don Diego's house. [*The Padlock* was published in Belfast by James Magee in 1769 and 1787]. Source: 15 May 1770

18 Fri. *Comus.* With a Grand representation of Comus's Court, the Bacchanalians and Bacchants dressed in their proper habits; the dresses entirely new. With *Miss in Her Teens.* Source: 18 May 1770

23 Wed. By Desire. *The Conscious Lovers.* Young Bevil–Ryder. With a comic-opera acted here but once called *The Padlock.* Mungo–Ryder. Source: 22 May 1770

25 Fri. *The Revenge.* With singing between the acts by Mrs. Bridges. With a new pantomime entertainment called *The Giant's Causeway; or, A Trip to the Dargle.* The scenery and machinery entirely new. Painted by Whitmore and executed by Geoghegan. In this entertainment will be exhibited an elegant view of the Giant's Causeway, the Dargle, the waterfall at Powerscourt. With all the scenes exhibited in *The Dargle* in Dublin. Source: 25 May 1770

30 Wed. *All in the Wrong.* Sir John Restless–Ryder. To which will added a farce called *Florizel and Perdita.* Source: 29 May 1770

June 1770

1 Fri. *The Beggar's Opera.* With a farce called *The Wrangling Lovers.* Source: 1 June 1770

5 Mon. *Hamlet.* The above tragedy was put off to this night on account of the wet weather. Source: 5 June 1770

12 Tues. By Desire. *The Maid of the Mill.* With a new farce called *A Trip to Scotland.* Source: 12 June 1770

13 Wed. *Love in a Village.* With *Catherine and Petruchio.* Source: 12 June 1770

15 Fri. *The Rival Queens.* In Act 2 will be introduced the Grand Triumphal entry of Alexander into Babylon with all the Grecian trophies, ensigns, banners, urns, vases and the Triumphal carr drawn by two captive

Kings. The trophies, ensigns entirely new and painted by Whitmore. With every other necessary decoration as performed at the Theatre Royal in Crow Street. The triumphal car executed by Geoghegan exactly after the manner of the so much admired one at the Theatre Royal in Crow Street, Dublin. With the celebrated comic interlude called *Linco's Travels*. As performed with universal applause at the theatres in Drury Lane and Crow Street by King. Written by Garrick. Source: 15 June 1770

18 Mon. *King Lear*. With *Polly Honeycombe*. Source: 15 June 1770

20 Wed. *Cato*. With *The King and the Miller of Mansfield*. Source: 19 June 1770

29 Fri. *The [Beaux'] Stratagem* and *Midas*. Source: 19 June 1770

July 1770

4 Wed. Benefit of Ryder. *The Foundling*. Young Bellmont–Ryder; Rosetta–Mrs. Ryder. Entertainments: End Act 1 a *"Sonnet to May"*; Act 2 a ramble through Dublin containing a visit to Stephen's Green; the College in College Green; a panegyrick on King William with a lick at modern economy and two Jew jugglers, written and to be sung by Ryder; Act 3 a song by Mrs. Bridges set to music by Sig. Thomaso Giordani, the words by Ryder; Act 4 *"Ailen a Roon"* by Mrs. Ryder. End of the play a comic interlude called *Lady Pentweazle of Blowbladder Street*. Lady Pentweazle–Ryder; Cormin–O'Keeffe. With a pantomime entertainment called *The Giant's Causeway; or, A Trip to the Dargle*. The whole to conclude with the celebrated song of *"Moderation and Alteration"* by Ryder. To begin on account of length of the performance exactly at half an hour past six o'clock. Nothing under full price will be taken. Source: 3 July 1770

6 Fri. By command of the Earl of Donegall. *The Beggar's Opera*. Macheath–Ryder. With a pantomime called *Harlequin in Derry; or, the Dutchman Outwitted*. To begin precisely at seven o'clock. Source: 3 July 1770

9 Mon. By desire of the Right Worshipful the Masters, Wardens and Brethren of the Ancient and Honourable Fraternity of Free and Accepted Masons of Belfast, Drumbridge. Benefit of Gemea. *Love for Love*. Ben–Ryder. Written by Congreve. A prologue to be spoke by Gemea in the character of a master mason. With the following entertainments: End Act 2 a song by Mrs. Bridges; Act 3 *"O let the Danger of a Son."* (from the Opera of *Artaxerxes*) by Gemea; End of the play *"Bucks have at ye all"* by O'Keeffe. With a farce written by Ryder and performed several nights in Dublin called *The Connaught Wife; or, The Honest Munster Man*. Thady Moriarty–Ryder. To conclude with an epilogue in the character of a country boy by Master Dawson. Pit 2s. 2d., Gallery 1s. 1d. To begin exactly at seven o'clock. Nothing under full price will be taken. Source: 6 July 1770

11 Wed. Benefit of S. Ryder. Never acted here. *Every Man in His Humour*. Bobadil–Ryder; Mrs. Kitely–Mrs. Ryder. Entertainments: End Act 1 *"The Soldier Tired"* by Mrs. Bridges; Act 2 a song by Gemea; Act 3 a favourite song called *"The Linnets"* by O'Keeffe; Act 4 *"The Chearful Linnets"* by Mrs. Bridges. With other entertainments as will be expressed in the bills. With a farce called *The Contrivances*. With all the original songs and music. Source: 6 July 1770

14 Sat.   Benefit of Fotteral. *The Mourning Bride*. Osmyn–Ryder; King–Fotteral; Almeria–Miss Hern; Zara–Mrs. Ryder. End Act 1 a song by Mrs. Bridges; Act 3 a favourite song called *"The Gods of the Greeks"* by Ryder; Act 4 a hornpipe by a young man of the town. End of the play an epilogue written by Garrick to be spoken by Master Dawson in the character of a fine gentleman. With a musical entertainment called *The Padlock*. Mungo–Ryder. Being positively the last night of performing it this season. The whole to conclude with *"Bucks have at you all"* (with alterations) by Fotteral, who humbly hopes the changing the night to Saturday will not be disagreeable as it is on account of a ball being given at Carrickfergus by the Right Hon. the Earl of Donegall on Friday evening. As it is to be on a Saturday night the curtain will rise at a quarter before seven and the performance will be over at eleven. Source: 10 July 1770

16 Mon. Benefit of Miss Hern. *The Merchant of Venice*. Shylock–Ryder; Portia–Miss Hern. With the following: End Act 1 a song called *"The Jest"* by Mrs. Bridges; Act 2 a song by O'Keeffe; Act 3 an Irish jigg by Logan and Mrs. Logan and an Irish song called *"Ellen a Roon"* by Mrs. Ryder. After the play a comic interlude called *The Disappointment; or, An Old Woman with a Colt's Tooth*. With a farce called *The Lottery*. Lovemore–Ryder; Chloe–Mrs. Ryder. Source: 13 July 1770

18 Wed. Benefit of Duffy. *The Miser*. Lovegold–Ryder. A prologue in the character of a country boy by Master Dawson. With the following entertainments End of Act 1 *"The Wood Lark"* by Mrs. Bridges; Act 2 a song by O'Keeffe; Act 4 a song called *"The Rapture"* by Mrs. Bridges; End of the play an epilogue written by Garrick to be spoken by Master Dawson in the character of a fine gentleman. After the play the celebrated comic interlude being positively the last time of performing it here this season called *Linco's Travels.* Linco–O'Keeffe. With a farce called *The Reprisal.* Ensign Maclamore–Ryder. Source: 17 July 1770

20 Fri.   Benefit of Stewart. By particular desire of several ladies and gentlemen. *Love Makes a Man.* Clodio–Ryder; Don Lewis–Stewart. With variety of singing between the acts by Ryder, O'Keeffe, and Mrs. Bridges. With the following entertainments for this night only: a humorous prologue upon an old man a boy and an ass indicating the difficulty of pleasing the million by Ryder; a humorous and sentimental paraphrase on Shakespear's *"Seven Ages"*, written by the celebrated Geo. Alex. Stevens, by O'Keeffe. Between the play and farce *"The Picture of a Playhouse; or, Bucks Have At Ye All"* (with alterations and additions as spoken originally by King) by Stewart. With a dramatic satire, never acted here, called *The What D'Ye Call It.* Timothy Peascod–Ryder; Thomas Philpot–O'Keeffe. To conclude with a comic satiric epilogue in the character of nobody addressed to everybody and to be spoke by somebody by Stewart. On account of the length of the night's entertainment the play will begin precisely at seven o'clock. Source: 17 July 1770

25 Wed.   Benefit of Mrs. Gemea and Miss Gemea. *The Wonder, A Woman Keeps a Secret.* Lissardo–Ryder. With a variety of entertainments as will be expressed in the bills. With a farce called *The Lying Valet.* Sharp–Ryder. Source: 24 July 1770

26 Thur. Never performed here. Benefit of O'Keeffe. *The Jovial Crew.* Oliver–Ryder; Hearty–O'Keeffe. Between the opera and farce will be performed a dramatick pastoral called *Colin's Welcome.* Written by O'Keeffe. The musick composed by Arne, Purcell and Sig. Tenducci. In this piece are described the most remarkable characters in a certain metropolis. With a farce called *The Mayor of Garratt.* Maj. Sturgeon–Ryder; Jerry Sneak–O'Keeffe. After the opera an interlude from Foote's farce of *The Minor* called *Mrs. Cole the Methodist.* Mrs. Cole–Ryder. By desire after Act 2 Carteret will dance a hornpipe. The whole to conclude with Stevens humorous and sentimental paraphrase on Shakespear's *"Seven Ages"* by O'Keeffe. Source: 24 July 1770

28 Sat.   Positively the last week but one of performing here. Benefit of Owens. *Barbarossa.* Sadi–Ryder; Barbarossa–Stewart; Othman–Fotteral; Aladin–S. Ryder; Officer–Duffy; Slave–McCarthy; Guard–Wilson; Guard–Gemea; Guard–Dawson; Achmet–Owens; Irene–Mrs. Bridges; Female Slave–Mrs. Logan; Zaphira–Miss Hern. With the following entertainments: Before the play an occasional prologue addressed to the ladies written and to be spoken by Owens; End of Act 1 *"The Soldier Tired"* by Mrs. Bridges; Act 2 a Hornpipe by a young man of this town. Act 3 *"De'el take the Wars"* by O'Keeffe. Act 4 *"The Linnets"* by O'Keeffe. Between the play and farce a comic interlude called *The Disappointment.* Widow Lovit–Ryder; Young Lovit–Duffy; Pimplenose–S. Ryder; Mrs. Macklin–Mrs. Logan. With a farce called *The Intriguing Chambermaid.* Drunken Colonel–Ryder; Valentine–Owens; Lord Pride–O'Keeffe; Goodall–Duffy; Puff–Fotteral; Security–Gemea; Oldcastle–Stewart; Slap–S. Ryder; Trusty–McCarthy; Lettice–Mrs. Bridges; Charlotte–Mrs. Maxwell; Mrs. Highman–Mrs. Logan. Before the farce Owens will speak the celebrated prologue to the author written by Foote with alterations and additions. To conclude with an epilogue by Master Dawson. On account of the length and variety of entertainments the curtain will rise at half an hour after six o'clock. The performance of the above play is deferred until tomorrow on account of Carteret's ball being this evening. Source: 27 July 1770

30 Mon. Positively the last week but one of performing. Benefit of Mrs. Ryder. *Venice Preserved.* Pierre–Ryder; Jaffier–O'Keeffe; Belvidera–Mrs. Ryder. After the play a comic interlude called *Lady Pentweazle of Blowbladder Street.* Lady Pentweazle–Ryder; Carmine–O'Keeffe. The above play and pantomime were to have been performed last Monday [23 July] but were obliged to be postponed till Monday next on account of the machinery for the pantomime not being entirely finished. Source: 27 July 1770

31 Mon. [The title of the mainpiece performed this night is not recorded]. For this night only a new pantomime entertainment called *Harlequin with Thurot; or, The Taking of Carrickfergus.* English Commodore–Ryder (with a song on our success in the late glorious war written by Ryder); Harlequin–Logan; French General–Duffy; Thurot–Fotteral; French Soldier–McCarthy; French Soldier–Dawson; French Soldier–Cannen; French Soldier–Owens; English Officer–S. Ryder; English Soldier–Gemea; English Soldier–Wilson; Sir Simon Scarecrow–Stewart; Jeremy Divel–O'Keeffe; Colombine–Miss Hern. In which will be exhibited a variety of new scenes particularly a view of Carrickfergus, Belfast, Joy's paper-mill, a landscape water-fall with cattle grazing, and an exact representation of a Patagonian man and woman brought from Patagonia by the *Dolphin* man-of-war in her voyage round the world. The painting by Whitmore. The machinery by Geoghegan. The whole to conclude with the song of *"Britannia rule the Waves"* taken from the celebrated masque of *Alfred* accompanied by a full chorus of English sailors. *Harlequin with Thurot; or, The*

Taking of Carrickfergus advertised to be performed yesterday evening Benefit of Mrs. Ryder is obliged to be postponed to Monday [31 July], on account of the machinery not being entirely finished

[On 21 February 1760 a diversionary force of three French war-ships led byCommodore François Thurot captured the fortress of Carrickfergus, Co. Antrim, a few miles north of Belfast, from a weak English garrison, which quickly ran out of ammunition and resorted to pelting the French soldiers with stones from the castle walls and using their coat buttons as bullets. The Army was saved from humiliation, when, on 27 February, three English frigates destroyed the entire French fleet in Carrickfergus Bay and killed Thurot. As a recent history observes, the episode "is a quintessentially Georgian mixture of valour and farce" (Bartlett and Jeffery, 1996, 226)]. Source: 31 July 1770

August 1770

1   Wed.   Benefit of Mrs. Bridges and Miss Bridges. *Rule a Wife and Have a Wife.* Copper Captain–Ryder; Estifania–Miss Hern. With singing by Mrs. Bridges and Miss Bridges and a farce called *Tom Thumb the Great.* Tom Thumb–Miss Bridges. Source: 31 July 1770

2   Thur.   Positively the last week of performing here. Benefit of S. Ryder and Fotteral. *Hamlet.* Hamlet–Ryder; Queen–Mrs. Ryder; Ophelia–Miss Hern. With the following entertainments End Act 1 a song by Mrs. Bridges; Act 3 a song from the masque of *Comus* (as sung by Tenducci) called *"Sweet are the pleasures"* by O'Keeffe; Act 4 *"The Chearful Linnets"* by Mrs. Bridges; Act 5 a humorous and sentimental paraphrase on Shakespear's *"Seven Ages"* written by Stevens to be spoken by O'Keeffe. With a farce called *The Reprisal.* Ensign Maclamore–Ryder; Harriet–Mrs. S. Ryder (her first appearance on the stage). The whole to conclude with a farewell address to the ladies and gentlemen written and to be spoken by Fotteral. S. Ryder and Fotteral being encouraged to take another benefit (as their first attempt failed) hope for the favour and countenance of the ladies and gentlemen of Belfast. Nothing under full price will be taken. Source: 31 July 1770

4   Sat.   Benefit of Wilson. *The Fair Penitent.* Lothario–Ryder; Altamont–Wilson. With the following entertainments: before the play a prologue on the charms of money by Wilson; End Act 1 a new song called *"The Sheep in a Cluster"* by Mrs. Bridges; Act 3 a song by Gemea; Act 4 *"Bucks have at ye All"* by Wilson; End of the play *"The Lilliputian Dance"* by Wilson and Logan. With *Chrononhotonthologos.* The whole to conclude with an epilogue of thanks or an address to the ladies of Belfast to be spoken by Wilson. Source: 31 July 1770

6 Mon. Benefit of [Preswick] Ryder Sr., Office-keeper, and Miss Hern. *The Revenge.* Zanga–Ryder; Leonora–Miss Hern. With entertainments, to which will be added a new pantomime entertainment called *The Giant's Causeway; or, A Trip to the Dargle.* With scenery and machinery entirely new. In this entertainment will be exhibited an elegant view of the Giant's Causeway and the Dargle, the water-fall at Powerscourt. With all the scenes exhibited in Dublin. Source: 3 Aug. 1770

7 Tues. Benefit of Mrs. Bridges. *Theodosius.* Varanes–Ryder. The stage during the greatest part of the play will be grandly illuminated and represent a stately temple with an altar shewing the Christian religion in its first magnificence then but lately established at Rome and Constantinople. With several new songs to be sung between the acts by Mrs. Bridges. With a farce called *The Vintner Tricked.* Vizard–Ryder. Nothing under full price will be taken. Mrs. Bridges being encouraged to take another benefit (her first attempt failed) hopes for the favour and countenance of the ladies and gentlemen of Belfast. Source: 7 Aug. 1770

8 Wed. Positively the last week of performing here. Benefit of Geoghegan, machinist. *Jane Shore.* Hastings–Ryder; Alicia–Mrs. Ryder; Jane Shore–Miss Hern. End of the play will be exhibited an exact model of Moore's famous and ingenious carriage that moves by self-impelling power executed by Geoghegan who will sit in it himself and move with a black behind several times up and down and round the stage. With a farce called *The Way to Keep Him.* [Published by James Magee in Belfast in 1760]. After the farce will be exhibited (for this night only) Whitmore's Italian shades as performed at the theatres in London and Dublin with universal applause. Source: 7 Aug. 1770

10 Fri. Benefit of Anderson, carpenter. *Douglas.* Douglas–Ryder; Lady Randolph–Mrs. Ryder. *The Honest Yorkshireman.* Source: 7 Aug. 1770

11 Sat. Positively the last night but two. Benefit of Owens. *The Orphan.* Chamont–Ryder; Castalio–Owens; Monimia–Miss Hern. With the following entertainments: before the play a prologue addressed to the ladies written and to be spoken by Owens. Several songs by O'Keeffe, Mrs. Bridges and Miss Whitemore. End of the play a comic pastoral called *Colin's Welcome.* Colin–O'Keeffe. Written by O'Keeffe and dedicated to the Right Hon. the Countess of Donegall. Before the farce the celebrated prologue to the author written by Foote to be spoken by Owens. With *The Citizen.* Young Philpot–Ryder; Young Wilding–Owens; Maria (with songs)–Mrs. Bridges. To conclude with a set of fire-works in miniature. The play will begin exactly at half after six and the whole entertainments be over before eleven. Owens, being encouraged to take a second benefit, as he lost considerably by his first and he humbly hopes for the countenance of the ladies and gentlemen of Belfast tomorrow evening. Source: 10 Aug. 1770

15 Wed. Benefit of Ryder and the last night of performing. *The Constant Couple* and *The Orators,* with the Trial of the Cocklane Ghost. Source: 14 Aug. 1770

1770–1771 SEASON

The Belfast Theatre was dark. During the summer and winter of 1770 and for the next two years Belfast life was disrupted by several "Hearts of Steel" riots occasioned by evictions resulting from the re-leasing of property and extortionate fines levied by the Earl of Donegall and other landowners.

1771–1772 SEASON

Venue: James Parker's company returned to Belfast and performed at "The Theatre in Mill Street."
Company: Atkins; Mr. and Mrs. Burden; Mr. and Mrs. Day; John Dumont (from King's Opera House, Haymarket); Peter Dumont; Mrs. Dumont; Farrell; Mrs. Farrell; Miss Farrell; [Brownlow] Forde; James Fotteral; Miss Gemea; Myrton Hamilton; John Kane; John Lynch; Mrs. Mozeen; James Parker (actor-manager); Pye; Mrs. Pye.

James Parker led his company to Belfast again this season. For his biography see 1768–68 season.

For biography of **Michael Atkins** see 1768–69 season.

Francis Berry, who had performed in Belfast during the 1765–66 season, received a benefit in January 1772 but is not known to have acted this season.

The *BD* relates the somewhat confusing career of the actor whom Clark identifies as **George Day** and who evidently made his only London stage appearance at Covent Garden in December 1762. The critics were not kind. Day (if it is the same man) disappears from the record for nearly eight years, resurfacing with his wife, for the 1770–71 season, in Dublin at Smock Alley on 8 December 1770 playing Lord Ogleby in *The Clandestine Marriage* and billed as "from the Theatre Royal, Covent Garden, first time in this Kingdom." There is no record of Day's having acted at Covent Garden prior to this time other than that of his supposed debut performance mentioned above. Earlier that season, on 6 November, Mrs. Day made her Dublin debut at the same theatre with the note that it was her "first appearance in this Kingdom."

The Days were not re-engaged in Dublin and spent the 1771–72 season with Parker's strolling company: first in Limerick for a brief stay in October 1771 and then for most of the remainder of the year in Belfast. In February 1773 they appeared for a time in Kilkenny, but, again, they disappear from the record for several seasons, reappearing for the 1778–79 Crow Street season.

In early December 1778 George Day, but not his wife, visited Belfast (billed as "From the Theatre Royal, Dublin") with Michael Atkins's company and performed there first on 18 December 1778, remaining until his last mention in the Belfast bills on 12 February 1779. He then returned to Dublin and reappears in the Crow Street bills on 25 February 1779.

Mr. and Mrs. Day are found again in Belfast in the spring and summer of 1780, and then, after disappearing for two years, are acting in Derry in October 1782 and then at Crow Street for the remainder of 1782–83 season. Evidently, the Days confined their activities to the Irish provinces thereafter because the only other record of their activities is in Cork in August 1794 (Day only, the last record of him). Thereafter, Mrs. Day is known only to have appeared in Limerick in October 1798 and in Cork in the spring of 1800.

The **Dumont** who reappears in Dublin at Smock Alley during the 1747–48 season was probably John Dumont, who, with his wife, had performed regularly in the Dublin theatres between 1732–33 and 1743–44. Dumont made his London debut at Drury Lane in the 1741–42 season and also danced at Sadler's Wells that summer. The following year he performed entr'acte dancing at Covent Garden.

Madame Dumont and her husband danced separately at various times. She was in Edinburgh at some point during the 1740s and danced at Covent Garden in 1746–47 and again in 1748–49, after which time, the BD believes, her name disappears from the bills. However, the Dumont family that danced in Belfast during the 1771–72 season was the one who had performed in Dublin thirty years earlier. Evidently, at some time near the end of the decade of the 1740s the Dumonts went onto the Continent where they performed for many years, returning to the north of Ireland in the spring of 1767. The BNL 21 Apr. 1767 prints an advertisement placed by "Mr. Dumont, dancing master" announcing the opening of a school for dance at the Market House in Downpatrick, Co. Down. We are told that Dumont has returned to Ireland after "many years and at several courts abroad." He has been a "principal dancer at the Dublin theatres, at the King's Opera House, Haymarket, London, and in the courts of Europe."

From 1767 John Dumont and his son, Peter, taught dance and acted as masters of ceremony for balls in the north of Ireland. On 1 January 1768 the entire Dumont family presented a set of popular dances from current plays at the Market House in Newry. The advertisement gives the names of the various dancers: in addition to Mr. and Mrs. Dumont were Misses Polly, Clementine, and Nancy Dumont and a son, Peter Dumont. For the next forty years, the Dumonts gave dancing lessons and hosted balls in Belfast, Lisburn, Armagh, Newry, Downpatrick, Moira, Comber, Carrickfergus, and Dundalk.

Mrs. Dumont died at Newry on 9 January 1777 after a long illness and was survived by her husband and children. In January 1780 Dumont's brother, billed as "John Dumont, Junior," also took up teaching dance in the north in conjunction with his brother and nephew. In subsequent advertisements the principal name is that of John Dumont, and it is not now possible to determine if this is the elder man or his brother. The last surviving record of the Dumonts is in the *BNL* in early December 1798.

Clark (1965, 358) indicates that the "Misses" **Farrell** performed in Belfast this season; however, I am able to find reference to only one Miss Farrell in the bills. See the 1768–69 season for biographies of the Farrells.

Brownlow Forde made his acting debut in Dublin at Crow Street on 6 April 1768 as Scrub in *The Beaux' Stratagem*, billed as a "Young Gentleman, his first appearance on any stage." *FDJ* 10–12 Mar 1768 reported: "We hear that a young Gentleman of this Kingdom who has been educated in our University and taken his Degrees there, has determined to pursue the profession of the Stage and will shortly make his Appearance in a principal Character in Comedy." His debut season seems to have been a fairly successful one.

The *BD* suggests the confusion about Brownlow Forde's early years. On the one hand, George Parker (in 1781) wrote that Forde "having met with some disappointment in the Church, had thrown by the Cassock to put on the Sock. . . .", on the other, William Upcott in 1816 contended that Forde was "a native of Ireland, who studied medicine under Professor Cleghorn, after which he joined a company of strolling players, and closed his career by taking orders." Other evidence indicates that Parker was closer to the truth. In a letter to David Garrick dated March 1768, the actor Walker wrote: "We have a parson [Brownlow Forde] to appear in Scrub with Mr. Mossop's Archer; such an extraordinary metamorphosis will no doubt excite curiosity. The town cannot now complain that they have had no novelty; this is the greatest the stage ever knew—though it is thought the canonical gentlemen will be so scandalized as to influence a party against us; but however it happens it will bring one great house, at least, perhaps several; and if we can but escape civil, we do not much mind ecclesiastical censure. Excommunication is not half so terrible to our state as an execution." (Garrick 1963, 1:289).

Forde was not reengaged in Dublin the following season, and, after a brief appearance in Kilkenny in August 1769, he disappears from the record until he makes his London debut, at the Haymarket Theatre on 29 May 1769 as the Minor in the play of that title. He was evidently unsuccessful, because he is not listed in further Haymarket productions that summer.

Forde (and for the first time Mrs. Forde) is next recorded as a member of the strolling company led by James Parker in Belfast in July 1771–January 1772. In addition to acting in the role of Scrub, Forde brought forward his only farce, never performed before, called *The Miraculous Cure; or, The Citizen Outwitted*, an adaptation of Cibber's *The Double Gallant* (published by George Stevenson, Newry, 1781). Immediately after the company left Belfast, Ford (billed as "his first appearance upon that stage") was engaged with the Smock Alley company for the remainder of the 1771–72 season.

Forde spent the next year acting in Kilkenny and Waterford (1772–73). According to the *BD*, Forde had a sideline as a printer in Dublin and evidently engaged in that business for the next few years, for there is no record of his having acted during that time.

At the beginning of the 1776–77 season Forde is found in Cork (July–October). He was not engaged at either of the major Dublin playhouses that season, but did join the company of the newly formed Fishamble Street playhouse when it opened on 27 January 1777. He sang and acted in a variety of primary and secondary roles during that season and took two sole benefits, his first being "hurt, by a number of his friends being on circuit."

At this time Forde evidently decided to try his hand at management, for an item in *FDJ* 27–29 Aug. 1776 reports: "We have the pleasure of informing the public, that a plan is now on foot, and a theatre preparing for the purpose of performing operas, musical farces, and pantomimes, under the joint management of Mr. Pinto and Mr. Forde. From the excellence of the former as a musician, and the latter as an actor, we have not the smallest doubt of that species of entertainment being brought to greater perfection than any ever yet exhibited in this kingdom."

The plan was brought to fruition the following spring. Again, the *FDJ* 22–25 Mar. 1777 reports: "Italian Opera. The director of the Italian Company most respectfully acquaints the nobility and gentry, that he has contracted with the managers of the new theatre in Fishamble Street for fifteen nights representation of Italian operas. The most eminent and capital performers have been engaged for that purpose; and the first exhibition will be the 8th of April; the characters of the piece and the names of those who are to perform in it, timely notice will be given to the public."

However, the Forde-Pinto partnership was a failure. Arthur Young, in his *Tour of Ireland* (1780, 4) says that he lived more than two months in Dublin at this time and: "An ill-judged and unsuccessful attempt was made to establish the Italian opera, which existed, but with scarcely any life, for this one winter; of course they could rise to no higher than a comic opera. *La Buona Figliuola, La Frascatana, and Il Geloso in Cimenti* were repeatedly performed, or rather murdered, except the parts in Sestini. The house was generally empty and miserably cold."

With the collapse of the Fishamble Street venture, Forde was reengaged at Crow Street and he spent the 1777–78 season there. As proof that he had married at least a decade earlier, an item in *Saunders's Newsletter* of 13 December 1777 placed by Brownlow Forde, the actor, indicates that his nine-year-old son, Arthur, has "strayed from his father's house in Cope Street" and may be endeavoring to walk to Cork. His parents offer a reward for information about the boy. Forde is found with the Crow Street company as a part of the company that regularly visited Cork in the summers of 1777 and 1778.

The urge to manage evidently did not desert Forde. He traveled to London and is found acting, for one special performance, at the Haymarket Theatre in March 1780. He applied for and was granted a license to stage plays and other entertainments at the Haymarket Theatre in 1782; however, he never availed of the license. The *BD* believes that the Mrs. Forde who acted in Portsmouth in August 1782 may have been the wife of Brownlow, but this seems unlikely.

In 1784 Brownlow Forde is found preaching again in London, apparently having given up the stage. He was the ordinary at Newgate prison for a time, but was dismissed from the post in 1814. He disappears from the record thereafter.

For biography of **James Fotteral** see the 1769–70 season.

For biography of **Miss Gemea** see the 1769–70 season.

For a biography of **Myrton Hamilton** see the 1768–69 season.

The earliest record of the actor **John Kane** is found in an R. J. Broadbent's article entitled "Old Circuit Days: Austin and Whitlock's Circuit," which indicates that in 1767 the two "brought a company from the [Theatre] Royal Dublin," including John Kane (quoted in *BD*).

There is no evidence of an actor named Kane in Dublin prior to this time. The Smock Alley box keeper named Kane probably assumed that post at the beginning of the 1765–66 season, but he is not known to have acted, and he was functioning regularly as box keeper at the time that John Kane is known to have been on Whitlock's circuit and also during the 1767–68 and 1768–69 seasons. Kane is found with the company at Cork in the summer and autumn of 1769.

When Mossop moved his company to Crow Street for the 1769–70 season Kane went with him. That season too an actor named Kane begins to appear regularly in the Crow Street bills. It is not now possible to determine if the box keeper and the actor, who played tertiary and a few secondary roles, are the same person, but it seems unlikely. The following season saw Kane acting at the ill-starred Capel Street theatre until it closed on 22 March 1771 and the company moved to Crow Street under Dawson's management. Again, the box keeper is Kane.

The following season the actor Kane is found in Belfast with Parker's strolling company from July 1771–January 1772. He is then recorded acting secondary and tertiary in Dublin, now at Smock Alley, for the 1772–73 through 1775–76. Kane's name is included among the companies that performed in Cork in the early autumns of 1775, 1776 and 1778. It is clear from the benefit playbills that two, different, Kanes are active at Smock Alley at this time, one an actor, the other the box keeper. Indeed, when the post of box keeper was taken over by Cullen, the actor continued to perform in Dublin.

The following season Kane moved to the new Fishamble Street theatre which opened on 27 January 1777 but he is found again at Crow Street in the summer after the opera company took residence at Fishamble Street. Kane acted in Belfast during the 1778–79 season, and, when he returned to Dublin, he moved to Smock Alley for the 1780–81 season through the 1782–83 seasons. Again, he visited Cork with the regular visiting company in the autumns of 1780, 1782 (and Limerick), and 1783. Kane visited Belfast again during the 1783–84 season. The last record of Kane's acting is in Derry in April 1799.

John Lynch evidently began his acting and dancing career in the Irish provinces. He is first noticed in the summer and autumn of 1771 in Belfast with James Parker's strolling company playing tertiary characters. Subsequently he is found in Cork in the early autumn of 1780, the last season the Cork theatre was managed exclusively by Tottenham Heaphy, without Daly's involvement. It was probably at this time that Lynch became acquainted with Daly. In any event, he was engaged for the following 1780–81 season at Daly's Smock Alley playhouse where he danced and played a variety of tertiary characters.

Lynch remained at Smock Alley for the 1781–82 through the 1786–87 seasons. In 1781 Mrs. Lynch is first noticed in the Smock Alley bills. She and her husband acted at Smock Alley for the 1782–83 season, but only he is mentioned in the Smock Alley bills in 1783–84 and thereafter. The name of John Lynch appears among those of the Smock Alley company who signed an affidavit that was published in *FDJ* 28–31 Jan. 1786 supporting Daly's character and reputation in the slander and libel controversy. Lynch's name disappears from the playbills for a time after the 1786–87 season.

During this period Lynch is frequently found in the Irish provinces: in Cork in August 1781; in Cork and Limerick in July and August 1782; in Cork in the autumn of 1783, 1784, and 1786. After his long stint in Dublin, Lynch, his wife (who made her stage debut at Belfast on 17 December 1788) and daughter became a stalwart of Michael Atkins's Belfast company, appearing there and in Derry in the 1788–89, 1789–90, 1791–92, 1792–93, 1793–94, 1794–95, and 1795–96 seasons. In the spring of 1798 he acted in Derry during the short season there. Finally, Lynch may have acted in Carrickfergus in December 1799.

The *BNL* 14 Feb. 1800 carried the following death notice: "Died on Thursday [13 February 1800] Mr. Lynch, comedian, whose death will be long regretted by the admirers of Dramatic merit. The liberality of a Belfast audience whose principal favourite he was for many years was amply evinced at his benefit the night preceding his final exit. He has left an afflicted wife and five children to mourn his loss."

For a biography of **Mrs. Mozeen** see the 1754–55 season.

For a biography of **Mr.** and **Mrs. Pye** see the 1768–69 season.

Repertory, July 1771–January 1772

This season James Parker attracted audiences by staging a relatively large number of popular plays that were new to Belfast, if not always to Irish audiences generally. *Cymon, Lionel and Clarissa, The School for Rakes, The West Indian* and *Tom Jones* had all premiered in Dublin in the recent past and had been successful there. Clearly, Parker was particularly interested in bringing new musical pieces to Belfast. The programs of this season are also interesting because, for the first time in Belfast, they regularly include (new) musical interludes, in addition to main and afterpieces.

Total Performances: 46 of 34 different named mainpieces; 42 of 28 named afterpieces.
   Shakespeare: 6.
   New Mainpieces: 8.
   New Afterpieces: 4.

(For a key to repertory symbols see above, page 11)

Mainpieces: *All in the Wrong; The Beaux' Stratagem* (2); *The Beggar's Opera; The Busy Body* (2); *The Clandestine Marriage; The Constant Couple* (2); *Cymon**▣; *The Distrest Mother; The Earl of Warwick**; *The Fair Penitent; False Delicacy; The Ghost; The Inconstant; Jane Shore; The Jealous Wife* (2); *King Henry IV, Part One; King Henry V*▣; *King Richard III; Lionel and Clarissa** (4); *Love in a Bog**; *Love in a Village; Macbeth; The Maid of the Mill; The Merchant of Venice; The Miser* (2); *The Mourning Bride; The Provoked Husband; The Rival Queens; Romeo and Juliet; The School for Rakes**; *Tamerlane* (2); *Tom Jones** (2); *The West Indian** (2).

Afterpieces: *The Anatomist* (2); *The Chaplet*†; *The Citizen* (2); *The Contrivances; Damon and Phillida; The Deuce is in Him* (2); *The Devil to Pay; The Elopement**; *The Fashionable Wife; Florizel and Perdita; The Guardian** (2); *Harlequin in the Shades* (2); *High Life Below Stairs; The Honest Yorkshireman* (3); *The Humours of Humbug; The King and the Miller of Mansfield; The Lying Valet; The Mayor of Garratt; The Mentalist**; *Midas; The Miraculous Cure*Θ; *Miss in Her Teens; The Old Maid* (3); *The Padlock* (2); *Polly Honeycombe* (2); *The Reprisal;* Unspecified "farce"(2); *The Virgin Unmasked; Wit's Last Stake*† (2).

Interlude: *The Farmer's Return from London*†; *The Female Officer*†; *Harlequin Skeleton*†; *The Magical Soldier*†.

Entr'acte entertainments: Singing: 11. Dancing: 3

Curtain time: 7 o'clock.

Benefits (16): Atkins; Francis Berry; Burden; Mrs. Burden; Burden and Mrs. Burden; Day; Mrs. Day; Farrell and Miss Farrell; Mrs. Farrell; Forde; Hamilton; Kane; Parker; the Poor; Pye; Mrs. Pye.

July 1771

29 Mon.   *The Jealous Wife*. With a farce and entertainments. The Theatre in Mill Street is repairing and will be opened in a few days with a play and farce, the particulars of which will be inserted in this paper. As the Company are determined to use their utmost abilities to merit a continuance of the favours the town of Belfast has been pleased to confer on them heretofore they have got all the new pieces ready, viz. *The West Indian, Lionel and Clarissa, The Brothers* [no record of its being performed this season], *The School for Rakes, The Earl of Warwick, Tom Jones* with which they propose to entertain the Ladies and Gentlemen during their short stay. Source: 16 July 1771

August 1771

2 Fri.   *Macbeth,* with all the original music, and necessary Decorations. Days of playing are Mondays, Wednesdays, and Fridays. The doors to be opened at six, and to begin exactly at seven. With a farce called *The Honest Yorkshireman.* Source: 2 Aug. 1771

7 Wed. Never performed here. *The Earl of Warwick.* With singing and a farce called *Miss in Her Teens.* Source: 6 Aug. 1771

9 Fri.   *The Provoked Husband.* With singing by Mrs. Mozeen and Mrs. Day. No person can be admitted behind the scenes. With *Damon and Phillida.* Source: 6 Aug. 1771

16 Fri.   *The   Distrest   Mother.*   Orestes–Atkins;   Pyrrhus–Fotteral; Pylades–Pye; Phoenix–Lynch; Andromache–Mrs. Mozeen; Hermione–Mrs. Pye; Cleone–Miss Gemea; Cephisa–Mrs. Farrell. *The Devil to Pay.* Source: 16 Aug. 1771

21 Wed. Never performed here. *Lionel and Clarissa.* With proper scenes, particularly, the library, moonlight, garden, painted for the occasion by

Atkins. [Published in Belfast by James Magee in 1778]. With a farce called *The Fashionable Wife*. Source: 20 Aug. 1771

23 Fri.   Never performed here [but see 21 Aug. 1771]. *Lionel and Clarissa*. With *Polly Honeycombe*. Source: 20 Aug. 1771

28 Wed.   By particular Desire, for the third time. *The West Indian*. With a farce as will be expressed in the Bills. Source: 27 Aug. 1771

30 Fri.   *Love in a Village*. With *Wit's Last Stake*. Source: 30 Aug. 1771

September 1771

4 Wed. *The [Beaux'] Stratagem*. Archer–Atkins; Aimwell–Fotteral; Boniface–Kane; Sullen–Burden; Gibbet–Hamilton; Foigard–Farrell; Sir Charles–Pye; Scrub–Forde; Mrs. Sullen–Mrs. Mozeen; Dorinda–Mrs. Day; Lady Bountiful–Mrs. Farrell; Gypsy–Miss Gemea; Cherry–Mrs. Pye. With *The Old Maid*. Source: 3 Sept. 1771

6 Fri.   Never performed here. *King Henry V*, altered from Shakespeare by Aaron Hill. With a comic Opera called *The Padlock*. Source: 6 Sept. 1771

11 Wed.   *The Rival Queens*. In Act 2 a Grand Procession, with all Trophies, Standards, Banners, and every necessary Decoration. With a farce called *The Mock Doctor*. Source: 10 Sept. 1771

13 Fri.   *The Miser*. With *The King and the Miller of Mansfield*. Source: 13 Sept. 1771

18 Wed.   *All in the Wrong*. With a farce called *The Contrivances*. Source: 17 Sept. 1771

20 Fri.   *The Mourning Bride*. With a farce called *The Guardian*. Source: 20 Sept. 1771

25 Wed.   *The Fair Penitent*. With a farce called *The Lying Valet*. Source: 24 Sept. 1771

27 Fri.   *The School for Rakes*. Written by a Lady of this Kingdom [Mrs. Elizabeth Griffiths]. With singing between the acts by Burden and Mrs. Day and a farce called *The Ghost*. Source: 27 Sept. 1771

October 1771

2   Wed.   By particular desire. *The Provoked Husband*. With a farce called *The Guardian*. With singing between the acts. Source: 1 Oct. 1771

4   Fri.   By particular desire. *Romeo and Juliet*. In Act 4 a Funeral Procession. With *The Padlock*. Being the last time of performing it this season. Source: 4 Oct. 1771

9   Wed.   *Jane Shore*. With singing by Burden and Mrs. Day. With a farce, never performed before, called *The Miraculous Cure; or, The Citizen Outwitted* compiled by Brownlow Forde [an adaptation of C. Cibber's *The Double Gallant*]. Source: 8 Oct. 1771

11   Fri.   *Lionel and Clarissa*. Being the last time of performing it this season. With a farce called *The Miraculous Cure; or, The Citizen Outwitted*. Source: 11 Oct. 1771

16   Wed.   *The Busy Body*. With a pantomime entertainment (second time) called *The Elopement; or, Harlequin Wizard*. With new scenery, machinery, music, dresses, and every necessary decoration. Source: 15 Oct. 1771

23   Wed.   *Cymon*. With proper scenery, machinery, music, as it was performed last season at the Theatres in Dublin upwards of seventy nights, with universal applause. With a farce called *The Deuce is in Him*. Source: 22 Oct. 1771

25   Fri.   *King Henry IV, Part One*. With the Humours of Sir John Falstaff. With *The Humours of Humbug*. Source: 25 Oct. 1771

30   Wed.   *Tom Jones*. Squire Western–Parker; Alworthy–Fotteral; Supple–Burden; Nightingale–Kane; Young Nightingale–Pye; Blifil–Lynch; Sportsman–Hamilton; Sportsman–Farrell; Tom Jones–Day; Mrs. Western–Mrs. Pye; Honor–Mrs. Mozeen; Nancy–Miss Gemea; Landlady–Mrs. Farrell; Sophia–Mrs. Day. The celebrated comic opera of *Tom Jones* taken from Fielding's excellent novel of that name. With a farce called *The Deuce is in Him*. Source: 29 Oct. 1771

November 1771

1   Fri.   *Tom Jones*. Cast as 30 Oct. With *High Life Below Stairs*. Source: 1 Nov. 1771

4   Mon.   *Tamerlane*. Source: 1 Nov. 1771

8 Fri.   By desire of the officers of his Majesty's 42nd Regiment of Foot. *The Jealous Wife*. With a farce called *The Citizen*. Those ladies and gentlemen who have tickets by them, are requested to bring them in this night, as the benefits begin on Monday, after which they will be of no use. Source: 8 Nov. 1771

15 Fri.   Benefit of Parker. *The Constant Couple*. With the following dances by M. Dumont and his family, from the King's Opera-House in the Haymarket, London. After Act 1 *"The Millers"* by Dumont and Mrs. Dumont; After Act 3 a Hornpipe by P. Dumont; After the Play, *"The Wood-Cutters"* by Dumont, P. Dumont and Mrs. Dumont in which will be introduced a Cotilion in the modern taste. With a new Comedy of two acts, called *The Mentalist; or, Doctor of the Passions*. Principal Characters by Atkins; Kane; Burden; Hamilton; Pye; Forde; Mrs. Burden; Mrs. Pye; Mrs. Mozeen. Written by a gentleman of the County Down [Brownlow Ford?], being the only time it will be performed this season. As Dumont's business does not call him from hence till Thursday next, he has been so kind as to offer Parker his performance for his benefit, which the public may be assured is the last time it will be in his power to dance here this season. Source: 15 Nov. 1771

20 Wed.   Benefit of Burden. *The Beggar's Opera*. After Act 1 *"Bucks Have At Ye All"* to be spoke by Mrs. Burden. A favourite interlude, taken from *The Female Officer; or, The Humours of the Army*. Female Officer–Mrs. Burden. With the Prussian Exercise, firing Mrs. Burden. To which (by particular desire) will be added a farce called *The Reprisal*. Source: 19 Nov. 1771

22 Fri.   Benefit of Mrs. Pye. *The Merchant of Venice*. With singing between the acts, by Mrs. Day. With a farce, called *The Honest Yorkshireman*. To conclude with an Italian pantomime called *Harlequin in the Shades*. Source: 22 Nov. 1771

27 Wed.   Benefit of Mrs. Farrell. *The West Indian*. With *The Mayor of Garratt*. With a Highland dance. Source: 26 Nov. 1771

29 Fri.   Benefit of Kane. *The Maid of the Mill*. A Prologue in the character of a master mason, in proper cloathing, and jewels, to be spoken by Kane; Mason songs, between the acts, by the brethren of the company, who will form themselves in the same manner as the Grand Lodge do in the Theatre-Royal in Dublin. An Epilogue, in the character of a Free Mason's wife, to be spoken by Mrs. Burden. With a farce called *Florizel and Perdita*. Source: 29 Nov. 1771

December 1771

4 Wed. Benefit of Forde. Not acted here these three years. *The Inconstant.* With a farce called *The Guardian.* With a variety of entertainments between the acts, particularly *Linco's Travels* and a paraphrase on Shakespeare's *"Seven Ages"*. As it is the universal desire of the ladies and gentlemen of Belfast, that the pit and gallery should be at one price on the above night, Forde hopes his complying therewith will not give any offence to the publick. Forde takes this opportunity of returning his sincere thanks to the writer of a letter, signed "A Countryman" for his good wishes; but is very sorry that it is not in his power to comply with his request of reviving the farce he mentioned, as *The Guardian* seems to be entirely agreeable to the ladies and gentlemen of Belfast, whom he would choose to oblige to the utmost of his power, as they have already manifested so remarkable an attention to his interest as demands his warmest gratitude; he therefore hopes his unknown correspondent will not take it amiss, if he should prefer their entertainment to that of a stranger; and if the author of the aforesaid letter has that particular attachment to him which he is pleased to express, he flatters himself he will not withdraw his friendship from him on this occasion for an affair of so little consequence as a farce. Source: 3 Dec. 1771

6 Fri. Benefit of Mrs. Day. Not acted here these 3 years. *False Delicacy.* With entertainments of singing between the acts. At the end of the play Mr. Day will present the audience with *"A Lottery Ticket for the Year 1771; or, The Sure and Speedy Way to Win a Prize."* With a farce (for the last time this season) called *The Citizen.* Source: 6 Dec. 1771

13 Fri. Benefit of Pye. By desire. *The Beaux' Stratagem.* A song called *"Jubal's Lyre"* by Mrs. Mozeen. With (for the third time) a farce called *The Devil to Pay.* The whole to conclude with an Italian pantomime called *Harlequin in the Shades.* Source: 13 Dec. 1771

18 Wed. Benefit of Day. *The Rival Queens.* With singing between the acts by Mrs. Day. Between the Play and Farce, a pantomimical interlude called *The Magical Soldier; or, Harlequin's Mouth Opened.* With *Wit's Last Stake.* Source: 17 Dec. 1771

20 Fri. Benefit of Hamilton. *The Miser.* With singing between the acts by Mrs. Mozeen and Mrs. Day. Between the Play and Farce a comic interlude called *The Farmer's Return from London after the Coronation.* With (by desire) a farce called *The Old Maid.* Source: 20 Dec. 1771

27 Fri.   By particular desire. Benefit of Farrell and Miss Farrell. *The Busy Body*. End Act 2 *"Lilliputian Dance,"* by Farrell; End Act 3 a pantomimical interlude between Harlequin and Queen Mab. End of the Play, an Epilogue by Farrell and Miss L. Farrell. With a Musical entertainment *The Chaplet*. Source: 24 Dec. 1771

January 1772

1 Wed.   By particular Desire. Benefit of Burden and Mrs. Burden. *Tamerlane*. With a favourite pantomime interlude called *Harlequin Skeleton*. With a Musical entertainment. *Midas* Source: 31 Dec. 1771

3 Fri.   Benefit of Atkins. *Lionel and Clarissa*. End of the Play (by desire) a hornpipe by Mr. Atkins. With (not acted here this Season) a Farce called *The Anatomist*. Source: 3 Jan. 1772

15 Wed.   Benefit of Francis Berry. *King Richard III*. With a farce called *The Old Maid*. Source: 14 Jan. 1772

17 Fri.   Benefit of the Poor. *Lionel and Clarissa*. Col. Oldboy–Parker; Lionel–Atkins; Sir John Flowerdale–Fotteral; Harman–Pye; Jenkins–Hamilton; Jessamy–Day; Clarissa–Mrs. Mozeen; Lady Mary Oldboy–Mrs. Farrell; Jenny–Mrs. Day; Diana–Mrs. Pye. With a farce called *The Honest Yorkshireman*. Admittance to any part of the House 2s. 2d. Source: 14 Jan. 1772

22 Wed.   Never performed before. *Love in a Bog*. Written by Dr. Maryat author of *The Sentimental Fables for the Ladies*. The Music entirely new and composed by Atkins. With a farce called *Polly Honeycombe*. This will be the only Night of performing *Love in a Bog* this Season. The Comedians take this Opportunity of returning their most sincere Thanks to the Town of Belfast for the very genteel Treatment they have received and beg Leave to assure the Ladies, Gentlemen, etc., that it will ever be their Study to merit Continuance of the Encouragement they have met with this and the former Season. Those who have any Demand upon the Company are requested to furnish Bills immediately as they leave Town early next Week. Source: 14 Jan. 1772

23 Thur.   Benefit of Farrell and Miss Farrell who were so unfortunate to fail in their former Attempt. Second time. *The Clandestine Marriage*. With Singing and Dancing between the Acts. With a farce called *The Virgin Unmasked*. Source: 21 Jan. 1772

24 Fri. Benefit of Mrs. Burden. Positively the last Night of the Company's performing in Belfast this Season. By particular Desire. *The Constant Couple.* Singing between the Acts by Mrs. Day and Mrs. Mozeen. With a farce called *The Anatomist.* Source: 21 Jan. 1772

1772–1773 SEASON

[The Belfast Theatre was dark].

1773–1774 SEASON

Venue: Theatre in Mill Street.
Company: Mr. and Mrs. Michael Atkins; Mr. Thomas and Mrs. (Elizabeth) Farrell and the Misses Farrell; Myrton Hamilton; Mr. and Mrs. Kenna (from the theatre in Smock Alley Dublin); Mrs. Richard Knipe; Mr. and Mrs. Pye; Mr. and Mrs. Joseph Waker.

Michael Atkins took over the Belfast theatre in Mill Street in 1773 and thenceforth "Belfast was to be the home base of an acting company that would go out on yearly tours, of considerable duration sometimes, to north-of-Ireland towns" (Clark 1965, 233). For biographies of Mr. and Mrs. Michael Atkins see the 1768–69 season.

For biographies of **Mr.** and **Mrs. Farrell** see 1768–69 season. The "Misses Farrell" who appeared in Belfast this season were almost certainly their daughters, one of whom, known only as "Miss L. Farrell," acted in Belfast during the 1779–80 season.

For a biography of **Myrton Hamilton** see the 1768–69 season.

The Mr. and Mrs. "Kennay" who first appear in Dublin during the 1770–71 season are almost certainly the same couple who that season are billed as **Mr.** and **Mrs. "Kenna,"** leading Clark and *BD* to mistakenly believe them to be two different couples, who sometimes spell the name "Kinney." However, there seems little doubt that they are in fact the same husband and wife. In 1773 Mr. Kenna was in Belfast, and in 1774, with his son John, acted at the Haymarket in London. Kenna evidently remained in London through the 1777–78 season (acting probably as "Kenny"). At some time in the mid-1780s Kenna and his family emigrated to America, making their debuts at the John Street Theatre in New York in 1786.

Kenna later opened theatres in Newbern, North Carolina, and Wilmington, Delaware. He acted in Philadelphia and in Charleston, South Carolina, until as late as 1794 when he disappears from the record.

For biographies of **Mr.** and **Mrs. Richard Knipe** see the 1765–66 season. Clark (1965, 233) places Richard Knipe in Belfast at this time, but I can find no record of him during this season.

For biographies of **Mr.** and **Mrs. Pye** see the 1768–69 season.

For biographies of **Mr.** and **Mrs. Joseph Waker** see the 1768–69 season.

Repertory, 1773–1774 Season

Michael Atkins's strategy this season seems to have been to perform a relatively large number of stock plays, interspersed with the occasional new piece. Bickerstaffe's *The Hypocrite*, Cumberland's *The Fashionable Lover*, and Goldsmith's *She Stoops to Conquer* all premiered in Dublin in this or in the previous season and were very successful. Hugh Kelly's tragedy *Clementina* had also enjoyed a run in Dublin and was probably of interest because of the political involvement of its Irish author. Atkins also staged several new pantomimes, although none of these seem to have been performed outside of Belfast and suggest that Atkins himself may have had a hand in the composition of both *The Hermit* and *The Witches*. Garrick had written his farce *The Irish Widow* especially to show off one of his favorite actresses in an Irish part, and must certainly have excited the curiosity of the Belfast audience as it had in Dublin the previous November.

Total Performances: 41 of 26 named mainpieces; 42 of 22 different named afterpieces.
  Shakespeare: 4.
  New Mainpieces: 3.
  New Afterpieces: 4.

(For a key to repertory symbols see above, page 11)

Mainpieces: *All in the Wrong; The Beaux' Stratagem* (2); *The Busy Body; The Clandestine Marriage* (2); *Clementina*† (2); *The Constant Couple; Douglas; The English Merchant*†; *The Fashionable Lover** (3); *The Grecian Daughter*†(3); *Hamlet; The Hypocrite**(3); *The Inconstant; Isabella*†(2); *The Jealous Wife; King Richard III; Lionel and Clarissa*(2); *Love Makes a Man; The Merchant of Venice; The Miser*(2); *The Provoked Husband; Romeo and Juliet; She Stoops to Conquer**(2); *The Suspicious Husband; Tamerlane; The West Indian.*

Afterpieces: *The Anatomist (2); The Apprentice; Catherine and Petruchio; The Chaplet* (2); *The Citizen; The Deuce is in Him; The Ghost* (3); *The Guardian; The Hermit*; High Life Below Stairs* (2); *The Honest Yorkshireman*(2); *The Irish Widow**(3); *The King and the Miller of Mansfield; Marriage a la Mode†; Midas* (2); *The Mock Doctor; The Old Maid; The Padlock* (2); *A Trip to Portsmouth†* (5); *A Trip to Scotland▶*(2); *The Virgin Unmasked; The Witches**(2).

Interlude: *Linco's Travels.*

Entr'acte entertainments: Singing: 0. Dancing: 2

Curtain time: 7 o'clock.

Benefits (15):   Atkins(2); Farrell and the Misses Farrell; Misses Farrell; Hamilton; Kenna(2); Mrs. Knipe; Lee; the Poor; Mrs. Pye; Waker(2); Ward.

September 1773

6   Mon.   By permission of the worshipful Shem Thompson Sovereign of Belfast, the Theatre will be opened with a tragedy called *Douglas.* Lady Randolph–Mrs. Kenna; Glenalvon–Kenna (from Smock Alley Dublin); Douglas–Atkins;   Lord   Randolph–Pye;   Old   Shepherd–Hamilton; Anna–Mrs. Waker. After the play a Highland Dance by Farrell. With a farce *The Mock Doctor.* Mock Doctor–Waker (first appearance on the stage these five years); Dorcas–Mrs. Pye. To begin at seven o'clock. Source: 31 Aug.–3 Sept. 1773

8   Wed.   *Lionel and Clarissa.* Clarissa–Mrs. Atkins (first appearance on this stage);   Oldboy–Hamilton;   Lionel–Atkins;   Harman–Pye;   Sir John Flowerdale–Waker; Jenkins–Farrell; Servant–Miss Farrell; Jessamy–Kenna; Diana–Mrs. Pye; Lady Mary Oldboy–Mrs. Farrell; Margery–Mrs. Waker; Jenny–Mrs. Kenna. With a new farce never performed here called *A Trip to Scotland.* The days of performing are Mondays, Wednesdays and Fridays. No person whatever will be admitted behind the scenes. Source: 3–7 Sept. 1773

17 Fri.   Never performed here. *She Stoops to Conquer.* [Published in Belfast by James Magee this year.] With *The Virgin Unmasked.* Source: 14–17 Sept. 1773

23 Wed.   *The Miser.* With the last new farce never performed here called *The Irish Widow.* [*The Irish Widow* was published by James Magee in Belfast this year]. Source: 17–21 Sept. 1773

24 Fri.   Never acted here. *The Fashionable Lover.* [Published in Belfast by James Magee in 1772]. With *The Irish Widow.* Nothing under full price will be taken during the whole performance. Source: 21–24 Sept. 1773

29 Wed.   *The Fashionable Lover* and *Midas.* Source: 24–28 Sept. 1773

October 1773

1 Fri.   *The Clandestine Marriage.* With *The Honest Yorkshireman.* Source: 28 Sept.–1 Oct. 1773

6 Wed.   *The Inconstant.* With *The Deuce is in Him.* Source: 1–5 Oct. 1773

13 Wed.   *The Grecian Daughter.* With a new pantomime with new scenery, machinery, dresses, music called *The Hermit; or, Harlequin Victorious.* Source: 8–12 Oct. 1773

15 Fri.   By particular desire. Third time. *The Fashionable Lover.* With (second time) a comic opera called *The Padlock.* Source: 12–15 Oct. 1773

20 Wed.   By particular desire. *The [Beaux'] Stratagem.* With *The Citizen.* Source: 15–19 Oct. 1773

22 Fri.   *The Suspicious Husband.* With *The Ghost.* Source: 19–22 Oct. 1773

27 Wed.   *Hamlet.* With *The Irish Widow.* Source: 22–26 Oct. 1773

29 Fri.   *The English Merchant.* With *The Apprentice.* Source: 26–29 Oct. 1773

November 1773

4 Wed.   *The Constant Couple.* With *The Witches; or, Harlequin's Vagaries.* Source: 19–23 Nov. 1773

5 Fri.   *Romeo and Juliet.* With *The Ghost.* Source: 2–5 Nov. 1773

12 Fri.   By desire of the Right Hon. Earl of Balcarras. *The Fashionable Lover.* With *Polly Honeycombe.* Source: 9–12 Nov. 1773

17 Wed.   *The Merchant of Venice.* With a musical entertainment called *The Chaplet.* Source: 12–16 Nov. 1773

19 Fri.   *Clementina.* With a new pantomime called *The Witches; or, Harlequin's Vagaries.* With new scenery, machinery, dresses, and music.

Nothing under full price will be taken during the whole performance. Children and servants cannot be admitted without paying. Source: 16–19 Nov. 1773

December 1773

1 Wed. By desire. *The Jealous Wife*. With *The Old Maid*. Source: 26–30 Nov. 1773

3 Fri. Second time. *Lionel and Clarissa*. With, third time, *A Trip to Portsmouth*. [*A Trip to Portsmouth* was published by James Magee in Belfast in 1774]. Source: 30 Nov.–3 Dec. 1773

6 Mon. [No program cited]. The Misses Farrell think it a duty incumbent on them to return their sincere thanks to the ladies and gentlemen of Belfast for the favours conferred on them at their benefit on Monday last. Source: 7–10 Dec. 1773

8 Wed. *The Grecian Daughter*. With, fourth time, a new comic sketch called *A Trip to Portsmouth*. Source: 3–7 Dec. 1773

10 Fri. Never performed here. *The Hypocrite*. With, fifth time, *A Trip to Portsmouth*. Source: 7–10 Dec. 1773

15 Wed. *The Busy Body*. With *Catherine and Petruchio*. Source: 10–14 Dec. 1773

17 Fri. *The West Indian*. With, sixth time, a new comic sketch called *A Trip to Portsmouth*. Source: 14–17 Dec. 1773

22 Wed. *The Hypocrite*. With *The Anatomist*. Being the last night of performing till Monday the 27th. Source: 17–21 Dec. 1773

29 Wed. *She Stoops to Conquer*. With *A Trip to Scotland*. Source: 24–28 Dec. 1773

31 Fri. *Tamerlane*. With, second time, *The Honest Yorkshireman*. Source: 28–31 Dec. 1773

January 1774

3 Mon. By particular desire. Benefit of Waker. *The Beaux' Stratagem*. Scrub–Waker. With several entertainments between Acts to which by desire will be added *The Ghost*. Roger–Waker. Source: 28–31 Dec. 1773

5 Wed. Benefit of Kenna. *Isabella.* With *"Bucks Have at You All"* by Kenna and *The Irish Widow.* Source: 31 Dec. 1773–4 Jan. 1774

7 Fri. Benefit of Mrs. Pye. *The Provoked Husband.* With entertainments between acts. And *The Padlock.* [Last mention of Mrs. Pye in the bills. 12–15 April 1774 announces the death in Belfast of the "comedian" Mrs. Pye, "after a tedious illness"] Source: 4–7 Jan. 1774

[In 11–14 Jan. 1774 Atkins thanks the inhabitants of Belfast for honouring him with their presence at his "late benefit"; however, there is no other record of a benefit for Atkins until 28 January].

14 Fri. Benefit of Hamilton. *The Clandestine Marriage.* With (seventh time) *A Trip to Portsmouth.* Source: 11–14 Jan. 1774

19 Wed. Benefit Mrs. Knipe. *King Richard III.* With *Marriage a la Mode.* Source: 14–18 Jan. 1774

28 Fri. Benefit of Atkins. *All in the Wrong.* Between the play and farce *Linco's Travels.* With *High Life Below the Stairs.* [Atkins thanks the Belfast audience for supporting this benefit in 28 Jan.–1 Feb. 1774]. Source: 25–28 Jan. 1774

February 1774

2 Wed. Benefit of Farrell and the Misses Farrell. *The Hypocrite.* With *Midas.* Variety of dancing between the acts. Source: 28 Jan.–1 Feb. 1774

6 Mon. By particular desire Benefit of Kenna. *Clementina.* Being positively the last time of performing it this season. With *The Anatomist.* Source: 1–4 Feb. 1774

9 Wed. Benefit of Ward. *Love Makes a Man.* With entertainments between the acts. With *The Chaplet.* Source: 4–8 Feb. 1774

11 Fri. By desire. Benefit of Waker. *The Miser.* By desire the Highland dance by Farrell and a humourous song in character of a drunken Butler by Waker. With *The King and the Miller of Mansfield.* Waker presents his most humble respects to the ladies and gentlemen of Belfast and hopes the second attempt will meet with their favour and approbation as he failed in his former benefit. Source: 4–8 Feb. 1774

16 Wed. Benefit of Lee. *The Grecian Daughter.* With *High Life Below Stairs.* Source: 11–15 Feb. 1774

18 Fri.   Last night performing here this season. Benefit of the Poor. Second time. *Isabella*. With *The Guardian*. Source: 15–18 Feb. 1774

1774–1775 SEASON

[Atkins's company spent the 1774–75 season at his newly-built playhouse in Derry].

1775–1776 SEASON

Venue: Mill Street Theatre.
Company: Mr. and Mrs. Michael Atkins; Mr. and Mrs. Booth; Mrs. Burdett; John Collins; Myrton Hamilton; Pye; Miss Villars; Mr. and Mrs. Wilmot and Miss Wilmot. Summer: Signora Rossi from Venice with her daughter.

For biographies of **Mr.** and **Mrs. Michael Atkins** see the 1768–69 season.

An actor named **Booth** played one of the Witches in *Macbeth* at Smock Alley in March 1761, but it is not now possible to determine if he was the same Booth who acted with the Capel Street company in May 1770. That Booth was a member of the company that visited Cork in the autumn of that year. Booth spent the remainder of his career in Belfast where he acted for the 1775–76 and 1778–79 seasons.

Mrs. Booth's career parallels that of her husband until his death, which occurred sometime between March 1779 and December 1790, when she again is found acting in Belfast, but now as Mrs. Mason "formerly Mrs. Booth, an old theatrical favourite of this town." Mrs. Mason was a regular with Atkins's company acting in Derry in March 1790 and the spring of 1791 and again in Belfast in the 1790–91 and 1791–92 seasons. Thereafter she disappears from the record, unless she is the Mrs. Mason "from the Theatre Royal, Edinburgh, first appearance here" who with her husband acted in Dublin during the 1807–08 and 1808–09 seasons.

Evidently, **Mrs. Burdett** confined her acting to the Irish provinces. She left no record in London or in Dublin. She is found at Kilkenny during the 1772–73 season, in Waterford sometime in 1773 and in Belfast for the 1776–77 season. Thereafter she disappears from the record.

Born in Bath in 1742, **John Collins** turned to the stage in his native city at an early age and by the time he was twenty, according to the *BD*, had "developed an extensive repertoire of roles 'extending to tragedy, genteel comedy, low comedy, and old men and country boys in farces and opera.'"

Collins is first noticed in Dublin at Smock Alley 7 November 1764 as Young Mirabell in *The Inconstant*, billed as from Theatre Royal, Edinburgh. That season he played a wide variety of primary and secondary roles before returning to the English provinces for a time. Collins was unsuccessful in securing an engagement with Garrick at Drury Lane and turned, instead, to performing amusing monologues and was to become the foremost monologist of his time. Over the next thirty years he perfected his *"Evening Brush,"* a mixture of recitation, music, and poetry "the lyrics written by himself and punctuated with imitation of the most famous stage personalities of the time," according to the *BD*. Collins performed his *"Evening Brush"* under a variety of titles at various assembly rooms in and around London until February 1776 when he joined Michael Atkins's Belfast company and delivered his *"Lecture upon Oratory and the Use and Abuse of Speech"* in addition to playing Falstaff. The *BD* does not note Collins's presence in Dublin at Fishamble Street later in February 1776 when he is advertised as performing on at least five nights his *"Attic Evening's Entertainment*, consisting of a satirical monologue against orators, speechifiers, preachifiers, etc., as performed 45 nights in London and Oxford." Later that season he was engaged by Arne for six nights of acting at Crow Street in addition to which he presented "an imitative interlude (which was repeated twenty successive evenings in London) called '*The Mimic's Looking Glass*'."

Collins married Miss Shellard on 24 January 1768 at Bath. It is not known if she had previous acting experience or what her activities involved before Mrs. Collins ("her first appearance in this kingdom") made her Crow Street debut on 26 March 1776 for her husband's benefit as Portia in *The Merchant of Venice*. In addition to playing Shylock, Collins introduced a favorite piece called *"The Diversions of the Morning"* wherein he presented the audience with the following characters from his *"Attic Evening's Entertainment"* "viz. the Bellower and Growler, the Ranter and Whiner, the Stammerer, Lisper and Snuffler, the Pulpit Pedant, the Rhetorical Barber, the Field-preaching Swadler, the Lancashire Justice, the Bath Collier, the Scotch Bagpipe, the Welsh Juryman, and Darby O'Wholligan Macholdup O'Byyourleave, the Irish Chairman. The whole consisting of Orators, Speechifiers, and Preachifiers; also several new imitations from Foote's Puppet shew, Shuter's London Crier, and the Comic Mirror, or the Theatrical World as it wags. With the humours of the Sock and the Buskin; the present state of the stage, and the powers of pageantry; particularly the attraction of Giants, Dwarfs, swans, elephants, etc."

For the next fourteen years Collins confined his activities largely to London, although he did appear briefly in Belfast in the spring of 1781, and his wife is found there in April 1787. In the summer of 1790 Collins performed his *"Evening Brush for Rubbing off the Rust of Care; or, Comic Review of the English Stage"* at Crow Street with great success.

In February of the following season Collins returned to Crow Street and again performed his *"Evening Brush"* on several occasions, again with great success. For his benefit on 2 March 1791 Collins chose to play Shylock in *The Merchant of Venice*. It was billed as "Being positively his last appearance on any stage." At the end of Act 4 Collins would include a "Judaical Metamorphosis; or, Shylock Transformed to a Modern Israelite with a song in character in the high German Jews dialect by Collins."

This was not, of course, Collins's last appearance on any stage. While his wife acted at Kilkenny, Waterford and Wexford in 1792, Collins performed his *"Evening Brush"* at the Lyceum Theatre, London. Thereafter, he played briefly in Birmingham, but then left the stage for a time and took up tavern-keeping at Plymouth and later yet auctioneering in Bath.

Mrs. Collins returned to Ireland several times during this period: in Waterford in March 1793 and in Galway in September 1795. Thereafter, she disappears from the record. According to the *BD*, she died at an unknown date "as the result of an operation for breast cancer."

Collins's final stage appearance was at York in 1795. He then bought an interest in the *Birmingham Chronicle* newspaper to which he frequently contributed poems and essays. He died at Birmingham on 2 May 1808 at the age of 66.

For a biography of **Myrton Hamilton** see the 1768–69 season.

A **Mr. Hutton** received a benefit on 13 March 1776 but does not seem to have been a performer.

For a biography of **Mr. Pye** see the 1768–69 season.

A **Miss Villars** is first noticed at Smock Alley on 23 April 1773 as Valeria in *The Roman Father*. The fact that her first recorded appearance is not commented on in the playbills suggests that she may have been acting there for some time without notice.

The Mrs. Villars who on 19 October 1774 played Lucinda in *The Brave Irishman* at Smock Alley and many other ingenue roles that season may have been the same Miss Villars who played at the same theatre two seasons earlier but it is not now possible to determine this with certainty. Although that was the only season she is known to have performed in Dublin, she is found in Kilkenny in the 1772–73 season and in Belfast in the spring of 1776. She married William Pero in Belfast on 24 March 1778 while she was appearing there. She returned to Belfast with her husband and step-daughter in the spring of 1779 and also performed at Kilkenny in June 1779.

Pero went on to manage the provincial English theatres in Stamford, Nottinghamshire, and Derby, and presumably his wife accompanied him, but the record is silent. She died in England at Retford on 14 September 1804 at the age of 73.

Mr. and **Mrs. Wilmot,** who both played tertiary and, occasionally, secondary parts for nearly thirty years in Dublin and the Irish provinces, are first noticed, in Kilkenny, at the beginning of the 1770–71, season and in 1771–72 Wilmot, but not his wife, was acting at Waterford with Ryder's company.

Mr. Wilmot is first mentioned in the Dublin playbills at the beginning of the 1771–72 season during which he played a variety of secondary roles at Smock Alley. The fact that his notices do not indicate that any of the roles are new for him or that he has recently begun playing at Smock Alley strongly suggests that he was not new to the Dublin stage. Wilmot was engaged at Smock Alley again the following season, though his wife's name is not found in the playbills until late in March. The following season Wilmot, but not his wife, was again performing at Smock Alley and in the 1774–75 season, Mrs. Wilmot performed once, her husband not at all. Earlier that autumn Wilmot is found in Derry with Atkins's company during the first season of the new Ship Quay theatre.

Wilmot and a **Miss Wilmot**, presumably his daughter, are found acting with Parker's company in Belfast in the spring of 1776 and Mr. and Mrs. Wilmot again in the spring of 1778. Later that year they are in Newry, where, Clark tells us (1965, 192) Wilmot deputized for Atkins when the latter returned to Dublin, and Wilmot managed the company for the remainder of the season, taking it to Derry in April.

The couple returned to Newry in the spring of 1779 but evidently traveled to England, for Wilmot acted in Brighton that year. The Wilmots returned to Belfast in March 1781. Wilmot, but not his wife, spent the 1780–81 season at Crow Street. Mrs. Wilmot made her Drury Lane debut on 26 December 1782 playing Monimia in *The Orphan*. Mr. Wilmot is not recorded in London that season, although he and his wife were in Brighton in July 1783. Wilmot is listed playing a minor role at Crow Street on 3 February 1783 and disappears from the record thereafter. The *BD* believes that the Mrs. Wilmot acting in Brighton in September 1801 is our subject. Thereafter, she too disappears from the record.

Sga. Marina Rossi was already an accomplished performer when she is first recorded in Bristol in February 1768 rope dancing, playing the mandolin and acting in pantomime.

Sga. Rossi is first noticed in London at Sadler's Wells dancing on the slack rope and playing the flute in April 1768. She evidently spent the intervening years on the Continent; when she returned to Bristol in March 1775 she was billed as "from Spain." She performed in Merchant Taylors' Hall in London in November 1775, and in January 1776 she and her daughter were at Smock Alley for twelve nights. "Signora Marina Rossi," we learn, "has had the honour to perform before several monarchs in Europe, with great applause, the most surprising feats on the rope; she will play on the violin on the rope, in six different positions equally neat and agreeable; she dances with or without the pole, and cute capers as well on the rope as any dancer can on the ground; she plays on two instruments (never seen here) at the same time on the rope, and performs many feats with two flags, far superior to any yet exhibited in Europe. Her young daughter will likewise perform several surprizing and amazing feats standing on a table, etc."

For her own benefit on 26 April 1776 she advertised the following entertainments, divided into three parts: "Part One: 1. Her fencing on the rope with her petticoat on, and with a pole, several leaps and capers. 2. Dancing with eggs tied to her feet, without breaking them. 3. Dancing without a pole and playing at the same time on a violin, in six different positions. 4. The surprizing performance of walking on the rope, down its descent to the rack of the pit, and returning backwards. Never attempted here by any woman. Part Two: 5. She will play a sonato, with variations on the psalter, a most delicate instrument, never played on in Ireland before. Part Three: 6. She dances on the rope tied up in a sack. 7. She will dance with a large earthen pitcher, tied to each foot."

In August 1776 Sga. Rossi and her daughter performed for a few nights in Belfast, billed as "from Venice." Their amusements included feats on the rope and performances on "different instruments pieces of Italian musick never done before by any woman." After this engagement Sga. Rossi traveled to Edinburgh and performed there from November through January 1777. Her last recorded performance is in May of that year at Sadler's Wells.

Repertory, 1775–76 Season

Atkins staged little besides tried-and-true stock pieces this season. The only new plays were the very popular afterpieces, *Bon Ton* and *The Deserter*, both of which had premiered successfully in Dublin within the past two years. The new pantomime of *The Revels; or, Harlequin Villager* seems to have been popular in Belfast, but is not known to have been performed elsewhere.

Total Performances: 34 of 28 different mainpieces; 30, of 24 named afterpieces.
Shakespeare: 4.
New Mainpieces: 0.
New Afterpieces: 3.

(For a key to repertory symbols see above, page 11)

Mainpieces: *As You Like It; The Brothers†; The Constant Couple; The Countess of Salisbury; The Earl of Essex; The Fair Penitent; The Fashionable Lover; Hamlet; The Hypocrite; Isabella; Jane Shore; Jealous Wife; King Henry IV, Part One; King Richard III* (2); *Love in a Village; Love Makes a Man; The Miser; Othello; The Provoked Husband; The Recruiting Officer; The Revenge; The Rival Queens; The Rivals†*(2); *The School for Wives†; She Stoops to Conquer; Tamerlane* (2); *The West Indian; The Wonder.*

Afterpieces: *The Anatomist; Bon Ton**(2); *The Brave Irishman; Catherine and Petruchio; The Citizen; The Contrivances; Damon and Phillida* (2); *The Deserter**(2); *The Devil to Pay; The Fashionable Wife; The Ghost; The Guardian; High Life Below Stairs; The Intriguing Footman†*(2); *The King and the Miller of Mansfield; The Lottery; The Lying Valet*(2); *The Mayor of Garratt; Midas* (2); *The Old Maid; The Padlock; The Revels*; A Trip to Portsmouth;* Unspecified "farce"; *The Virgin Unmasked.*

Interludes: *Henry and Emma†; Linco's Travels.*

Entr'acte entertainments: Singing: 4. Dancing: 0

Benefits (11): Atkins; Mrs. Atkins; Mrs. Booth; Freemasons; Hamilton; Hutton; the Poor; Pye; Mrs. Villars(2); Mr, Mrs. and Miss Wilmot.

November 1775

The Theatre in Mill Street will be opened in a few days with a play and farce as will be expressed in the bills. A few free tickets for the season will be disposed of, transferrable, at a guinea and a half each, to be had of Atkins. [Presumably, several unrecorded performances were given between 14 and 22 November] Source: 10–14 Nov. 1775

22 Wed. *The Wonder, A Woman Keeps a Secret.* With *The Guardian.* Source: 17–21 Nov. 1775

24 Fri. *Tamerlane.* With *The Intriguing Footman,* with the Humours of Humbug. Source: 21–24 Nov. 1775

December 1775

1 Fri. *King Richard III.* A song, accompanied on the drum, by Booth. With *The Lying Valet.* Source: 28 Nov.–1 Dec. 1775

6 Wed. *The [Beaux'] Stratagem.* With *The Ghost.* Source: 1–5 Dec. 1775

8 Fri. *Love in a Village.* Rosetta–Mrs. Burdett (first appearance on this stage). With *The Fashionable Wife* with the Humours of Barnaby Brittle. Source: 5–8 Dec. 1775

13 Wed. *Hamlet.* [Published in Belfast by James Magee in 1776]. With *Damon and Phillida.* Source: 8–12 Dec. 1775

15 Fri. *The Recruiting Officer.* With *Midas.* Source: 12–15 Dec. 1775

22 Fri. *The Rival Queens.* With *The King and the Miller of Mansfield.* Source: 19–22 Dec. 1775

27 Wed. *The Rivals.* With *A Trip to Portsmouth.* The piece to conclude with a grand view of the British fleet. Source: 22–26 Dec. 1775

29 Fri. *The Fashionable Lover.* With *The Virgin Unmasked.* Source: 26–29 Dec. 1775

January 1776

5 Fri. By particular desire. *Jane Shore.* A song called *"Advice"* by Mrs. Burdett; the song of *"Down the burn Davey"* by Booth and a farce called *The Citizen.* Source: 2–5 Jan. 1776

12 Fri.   *The Constant Couple*. With *Catherine and Petruchio*. Source: 9–12
Jan. 1776

17 Wed.   *She Stoops to Conquer*. With a farce as will be expressed in the Bills
of the Day. Source: 12–16 Jan. 1776

19 Fri.   The last time this season. *The Rivals*. With *The Lottery*. Source:
16–19 Jan. 1776

24 Wed.   *The Brothers*. To which will be added a Comic Opera (for the
second time) called *The Deserter*. Source: 19–23 Jan. 1776

26 Fri.   *Tamerlane*. To which will be added a Comic Opera (for the third
time) called *The Deserter*. Source: 23–26 Jan. 1776

February 1776

2   Fri.   *The West Indian*. Maj. O'Flaherty–Collins (for his amusement).
After the play (for this night only) Collins will deliver his *"Lecture upon Oratory
and the Use and Abuse of Speech."* Nothing under full price will be taken during
the whole performance. Source: 30 Jan.–2 Feb. 1776

7   Wed.   *King Henry IV, Part One*. Falstaff–Collins (for his amusement). To
which will be added a comic opera called *The Padlock*. Source: 2–6 Feb.
1776

16 Fri.   *The Fair Penitent*. With (fourth time) a Pantomime Entertainment
called *The Revels; or, Harlequin Villager*. (For the last time this Season). Source:
13–16 Feb. 1776

23 Fri.   *The Countess of Salisbury*. With *The Brave Irishman*. Capt. O'Blunder
(by desire)–John Barron (for this night only). Nothing under full price will
be taken during whole performance. [Barron seems to have been a Belfast
scrivener and writer as well as a "Mason and a novice actor" (Clark 1965,
235). See benefit performance of 3 April 1776 below]. Source: 20–23 Feb.
1776

28 Wed.   *Love Makes a Man*. End of Act 3 a new song called *"Be quiet"* by
Booth; End of Act 4 a new Scotch song by Booth; End of the Play an
Epilogue by Mrs. Booth; Between the Play and Farce a musical interlude
called *Linco's Travels*. Linco–Atkins. To which will be added (second time)
a new Comedy of two acts called *Bon Ton*. Source: 23–27 Feb. 1776

March 1776

6   Wed.   Benefit of Mrs. Atkins. Not acted here these four years. *The Earl of Essex*. With entertainments and *The Anatomist*. Source: 1–5 Mar. 1776

8   Fri.   Benefit of Mrs. Booth. *Isabella*. With *High Life Below Stairs* and a variety of entertainments as will be expressed in the bills of the day. Source: 5–8 Mar. 1776

13 Wed.   Benefit of Hutton. *The Revenge*. Written by Dr. Young. With several entertainments between the Acts and *The Intriguing Footman*. Source: 8–12 Mar. 1776

15 Fri.   Benefit of Atkins. *The Provoked Husband*. With entertainments between the Acts to which will be added *The Devil to Pay*. Source: 12–15 Mar. 1776

20 Wed.   Benefit Hamilton. *The Hypocrite*. With a variety entertainments between the Acts to which will be added *Midas*. Source: 15–19 Mar. 1776

22 Fri.   Benefit of Pye. *As You Like It*. With entertainments between the Acts and a farce (third time) called *Bon Ton*. In 24–26 Mar. 1776 Pye thanks the public for honoring his benefit. Source: 19–22 Mar. 1776

27 Wed.   Benefit of Mrs. Villars. *The School for Wives*. [Published in Belfast by James Magee in 1774]. With the farce of *The Contrivances*. 22–26 Mar. 1776

29 Fri.   Benefit of Mr. and Mrs. Wilmot and Miss Wilmot. *Othello*. Between the Play and Farce a new poetical interlude called *Henry and Emma; or, The Nut Brown Maid*. To which will be added *Damon and Phillida*. Source: 26–29 Mar. 1776

April 1776

3   Wed. Benefit of Barron. By desire of the Masters, Wardens, and Brethren of the Lodges Nos. 272, 418, and 491 of Free and Accepted Masons who are to appear at the Theatre where the Throne will be placed on the Stage for the Worshipful Master and seats for the rest who will appear in their proper cloathing. *The Jealous Wife*. Capt. O'Cutter (with the Brogueanerean songs in Character)–Barron. Prologue, Mason songs, and other entertainments between the Acts. With *The Mayor of Garratt*. Matthew Mug–Barron. On account of the extraordinary length of the entertainments the door will be opened at half an hour after five and the curtain will rise precisely half an hour past seven o'clock to whatever company shall be then in the House. John Barron takes this method of returning his most grateful thanks to those Ladies and Gentlemen who were pleased to honor him with their Company at the Theatre on Wednesday Night. He hopes they'll pardon his imperfections on that night which did not proceed from negligence but his being hurried with business (entirely new to him) the preceding days. N. B. He continues to carry on the scrivening or writing business in the most extensive manner as usual (5–9 Apr. 1776). Source: 29 Mar.–2 Apr. 1776

8 Mon. Benefit Mrs. Villars, who having failed in her former attempt is induced by the advice of several friends to try a second. *King Richard III.* With *The Old Maid.* Source: 2–5 Apr. 1776

10 Wed. Benefit of the Poor. Second time. *The Miser.* With the Farce of *The Lying Valet.* The pit and the gallery to be thrown into one and nothing under full price will be accepted of during the whole of the Entertainment nor any servant admitted. [18–21 February 1777 gives the receipts for the play benefitting the Poor]. Source: 5–9 Apr. 1776

August 1776

2 Fri. Performed by the celebrated Signora Rossi from Venice with her daughter who performed last winter at the Theatre-Royal, Smock Alley, with great applause. Consisting of Feats on the Rope. She will play on different instruments pieces of Italian Music never done before by any woman. Source: 30 July–2 Aug. 1776

19 Mon. Performed by the celebrated Signora Rossi from Venice with her daughter who performed last winter at the Theatre-Royal, Smock Alley, with great applause. Consisting of Feats on the Rope. She will play on different instruments pieces of Italian musick never done before by any woman. She performs for the last time on Monday evening next. Source: 13–16 Aug. 1776

1776–1777 SEASON

[The Belfast Theatre was dark this season. Atkins's company spent the 1776–77 season "at least partly" in Derry (Clark 1965, 235)].

1777–1778 SEASON

Venue: Presumably, the Mill Street theatre was used this season.
Company: Mr. and Mrs. Michael Atkins; Mrs. Booth; Myrton Hamilton; Mr. and Mrs. Walter (or William) Pero and Miss M. Pero; Pye; Mr. and Mrs. Richard Coxe Rowe; Mr. and Mrs. Wilmot.

For biographies of **Mr.** and **Mrs. Michael Atkins** see the 1768–69 season.

For biography of **Mrs. Booth** see the 1775–76 season.

For biography of **Myrton Hamilton** see the 1768–69 season.

For biographies of **Mr.** and **Mrs. Walter (or William) Pero** and **Miss M. Pero** see the 1775–76 season under Mrs. Villars.

For a biography of **Pye** see the 1768–69 season. Clark (1965, 239) places both Mr. and Mrs. Pye in Belfast this season, but I find no record of Mrs. Pye and no record that Pye performed at the theatre. However, the notice below states that he would be offering flute lessons to the public "during his stay in Belfast," suggesting a brief engagement.

We learn from his obituary that **Richard Coxe Rowe** was born at Dublin in 1753 and "destined by his parents for a mechanical employment," but took to the stage instead. Rowe is first noticed acting at Cork with Tottenham Heaphy's company in September 1775. He was engaged to play at Crow Street the following 1775–76 season and appeared in a variety of secondary roles, mainly in the line of older men, although he did play a few primary parts, such as Lovegold in *The Miser*. The fact that no notice is taken of Rowe's debut suggests that he was already known to the Dublin audience. He appeared again with the Cork company in the autumn of 1776.

Mrs. Rowe (née Ashmore) made her stage debut at Crow Street on 13 February 1773 as a Pastoral Nymph in *Comus*. During the summer season she moved to Smock Alley and played tertiary roles, most involving some singing. The following season she was promoted to more important roles at Crow Street and she sang at the Dublin Ranelagh Gardens concerts in the spring and summer.

At some time between the summer of 1774 and April 1778 Miss Ashmore married Richard Coxe Rowe. The couple visited Belfast in the spring of 1778, and Newry during the 1778–79 season, after which they are found in

Derry in August 1779. Her husband acted in Newry during the 1778–79 season.

On 22 November 1780 at Crow Street Mrs. Rowe played Lucy in *The Virgin Unmasked* and it was noted that this was her "first appearance here these four years." With her husband she performed in a wide variety of secondary and tertiary roles that season and appeared occasionally the next (without her husband, whose whereabouts that season are unknown).

After the 1781–82 season Mrs. Rowe disappears from the record but Richard Rowe continued to act in the Irish provinces for another decade. He acted briefly in Sligo in the summer of 1783 and in Limerick in November 1784. He performed in Belfast in January 1782 and thereafter became a mainstay of Atkins's company, which acted in Belfast and Derry from 1783 through 1792 seasons.

Richard Coxe Rowe died a favorite of the northern Irish audiences "after long languishing in a hopeless disorder" in Belfast on 7 May 1792. His popularity was such at the time of his death that by public subscription an inscribed headstone was erected over his grave in Newtownbreda, "the first public memorial to an actor in Ireland," according to Clark.

For biographies of **Mr.** and **Mrs. Wilmot** see the 1775–76 season.

Repertory, 1777–1778 Season

The performance record for this season is very sketchy. From the playbills that have survived, it seems that Atkins was, in general, content to stage stock pieces, and relied on multiple performances of a few popular new plays to attract audiences. Goldsmith's *The Good Natured Man* had premiered in Dublin the previous May with some success, and *The Governess*, Thomas Ryder's piracy of Sheridan's *The Duenna*, had been attracting large audiences in Dublin since February. This season also probably saw the Belfast premiere of Francis Dobbs's tragedy, *The Patriot King*, which had been performed in Dublin, with little success, in 1773. Although rarely performed, it was published in Dublin in 1775 and in Philadelphia in 1777, suggesting that it had some abiding political interest. Interesting, too, is the unpublished satirical interlude entitled *Twiss in Ireland*, by a "Gentleman of Trinity College," which evidently is a hit at the English travel writer Richard Twiss, who, in a book entitled *A Tour in Ireland in 1775*, had made several unflattering observations about that country to the indignation of the Irish.

Total Performances: 17 of 14 different named mainpieces; 16 of 12 different named afterpieces.

Shakespeare: 3.

New Mainpieces: 3.

New afterpieces: 1.

(For a key to repertory symbols see above, page 11)

Mainpieces: *As You Like It; The Gamester; The Good Natured Man*; The Governess**●*(4); *Jane Shore; The Jealous Wife; King Henry IV, Part One; Love Makes a Man; Macbeth*■(2); *The Patriot King*; Percy*†; *The Rivals; The Roman Father*†; *Theodosius*■.

Afterpieces: *Chrononhotonthologos; The Deserter; The Guardian; The Honest Yorkshireman; The Irish Widow*(2); *The Lottery; The Lying Valet; A Man of Quality**●□; *The Padlock*(2); *The Spell*†; *Thomas and Sally* (2); Unspecified "farce"(2); *The Waterman*†.

Interludes: *Lady Pentweazle; Twiss in Ireland**▲.

Entr'acte entertainments: Singing: 0. Dancing: 0

Benefits (4): Mr., Mrs. and Miss Pero; the Poor; Mr. and Mrs. Rowe; Mrs. Wilmot.

October 1777

24 Fri.   *The Gamester.* To which will be added *The Irish Widow.* By permission of the Worshipful Stewart Banks, Sovereign. The Theatre in Belfast will be shortly opened. Atkins begs leave to inform the ladies and gentlemen of Belfast that he has prepared several new pieces for the season and he flatters himself that the merit of his company joined with the most unwearied attention to please will entitle them to the same patronage and protection they have so often experienced from the town. A few tickets for the season to be disposed of at the usual price. During the Company's stay in town Pye will instruct young gentlemen on the German flute. Source: 17–21 Oct. 1777

November 1777

7   Fri.   Never acted here. *The Good Natured Man.* With *The Lying Valet.* Source: 4–7 Nov. 1777

10 Wed.   Never acted here these seven years. *Theodosius.* The play opens with a new transparent Altar scene with Atticus the High Priest officiating the duties of the Christian religion. Over the altar will be seen the bloody cross. With a farce as will be expressed in the bills of the day. Source: 7–11 Nov. 1777

14 Fri.   *The Jealous Wife*. With the farce of *The Padlock*. Source: 11–14 Nov. 1777

19 Wed.   By particular desire. *The Roman Father*. To which by desire will be added the farce of *The Irish Widow*. Source: 14–18 Nov. 1777

21 Fri.   *King Henry IV, Part One*. To which by desire will be added the farce of *The Waterman*. [*The Waterman* was published in Belfast by James Magee this year]. Source: 18–21 Nov. 1777

December 1777

12 Fri.   *As You Like It*. With the farce of *Thomas and Sally*. Source: 9–12 Dec. 1777

15 Mon.   *The Patriot King; or, The Irish Chief*. Written by Francis Dobbs. With a farce as will be expressed in the bills. Source: 9–12 Dec. 1777

January 1778

7   Wed.   Not acted here in seven years. *Macbeth*. With the original music, scenery, machinery, sinkings, flyings, witches, apparitions, invocations. With a musical Farce called *Thomas and Sally*. Source: 2–6 Jan. 1778

14 Wed.   Never performed here. *The Governess* as it is now performing at the Theatre-Royal Dublin with universal applause. In which will be introduced all the favourite Airs, Songs, Catches, Glees, Duettos, and Choruses in the celebrated Opera of *The Duenna*. To which will be added *The Guardian*. Source: 9–13 Jan. 1778

16 Fri.   Second time. *The Governess* as it is now performing at the Theatre-Royal in Dublin with universal applause. With *Chrononhotonthologos*. Source: 13–16 Jan. 1778

28 Wed.   By particular desire. *The Governess*. With the farce of *The Guardian*. Source: 23–27 Jan. 1778

February 1778

11 Wed.   *The Governess*. Being the last time of performing it this season. With the Pantomime entertainment of *The Spell; or, Harlequin's Funeral*. With new scenery, machinery, music, and dresses. Nothing under full price will be taken during the whole performance. Source: 6–10 Feb. 1778

April 1778

1 Wed. *Love Makes a Man.* With entertainments between the acts and the farce of *The Lottery.* Source: 27–31 Mar. 1778

10 Fri. Benefit of Mrs. Wilmot. Not acted this season. *Jane Shore.* Lord Hastings–Atkins; Shore–Pero; Alicia–Mrs. Booth; Jane Shore–Mrs. Wilmot (first appearance in that character). With several entertainments to which will be added a comedy of three acts never performed here called *A Man of Quality.* Sir Tunbelly Clumsey–Wilmot; Miss Hoyden–Mrs. Wilmot. As now performing in London and Dublin with great applause. Source: 7–10 Apr. 1778

[On 13 April 1778 John Paul Jones, the American privateer, entered Belfast Lough and carried off the British sloop *Drake.* With the aim of defending their coast from French invasion a second company of Volunteers was formed in Belfast at about this time].

20 Mon. By particular desire. Benefit of Mr. and Mrs. Pero and Miss M. Pero. *Percy, Earl of Northumberland.* [Published in Belfast by James Magee this year]. Between the play and farce a new interlude called *Twiss in Ireland; or, Fop in Disgrace.* Written by a gentleman of Trinity College. With a comic opera of *The Deserter.* Source: 14–17 Apr. 1778

24 Fri. Benefit of Mr. and Mrs. Rowe. *The Rivals.* With several favourite songs and *The Honest Yorkshireman.* The whole to conclude with the celebrated interlude *Lady Pentweazle of Blowbladder Street.* Lady Pentweazle–Rowe; Carmine–Wilmot. Source: 21–24 Apr. 1778

27 Mon. Benefit of the Poor. *Macbeth.* With the original scenery. With *The Padlock.* [4–7 May 1779 gives the receipts for this performance]. Source: 21–24 Apr. 1778

1778–1779 SEASON

Venue: Ann Street Theatre.
Company: Mr. and Mrs. Thomas Betterton; Mr. and Mrs. Booth; Day (from Theatre Royal in Dublin); Mr. and Mrs. Farrell and Miss Farrell; Myrton Hamilton (actor-manager); William Hamilton (from the Theatres

Royal Covent Garden and Dublin); Kane (from the Theatre-Royal in Dublin); Antony Lebrun; Mr. and Mrs. Pero and Miss Pero; Pye; Mr. and Mrs. Quin; Mr. and Mrs. William Talbot Richards and Miss Elizabeth Rebecca Richards (from the Theatres-Royal of Edinburgh and Dublin); Mrs. Walter Smith (her first appearance in Belfast); Mrs. Tisdall.

Musicians: Byrne and Rauppe.

During the late summer of 1778 a "major rift" developed in Atkins's company during its stay at Newry, which resulted in Myrton Hamilton's setting up in opposition to Atkins. Atkins "no doubt much disgusted by this revolt, found it a good cause for cutting loose from his Belfast stage connexions" and he joined Ryder's Crow Street company at Cork. Hamilton took up the management in Belfast. "He reconstructed a building that was located somewhere in Ann (formerly Bridge) Street. . . ." (Clark, 1965, 238).

For biography of **Myrton Hamilton** see the 1768–69 season.

According to the *BD*, **Thomas William Betterton** was the grandson of the sexton of St. Andrew's Church, Dublin, whose name was Butterton. When he took to the stage, acting tertiary roles with Waddy, Sparks, and Vandermere's Fishamble Street company in the 1776–77 season, he adopted the name Betterton (presumably to associate himself with the great actor of the previous century). In the summer of 1778 Betterton is found, again in minor roles, at Crow Street.

In 1778 Betterton was in Belfast with Myrton Hamilton's company at the new Ann Street theatre. On 21 December 1778 he married the widow of the recently-deceased northern manager, James Parker, and the couple remained in Belfast until the end of the 1778–79 season. Betterton spent March through July 1780 in Belfast, although none of his roles are recorded.

The Betterton's whereabouts during the 1781–82 season are not known, but both he and his wife were engaged and played secondary roles at the new Capel Street theatre during its brief existence. When it closed, he evidently moved to Crow Street and on 21 December 1782 (later playbills twice make the claim that they are his first performance at Crow Street). The following year Betterton decided to launch out on his own, and, after raising a considerable sum by subscription from the citizens of Newry (and using a great deal of his own money), he built a new theatre in Hill Street which probably opened in November 1783. But if he had hoped to make his fortune as an impresario he was bitterly disappointed. After a summer season, he was being hounded by creditors and took to his heals.

Betterton performed a few nights at Smock Alley in November 1785, billed as his "first time on this stage." Later that season he and his wife are found in Edinburgh, and later still with Tate Wilkinson's York company. Betterton was such a favorite there that he probably remained with Wilkinson through 1788–89. He was then engaged by Richard Daly to perform at his theatres in Ireland. On his way back to Ireland he played first at Liverpool in the summer of 1791. He returned to Newry in 1792 and then played in Drogheda later that season. On 7 November 1792, billed as "from the Theatre Royal, Liverpool, his first time on this stage," Betterton began the 1792–93 season at Crow Street. He attempted a variety of roles, from primary singing parts, such as Jessamy in *Lionel and Clarissa,* to supernumerary peasants. On 9 January 1793 Betterton's daughter, Julia, recited Collins's *"Ode on the Passions,"* billed as "a child only ten years of age, who will also at the end of the play speak a favourite epilogue."

In the following months Betterton traveled in the Irish provinces: to Waterford in March, Wexford in April and May, Kilkenny in June and July and Galway in July and August 1793. Evidently, Mrs. Betterton had died sometime soon after January 1793, she had been ill and unable to perform during their engagement at Drogheda in October and November 1792 and is not known to have performed thereafter.

What remained of the Betterton family then traveled to the English provinces, Betterton and his daughter performing with Watson's company in Hereford in 1794 and with Dimond and Keasberry in Bath and Bristol in 1795–96 and 1796–97. Julia's obvious talent secured the Bettertons, including a son whose name is not now known, an engagement at Covent Garden in October 1797. Betterton continued at Covent Garden until 1801. From 1802 until 1804 he performed with Cross's Royal Circus, acting occasionally in the provinces, specifically in Manchester and Stockport, and may have remained in the provinces from 1805 until 1813, although the record is largely silent. A Betterton is found acting in farces with Davis's circus which performed in Dublin's Royal Amphitheatre, Peter Street, in the winter of 1801, although it is not now possible to tell if this was the father or the son. The Betterton found acting and dancing at the Royal Hibernian Theatre in Dublin during the 1809–10 season was almost certainly John (d. May 1816).

By 1816 Thomas Betterton had crossed the Atlantic to New York, where he performed in April. Thereafter he is found in various North American cities: in Philadelphia in 1818, in Halifax, Nova Scotia, during the 1818–19 season, and in Boston in 1819. He returned to London's Sadler's Wells as late as April 1820 after which he evidently retired from the stage. He died in London in 1834.

For biographies of **Mr.** and **Mrs. Booth** see the 1775–76 season.

For a biography of **George Day** see the 1771–72 season. Clark (1965, 238) places Mrs. Day with the company this season, but I can find no record of her performing in Belfast at this time.

For biographies of the **Farrells** see the 1768–69 season.

William Hamilton (fl. 1735–1805?): It is difficult to distinguish between the various performers bearing the name of Hamilton who were active on the Irish stage during the eighteenth and early nineteenth centuries. The first Hamilton of whom we have record, first name unknown, married Sarah Lydall (fl. 1727–1776), the actress, by the 1727–28 season, when she began using his name. The Hamiltons had at least five children, all of whom became actors. Of the sons the *BD* contains entries for William Hamilton (fl. 1735–1805?) and James Hamilton (fl. 1735–1746).

The Hamilton active at Smock Alley in 1750–51 through 1766–67 in the line of young men strongly suggests one of the Hamilton sons, and the *BD* is probably correct in ascribing most of these roles to William Hamilton. He is frequently noted for his "Statue Scene" in pantomimes, and his status in the company gradually increases, beginning as a sharer in a multiple benefit and moving to being the occasional recipient of a sole benefit by 1752–53. Except in pantomime, however, his roles seldom rose above the tertiary.

After the 1766–67 season the name of Hamilton disappears from the Dublin record until the 1774–75 season. The *BD* indicates that William Hamilton had traveled to London with Spranger Barry in the summer of 1766 and played at the King's Theatre and that he returned there in the summers of 1767 and 1768. He made his Covent Garden debut in November 1768 where he remained until March 1773, playing each summer through 1773 at the Haymarket Theatre. It is said that in the spring of 1773 William Hamilton was discharged from Covent Garden for his "inattention and volatility," and he turned to the provinces; however, the record indicates that William Hamilton was again performing at Covent Garden during the 1773–74 season. At the end of that season he moved to Edinburgh, where he acted through the 1776–77 season making his Belfast debut (managed by his brother Myrton) in March 1779.

A Hamilton (playing many of the same roles the earlier Hamilton had, and, thus, probably William) and a Hamilton, Jr. are found acting at Crow Street in the 1774–75 season and this Hamilton continues in bills there until 1778–79. In that season Hamilton is not listed as having acted, but rather, is noticed as the designer of the machinery for the new pantomime *The Elopement; or, A Trip to the Dargle.*

The Hamilton who was a member of the Smock Alley company during the 1780–81 season was Myrton, judging from a petition signed by the members of that company in support of Daly's management and bearing the signature of "M. Hamilton." However, that season a Hamilton played roles that are indistinguishable from those played by the William Hamilton since 1751–52, so it is possible that both William and Myrton Hamilton were engaged at Smock Alley that season.

The name of Hamilton again disappears from the Dublin record for several years until 22 December 1784 when at Fishamble Street a Hamilton played Papillion in *The Lyar,* and the performance is billed as his "first appearance in this city these eight years." This is probably William Hamilton. In later bills that season two actors named Hamilton are listed: one actor is designated as "M. Hamilton" the other simply as "Hamilton." The former was almost certainly Myrton Hamilton, the latter probably his elder brother William.

The name of Hamilton disappears from the Dublin record for many years after the 1784–85 season, except for one mention of a Hamilton in Crow Street playbill in the 1789–90 season in a supernumerary role. The whereabouts of William Hamilton after this time is uncertain. An actor named Hamilton was with the Manchester company in 1788, a company at Leigh in 1789 and in Salisbury and Windsor in 1790 and 1791. A William Hamilton performed old men's parts in Charleston, South Carolina, between February 1793 and April 1795. Hamilton was evidently still alive about 1805 but nothing is known about him after that year.

For a biography of **John Kane** see the 1771–72 season.

Antony Lebrun evidently never appeared in London, for he is not mentioned in *BD*. George Dunlop, Frederick Cooke's biographer, describes Lebrun as "a humourous vagabond." The earliest record we have of him is with Myrton Hamilton's company at the new Ann Street theatre in Belfast this spring. He acted at Cork in August and September 1779, and again in September 1780 before joining the Smock Alley company for the 1780–81 season. At that time he played mainly secondary roles in comedy.

Lebrun and Mrs. Lebrun were engaged at Smock Alley for the 1781–82 season but then left Ireland. He was at Liverpool in 1782, and it was probably our figure who served as prompter at Margate Theatre as late as 1803.

For biographies of **Mr.** and **Mrs. Walter (or William) Pero** see the 1775–76 season under Mrs. Villars.

For a biography of **Pye** see the 1768–69 season.

The *BD*, without much enthusiasm, suggests that the **Mr. Quin** who with his wife appeared with Myrton Hamilton's Ann Street company this spring in secondary roles and in Kilkenny twenty years later, may be the same Quin who acted at Covent Garden for one performance in February 1798. A Quin also appeared at Norwich in 1786 and 1787, Brighton in 1788, Barnstable or Richmond in 1792, and with the Royal Circus as an equestrian in 1794. The last notice of Quin is at Edinburgh in January 1800.

The Richards who is found playing tertiary roles at Smock Alley during the 1765–66, at Crow Street during the 1769–70 and at Capel Street during the 1773–74 seasons may have been **William Talbot Richards**, although it is not now possible to say with any certainty. Clark places Mr. and Mrs. William T. Richards, billed as "from Edinburgh" at Cork in August through November 1778.

A curious, perhaps unique phenomenon occurs with the Richards family who for a time at the beginning of the 1778–79 season seem to have performed in both Dublin and Belfast (from December 1778 through January 1779). Richards, billed as "first appearance on this stage," is first found at Crow Street beginning on 20 November 1778 and his wife made her Crow Street debut the following night. Richards performed at Crow Street again on 25 November, then on 11 and 29 December 1778. Mrs. Richards is not listed among the Crow Street company again until 9 January 1779. After that time the Richards left Dublin and are believed to have taken up residence in Belfast for the remainder of the season 1779, billed as "from the Theatres-Royal of Edinburgh and Dublin."

An item in the *BNL* 11–15 Dec. 1778 praises Myrton Hamilton for his industry and for providing so many "respectable performers," and is sorry to hear that Mrs. Richards, "who is without doubt the best vocal performer in this kingdom," will be staying such a short time. On 12 February 1779 Miss Elizabeth Richards, who was to become one of the most important actresses and singers of the early nineteenth century, made her first recorded stage performance singing the favorite song of "*My Jocky*." At the end of the play an occasional epilogue was spoken by Miss Richards. (Several details of Elizabeth Richards's career presented in the *BD* and Clark are erroneous and have been corrected here. For example, the debate over her year of birth (1773 according to Clark, 1771 according to the *BD*) seems to be resolved by the notations in the calendar below specifying her age as 6 years in 1779 and as 8 in 1781).

After spending the months of September and October at the Cork theatre, the Richards returned to Crow Street for the 1779–80 season, a popular attraction being R. B. Sheridan's comedy *The Camp*, when in the character of a Female Volunteer Mrs. Richards introduced "the manual exercise. The last scene exhibits a most striking and exact view of the camp at Coxheath with all the general officers, and soldiers, marquees and tents, artillery, colours with the different corps under arms and exercising by beat of drum." Miss Richards performed her first acting role as Queen Mab in the afterpiece of that title. (The Richards whom Clark finds acting at Kilkenny on 16 December 1779 cannot be William T. since he was playing at Crow Street on that night).

The Richards family remained at Crow Street for the 1780–81 and 1781–1782 seasons. Miss Richards, billed in 1781 as "a child of eight years old," continued to increase her repertoire with such roles as Priscilla in *The Romp* for her own and her father's benefit. Her popularity was such that before the end of the summer of 1781 she was given two sole benefits. The following season she played and sang regularly in a wide variety of roles.

The next few years the peregrinations of the Richards family are difficult to follow. According to the *BD*, a Miss Richards shared in tickets at Drury Lane in May 1783 and 1784. At about this time, however, Miss Richards left the stage temporarily. According to *The Monthly Mirror* "her health became, in a degree, impaired from her public exertions at those tender years." Her career re-commenced when she was 15 years old (i.e., in 1788) at York. Thereafter she is found at Richmond in the summer of 1790 and with Wilkinson's company in York during the 1790–91 season. Elizabeth Richards went with her mother to Margate in the late spring of 1791.

As Elizabeth's career rose, those of her parents declined. The last record of their performing is in Derry in May 1794. Elizabeth married the popular actor John Edwin late in 1791 and first appeared under her new name at the Haymarket Theatre in June 1792 and was to achieve great fame as Mrs. Edwin.

Henrietta Scrace Smith (**Mrs. Walter Smith**) was the daughter of the actor Richard and Martha Scrace (fl. 1749–1764) and sister of the actress Patty Ann Scrace (Mrs. James Bates, d. 1784). Henrietta could not be the Mrs. Smith who acted in a few tertiary roles at Capel Street in the 1773–74 season, since she did not marry until 1776.

As Miss Scrace "from Theatre Royal, Bath, her first appearance here" she made her Dublin debut at Crow Street on 21 October 1776 as Louisa Dudley in *The West Indian* and continued to perform in primary roles through that season. *The Hibernian Journal* of 28 May 1777 reports the recent marriage of Mr. Walter Smith, the provincial actor, and Miss Scrace, both of Crow Street. As early as 29 May 1777 the name of Mrs. Smith begins to replace that of Miss Scrace. We can assume that the "Miss Smith" who appears in three playbills in the roll of Anna in *Douglas* near the end of the season are compositor's errors, for Mrs. Smith had played that role earlier in the season.

The Smiths continued to act at Crow Street through the regular and summer 1778–79 seasons. The couple were with the company in Cork in the autumns of 1777 and 1778. Mrs. Smith but not her husband is found in Belfast in March 1779 and in Cork in the autumn of that year. From about this time on it is clear that Mrs. Smith was considered by the managers to be a more valuable asset than her husband.

Mr. and Mrs. Smith joined Tate Wilkinson's company at Hull, York, and Sheffield during the 1779 season and remained with that company until 1786, with short stints in Edinburgh in 1783 and 1784. In the fall of 1782 Mrs. Smith and the great actress Dorothy Jordan, both with Wilkinson's company, were locked in a bitter rivalry for the best roles. As the *BD* indicates, "Mrs. Smith was pregnant, but she continued acting rather than yield her parts to Mrs. Jordan and acted until the last minute before going into labor. Less than two weeks after delivering her baby she insisted on making the journey from Doncaster to Sheffield, where the company was performing. She arrived "with a fixed lameness in her hip," according to Wilkinson, but performed anyway and became ill for several months.

Her jealousy of the other actresses in the company after this caused Mrs. Smith to leave Wilkinson's company in May 1786, and she made her London debut in *The Conscious Lovers* at the Haymarket Theatre in July. She evidently acquitted herself well. Thereafter she is found in Norwich and Brighton in 1787. In 1788 the Smiths were at Manchester, described as "from Dublin." Walter and Henrietta Smith then took up residence with the Bath company where he acted from 1789–90 through 1804–05, with the possible exception of the 1792–93 season. After 1798 he also served as the company's treasurer until his death in 1809. Mrs. Smith acted in Bath through the 1799–1800 season, after which she left the stage. She died in Edinburgh on 31 December 1822 at the age of 70.

Except for its broad outlines, little is known about the career of **Mrs. Tisdall**. The *BD* thinks that she made her stage debut at the Haymarket Theatre on 22 May 1769 and acted there from July to August of that year. She spent the remainder of her career in Ireland: her first recorded Dublin appearance, at Smock Alley on 21 October 1774 as Lucy in *The Beggar's Opera*, was not commented on in the playbills suggesting that she was already known to Dublin. During the 1774–75 season she played regularly in a wide variety of secondary roles, most involving singing. She appeared the following September in Cork.

Mrs. Tisdall spent the 1775–76 season at Crow Street, again acting and singing in secondary roles (not noticed by *BD*). Her whereabouts are not known in 1776–77 or 1777–78, but she is found among Myrton Hamilton's Ann Street company in Belfast for at least a part of this 1778–79 season. On 15 July 1779 Mrs. Tisdall played Cherry with a group of amateurs at Crow Street for the benefit of Cartwright, the musician. On the evening of 20 October 1779 Mrs. Tisdall took a benefit at the Patagonian Theatre, Fishamble Street. In addition to a variety of musical entertainments Mrs. Tisdall recited *"Bucks Have at Ye All"* in the character of a Volunteer. Remarkably, *Saunders's Newsletter* 22 October 1779 reports that on the evening of her benefit on 20 October 1779 Mrs. Tisdall, comedian, "died suddenly, at her lodgings in Chancery-lane," Dublin.

On 18 May 1762 at Crow Street a **Byrne** shared a benefit with Dowdall, McGowran, and Stockdill. Since the others were certainly Crow Street musicians, it seems probable that this is Byrne the violinist. The following two seasons Byrne shared benefits at Crow Street with musicians: on 5 April 1763 with Hodgins, Dowdall, and Tuke; on 22 May 1764 with McBride and Frazer.

While it is not possible to say with certainty, the Byrne who performed a violin solo at Hamilton's Ann Street Theatre, Belfast, on 23 October 1778 may have been the same musician. Again, the name of Byrne appears sharing a benefit with the other Crow Street musicians Campbell, Jones, Tuke, McMahon on 28 May 1779. It was probably the violinist Byrne who, by desire Belfast Musical Society, took a sole benefit at the Ann Street

Theatre in Belfast on 28 January 1782. Presumably, he had been performing in Belfast prior to the benefit, but the record is silent.

A Byrne took a sole benefit at Crow Street on 24 July 1778. The Byrne who played the supernumerary role of a Haymaker in the prelude *A Fig for the French; or, News from Bantry Bay* at Crow Street on 6 July 1779 may have been the musician, but it is more likely that he is the same Byrne who played a French Prisoner in the farce *The Liverpool Prize; or, The British Flag Triumphant* at Crow Street on 25 April 1780 and who performed in several tertiary roles at Capel Street during the 1782–83 season.

Johann Georg Rauppe, 1762–1814, was born in Stettin in Germany on 7 July 1762 and studied violoncello under Duport in Berlin in his youth. At this point in Rauppe's biography the *BD* overlooks several important details of the musician's life which may be gleaned from the Irish stage record. It is clear that he was a member of a family of musicians who went on tour to Ireland between 1778 and 1779, when he would have been about 16 years old. With him was his father and at least one brother (first names unknown), all apparently violoncellists.

On 11 June 1778 the Dublin newspapers announced that "Mr. Rauppe and sons from Germany will perform several solos and concertos on the violoncello in the house" in Ranelagh Gardens, Dublin. On 30 June at Ranelagh the bills announced that "Master Rauppe will entertain in the house by playing several solos on the violoncello, being the last time." On 6 July 1778 Rauppe and Sons took a benefit at Ranelagh and announced that "Master Rauppe will perform two solos and two quintettos in each act and wind music in the garden." When the musician and composer Robert Tuke announced his benefit on 15 July at Ranelagh his bills advertised that "The Masters Rauppes are engaged for that night and will perform solos and concertos on the violoncello."

The Rauppes remained in Ireland, appearing in Belfast with Hamilton's Ann Street Company during the winter of 1779. On 24 February 1779 the Messieurs Rauppe took a benefit with the note that they "have had the honour of performing before their Majesties and most of the Nobility of Great Britain and are esteemed to be the most capital performers on the Violoncello in Europe." Johann Georg Rauppe traveled to Denmark and Sweden as principal cellist at the German Opera in Amsterdam in 1782. He visited England and France in 1784 and returned to Amsterdam in 1786 where he performed for the remainder of his long career. Evidently the death of his wife in 1813 caused him such distress that his mind became unbalanced and he died the following year leaving a son and daughter.

There is no *BD* entry for **Monsieur Bissons** (or Bisset or Bissent) suggesting that he never performed at a major London theatre.

On 28 January 1774 at Smock Alley the bills advertised as a part of that night's program "several new and surprising performances on the Wire by the celebrated Monsieur Bissons, from Paris, never yet attempted by the Turk, Maddocks, Matthews, or Saunders" (other popular equilibrists of the day). Bissons performed in Dublin for the second time on 4 February and the bills indicated that "Bissent [*sic.*] will balance on Egg upon a Straw, never yet attempted by any other Person. Likewise several Performances in the Slack Rope, with an amazing Leap from the Rope, superior and more difficult than the Lion's Leap, as exhibited by Signior Le Namora. He will also throw himself from the Rope, and hang by his Neck, while the Rope is in full Swing; with several entertaining Feats of Ladder Dancing by the famous Polander, the Sieur Potowskie and M. Bissent. The Ladder is eleven Feet high, and will be placed upon two Pinnacles, and is so Light, it can be blown away by a Pair of Bellows, while they perform the Snakes, never yet exhibited in the City but once." Bisset repeated these performances several times before the end of the season when he disappears from the record for several years.

The *BNL* 16–19 Feb. 1779 reported that on 23 February 1779 "at the Old Theatre in Mill Street Belfast. For that Night only. Mr. Bisset will exhibit several surprising Equilibres on the Slack-Wire, Rope Ladder, Tumbling, etc. On the same Night the Lion's Leap will be performed on the Rope. He will also stand on his Head on a Bottle on the Wire, the Wire in full Swing; not done by any other. The Avizinia or Bird of Knowledge, will also exhibit his amazing Performances which astonishes every Beholder there is not a Bird in the World equal to this. Also will be exhibited a Lion Porcupine and two other curious Animals. Pit 1s. 6d., Gallery 6d. As Mr. Bisset is engaged this Season in Dublin in Order that no Person may be disappointed said Bird will be exhibited before any Number of Ladies or Gentlemen (at Mr. Bisset the Proprietor's House) or at their own Houses if desired at one Shilling each. Mr. Bisset will stop a few Days at Lisburn, Newry and Drogheda on his Road to Dublin." There is record of his performing in a Dublin theatre at that time.

It is probable that Bisset finally settled in Belfast and that the earlier equilibrist is the "John Bisset of Belfast" whom *FDJ* 29–31 Jan. 1784 reported had "died last week at Chester." He was "the most remarkable man that probably ever lived for cultivating an intimacy with the dumb creation. He made a figure in London several years ago, as conductor of the Cats Opera; since which time he has instructed, in the most curious tricks and deceptions, several dogs, horses, turtles, birds, etc. and latterly a small pig, which was lately shewn in the North and this city, and with which he was on his way to London when he died."

Repertory, 1778–1779 Season

Political fevers were running high in both Dublin and Belfast during this time. The Patriot faction in the Irish parliament, with the support of the Volunteers, was exerting pressure on the British government for legislative independence and the easing of commercial restrictions. In keeping with the times perhaps, Myrton Hamilton this season offered Belfast a relatively large number of new main and afterpieces, most by Irish playwrights. R. B. Sheridan's wildly popular *The School for Scandal* had brought handsome profits to the Dublin managers after its premiere at Crow Street in January 1778. In Belfast, the piece almost certainly received more performances that the one of which we have record. Of particular interest this season is the performance of Henry Brooke's tragedy, *Gustavus Vasa*. The piece had been refused a licence in London in 1739 because of its anti-Walpole allegory and was never performed there. Brooke revised it under the title of *The Patriot*, and it was performed three times at Smock Alley in December 1744. When it was performed (under its original title) in Dublin in 1772 the play was publically identified with the memory of the patriot Dr. Charles Lucas. It seems likely that the presentation of the tragedy in Belfast at a time when the Volunteer movement was so active and influential was intended as a political statement. Arthur Murphy's comedy *Know Your Own Mind* was performed only six months after its Dublin premiere. Hugh Kelly's *A Word to the Wise* had been hissed off of the Drury Lane stage when it was first brought forward in 1770 because of Kelly's anti-Wilkesite activities, but when it was revived for a few performances in London in 1777 at the Haymarket Theatre and Covent Garden it drew little attention. The play received its Dublin premiere at Capel Street in 1774 but was only performed twice. Hamilton staged three genuinely new afterpieces: Isaac Jackman's *All the World's a Stage* had premiered in Dublin the previous season and was very popular, as was the Bickerstaffe/Dibdin farce *The Sultan*, which had received its first Dublin performance the previous July at Crow Street. An adaptation of their two-act musical farce *The Romp* was also very popular in Dublin the previous season. Although Macklin's *Love a la Mode* was new to Belfast, it had been acted regularly in Dublin for several decades.

Total Performances: 32 of 24 named mainpieces; 29 of 20 different named afterpieces.

Shakespeare: 5.
New Mainpieces: 2.
New Afterpieces: 3.

(For a key to repertory symbols see above, page 11)

Mainpieces: *As You Like It; The Beaux' Stratagem* (2); *The Beggar's Opera* (2); *Cymon; The Fair Penitent; The Fashionable Lover; The Governess; Gustavus Vasa*; Hamlet; The Hypocrite; King Lear; Know Your Own Mind†; Lionel and Clarissa* (3); *The London Merchant; Love in a Village; The Merchant of Venice; The Miser; Much Ado About Nothing†; Othello; Rule a Wife and Have a Wife■; The School for Scandal†; She Stoops to Conquer; Tamerlane* (2); *A Word to the Wise** (2).

Afterpieces: *All the World's a Stage*; The Apprentice; The Author; Bon Ton; Catherine and Petruchio; The Citizen* (3); *Cross Purposes†; The Deserter* (2); *The Deuce is in Him; Florizel and Perdita; The Ghost; The Guardian* (2); *Love a la Mode*; The Old Maid; The Padlock* (3); *The Romp†*(2); *The Sultan*; Thomas and Sally;* Unspecified "farce" (3); *The Virgin Unmasked; The Waterman.*

Interludes: *The Recruiting Serjeant†; The Tavern Bilkers†.*

Entr'acte entertainments: Singing: 8. Dancing: 1

Benefits (10): Mrs. Booth; Farrell; Hamilton; Kane and Lebrun; Lebrun; Pero; Mrs. Pero; Messrs. Rauppe; Richards; Mrs. Richards; Miss Richards.

October 1778

23 Fri.   This present evening the New Theatre in Ann Street will be opened with the occasional prologue written by a gentleman of Belfast to be spoken in the character of a sailor by Hamilton after which will be presented (not acted here in ten years) the comedy of *Rule a Wife and Have a Wife.* Altered and adapted to the stage by Garrick. After the play an epilogue written by a gentleman of Belfast to be spoken by Mrs. Booth. A solo on the violin by Byrne. With *The Guardian.* Hamilton with the most profound respect begs leave to inform the ladies and gentlemen of Belfast that with great expence and fatigue he has at length compleated a most elegant and commodious theatre. Thoroughly sensible of the goodness and hospitality of his patrons he humbly submits himself and company to their protection and is willing to hope their assiduity and earnest endeavour to please will secure them the encouragement of the generous public. [Hamilton's opening-night prologue is printed in *The Hibernian Magazine,* Appendix, 1778, 751] Source: 20–23 Oct. 1778

28 Wed.   *The [Beaux'] Stratagem.* With *Bon Ton.* Source: 23–27 Oct. 1778

30 Fri.   *The Miser.* With a song by Booth. With *The Deuce is in Him.* Source: 27–30 Oct. 1778

November 1778

4 Wed. By desire of the Belfast Volunteers. In commemoration of the anniversary of the birth of King William III of glorious and immortal memory. *Tamerlane.* With the Fall of Bajazet, Emperor of the Turks. With the farce of *Catherine and Petruchio.* Source: 30 Oct.–3 Nov. 1778

11 Wed.   *The London Merchant.* To which will added the farce of *Cross Purposes.* Boxes 2s. 3d., pit 1s. 6d., gallery 9d. Source: 6–10 Nov. 1778

13 Fri.   *She Stoops to Conquer.* With the farce, never performed here, of *All The World's a Stage.* Source: 10–13 Nov. 1778

20 Fri.   *The Fashionable Lover.* With the farce of *The Ghost.* Source: 17–20 Nov. 1778

25 Wed.   *Much Ado about Nothing.* In Act 1 a masquerade scene dance. With a farce as will be expressed in the bills. Source: 20–24 Nov. 1778

December 1778

2 Wed. *The Fair Penitent.* Sciolto–Kane (from the Theatre-Royal in Dublin). With a musical farce called *Florizel and Perdita.* Source: 27 Nov.–1 Dec. 1778

4 Fri.   *The Beggar's Opera.* Macheath–Richards; Polly–Mrs. Richards (from the Theatres-Royal of Edinburgh and Dublin). With *The Virgin Unmasked.* Miss Lucy–Mrs. Richards. [An item in 11–15 December 1778 praises the manager for his industry and for providing so many "respectable performers." The correspondent is sorry to hear that Mrs. Richards, "who is without doubt the best vocal performer in this kingdom," will be staying such a short time]. Source: 1–4 Dec. 1778

9 Wed.   *Lionel and Clarissa.* Lionel–Richards; Diana–Mrs. Richards. With the farce of *The Citizen.* Source: 4–8 Dec. 1778

11 Fri.   *The Hypocrite.* With *The Padlock.* Leonora–Mrs. Richards. Source: 8–11 Dec. 1778.

[*BD* 2: 99 says "Widow Parker" (i.e., the widow of James Parker) of the "New Theatre" and Thomas Betterton were married on 21 December.]

28 Mon.   *Othello.* Othello–Day (from the Theatre-Royal, Dublin). And by desire *The Padlock.* Source: 22–25 Dec. 1778

30 Wed.   By particular desire. *Lionel and Clarissa.* Jessamy–Day; Clarissa–Mrs. Tisdall. With *The Apprentice.* Source: 25–29 Dec. 1778

January 1779

1   Fri.   Never performed here. *A Word to the Wise.* A prologue for New Year's Day by Hamilton. With *The Guardian.* Source: 29 Dec. 1778–1 Jan. 1779

8   Fri.   *A Word to the Wise.* With *The Deserter.* Source: 5–8 Jan. 1779

13 Wed.   *The Governess.* In which will be introduced all the favourite airs songs catches glees duettos and chorusses in the celebrated opera of *The Duenna.* With a farce as will be explained in the bills. Source: 8–12 Jan. 1779

22 Fri.   Benefit of Farrell. *The Merchant of Venice.* "*Tell me Cruel Cupid*" a song by Mrs. Tisdall; "*The Highland Dance*" and "*Dusty Miller*" by Farrell. With the musical farce of *Thomas and Sally.* Source: 19–22 Jan. 1779

27 Wed.   Never performed here. Benefit of Pero. *Gustavus Vasa.* With a farce and entertainments as will be expressed in the bills. Source: 22–26 Jan. 1779

29 Fri.   Benefit of Lebrun. *Hamlet.* A song by Mrs. Tisdall. With (never performed here) the farce of *The Author.* Written by the late facetious Foote. Source: 26–29 Jan. 1779

February 1779

5   Fri.   *Lionel and Clarissa.* Between the play and farce a pantomime interlude in grotesque characters called *The Tavern Bilkers; or, Harlequin Rake.* With *The Citizen.* Source: 2–5 Feb. 1779

12 Fri.   Benefit of Richards. By permission of the author for that night only. *The School for Scandal.* Sir Peter Teazle–Richards; Sir Oliver Surface–Pero; Charles Surface (with the original song)–Day; Sir Benjamin Backbite–Pye; Rowley–Kane; Crabtree–Lebrun; Moses–Booth; Col. Careless–Quin; Trip–Miss Pero; Joseph Surface–Betterton; Lady Teazle–Mrs. Booth; Maria–Miss Farrell; Lady Sneerwell–Mrs. Quin; Maid–Mrs. Betterton; Mrs. Candour–Mrs. Pero. (By permission of the author, R. B. Sheridan). End Act 3 the favourite song of *"My Jocky"* by Miss Richards; end of the play an occasional epilogue by Miss Richards. With the comic opera of *The Padlock.* Don Diego–Hamilton; Leander–Pye; Scholar–Quin; Scholar–Lebrun; Mungo–Richards; Leonora–Mrs. Richards; Ursula–Mrs. Pero. The theatre will be illuminated with wax. Source: 9–12 Feb. 1779

19 Fri.   Benefit of Mrs. Booth. *Tamerlane.* With the Fall of Bajazet Emperor of the Turks. An Epilogue by Mrs. Booth. With the farce of *The Waterman.* Source: 16–19 Feb. 1779

23 Tues.   At the Old Theatre Mill Street Belfast. By Permission of George Black, Sovereign. (For that Night only). On Tuesday 23 February the celebrated Mr. Bisset will exhibit several surprising Equilibres on the Slack-Wire, Rope Ladder, Tumbling, etc. On same Night the Lion's Leap will be performed on the Rope. He will also stand on his Head on a Bottle on the Wire the Wire in full Swing not done by any other. The Avizinia or Bird of Knowledge, will also exhibit his amazing Performances which astonishes every Beholder there is not a Bird in the World equal to this. Also will be exhibited a Lion, Porcupine and two other curious Animals. Pit 1s. 6d., Gallery 6d. As Mr. Bisset is engaged this Season in Dublin. In Order that no Person may be disappointed said Bird will be exhibited before any Number of Ladies or Gentlemen (at Mr. Bisset the Proprietor's House) or at their own Houses if desired at one Shilling each. Mr. Bisset will stop a few Days at Lisburn, Newry and Drogheda on his Road to Dublin. Source: 16–19 February 1779

24 Wed.   New Theatre Ann Street. Benefit of Messieurs Rauppe who have had the honour of performing before their Majesties and most of the Nobility of Great Britain and are esteemed to be the most capital performers on the Violoncello in Europe. *The Beggar's Opera.* The songs to be accompanied by Messieurs Rauppe. Between the acts of the Opera will be performed several solos and select Irish tunes on the Violoncello by Messieurs Rauppe. With *The Old Maid.* Source: 19–23 Feb. 1779

26   Fri.   *King Lear and his Three Daughters.* With *The Deserter.* Louisa–Mrs. Richards, in which character she will introduce the Scotch song of *"De'el Take the Wars".* Source: 23–26 Feb. 1779

March 1779

2   Tues.   By particular desire at the Old Theatre Mill Street Belfast. The celebrated Mr. Bisset will exhibit several surprising equilibres on the slack-wire, rope ladder, tumbling, etc. On the same night the lion's leap will be performed on the rope. He will also stand on his head on a bottle on the wire, the wire in full swing not done by any other. The Avizinia or Bird of Knowledge will also exhibit his amazing performances which astonishes every beholder. There is not a bird in the world equal to this. Pit 1s. 6d., gallery 6d. As Mr. Bisset is engaged this season in Dublin in order that no person may be disappointed said bird will be exhibited before any number of ladies or gentlemen (at Mr. Bisset the Proprietor's House) or at their own houses if desired at one shilling each. Mr. Bisset will stop a few days at Lisburn, Newry, and Drogheda on his road to Dublin. Source: 23–26 Feb. 1779

3   Wed.   Benefit of Mrs. Pero. *Know Your Own Mind.* With a farce (never performed here) written by Macklin called *Love a la Mode.* Source: 26 Feb.–2 Mar. 1779

5   Fri.   Benefit of Hamilton. *As You Like It.* After the play the interlude of *The Recruiting Serjeant.* With *The Citizen.* Maria (with a Song in Character)–Mrs. Smith (first appearance in Belfast). Source: 2–5 Mar. 1779

12   Fri.   The last night but one. Benefit of Mrs. Richards. Third time. *Love in a Village.* Rosetta–Mrs. Richards, in which character will be introduced *"Come Live with Me and be my Love".* In Act 1 (never sung here) the last new Scotch Song called *"My Bonny Jemmy O"* by Mrs. Richards; in Act 2 the favourite song of *"The Rose"* from *Selima and Azor* by Miss Richards; in Act 3 a song by Miss Richards; End of the Play an Epilogue by Miss Richards. With (for that night only) the Musical Entertainment of *The Romp.* Watty Cockney–Richards; Miss Priscilla Tomboy–Mrs. Richard. The Theatre will be illuminated with wax. Source: 9–12 Mar. 1779

19   Fri.   Benefit of Kane and Lebrun. *The [Beaux'] Stratagem.* Scrub–William Hamilton (from the Theatres Royal Covent Garden and Dublin; first appearance in Belfast). The song of *"My Bonnie Jemmy O"* by

Mrs. Richards and a farce (never performed here) called *The Sultan.*
Solyman–Betterton; Haly Hassan–Farrell; Grand Carver–Lebrun;
Osmyn–Richards; Roxalana–Mrs. Booth; Elmira–Mrs. Farrell; Ismene
(with Songs in Character)–Mrs. Richards. As performed last season at the
Theatres Royal of London and Dublin with universal applause. Kane and
Lebrun having unfortunately failed in their first Benefit have at the request
of many of their friends undertaken a second and humbly hope for the
patronage and support of the ladies and gentlemen of the town of Belfast
and its environs. They likewise pledge themselves to the ladies and
gentlemen who intend to honour them with their presence that whatever
is inserted in the bills will be performed with the strictest attention. As the
inclemency of the weather prevented the performance on Wednesday last
tickets delivered for that night will be admitted. Source: 16–19 Mar. 1779

[23] Tues. [date uncertain] By particular Desire. Benefit of Miss Richards.
Cymon. Cupid–Miss Richards. End Act 3 a song by Miss Richards; end of
the Play a favourite Epilogue by Miss Richards. To which (by general
desire) will be added *The Romp.* The Romp–Mrs. Richards. Source: 19–23
Mar. 1779

The receipts for the unrecorded charity "plays" customarily given at the
conclusion of the Belfast season are reported in 4–7 May 1779

1779–1780 SEASON

Venue: Ann Street Theatre.
Company: Mr. and Mrs. (née Mary Russell) Best; Thomas Betterton; Mr.
and Mrs. Day; Miss Farrell; Myrton Hamilton (actor-manager); Pye; Walsh
(from Theatre Royal, Crow Street).

The Belfast Theatre was managed again this season by **Myrton
Hamilton,** for whose biography see the 1768–69 season.

Very little is known about the acting careers of **Mr.** and **Mrs. Best.**
According to their *BD* entry, a Mr. Best played Harlequin at the
Haymarket Theatre in March 1779, and the authors believe the same man
also appeared in Belfast this season. Again, according to the *BD*, in Belfast
"shortly before 1 June 1785, he married Miss Mary Russell, an actress who
played at the Haymarket in 1777–78." The *BNL* 3–7 June 1785 announces
that Mr. Best "comedian" has married Miss Mary Russell in Belfast.
Perhaps this was Best's second marriage. There is no Dublin record for any
actor named Best.

For a biography of **Thomas Betterton** see the 1778–79 season.

For biographies of **Mr.** and **Mrs. Day** see the 1771–72 season.

For biographies of the **Farrells** see the 1768–69 season.

For a biography of **Pye** see the 1768–69 season.

The Mr. Walsh, advertised as from Theatre Royal, Crow Street, may have been the singer and musician **Henry Green Walsh,** who, the *BD* tells us, "passed most of his adult career in Dublin." There is no record of Walsh having performed at Crow Street, although he may have been a musician there and have gone unrecorded. Henry Green Walsh later participated in the Handelian concerts in Westminster Abbey (1794) and was a member of the Irish Musical Fund in 1804. He was supposed to have played in the orchestra for the annual Dublin Handel commemoration as late as 1809 but was fined for being absent.

Repertory, 1779–1780 Season

Almost certainly many more performances took place this season than the surviving record indicates; however, the surviving playbills indicate that only one relatively new play was performed in Belfast this season: Gen. Burgoyne's two-act comic opera *The Maid of the Oaks*, which had premiered in Dublin in 1777 with modest success. Volunteer activity continued in Belfast and the theatre programs reflect support for that organization.

Total Performances: 13 of 11 different named mainpieces; 11 of 9 different named afterpieces.
    Shakespeare: 3.
    New Mainpieces: 1.
    New Afterpieces: 0.

(For a key to repertory symbols see above, page 11)

Mainpieces: *As You Like It; The Conscious Lovers; Macbeth; The Maid of the Oaks*† (2); *The Miser; Much Ado About Nothing; The School for Scandal* (2); *Tamerlane; Venice Preserved; The Way to Keep Him.*

Afterpieces: *Catherine and Petruchio; Cymon; The Deuce is in Him; The Devil to Pay; The Duenna* (2); *The Honest Yorkshireman; The Jubilee*† ; *The Mock Doctor; The Padlock; The Romp;* Unspecified "farce."

Interludes: *The Recruiting Serjeant.*

Entr'acte entertainments: Singing: 1. Dancing: 0

Benefits (6): Mr. and Mrs. Best; Betterton (2); Mrs. Day; the Poor; Pye.

November 1779

4   Thur. Theatre Ann Street. By permission of the Worshipful Samuel Black, Sovereign of Belfast. Anniversary of the birth of King William. *Tamerlane*. With a farce as will be expressed in the Bills. Source: 29 Oct.–2 Nov. 1779

10 Wed.   *The School for Scandal*. With the Comic Opera of *The Duenna*. The Songs Catches Duets accompanied by the Band belonging to his Majesty's 36th Regiment. Source: 5–9 Nov. 1779

17 Wed. By Desire of the Officers belonging to his Majesty 36th Regiment of Foot. *The School for Scandal*. With the Comic Opera of *The Duenna*. Before the Play and between the Acts several select pieces of Music by the Band belonging to the above regiment. Source: 12–16 Nov. 1779

January 1780

8   Sat.   Benefit of the Poor. *The Honest Yorkshireman* with an interlude called *The Recruiting Serjeant* and the farce of *The Mock Doctor*. The characters by young gentlemen of this town. To begin exactly at seven o'clock. Source: 4–7 Jan. 1780

February 1780

14 Mon.   *The Maid of the Oaks*. [Reviewed in source issue]. Source: 15–18 Feb. 1780

18 Fri.   *The Maid of the Oaks*. [second night]. Source: 15–18 Feb. 1780

March 1780

1   Wed. Benefit of Betterton. *Macbeth*. End of the play a new comic dance to which will be added the dramatic romance of *Cymon*. The whole to conclude by particular desire with *"The Bower Dance."* Source: 25–29 Feb. 1780

3   Fri.   Benefit of Pye. *As You Like It*. Singing between the acts with the farce of *Catherine and Petruchio*. Source: 29 Feb.–3 Mar. 1780

10 Fri.　*Much Ado About Nothing.* To which will be added the comic opera of *The Padlock.* Mungo–Walsh (from the Theatre-Royal Crow Street). Source: 7–10 Mar. 1780

15 Wed.　By particular desire of several ladies and gentlemen. Benefit of Mr. and Mrs. Best. *The Way to Keep Him.* With the much admired farce of *The Romp.* With a variety of other entertainments. Source: 10–14 Mar. 1780

27 Mon.　Benefit of Mrs. Day. *The Conscious Lovers.* To which by desire will be added the entertainment of *The Jubilee.* With songs, duets, rondos, serenades and decorations from *Henry VIII* in which will be introduced the grand procession and exact representation of the coronation of Anne Bullen with the ceremony of the champion on horseback in full armour. Source: 17–21 Mar. 1780

July 1780

10 Mon.　[No program available]. By permission of Samuel Black, Sovereign the Theatre in Ann Street will be opened and continue so during the week of the review [of Irish Volunteers]. Source: 30 June–4 July 1780

11 Tues.　*The Miser.* Between the play and farce a new Volunteer epilogue written by a gentleman of Belfast to be spoken by Miss Farrell. With *The Deuce is in Him.* Source: 7–11 July 1780

19 Wed.　Benefit of Betterton. *Venice Preserved.* Pierre–Day. And *The Devil to Pay.* Nell–Mrs. Day. Source: 14–18 July 1780

1780–1781 SEASON

Venue: Ann Street Theatre.
Company: Michael Atkins (actor-manager); John Collins; Mr. and Mrs. Wilmot.

Michael Atkins recommenced management of the Belfast company and Myrton Hamilton moved to Dublin to act at Smock Alley. For biography of Atkins see the 1767–68 season.

For a biography of **John Collins** see 1775–76 season.

For biographies of **Mr.** and **Mrs. Wilmot** see the 1775–76 season.

Repertory, December 1780–May 1781

There were certainly many more plays staged this season than the calendar indicates. The only new piece of which we have record is Dibdin's *The Quaker*, which had premiered in Dublin the previous April.

Total Performances: 3 of 3 different named mainpieces; 3 of 3 different named afterpieces.
   Shakespeare: 0.
   New Mainpieces: 0.
   New Afterpieces: 1.

   (For a key to repertory symbols see above, page 11)

Mainpieces: *The Fashionable Lover; The Wonder; A Word to the Wise.*

Afterpieces: *Daphne and Amintor†; The Mock Doctor; The Quaker*.*

Entr'acte entertainment: Singing: 1. Benefits: 0.

Benefit (1): Freemasons.

December 1780

Atkins with the utmost respect and gratitude begs leave to inform the ladies and gentlemen of Belfast that he has obtained permission from the worshipful Sam. Black to open a theatre in a few weeks. He will not say any thing of the merits of his company as from experience he is certain if they prove deserving that they will meet with that candour politeness and approbation which has ever been the particular characteristics of the inhabitants of Belfast. A few tickets for the season will be disposed of at one guinea and a half each. Source: 26–29 December 1780

March 1781

23 Fri.   *A Word to the Wise.* To which will be added a new musical entertainment never performed here *The Quaker*. [*The Quaker* was published in Belfast by James Magee in 1782]. Source: 16–20 Mar. 1781

May 1781

9 Wed. By desire of the right worshipful the master wardens and brethren of the Ancient and Honourable Society of Free and Accepted Masons of the Orange Lodge of Belfast No. 257. *The Wonder, A Woman Keeps* *a Secret*. A new occasional prologue in character of a Knight Templar written by Amyas Griffith to be spoken by Brother Mason Wilmot. Songs between the acts by the brethren. An occasional epilogue in character of a Mason's wife by Mrs. Wilmot. With a musical entertainment never performed here called *Daphne and Amintor*. The worshipful master and wardens expect the attendance of the brethren at the Lodge Room at six o'clock in order to proceed from thence to the theatre where a throne and amphitheatre will be erected on the stage for their reception. Source: 4–8 May 1781

30 Wed. *The Fashionable Lover*. Collin Macleod (for one night only)–Collins. Written by the author of *The West Indian, The Brothers* etc. [Richard Cumberland] at the joint request of several of his friends. After the play Collins by particular desire will exhibit the following characters from his Comic Lecture on Modern Orators and Modern Oratory as it has been exhibited in London, Dublin, Oxford, Cambridge and every principal city in the three Kingdoms to crouded audiences with universal applause, viz. A Macaroni orator, a Scholastic Orator, an illiterate work-grubber, a clipper of English, two droning schoolboys, a superannuated schoolmistress, and a flogging schoolmaster with a picture of the modern school; to conclude with the ludicrous oratory of a stammerer, a lisper, and a snuffer, with all their heads dressed in character and introduced in *propriis personis*. To which by desire will be added *The Mock Doctor*. Mock Doctor–Collins. Source: 25–29 May 1781

1781–1782 SEASON

Venue: Ann Street Theatre.
Company: Michael Atkins; Byrne (violinist); Richard Coxe Rowe; Mrs. Sparks (from Crow Street); Tyrrell; Mr. and Mrs. Wilmot.

For biography of **Atkins** see the 1767–68 season.

For biography of **Byrne** (violinist) see the 1778–79 season.

For a biography of **Richard Coxe Rowe** see the 1777–78 season.

In early January 1772 **Miss Frances Ashmore**, a young actress who had appeared in Ireland from as early as 1765, married Richard Sparks, the youngest member of the Sparks dynasty of Irish actors. Mr. and Mrs. Sparks acted together at Ryder's Smock Alley theatre for the 1772–73 season, and they remained in Dublin playing with great regularity for the next twenty years. They moved to the new Fishamble Street theatre for the 1776–77 season where Sparks was co-manager with Vandermere and Waddy, and, when that venture failed, returned to Crow Street from 1776–77, advertised as their first performances there in four years. The Crow Street company went bankrupt at the end of that season, and the Sparkses are not found in any Dublin playbills for the 1779–80 season. They resurface at Smock Alley at the beginning of 1780–81 and they performed there until late April when Sparks was imprisoned for debt, evidently at manager Daly's instance. Ryder, the Crow Street manager, offered Sparks the use of his theatre, and he took a benefit there late in May.

Sparks was evidently released from confinement soon thereafter, but he left Ireland temporarily, perhaps wishing to avoid other creditors. Whether or not he performed in Edinburgh during the 1781–82 season, when his wife certainly performed there, is not now known. The *BD* believes that the Sparks acting in Edinburgh that season was Hugh Sparks and not Richard. Nevertheless, when Mrs. Sparks reappears in Dublin at Crow Street for the 1782–83 season it is billed as her first appearance there in three years. Sparks acted at Crow Street also and evidently had a hand in the management of the company, for in the spring of 1783 the company voted to turn the sole management of the company over to Clinch because it was coming apart under the co-direction of Dawson, Glenville, Hurst, Sparks, and Owenson. Sparks acted no more that year.

The following season the Sparkses were once more engaged at Smock Alley theatre, their first appearances there in three years. They remained at Smock Alley until the end of the 1784–85 season when they once again disappear from the record until the 1792–93 season. Then, on 7 May 1793 they were given a benefit at Crow Street although they were not present themselves. Evidently, they had been performing in Scotland for a time and had been arrested for debt. The playbills add: "A free benefit for the Sparks's, who are both in distressed circumstances in Scotland — yet, alas! a very indifferent house." The record again is silent until on 20 August 1798 at Crow Street Mrs. Sparks "for many years a deserving favourite of the Irish nation" appeared for one night as Nell in *The Devil to Pay*.

It seems likely that it was at about this time that Richard took up a post at the Custom House in Dublin. Subsequent references in the playbills to a "Mr. Sparks" may be to the actor and singer G. Hugh Sparks, who was probably related to them.

Considering his long association with both the Crow Street and Smock Alley theatres it is perhaps surprising that Richard Sparks appeared so seldom in the provincial theatres. His record includes: Kilkenny, June and August 1776, and October 1779; Cork in August 1783. There is some question about the identity of the "Mr. Sparks" who appeared in Belfast with Atkins's company February–early May 1800. That performer was principally a singer of comic songs and neither Richard Sparks nor Hugh Sparks have records as singers. Hugh Sparks would have had the opportunity to travel to Belfast at that time judging from the Drury Lane record for the spring of 1800 when he is absent for precisely those months.

Mrs. Sparks spent more time away from Dublin. Before her marriage, as Miss Ashmore, she is found in Cork in the autumn of 1769, (Clark errs in finding her in Belfast in the summer of 1770). As Mrs. Sparks she is noticed in Cork and Limerick in the summer and fall of 1773 and again in the summer and fall of 1774: The *FDJ* 13–15 Oct. 1774 announces that "Mrs. Sparks, the celebrated Actress, was delivered last Monday of two Sons, at Silvermines in the County of Tipperary, on her Way from Limerick to Dublin, and she and the Children are in a fair Way of doing well." She returned to Kilkenny in the summer of 1776 and again in the autumn of 1779; she is found in Belfast in September 1781, in Derry in the fall of 1782, in Cork and Limerick in the fall of 1783 and in Carlow in October 1797.

The Mrs. Sparks performing in a few older women's roles at Crow Street during the 1799–1800 and 1800–01 seasons may have been Mrs. Richard Sparks and probably not the Mrs. Sparks who, with a "Miss Sparks," performed younger women's roles at Peter Street the previous season.

A **Mr. Tyrrell** is first noticed in Dublin on 14 November 1771 at Crow Street playing tertiary roles. In October 1771 he is found at Limerick with the company of Crow Street actors Heaphy had engaged, and Tyrrell probably also visited Cork at that time, although the record is silent. He was with Brownlow Forde's strolling company in Kilkenny for much of the 1772–73 season. Tyrrell was engaged at Smock Alley for the 1774–75 and 1775–76 seasons, acting, now, in mainly secondary roles.

In the autumn of 1776 Tyrrell visited Cork briefly, before beginning an engagement at the new Fishamble Street theatre. That season Mrs. Tyrrell appears in the record for the first time, initially at Kilkenny in the autumn, and then with her husband at Fishamble Street in tertiary roles. The whereabouts of the Tyrrells for the 1777–78 season is unknown. They are found together at Newry in December and April 1778–79, probably with

Atkins's company from Belfast and not with the short-lived breakaway company that had set up in competition to Atkins headed by Hamilton and Pero. Tyrrell, usually without his wife, is for several seasons thereafter found with Atkins company acting in Belfast (1781, 1783 (with his wife), 1784 1787 and 1788) and Derry (1782 and 1784). Thereafter, he disappears from the record. Perhaps he is related to the William H. Tyrrell, who acted as printer to the theatre with offices in 44 (later No. 17), College Green, who regularly printed music and Dublin theatre tickets and playbills at the beginning of the nineteenth century.

Although we have no record of her activity from 1779 to 1784, Mrs. Tyrrell was engaged as a member of the Fishamble Street company for the 1784–85 season but that is the last record of her activities.

For biographies of **Mr.** and **Mrs. Wilmot** see the 1775–76 season.

Repertory, September 1781–January 1782

This season again Atkins seems not to have advertised regularly in the newspapers and the record is accordingly sparse. The only new offering was Mrs. Cowley's *The Belle's Stratagem*, which had premiered in Dublin in December 1780 with great success.

Total Performances: 10 of 7 different named plays; 9, of 7 different named afterpieces.
Shakespeare: 0.
New Mainpieces: 1.
New Afterpieces: 0.

(For a key to repertory symbols see above, page 11)

Mainpieces: *The Belle's Stratagem** (3); *Cato* (2); *The Foundling; The Grecian Daughter; The Jealous Wife; Love in a Village; The Twin Rivals.*

Afterpieces: *The Ephesian Matron*†; *The Intriguing Footman; The Lottery; The Padlock; The Quaker; The Romp* (2); *The Sultan;* Unspecified "farce".

Entr'acte entertainments: Singing: 2. Dancing: 1

Benefits (4): Byrne; the Poor; Rowe; Tyrrell.

September 1781

7 Fri. *The Grecian Daughter*. Atkins has engaged Mrs. Sparks from the Theatre Royal, Crow Street, Dublin. Source: 31 Aug.–4 Sept. 1781

October 1781

25 Thur. By particular desire. *The Foundling.* With the musical farce of *The Romp.* Source: 19–23 Oct. 1781

November 1781

7 Wed. Never performed here. *The Belle's Stratagem.* In Act 4 a Grand Masquerade. With a farce and entertainments as will be expressed in the bills. Source: 2–6 Nov. 1781

14 Wed. By desire of the Belfast Battalion. *The Belle's Stratagem.* With the farce of *The Padlock.* Source: 9–13 Nov. 1781

16 Fri.   Anniversary of the landing of King William at Torbay by desire of the Belfast Volunteer Company. *Cato.* Singing by Atkins, Tyrrell and several pieces of music between the acts by the band of 49th Regiment. With the farce of *The Sultan.* Source: 13–16 Nov. 1781

21 Wed. Benefit of Tyrrell. *The Twin Rivals.* Written by Farquhar. With the farce of *The Lottery.* Source: 16–20 Nov. 1781

December 1781

5 Wed. Benefit of Rowe (by particular desire) *Cato.* With *The Quaker.* Source: 30 Nov.–4 Dec. 1781

January 1782

4 Fri.   Benefit of Rowe. By particular desire. *The Belle's Stratagem,* with the musical farce *The Romp.* Source: 1–4 Jan. 1782

16 Wed. Benefit of the Poor. *The Jealous Wife.* With the entertainment of *The Ephesian Matron.* [15–19 Mar. 1782 gives receipts of Belfast Charitable Society for a benefit play for the Poor this season]. Source: 11–15 Jan. 1782

25 Fri.   By desire Belfast Musical Society. Benefit of Byrne. *Love in a Village* with favourite catches and glees between the play and farce of *The Intriguing Footman.* Source: 22–25 Jan. 1782

1782–1783 SEASON

Venue: Although few bills have survived, the Belfast company seems to have performed at Ann Street Theatre from early February until mid-May 1783.

Company: Michael Atkins; Mr. and Mrs. John Bernard; Mr. and Mrs. Andrew Cherry (née Knipe [*BNL* 25–28 Mar. 1783 announces that Andrew Cherry and Miss Knipe "both of our theatre" were recently married]); Captain Garvey; Jacob Hammerton; Mrs. Charles Hoskins (often Hoskin); Miss Ann Hoskins; Miss Mary Jameson; John Kane; Kennedy; William Macready; John Shane O'Neill; Richard Rowe; Mr. and Mrs. Tyrrell.

For biography of **Michael Atkins** see the 1767–68 season.

John Bernard is probably best remembered for his very interesting *memoirs* which furnish one of our most vivid and detailed pictures of the strolling actor's life in the last quarter of the eighteenth and first quarter of the nineteenth centuries. The son of an Irish lieutenant in the British navy, Bernard was born at Portsmouth in 1756. He grew up there and was attracted to the stage at an early age over the protestations of his mother. He was sent away to grammar school at Chichester and then his family tried to get him to begin a career in the navy or in the law but John ran away from home at the age of about 17 and joined several obscure strolling companies in the English provinces. In Weymouth he was arrested and returned home to his mother, but his parents finally consented to allow him to try his luck on the stage.

Bernard soon joined another strolling company on the Braintree-Needham-Dedham circuit, was seen by some influential patrons and recommended to Griffith of Norwich where he was engaged. At Norwich in 1774 at the age of 18 he married a Mrs. Cooper, an experienced actress six years his senior who was also acting with the Norwich company. The Bernards played at Exeter, Taunton, Barnstaple and Plymouth during 1775–76, and they joined Wilkinson's company in the summer of 1776 and appeared at York, Halifax and Wakefield, before returning to Exeter in 1776–77. The Bernards made their Bath debuts in the 1777–78 season, then are found again in Exeter 1778–79, at Barnstaple and Taunton in the summer of 1779 and then at Weymouth until 1782.

Evidently with an eye to engaging them at Crow Street for the 1782–83 season, Richard Daly invited the Bernards to join his company in Limerick in August and in Cork in September and October 1782 where Bernard, but not Mrs. Bernard, who was ill, acted with the visiting London actors John and Stephen Kemble, West Digges, Mrs. Barsanti, Mrs. Melmoth and others. Daly evidently changed his mind about engaging the Bernards, and they signed instead with the new Capel Street managers Truby and Watts. When Truby and Watts decamped in early December 1782 after the Lord Mayor withdrew his license because of the complaints of the theatre patrons who had been rooked at their back-room gambling table, the Bernards, having little option, continued to perform at Capel Street for their own benefit on shares. According to playbills Bernard's last performance at Capel Street was on 29 January 1783 when the company finally collapsed; however, notices in the *BNL* indicate that Bernard and his wife first appeared in Belfast with Michael Atkins's company on 27 January 1783.

Bernard tells us that Atkins entrusted him with the management of his company when it traveled to Sligo in the summer and to Derry for the 1783–84 season. The Bernards returned to Belfast for the 1784–85 season and acted in Waterford in the autumn. Thereafter, they returned to England and were engaged with the Bath company for three seasons during which, Bernard tells us, he was the "ruling favourite of the theatre." Accordingly, the Bernards were engaged by Harris of Covent Garden to perform for four seasons. Beginning in 1787–88 the Bernards performed frequently at Crow Street in a wide variety of mostly secondary roles through 1790–91, after which Bernard played in Plymouth for a time.

According to her husband's memoirs, Mrs. Bernard died in 1792, but convincing evidence assembled by the authors of the *BD* indicates that it is more likely that she left him for a Mr. Tayleure whom she married sometime after 1794. (Indeed, there is some doubt about whether Bernard ever actually married the former Mrs. Cooper). Thus, Clark errs when he finds two Mrs. Bernards active in the Irish provinces. Mrs. John Bernard and the Mrs. Bernard who performed in Belfast with Atkins's company in the winter and spring of 1793 and at Derry in the spring of 1794 were the same person. After that time Mrs. Bernard disappears from the record. She probably was still alive in 1805.

John Bernard returned to Covent Garden for the 1793–94 and 1794–95 seasons. His successful musical entertainment, *The Poor Sailor,* music by Attwood, had its Covent Garden premiere on 29 May 1795. By 1795 Bernard had obtained interests in the theatres in Plymouth, Brighton, Dover and Guernsey but was not successful in any of these ventures. He signed articles to appear in Philadelphia with Wignell's company, and, with his second wife, the former Miss Fisher of Guernsey, whom he married in 1796, performed in Philadelphia, New York, and Boston until the death of his wife in 1806, after which he returned to England only long enough to marry his third wife, a Miss Wright, and to engage entertainers from London.

Returning to Boston in 1806, Bernard was joint-manager of the Federal Street theatre until 1811. He also acted in Canada, Baltimore, Kentucky, and managed the Green Street Theatre in Albany, New York, before finally returning to England in 1819. Evidently, John Bernard was never able to reestablish himself financially in England, and he died, destitute, on 29 November 1828. His *memoirs* entitled *Retrospections of the Stage* was published in 1830 by his son.

As Miss Knipe, the future **Mrs. Andrew Cherry** made her stage debut in Belfast on 20 January 1766 singing with her parents (for whose biographies see above in the 1765–66 season). She made her acting debut at Crow Street (not at Smock Alley in 1786 as Clark indicates) playing the Duke of York in *Richard III* in May 1768.
Andrew Cherry first appears in the record in Newry for the 1778–79 season and again that autumn in Derry. If this is his stage debut he was about 16 years old at the time. Cherry acted again in Derry in December 1782. Clark locates Cherry at Crow Street in 1779, but I can find no record of a Dublin performance for him that season. In fact, Cherry made his Crow Street debut on 4 January 1783 when he played Brush in *The Beaux' Stratagem*. This was probably not Cherry's first Dublin appearance, however. In the earlier playbills for the 4 January performance a note stated that it was Cherry's "first appearance in this city," but that was later changed to "his first appearance on this stage." This is the only known role for Cherry that season. Thereafter, he and his wife are found (from 27 January 1783) in Belfast with Atkins's company and in Derry in the summer of 1783. An item in *BNL* 25–28 Mar. 1783 indicates that Andrew Cherry and Miss Knipe "both of our theatre" were recently married. The Cherrys spent the 1783–84 season with the company headed by John Bernard in Atkins's stead, performing perhaps in Sligo in the summer and then in Derry. Cherry (but evidently not his wife) were in Belfast for the opening of the Rosemary Lane Theatre in March 1784 and he remained there through the 1784–85 season.

Mrs. Cherry made her Smock Alley debut ("her first appearance here") on 13 November 1786 as Lucinda in *Love in a Village*, and Cherry made "his first appearance" the following night. They continued at Smock Alley in secondary roles with some regularity until the end of the 1787–88 season. Clark must err in finding Mr. and Mrs. Cherry acting in Belfast on 19 January 1787. There is no evidence that Mrs. Cherry performed there that year. The playbill that appeared in *The Londonderry Journal* of 30 January 1787 (followed by Clark) must also err when it finds Cherry in Belfast because the Dublin playbills clearly indicate that Cherry appeared at Smock Alley that month, specifically on 15 and 22 January 1787. It is highly unlikely that he would have made the two-day journey to Belfast for one performance.

In October 1787 Cherry was with the Smock Alley company when it visited Waterford. After his own benefit on 13 May 1788 Cherry presented *"A Dramatic Olio; or, The Faithful Indian,"* which seems to have been a sort of comical recitation of his own composition.

The Cherrys moved to Crow Street for that summer season. They returned for the 1788–89 season, and Cherry had considerable success. Judging from the wide variety of roles he played, he was a versatile mainstay of the company. Perhaps his importance is suggested by the fact that near the end of the season he attracted the wrath of the publisher of the *Dublin Evening Post*, John Magee, who at this time had launched a bitterly libelous campaign against Daly and his company. In an adverse review in *DEP* 13 June 1789 Cherry is characterized as miscast in Sir Peter Teazle and is called "the lowest buffo of the stage." Cherry replied to this in a card in the *Hibernian Journal* 15 June 1789 threatening a libel action.

The Cherry's continued to act regularly at Crow Street through the 1791–92 season. For his own benefit on 17 May 1791 Cherry brought forward for the first time his own "Comic-satiric-musical interlude" entitled *Shelty in Dublin.* Clark errs when he finds Cherry acting in Belfast on 24 October 1792 (should read 1794) since the new Arthur Street Theatre did not open that season until 25 February 1793. During their four seasons with the Crow Street company the Cherrys traveled with it on its annual tours of the provinces: to Cork in the autumns of 1787, 1788, 1789; and Waterford 1787 and 1789 (after which Mrs. Cherry disappears from the provincial record).

Evidently, the Cherrys spent the 1793–94 season in York with Tate Wilkinson's company, for in his *memoirs* Wilkinson tells us that during the summer Daly sent Hitchcock to Yorkshire to engage Cherry to support Miss Farren during her visit to Dublin. The Cherrys acted the 1794 summer season at Crow Street, billed as their "first appearance in three years." Cherry, but not his wife, is found in Belfast in October and November of 1794 for a limited engagement. After his first appearance on 24 October 1794 the *BNL* observed that "It is several years since this town has been gratified by such excellent playing as Cherry as Lazarillo in Jepson's *The Hotel.*" *The Northern Star* 10 Nov. 1794 observed that Cherry's benefit drew "the greatest audience ever known in the North of Ireland"; there was "an overflow in every part of the house." Cherry's receipts were £87.

The Cherrys remained for two seasons at Crow Street, during which, Wilkinson says, "he wrote for the theatre two operatical pieces which were performed with approbation." The first of these, which premiered on 18 March 1795, was *The Grateful Child; or, Walter's Wedding,* a sequel to Morton's *The Children in the Wood.* On 17 November 1794 a Miss Cherry, their daughter, enters the Crow Street playbills for the first time, playing a child's role, the Dauphin in *The Maid of Normandy.* Before the season was out she had played in a wide variety of roles with considerable success. Cherry acted with Atkins's company in Derry in the autumn of 1795 and then returned to Crow Street that autumn.

For his family's benefit on 1 March 1796 Cherry brought out his second play: *The Outcasts; or, Poor Bess and Little Dick,* a variant of *Sylvester Daggerwood,* "for this night only a new comic opera never performed." Cherry was unable to act that evening due to a "debility occasioned by a tedious and painful illness." Evidently, the Cherrys went to England after this. He wrote many pieces for the London stage, but did not act again.

Captain Garvey was a member of the Belfast company this season and on 27 January 1783, according to Bernard (1830 1:195), in *The School for Scandal,* Garvey played Careless and in Act 2, scene 3, "the solo part in the drinking song '*Here's to the Maiden!*' was sung by the very popular Captain Garvey."

Garvey and the Bernards joined the ill-fated Capel Street theatre under Truby and Watts for the 1782–83 season, and, after the venture failed at the end of January 1783, Garvey is found in the spring and summer in Belfast, Derry, and Sligo. **Mrs. Garvey** acted at Fishamble Street in 1792–93 and again in the 1797–98 season and then at Crow Street for the 1798–99 season. The last record we have of Mr. and Mrs. Garvey is in Belfast at Atkins's Arthur Street Theatre during the 1799–1800 season. Thereafter, they disappear from the record.

According to Clark (1965, 244 and 360) **Jacob Hammerton** was with Atkins's Derry company (then led by his deputy, John Bernard) when it traveled to Belfast in January–May 1783 and he also traveled to Kilkenny in February–June 1784 and to Waterford in July 1784.

The first recorded role for Hammerton was as Leeson in *The School for Wives* on 20 December 1784 the opening night of Robert Owenson's City Theatre in Fishamble Street, billed as Hammerton's "second appearance in this city." The first appearance is not recorded. Judging from the roles he played that season, most of which were primary or secondary, it is clear that Hammerton had been on the stage for some time before he made his Dublin debut.

Hammerton traveled to Cork and performed there from August–September 1785. On the opening night of the Smock Alley theatre for the 1785–86 season, Hammerton was advertised as "from Fishamble Street." Hammerton's whereabouts for the 1786–87 season are unknown, perhaps he was in London. He appeared again at Smock Alley briefly in the summer of 1787, in Waterford in October, and at Smock Alley again until early December 1787. Where he spent the remainder of the season is not known.

Hammerton moved to Crow Street for the 1788–89 season playing a variety of rules. He is found in Cork in August 1788 then again at Crow Street for the 1789–90, 1790–91, and 1791–92 seasons, acting in primary and secondary roles. Hammerton is found in Waterford in June 1789 and in Cork in September 1790.

Hammerton's whereabout after the 1791–92 season are unknown for a time. When he resurfaces in Dublin it is at Fishamble Street on 12 January 1798 as Rover in O'Keeffe's *Wild Oats*. The bills state that it is Hammerton's "first appearance these five years." He played a variety of other characters that season, several primary. Hammerton moved to Crow Street for the 1798–99 season, and we learn from a pamphlet entitled "Theatrical Fund, for the Relief of Decayed Actors and Actresses, Their Widows and Children, Instituted at the Theatre Royal, Dublin, 3d of March, 1799," that he was an original member of the board of the Irish Theatrical Fund.

When Hammerton took his benefit on 17 April 1799 he is billed as "The Manager of the Theatre Royal." Hammerton led the Crow Street company to Cork in August 1799 and it was Jacob Hammerton, signing his name as deputy manager of the theatre royal, who called the Crow Street actors to town at the beginning of the 1799–1800 season. Hammerton's last season as deputy manager at Crow Street was 1800–01 after which he traveled to Belfast and Holman assumed the post of Jones's deputy. Thereafter, Hammerton's whereabouts are unclear. It seems unlikely that the actor and singer who performed in Dublin from 1816–17 through 1819–20 is Jacob. It may be a son.

The early careers of **Mr.** and **Mrs. Charles Hoskins** are something of a mystery. She is first noticed in Ireland on 26 February 1770 at Capel Street on its opening night playing Mrs. Harley in Kelly's *False Delicacy* and billed as "from the Theatre Royal, Drury Lane." However, there is no record of her having performed in London. Later that season, she acted in a variety of roles in the line of older women, suggesting, perhaps, that she had already had considerable experience on the stage. We learn from the bills for her benefit night later in the season that she is the "Widow of Mr. Hoskins, Constructor and Builder of the City Theatre." A benefit for Hoskins was advertised for 22 May, but was deferred on account of his illness, then the *PRFJ* 26 May 1770 announces the death of Charles Hoskins "at his lodgings in Capel Street . . . one of the proprietors of the City Theatre." He left a widow and a "disconsolate Family."

Rather than selling it, Mrs. Hoskins retained her husband's interest in Capel Street for a time, and when that theatre opened on 9 November 1770, in addition to playing Diana Trapes in *The Beggar's Opera*, Mrs. Hoskins joined with Mahon and Dawson as one of the "managers" of the theatre. She acted in Limerick in the autumn of 1771, and when Capel Street closed Mrs. Hoskins went, with most of her company, to Crow Street. She continued in her accustomed line for the remainder of that and the most of the following season. On 14 January 1772 her performance was billed as her first on that stage.

When Ryder opened the Smock Alley theatre for the 1772–73 season Mrs. Hoskins was with the company, and she remained there four seasons. On 26 December 1774 a Miss Hoskins played the child's role of the Duke of York in *King Richard III*, which was probably her stage debut. (The *BD* entry for Ann Hoskins seems to contain some spurious information which does not relate to Miss Hoskin). Mrs. Hoskins accompanied the Smock Alley company to Cork in October 1776.

When the new Fishamble Street theatre opened for the first time on 27 January 1777 Mrs. Hoskins was with the company for that season, although after 11 April 1778 she moved to Crow Street, performing once more at Fishamble Street before it closed for the season. She remained at Crow Street for the following season and until 1781–82. Her daughter reappears in the 1777–78 season playing more mature roles than formerly and continues with the company until she and her mother disappear from the Dublin record in 1782.

In addition to their appearances in Dublin, Mrs. Hoskins is found in Kilkenny in October 1779, and her daughter is listed among the Limerick company at the same time. They were together at Belfast in the winter and spring of 1783 and again in the winters of 1788 and 1789. Miss Hoskins appeared in Belfast without her mother during the 1786–87 season. After acting with her mother in Derry in May 1790 Miss Hoskins disappears from the record. Her mother continued to play regularly with Atkins's company in Belfast and Derry in the 1791, 1792, 1793, 1794–95 (her benefit bills beg the public to "rescue their poor old favourite from the greatest misery and distress, and enable her to support herself in her later days without soliciting charity. . . ."), and finally, in Derry in 1799.

Miss Mary Jameson was singing in London at Vauxhall Gardens as early as 1770, and, according to the *BD*, "was clearly one of the most popular of the pleasure garden singers." Songs she had popularized at Vauxhall were published regularly citing her name as the singer. She made her stage debut at Covent Garden on 29 September 1773 as Rosetta in *Love in a Village*, billed as "a Young Lady, a pupil of Dr. Arne's." She remained at Covent Garden for the 1773–74 season singing various primary roles, and then to the Haymarket for the winter of 1774–75.

Miss Jameson, whose name in Dublin playbills is spelled variously, most frequently as "Miss Jemmeson," sang at Smock Alley and Crow Street for the 1775–76 season and at Fishamble Street and at the Rotunda in 1777. After appearing in Cork and Kilkenny in 1779 and 1780, she is back at Smock Alley for the 1781–82 through 1785–86 seasons. In October 1786 she was billed in Cork as Mrs. Arnold, "late Miss Jameson." The *BD* points out that the marriage license of Stewart Arnold and Mary Jameson is dated 1788. She sang somewhere in Ireland as the "late Miss Jameson" on 12 April 1788. She disappears from the record thereafter.

For a biography of **John Kane** see the 1771–72 season.

Lawrence Kennedy was born in Dublin around 1729, and, according to the *BD*, was on the stage by the time he was six years old; however, the Dublin playbills make no reference to any Master Kennedy. Kennedy's father performed at Bath and London at Goodman's Fields and Covent Garden in the 1740s, and was manager of the theatres in Exeter, Portsmouth, and Plymouth in the 1750s. His mother was an actress who also played in London and Bath in the mid-1740s.

Judging from the number and status of the parts Lawrence himself played in his first season at Smock Alley, he probably had made his Dublin debut some time before his first recorded performance on 7 December 1748. During that season he is cited in the playbills in a variety of secondary young men's roles. In the spring of 1749 Kennedy married Elizabeth Orfeur, one of the daughters of the actors Mr. and Mrs. Orfeur. She had performed in Dublin from as early as the 1742–43 season and was certainly a member of the Smock Alley company from 1746–47 through 1749–50. Mrs. Kennedy also sang at Crow Street Music Hall concerts in March 1750.

The Kennedys acted, mainly in secondary roles, at Smock Alley from 1749–50 through the 1759–60 season with the exception of the 1755–56 season when Kennedy was engaged in Edinburgh. The *BD* relates how, upon his return to Dublin, the Smock Alley managers at first refused to re-engage Kennedy at a salary of more than 30s. a week, while his wife was earning £4. Kennedy was outraged and confronted one of the managers "with a pistol in each hand and demanded satisfaction." He was immediately signed at £3; thereafter Kennedy was known as "Bold Larry" Kennedy. He and his wife continued to act at Smock Alley until 1759–60. Kennedy's pugnacity seemingly made him a valuable asset in certain circumstances. During the 1759–60 season, for example, when both the great mimics of the age, Samuel Foote and Tate Wilkinson, were performing in Dublin, Wilkinson ridiculed Foote in one of his pieces. The next day he was paid a visit by Foote (accompanied by Kennedy) who demanded that Wilkinson desist or he would call him to account.

Mr. and Mrs. Kennedy traveled with the touring Smock Alley company to Cork in the autumns of 1756, 1757, and 1758. The Master Kennedy who played Tom Thumb at Mrs. Kennedy's benefit on 1 April 1757 and who acted in minor roles was their son, Thomas, making his stage debut (for his biography see 1795–96 season).

The Dublin Gazette 10–14 July 1759 announced that Mr. and Mrs. Kennedy sailed for Parkgate, suggesting that they planned to perform in Scotland or England during the summer, but the record is otherwise silent until they returned to Smock Alley where they acted until the end of the 1759–60 Smock Alley season after which they traveled to London.

Mrs. Kennedy made her Drury Lane debut on 10 October 1760 and her husband his on 29 December. Clearly, Mrs. Kennedy was a favorite with Garrick and well liked by the public, but her husband performed only very occasionally. The Kennedys remained at Drury Lane until the end of the

1761–62 season, she performing several capital roles while he was consigned to the occasional minor one. When their articles were not renewed at Drury Lane, the Kennedys once again took to the provinces. They are found in Cork in the autumn of 1762 and at Edinburgh and Norwich that winter.

Kennedy joined his friend Foote at the Haymarket Theatre in the summer of 1763, but he is lost in the provinces for a time thereafter. Mr., Mrs., and Master Thomas Kennedy appeared again at Smock Alley for the 1763–64 season (not noticed in *BD*) and returned with the Smock Alley company to Cork in the autumns of 1762, 1763, and 1764. The Kennedy family moved to Crow Street for the 1764–65 season but their whereabouts for the 1765–66 and 1766–67 seasons is not known. It is possibly one of these seasons to which the *BD* refers when it says that the Kennedys were engaged in Edinburgh "in 1764." They were certainly performing regularly in Dublin during the 1763–64 and 1764–65 seasons.

Kennedy was engaged in Edinburgh for the 1767–68 season and a Kennedy acted once at Crow Street in November 1768. Kennedy is found in Stratford in the spring of 1771. In 1772 he is known to have become manager of the new theatre company in Gloucester which also performed in Bristol in 1772 and the summer of 1773. The following year he managed the theatre in Richmond for a time, also acting at the Haymarket Theatre. On 4 May 1774, while staying at their friend Younger's London home, a fire broke out and Mrs. Kennedy was killed. Kennedy, while attempting to save his wife, was severely burned and his face badly scarred.

Lawrence Kennedy continued to perform at Crow Street for the 1777–78 season. It may have been he and not his son who acted at Cork in October 1779. It was probably Lawrence also who played Sir Archy MacSarcasm in Macklin's *Love a la Mode*, "his first appearance on this stage in three years," for Clinch's benefit on 6 March 1780 at Crow Street. Kennedy performed occasionally at Smock Alley during the 1780–81 season.

Kennedy, billed as "from the Theatre Royal, Drury Lane," acted in Belfast with Atkins's company during the winter and spring of 1783; however, Kennedy is not known to have acted after this engagement. Not long after he suffered a debilitating stroke and only survived because of the generosity of his friend and fellow actor John Henderson, who gave him a small stipend. When Henderson suddenly died in November 1785, Kennedy soon became destitute. He took his own life, with a razor, on 28 June 1786 at the age of 66.

Born in Dublin in 1755, **William Macready** (his name is spelled variously, M'Cready, McCready, but here regularized to the *BD* spelling) was the son of an upholsterer. He broke his apprenticeship bonds and ran away to the Irish provinces to take to the stage. In March 1815, Macready's grandfather, who died about three years earlier, was called by the newspapers "the Father of the City of Dublin, being the oldest representative in Common Council."

Since the first record we have of his acting is in Kilkenny in August 1776, by which time he would have been 21 years old, we can assume that Macready had some experience of acting before that time. Subsequently, we have record of him at Edinburgh in 1776–77, and the *BD* thinks it possible that he is the "M'Cready" who performed at the Haymarket Theatre in December 1779. He is also known to have acted in Kilkenny in March 1781, but the record is blank otherwise until he made his Dublin debut at Truby and Watts's Capel Street theatre on 11 November 1782.

When Capel Street closed early in 1783, Macready, with several other members of that ill-fated company, traveled to Kilkenny and Belfast for the remainder of the season. Macready was engaged at Smock Alley for the 1783–84 season, acting in secondary roles, and continued there through the 1784–85 and finished the season in Cork in September. Charles Macklin evidently secured a place for Macready with Mattocks's Manchester company in January 1786. There he met Miss Birch who was also with the company and they married in June 1787. *FDJ* 1–4 July 1786 reports that "Mr. McCready, late of Smock Alley theatre we hear is engaged for a particular line of characters for three years at Covent Garden," and subsequently he made his debut on 18 September 1786, although he was to remain there for the next eleven years and not just three. Macready was a serviceable actor in secondary and tertiary roles in the line of older men and Irishmen.

Macready returned to Dublin's Crow Street theatre with other Covent Garden travelers, including J. P. Kemble, for the summer seasons of 1788, 1789, 1790, 1792 ("his first appearance these three years"), and 1793 (he also appeared at Cork in 1792 and 1793). At the end of the 1794–95 season Macready, who had never attracted a very large salary, quit Covent Garden in a argument over money. He was engaged by the proprietors of the new theatre in Birmingham as manager where he remained for the following season. Thereafter Macready had mixed success as a provincial manager, and for a time gave variety performances at London's Royalty Theatre, Wellclose Square.

Each summer from 1796 he brought a company of London "stars" to Birmingham and, often, Manchester. When he lost the lease on the Birmingham theatre in 1807, he rented the new theatre in Manchester, but was disastrously unsuccessful, went bankrupt in 1809 and was arrested for debt. Thereafter he continued to manage companies in Birmingham, Leicester, Sheffield, and Manchester, visiting Dublin and Edinburgh in 1800.

Macready also wrote a number of farces, a few of which were moderately successful, including *The Irishman in London* (1792)and *The Bank Note* (1795).

William Macready continued to manage various theatres in the British provinces (Newcastle upon Tyne, Bristol, Swansea, Cardiff) for many years. Although he seldom rose above the second rate as an actor, as a manager he was generally praised for his honesty, friendliness, and rectitude regardless of the circumstances. He died at Bristol on 9 April 1829 leaving his second wife, née Sarah Desmond, a talented actress, and four children.

The 1782–83 season sees a burgeoning of O'Neills on Irish stages. By 26 December 1782 the Capel Street bills distinguish between J. (presumably John) O'Neill and G. O'Neill both of whom play minor parts. Surprising, considering the presence of so many O'Neills the previous season, the 1783–84 season passed without a single one appearing in a playbill. John O'Neill may have been related to the O'Neill who managed a strolling company in the Irish provinces from as early as 1757 (see the 1757–58 season for his biography).

The O'Neill who was engaged by Truby and Watts at their new Capel Street theatre is identified as **John "Shane" O'Neal** by John Bernard. This season also saw the Dublin stage debut of the Miss Eliza O'Neill ("the modern Juliet"). She is probably the "Miss O'Neill" who shared a benefit with two other novices in Belfast in March 1792, but for whom no other record is available. John O'Neill remained at Capel Street until that theatre failed in January 1783. It is clearly John "Shane" O'Neill who performed in Belfast with other members of the defunct Capel Street company in the winter of 1783. Clark finds O'Neill also in Sligo (1783) and in Cork (1786 and 1795).

The name O'Neill does not appear again in the Dublin playbills until the 1812–13 season when Eliza O'Neill is found at Crow Street acting in primary roles. An O'Neill, Jr., presumably her brother, is often included in the bills with her. Before the end of the season Miss O'Neill received overtures to appear at Covent Garden but she refused to leave Dublin unless the London managers would guarantee to engage her family. She continued at Crow Street for the 1813–14 season, when "Shane O'Neal" was billed occasionally with his daughter and son. This is the last reference to him in the record.

At the end of the 1813–14 season Miss O'Neill left Dublin for London (with her family) and made her Covent Garden debut on 6 October 1814 as Juliet and was immediately popular and acted there with great success until the 1819–20, when she returned to Dublin for the first half of the season. At the end of her Dublin engagement *Carrick's Newsletter* reported that on 18 December 1819, Miss O'Neill was married at Kilfane Church, county Kilkenny, to Mr. (afterwards Sir William) Beecher, the noted Kilkenny amateur and possessor of a large fortune. *DEP* 28 Dec. 1819 reports that Beecher allowed his bride to keep her own considerable fortune, which she settled on her parents, brothers and sister, and Beecher settled a further £1,000 on his wife. During the 1820–21 season Mrs. Beecher performed at Crow Street on 18 November as Belvidera and 20 November as Mrs. Beverley. Thereafter, she retired from the stage.

For a biography of **Richard Coxe Rowe** see the 1777–78 season.

For a biography of **Mr.** and **Mrs. Tyrrell** see the 1781–82 season.

Repertory, January–June 1783

Again, the performance record for this season is very sparse; there were almost certainly many more performances than have survived in the record. The only new plays in the repertory are Miss Lee's *The Chapter of Accidents*, which had been staged regularly in Dublin since 1780, and Sheridan's afterpiece *The Critic*, which had made its Dublin debut on 14 February 1781.

Total Performances: 5, of 3 different named mainpieces; 2 of 2 different named afterpieces.
    Shakespeare: 0.
    New Mainpieces: 0.
    New Afterpieces: 2.

(For a key to repertory symbols see above, page 11)

Mainpieces: *The Chapter of Accidents*†; *The School for Scandal*; *A Word to the Wise.*
Afterpieces: *The Critic**; *Poor Vulcan*†.

Entr'acte performances: Singing: 1

Benefits (3): Atkins; Bernard; Mrs. Bernard.

January or February 1783

By permission George Black, Sovereign the theatre in Ann Street will immediately be opened by Atkins who takes this method of acquainting the ladies and gentlemen of Belfast and its vicinity that he has at great expence and trouble made the most capital engagements in the kingdom in order to prove himself once more worthy of their countenance and protection. He has also procured every new piece of merit from London and Dublin among which are the celebrated productions of *Which is the Man? The Agreeable Surprise* and *The Son-in-Law*. Mr. and Mrs. Barnard from the Theatre Royal Bath and lately from Dublin, Mrs. Hoskins from the Theatre-Royal Crow Street, Kennedy from the Theatre-Royal Drury Lane, and the celebrated Miss Jameson, confessedly the first public singer in Ireland, form a part of that company who by their earnest endeavours and assiduity to merit the favour of Belfast are not in the least apprehensive of obtaining it. [An item in 14–18 February 1783 indicates that at some time prior to that date the actor Kennedy's London house burned down and his wife "perished in the flames"]. Source: 21–24 Jan. 1783

January 1783

27 Mon. *The School for Scandal.* Charles Surface–Bernard; Joseph Surface–Macready; Sir Peter Teazle–Rowe; Lady Teazle–Mrs. Bernard; Crabtree–Cherry; Careless–Garvey. In Act 2, scene 3 the solo part in the drinking song *"Here's to the Maiden!"* was sung by the very popular Captain Garvey. Source: [Bernard 1830, 1: 195].

March 1783

14 Fri.   By desire of the ancient and honorable Society of Free and Accepted Masons of the Orange Lodge Belfast. *The Chapter of Accidents.* With *Poor Vulcan.* [*Poor Vulcan* was published in Belfast by James Magee in 1784]. With Mason songs prologues epilogues between the acts. To begin precisely at 7 o'clock. Source: 7–11 Mar. 1783

April 1783

21 Mon. Benefit of Bernard. *A Word to the Wise* with a variety of interludes to which will be added a new entertainment of three acts never performed here called *The Critic*. Source: 15–18 Apr. 1783.

May 1783

16 Fri.   [Program unavailable]. Atkins thanks the ladies and gentlemen of Belfast who attended his benefit night at the theatre on this night. Source: 16–20 May 1783

19 Mon. [No program available]. [In the source issue Mrs. Bernard thanks the Earl of Donegall, the ladies and gentlemen of Belfast and other members of the "brilliant assemblage" that gathered on the occasion of her benefit night]. Source: 20–23 May 1783

June 1783

Commentary: (3–6 June 1783) Many of the ladies and gentlemen who have subscribed to the theatre for this season would be glad to know the manager's reasons for not sending them their transferable tickets on stock nights and whether he does this in order to prejudice such of the benefits of the performers as are yet to come as surely such treatment must greatly incense the subscribers in general who have had but very little entertainment for their money this season.

Commentary: (13–17 June 1783) Atkins takes this method of returning his thanks to those respectable gentlemen who have honoured him with a subscription for his new theatre and informs them he has taken a lot of ground in Rosemary Lane an excellent and central situation and assures them that the theatre will be opened early in the ensuing winter. From his experience of the liberality of the Belfast audience he is determined to spare no trouble or expence to render the building for beauty and convenience equal to any house in the kingdom. He will also make the capital engagement in regard to his performers. It shall be his constant study by the most attention to prove himself as deserving as possible of so respectable a countenance as that of the inhabitants of Belfast.

Commentary: [Clark 1965, 246, indicates that the project detailed below, proposed in opposition to Atkins's new theatre, failed to attract much support and the plan was put in abeyance]. (13–17 June 1783) Theatre Ann Street Belfast. Myrton Hamilton with the utmost respect begs leave to inform the ladies and gentlemen of Belfast that as the theatre in Ann Street being at times too small for the reception of the audience proposes to enlarge it by subscription on the following plan. That each subscriber shall pay ten guineas for which he shall be entitled to one transferable ticket to admit one person to the pit for each performance for ten years the benefits excepted. No more than twenty subscribers to be received. The proprietor binds himself to make the theatre ten feet wider and five feet higher than it now is and to have it boxed round after the manner of Smock Alley Theatre with a box-room in the front for servants to wait in. The subscription-money to be deposited in the hands of one of the subscribers as the proprietor of said theatre at his sole expence prepared it in the best manner the size would admit of for the reception of the publick. The old house in Mill Street being a disgrace to the drama he therefore flatters himself this second improvement will meet with their approbation. Those who choose to encourage this undertaking are requested to give their names to McIlwrath at Blow's, Robert Smith, Bridge Street Belfast, or to Hamilton Armagh.

1783–1784 SEASON

Venue: Rosemary Lane Theatre. [John Bernard took Atkins's Belfast company to the Derry theatre during the time that the Rosemary Lane Theatre was being built. The new theatre had opened by 3 March. Thereafter the old playhouse in Ann Street was used occasionally for amateur theatricals].
Company: Atkins; Mr. and Mrs. Bernard; Andrew Cherry; Duncan; Kane; Richard Rowe; Tyrrell.

For biography of **Michael Atkins** see the 1767–68 season.

For biographies of **Mr.** and **Mrs. John Bernard** see the 1782–83 season.

For a biography of **Andrew Cherry** see the 1782–83 season.

The *BD* probably errs in stating that **Timothy Duncan's** first notice was at Smock Alley in 1766. The Duncan who acted in the supernumerary role of Triton in the new pantomime of *Mercury Harlequin in Ireland; or, The Rape of Colombine* at Crow Street many times during the 1763–64 season may well have been our subject. Duncan then played tertiary roles at Smock Alley from 1766–67 through 1770–71. Duncan was with the combined company that Mossop took to Limerick in October 1768. The *HM* Apr. 1771 contains a "Scale of Merit" comparing the casts of the Smock Alley and Capel Street companies in *The West Indian* that season. Duncan is rated last of the men in the company, which included Mossop and Heaphy.

Duncan made his first voyage to England on 25 March 1771 and a few months later is found at Newcastle. For several years Duncan surfaces only intermittently. In the autumn of 1778 he was with Austin's company at Chester and there married the actress, Miss Legg, who had probably recently made her stage debut there. He and his wife continued at Chester until the autumn of 1780. They were probably acting at Liverpool in 1784, when their daughter, Maria Rebecca, was born.

The Duncans appeared in Belfast at Atkins's newly opened Rosemary Lane theatre for the 1783–84 season, although he is listed in only one role, that of Maj. O'Flaherty in *The West Indian*. *The Belfast Mercury* of 5 March 1784 praised him: "It is usual to represent the Major as a vulgar brogueineering Irishman; but Duncan with true propriety, tho' he still retained the Irish characteristics in his terminations, showed O'Flaherty the man of travel, of Mars, of the world." Later that season Duncan is listed singing a new song *"The Gift of the Gods; or, Establishment of Irish Freedom."* The nature of these performances suggests that by this time Duncan has established himself in the line of middle-class Irishmen.

The Duncans are found in Edinburgh for the 1784–85 season, then they made their London debut at Covent Garden in September 1788, billed as "from Chester." Evidently, they did not have great success in London and the Duncans were engaged at Crow Street for the 1788–89 season, billed as "from the Theatre Royal, Covent Garden, first appearance on this stage." Acting mainly in secondary roles, the Duncans remained at Crow Street as mainstays of the company through the 1794–95 season. Their daughter, Miss Maria Rebecca Duncan (later the very successful actress Mrs. Davison), made her stage debut sometime before 24 April 1789 when she played Tom Thumb billed as "a child of eight years; her second appearance." Mrs. Duncan's appearances were sporadic (in 1792–93 season she is not found in the record).

For the first time in nine years the Duncans did not appear at Crow Street for the 1795–96 regular season, playing instead with Atkins's company in Belfast and Derry. They returned to Crow Street for the 1796 summer season, during which Miss Duncan played a wide variety of ingenue roles with considerable success. They continued at Crow Street for 1796–97 and then traveled to England.

The Duncans are found at Leeds in June 1797 and at York in 1797, billed as "from Dublin." They continued there through 1800. They were engaged in Edinburgh in 1801, but Timothy Duncan died in February. Mrs. Duncan seems to have left the stage after her husband's death.

For a biography of **John Kane** see the 1771–72 season.

For a biography of **Richard Coxe Rowe** see the 1777–78 season.

For biographies of **Mr.** and **Mrs. Tyrrell** see the 1781–82 season.

Repertory, December 1783–July 1784

Despite the small number of surviving playbills it would seem that Atkins continued to provide his audiences with a considerable number of fairly new plays. O'Keeffe's very popular comic opera *The Dead Alive* had been attracting audiences in Dublin since 1781. The play evidently had a special attraction for the citizens of Belfast because that year it was published there by both James Magee and by a Company of Stationers. Delap's *The Royal Suppliants* had made its Dublin premiere in 1781 also, but with much less success, although it had been published by a company of booksellers in Dublin. The sole afterpiece to make its putative Belfast debut this year was O'Keeffe's *The Son-in-Law*, which also had come out for the first time in Dublin in 1781.

Total Performances: 11 of 9 different named mainpieces; 5, of 5 different named afterpieces.
    Shakespeare: 0.
    New Mainpieces: 0.
    New Afterpieces: 0.

(For a key to repertory symbols see above, page 11)

Mainpieces: *A Bold Stroke for a Wife; Cato; The Dead Alive*†; *The Fair Penitent; Gustavus Vasa; The Jealous Wife; The Royal Suppliants*†; *The Tempest;* Unspecified "play"; *The West Indian*(2).

Afterpieces: *The Agreeable Surprise*†; *The Devil to Pay; Miss in Her Teens; Robinson Crusoe*†; *The Son-in-Law*†; Unspecified "farce."

Entr'acte entertainments: Singing and Dancing: 0.

Benefits (5): Freemasons; Kane; the Poor(2); Rowe.

December 1783

11 Thur. Benefit of the Poor. *The West Indian* with *Miss in Her Teens.* The characters by the officers of this garrison. No person to be admitted behind the scenes on any account. [12–16 December 1783 gives the receipts for this performance and offers special thanks to the officers of the garrison regiment. The gross receipts totaled £49. 6s. 5d.; the net receipts "after defraying expenses" were £38. 10s. 3d. This is the first documentary evidence we have of "house charges" of the Belfast theatres and indicates that such charges were about £10, or one-fifth of the gross. Of course, these charges do not include a deduction for the actors' salaries since the play was performed by amateurs]. Source: 2–5 December 1783

March 1784

3 Wed. *The West Indian.* Belcour–Bernard; Old Dudley–Kane; Maj. O'Flaherty–Duncan; Varland–Cherry; Charlotte–Mrs. Bernard. With the musical entertainment of *The Son-in-Law.* Boxes and lattices 3s. 3d., pit 2s. 2d., gallery 1s. 1d. Ladies and gentlemen who take places in boxes are requested to send their servants to keep them at six o'clock and such servants will be admitted into the gallery that they may be always ready to answer the commands of their respective masters and mistresses. Half price after nine and no admittance on any account behind the scenes. Cast in *BM* 5 Mar. 1784, which observes of Duncan as Maj. O'Flaherty that: "It is usual to represent the Major as a vulgar brogueineering Irishman; but Duncan with true propriety, tho' he still retained the Irish characteristics in his terminations, showed O'Flaherty the man of travel, of Mars, of the world." [Clark 1965, 246 thinks this is the opening night of the new theatre in Rosemary Lane. While it was being erected "Atkins sent his players under John Bernard to perform in Derry and Sligo"]. Source: 27 Feb.–2 Mar. 1784.

April 1784

28 Wed. *The Dead Alive.* [Published in Belfast by James Magee in 1785]. Source: *BM* 30 Apr. 1784

May 1784

5 Wed. *The Fair Penitent* and *Robinson Crusoe; or, Harlequin Friday.* Source: *BM* 4 and 7 May 1784

7   Fri.   Benefit of the Masons of Orange Lodge 257. *Cato.* Cato–Rowe; Marcia–Mrs. Bernard. Source: 7–11 May 1784

26 Wed.   Benefit of Rowe. *A Bold Stroke for a Wife.* With the favourite farce of [*The Devil to Pay; or,*] *The Wives Metamorphosed.* Source: 21–25 May 1784

June 1784

23 Wed.   *The Royal Suppliants.* With a new song *"The Gift of the Gods; or, Establishment of Irish Freedom"* by Duncan. Source: *BM* 11 June 1784

25 Fri.   Benefit of John Kane. *The Tempest.* Source: *BM* 22 June 1784

July 1784

7   Wed.   Benefit of Cherry. *Gustavus Vasa.* Source: 2–6 July 1784

13 Tues.   *The Jealous Wife* and *The Agreeable Surprise.* [The afterpiece was published in Belfast by James Magee in 1785]. In honour of the Earl of Charlemont, commander-in-chief of the Irish Volunteers. Source: *BM* 20 July 1784

19 Mon.   Benefit of the Poor. [Play and farce as will be expressed in the bills]. [This performance was attended by twenty-four of the young ladies of Mr. Ware's select boarding school (Clark 1965, 250)]. Source: 13–16 July 1784

[In August the company moved its activities to Lisburn until mid-November].

1784–1785 SEASON

Venue: Because of rumors that a windstorm had damaged the roof of the Rosemary Lane playhouse, Atkins undertook repairs to the structure which delayed the opening of this season.
Company: Atkins; Cherry; Mrs. George Dawson; Kane; Richard Rowe; Mrs. James Swendall [usually spelled Swindall]; Miss Usher. In June Sarah Siddons and Miss Anne Kemble played in Belfast. Mr. Best "comedian" has married Miss Mary Russell in Belfast. (3–7 June 1785).

For biography of **Michael Atkins** see the 1767–68 season.

For a biography of **Andrew Cherry** see the 1782–83 season.

For a biography of **Mrs. George Dawson** see the 1769–70 season.

For a biography of **John Kane** see the 1771–72 season.

For a biography of **Richard Coxe Rowe** see the 1777–78 season.

Mrs. James Swendall (usually spelled Swindall in Ireland) née Jane Bannister, was the daughter of the singer Charles Bannister (1741–1804) and his wife, and the sister of the very popular actor John Bannister (1760–1836). She made her stage debut at the Haymarket Theatre in August 1783 and the following two seasons acted with her family at Drury Lane. In its biographical sketch of Jane Bannister the authors of the *BD* find an hiatus in her career from 1785 through the summer of 1788, and are unaware of her Belfast engagement this season.

The date of the Swendalls' marriage is problematic. The *BD* suggests that the marriage did not occur until sometime around the summer of 1790 (the couple was engaged with the Brighton company for the summer of 1788 and, again, in the summer of 1790). When they appeared at Crow Street for the 1789–90 season, Mrs. Swendall was billed as "the late Miss Bannister, her first appearance in this kingdom." It is, of course, possible that James Swendall married twice, but it seems more likely that the couple had married sometime before Mrs. Swendall's Belfast engagement in 1784.

After 1790 Mrs. Swendall's career parallels that of her husband. Although the record is spotty for the next decade, they performed at Stephen Kemble's new theatre in Edinburgh for the 1792–93 season then at Richmond (1795 and 1797), Manchester (1796), and Birmingham (1798). James made his last appearances in London at the Haymarket Theatre in June 1799, after which he and his wife are found again in Edinburgh in early 1800. Swendall acted at Coventry, Brighton, and on the Manchester-Chester circuit from 1803 through 1806, which theatres he managed for a time in 1802–03.

The Swendalls were still acting, in Brighton, in the summers of 1809 and 1810, but after that they disappear from the record. Mrs. Swendall was still alive in 1829.

Miss Usher was probably the daughter of the actors Mr. and Mrs. Howard Usher, for whose biographies see the summer season 1761 above. Little is known about her career. The *BD* quotes John Taylor's *The Records* *of My Life* (1832) where it is stated that Miss Usher "was a provincial actress of some repute." In addition to this Belfast appearance, she is known to have acted in Bristol (1778–79) and in Ennis (January and March 1790).

Mrs. Sarah Siddons was the greatest actress of the latter half of the eighteenth century and the details of her life are too well-known to merit more than a brief sketch here. Born in Wales in 1755, the eldest of twelve children, several of whom became famous on the English stage, Sarah Kemble got her early training as a member of her father's strolling company which played in the towns of northern and western England in the 1760s. She married the provincial actor William Siddons in November 1773 and made her London debut at Covent Garden in December 1775, shortly after giving birth to her first child. Her debut was inauspicious due, evidently, to her stage fright. She was released from Drury Lane and spent the next seven seasons acting in the provinces. At Bath her playing of pathetic roles reduced her audience to tears. She was cultivated by the Duchess of Devonshire, who induced the Drury Lane manager, R. B. Sheridan, to engage her in 1782, by which time she had delivered five children.

Her return to the Drury Lane stage occurred in October 1782 and from the first night it was clear that she would dominate the stage in tragic roles for years to come. Within a week the Drury Lane managers "ceremoniously gave her Garrick's dressing room on the stage level." Mrs. Siddons remained the principal actress of Drury Lane, and, later, Covent Garden theatre throughout her career. Such was her energy (and her acquisitiveness, according to her enemies) that at the end of most seasons she would go on tour in the English provinces, Scotland, and Ireland.

She visited Ireland frequently: in 1783 (Smock Alley, June–Aug; Cork, Aug); 1784 (Smock Alley, June–Aug; Cork, September; she was advertised to appear in Belfast this summer but canceled due to ill health); 1785 (Belfast, June); 1793–94 (Crow Street, December–May); 1802–03 (Crow Street, May–August; Limerick, August; Cork and Belfast, September–October; Crow Street November–March, Cork, March); 1805 (Crow Street, July–August); 1807 (Belfast, August)

Mrs. Siddons retired from the stage at the end of the 1811–12 season although she gave occasional benefit performances until 1819. She died on 31 May 1831 at the age of 76.

The **Miss Anne Julia Kemble** who played in Belfast this season was Sarah Siddons's younger sister, Ann (1764–1838). The seventh of the children of Roger and Sarah Kemble, she showed little interest in the stage in her early years but at about this time decided to try her hand at acting, a desire that her elder sister evidently indulged. She was probably the Miss Kemble who played Smock Alley with Sarah Siddons in the summer of 1783, although she was then billed as being from the Theatre Royal, Drury Lane, and there survives no record of her having performed in London at this time.

By October 1783 she had married a provincial actor named Curtis, but she was made destitute when it was discovered that Curtis was already married and the two separated. In 1792 she married William Hatton, who may have been an actor, and the two traveled to New York. In America she became noted for singing patriotic songs in the theatres, and for her play, *Tammany; or, The Indian Chief*, which was produced in New York, Philadelphia and Boston. She also gave readings of the works of Dryden, Milton, Sterne, and others.

By 1800 the Hattons were back in England. Ann was given an allowance of £100 a year by her sister, Sarah, and her brothers. Some allege that the allowance was given with the provision that she reside at least 100 miles from London. She and her husband settled in Swansea where they kept a hotel. In later life Ann Hatton wrote more than a dozen moderately successful novels and romances and several volumes of poetry. She died in 1838.

Repertory, December 1784–July 1785

The record of performances for the regular season, between December and May, is very sparse. The most novel attraction was *The Follies of a Day*, Giordani's rendition of Beaumarchais's *The Barber of Saville*, which had attracted large audiences in Dublin ever since its debut scarcely a month earlier, in February 1785. Frances Brooke's popular comic opera *Rosina* had first been performed in Dublin in March 1783, and the fact that the playwright was an Irishwoman no doubt helped it to draw.

Total mainpiece performances: 19 of 11 different named mainpieces; 11 of 7 different named pieces.
    Shakespeare: 1.
    New Mainpieces: 1.
    New Afterpieces: 0.

(For a key to repertory symbols see above, page 11)

Mainpieces: *Cato; Douglas; The Follies of a Day**; *The Gamester; The Grecian Daughter* (2); *Isabella*(3); *Jane Shore; Macbeth; The Mourning Bride; The Recruiting Officer;* Unspecified "play"; *Venice Preserved*(2).

Afterpieces: *The Agreeable Surprise; The Citizen; Peeping Tom*†(2); *The Poor Soldier*† (2); *Poor Vulcan*(2); *Rosina*†; *Thomas and Sally;* Unspecified "farce".

Entr'acte entertainments: Singing and Dancing: 0.

Benefits (4): Miss Kemble; the Poor; Mrs. Siddons; Volunteers.

December 1784

8 Wed. *Isabella.* Isabella–Mrs. James Swendall. With *Poor Vulcan.* Venus–Mrs. George Dawson. Source: *BM* 7 and 10 Dec. 1784

10 Fri. *The Grecian Daughter.* Euphrasia–Miss Usher (first time on this stage). Source: *BM* 10 Dec. 1784.

January 1785

19 Wed. By desire of the master wardens and brethren of the Orange Lodge 257. [Unspecified play and farce]. The particulars will be expressed in the bills of the day. Source: 14–17 Jan. 1785

March 1785

28 Mon. Never performed here. *The Follies of a Day; or, The Marriage of Figaro.* With (by desire) the farce of *The Poor Soldier.* [*The Poor Soldier* was published in Belfast by James Magee this year]. Source: 22–25 Mar. 1785

April 1785

11 Mon. Volunteers' Benefit. *Cato.* Cato–Rowe. Source: 22–25 Mar. 1785

June 1785

Commentary: (31 May–3 June 1785) A report being circulated that the roof and gallery of the playhouse were not sufficient. We by desire of a number of ladies and gentlemen of the town as well as Atkins have examined them and think them perfectly safe and secure. [signed] Roger Mulholland and John Russell. (31 May–3 June 1785) Atkins informs the ladies and gentlemen of Belfast and its vicinity that Mrs. Siddons engagement commences the second week in June. Timely notice will be given of the particular day. In the course of her nights she will perform her most favorite characters of Belvidera, the Grecian Daughter, Zara and Lady Randolph. Atkins with the greatest respect informs his friends that no credit can be given for tickets and that servants who keep places in the boxes cannot be admitted as usual into the gallery gratis. Boxes 6s. 6d., Pit 5s. 5d., Gallery 3s. 3d. [As early as December 1784 the *BNL* was announcing that Mrs. Siddons would visit Belfast, either before or after her engagement in Edinburgh (3–7 December 1784)].

6 Mon. *Venice Preserved.* Belvidera–Mrs. Siddons. The first of Mrs. Siddons's nights. The ladies were encouraged not to wear hats, bonnets or feathers to the performance so that "the ladies who have places in the second or back seats of the boxes will see equally well with those in the front." [Receipts: £64. 7s. 6d. Gross receipts for each of the ten of Mrs. Siddons's Belfast were published in the *BM* 28 June 1785 and are cited by Clark 257. A total of £716. 15s. [but see below, 27 June] was taken during her engagement of which she received £210. plus the £113. of her benefit night. Atkins had advertised that Mrs. Siddons would receive a fee of £30. per night and one benefit "clear of all house charges" (Clark 253)]. Source: *BM* 7 June 1785 and 31 May–3 June 1785

8 Wed. Mrs. Siddons second night. *The Mourning Bride.* Almeria–Miss Kemble; Zara–Mrs. Siddons. With the farce of *Peeping Tom of Coventry.* [*Peeping Tom* was published in Belfast by James Magee this year]. Receipts: £83. 7s. 6d. Source: 3–7 June 1785

10 Fri.   Mrs. Siddons third night. *Jane Shore.* Alicia–Miss Kemble. With *Thomas and Sally.* [Receipts: £116. 12s. 0d. Performance was reviewed very favorably in 10–14 June 1785]. Source: 7–10 June 1785

13 Mon. *The Grecian Daughter.* [Receipts: £101. 18s. 6d.] Source: 7–10 June 1785

15 Wed. *The Gamester.* Mrs. Beverly–Mrs. Siddons; Charlotte–Miss Kemble. With *Poor Vulcan.* The ladies and gentlemen of Belfast will do everything in their power to accommodate those ladies and gentlemen who may come from the country with places. [Receipts: £120. 0s. 6d.] Source: 10–14 June 1785

17 Fri.   *Isabella.* Isabella–Mrs. Siddons. With *The Poor Soldier.* [Receipts: £130. 0s. 0d.]. Source: 14–17 June 1785

20 Mon. *Douglas.* Lady Randolph– Mrs. Siddons; Old Norval–Rowe. and *Peeping Tom of Coventry.* [Receipts: £120. 9s. 0d.] Source: 14–17 June 1785

22 Wed. Benefit of Mrs. Siddons and the last night but one of her engagement. *Venice Preserved.* Belvidera–Mrs. Siddons. With *The Agreeable Surprise.* [Receipts: £113. 13s. 0d.] Source: 17–21 June 1785

24 Fri. Benefit of Miss Kemble. *Isabella.* Isabella–Mrs. Siddons. With the farce of *The Citizen.* Maria–Miss Kemble. [Receipts: £98. 17s. 6d.] Source: 21–24 June 1785

27 Mon. Benefit of the Poor. *Macbeth.* Lady Macbeth–Mrs. Siddons. [Receipts: £106. 0s. 0d. 28 June–1 July 1785 lists the total receipts for the ten nights of Mrs. Siddons's acting as £1036. Mrs. Siddons evidently had considered engaging in Belfast for another series of plays later in the summer, but she withdrew her engagement because "her late indisposition renders it impracticable for her to make good both her engagements to Cork and this place and be in London as early as the time appointed for her appearing there (13–17 August 1784). In July the *BNL* first suggested that Mrs. Siddons would not be coming to Belfast (20–23 July 1784), then it announced that "The expectation of Mrs. Siddons acting here is again revived through the friendly attention of Mrs. O'Neill" who had "positively engaged" Mrs. Siddons to act three nights "in the beginning of September" (27–30 July 1784)]. Source: *BM* 1 July 1785.

July 1785

13 Wed. *The Recruiting Officer* with a musical entertainment of *Rosina; or, Love in a Cottage.* There will be plays on Thursday, Friday and Saturday. Source: 8–12 July 1785

14 Thur. [Program unavailable, see performance of 13 July 1785].

15 Fri. [Program unavailable, see performance of 13 July 1785].

16 Sat. [Program unavailable, see performance of 13 July 1785].

29 Fri. *Dinwiddie's lecture on electricity.* Pit 2s. 2d., Gallery 1s. 1d. Source: 26–29 July 1785

1785–1786 SEASON

[The Belfast Company spent the 1785–86 season in Derry].

1786–1787 SEASON

Venue: Rosemary Lane.
Company: Atkins; Mrs. Achmet (from the Theatre Royal, Smock Alley); Byrne; Andrew Cherry?; Mrs. Collins; Master Collins; Mrs. George Dawson; James Fotteral (from Theatre Royal, Smock Alley); Mr. and Mrs. Freeman (from Theatre Royal, York); Miss Hoskins; Mr. and Mrs. Charles Lee Lewes (from Theatre Royal, Covent Garden); Tyrrell; Mrs. Thomas [Sarah Hoare] Ward. Summer season: Miss Anne Brunton.

For biography of **Michael Atkins** see the 1767–68 season.

Mrs. Achmet was the stage name of Catherine Ann Egan, later, Mrs. William Cairns. Catherine Ann Egan, the daughter of a Kilkenny surgeon and a Miss O'Neill of Dublin, was born in 1766. The *BD* suggests that Miss Egan was the toast of Dublin before her first appearance on the stage, and this perhaps helps to explain the unusual circumstance of her being engaged to play six nights at Smock Alley on 8 November 1784 billed as "a Young Lady, a pupil to Dr. [Samuel] White, her first time on any stage." The reviewer for the *DMP* 11 Nov. 1784 wrote that the first performance was witnessed by "a numerous and brilliant audience: the performance was anteceded by a prologue (written by Mr. White) fraught with the keenest strokes of wit, and admirably applicable to the present times. The young lady announced for the first appearance was received with every mark of approbation that her unrivaled performance could merit." However, "The indecencies of the play are such, that, we trust, it will not in haste insult the ears of a polite audience!—it was Imoinda's choice; Mr. Daly, therefore, stands perfectly excused."

At some point between December 1784 and November 1785 Miss Egan assumed the stage name of Mrs. Achmet. This was the result of her having married William Cairns (a.k.a. Patrick Joyce, of Kilkenny) the perpetrator of one of the most successful scams of this period. Posing as Dr. Achmet, an expatriate Turk, Cairns or Joyce, came to Dublin and convinced the populace of the efficacy of Turkish steam baths for their health. He constructed the Royal Patent Baths on Bachelor's Quay and until his disguise was penetrated was the darling of Dublin society with his elaborate adventure tales. He extracted considerable money to support the baths from the Irish parliament.

During the 1785–86 Smock Alley season, Mrs. Achmet continued to attract large audiences, particularly on the nights when she played in breeches parts, of which she performed several, such as Sir Harry Wildair in *The Constant Couple*. Again, she performed a limited engagement of six nights, which was later extended a further six.

Mrs. Achmet spent the beginning of the 1786–87 season with Michael Atkins's company in Belfast on a limited engagement which, again, was extended. According to the bills, Mrs. Achmet was "the first female ornament of the Irish stage, a lady possessed of most uncommon abilities for a number of nights." By this time she had come under the tutelage and protection of the actor Lee Lewes.

Her return to Smock Alley for the 1787–88 season was advertised as her "first appearance here these two years." Her roles were more substantial, and she was seen to perform well with Joseph Holman, the current rage of London, who was visiting Dublin after a dispute about salaries with the Covent Garden manager. She was articled this time for the full season and was given the unusual privilege of two benefits. The following season she played at Smock Alley again, and again was well received, particularly in breeches parts. As early as 29 November a correspondent in the *Dublin Evening Post* wrote: "Of Mrs. Achmet, what shall we say? for she has so often assumed the breeches during this season, that we know not whether to consider her as a woman or a man."

Perhaps at the encouragement of Joseph Holman, who had ended his squabble with the Covent Garden managers, Mrs. Achmet made her London debut there in September 1789. London reviewers admired her person but were unenthusiastic about her acting ability. Although she appeared occasionally in subsequent bills, she was not a success in London and by early winter 1790 she is found in Limerick and Ennis. In the provinces she evidently charmed "a Theatrical Baronet of Limerick who has an amiable wife and family," but the public was outraged and would no longer allow her to perform on stage there. By mid-April 1791 she had eloped from her husband and evidently traveled to England where she may have performed briefly at Shrewsbury and York. Thereafter she disappears from the record.

For biography of **Byrne** (violinist) see the 1778–79 season.

For a biography of **Mrs. John Collins** and **Master Collins** see 1775–76 season.

It is not possible to determine from the playbills if **Mrs. George Dawson**, whose husband, the popular comedian, had died in February 1787, acted in Belfast this season or merely was given a sympathy benefit. For a biography of Mrs. Dawson see the 1769–70 season.

For a biography of **James Fotteral** see the 1769–70 season.

The identities of the **Mr.** and **Mrs. Freeman** who are listed as members of Atkins's company in Belfast this season (not noticed in *BD*) and who were billed as "from the Theatre Royal, York," are unclear. They had no Dublin record. The authors of the *BD* speculate that Freeman may be the man who played at the Haymarket Theatre from as early as 1778 and again in 1780 and 1785.

Mr. and Mrs. Freeman returned to Belfast for the 1788–89 season and sang regularly. A Mr. and Mrs. Freeman are also found at Manchester in 1790, at Exeter in 1794 and at Liverpool in 1797. Mr. Freeman sang at the concert at Arthur Street, Belfast, in December 1798.

For a biography of **Miss Hoskins** see the 1782–83 season.

Charles Lee Lewes had a long career in London before appearing on the Dublin stage. Lewes began acting at an early age, and appeared in minor roles in London by 1760, although he spent most of his youth with various strolling companies in the provinces. By 1767 he had changed the spelling of his name from Lewis to Lewes, perhaps, the *BD* speculates, "to distinguish himself from Philip Lewis, still a member of the Covent Garden Company."

Lewes was particularly adept in pantomime and spent the 16 seasons from 1767 through 1782–83 with the Covent Garden company. At the end of that season, he quarreled with the Covent Garden manager, Harris, and left London for a time, delivering his version of Stevens's very popular *"Lecture upon Heads"* monologue in Paris. The following season he was engaged at Drury Lane, but there he was in competition for many of the parts in his line and his career began to decline. He visited Cork in the autumn of 1784.

In the autumn of 1786 Lewes and his third wife, Catherine Maria Lewes, visited Cork and Waterford. Lewes declined the salary offered by Harris for the 1789 season, acting instead in the provinces. Lewes returned briefly to London and then decided to seek his fortune in India, where he was unsuccessful, and he soon returned. In the summer of 1789 he was acting in Margate, but was acting in benefits at Covent Garden in the spring of 1790 and in following winter, but he was not engaged at either of the London theatres at the time.

Lewes's career was clearly in decline when he made his first appearance in Dublin in the 1792–93 season. He visited Dublin again in 1794 (also visiting Kilkenny and Cork). In December 1794 he gave six performances in Belfast acting in a few roles and delivering his *"Lecture upon Heads."* The appearance was billed as his "first here these eight years."

Lee Lewes acted at Crow Street for the 1796–97 season, and is found in Drogheda, Cork and Kilkenny in 1797. His last recorded Irish performance is in Belfast in 1800. Thereafter Charles Lee Lewes returned to England and acted, briefly, at Sheffield. He advertised that he planned to set sail in the near future for America but he evidently changed his mind. Lewes took his farewell benefit on 24 June 1803 at Covent Garden and he died two days later, on 26 June 1803. The *BD* says that John Genest "thought Lewes to be a good actor whose sense of self-importance caused the loss of his career."

Lewes's third wife, Catherine Maria, made her stage debut billed as "A Lady" in Belfast on 20 December 1786. A correspondent in *BNL* who reviewed the performance observed that "her person and voice threaten to be insuperable bars to her arriving at eminence in the profession." Indeed, her career was not brilliant. Subsequent to leaving Belfast she played at Derby in 1788–89 and 1789–90. She made her debut at Covent Garden on 16 July 1790 but acted only one night there and another at the Haymarket Theatre in March 1791. She is found in Edinburgh from 1792 through 1795, acting mainly secondary and tertiary roles, although she did attempt the occasional capital part, such as Lady Macbeth and Lady Randolph, in *Douglas*. Catherine Maria Lewes died in early March 1796 in Edinburgh.

For a biography of **Tyrrell** see the 1781–82 season.

The Mrs. Ward appearing in Belfast between February and April in young woman's roles, breeches parts, and singing Scottish songs is probably **Mrs. Thomas Achurch (Sarah Hoare) Ward.** Although Mrs. Ward was regularly engaged at Drury Lane from 1782–83 through 1792–93, the *London Stage* does not record any performances for her from 8 February to 14 April 1787, and it is conceivable that she was visiting Belfast with Lee

Lewes at this time. In any event, no other Mrs. Ward of sufficient talents to perform in the roles listed is known to have been active at this time.

The **Miss Anne Brunton** who visited Dublin and Belfast in July and August 1787 was the eldest daughter of the actor-manager John Brunton, Sr. (1741–1822). She was to become one of the most important Anglo-American actresses of the period 1786 through 1808.

Anne made her stage debut at Bristol in February 1785 at the age of 16 in the demanding role of Euphrasia in *The Grecian Daughter*. She was received enthusiastically in Bristol and in Bath, where she performed the part a few weeks later to thunderous applause. Such was her talent that in the summer of 1785 Harris, the Covent Garden manager, engaged her for three years in hopes of giving competition to the great Sarah Siddons, who was performing at Drury Lane.

Anne Brunton made her Covent Garden debut on 17 October 1785 as Horatia in *The Roman Father*. The critics were unanimous in their praise for her potential, but most also felt that she was "being brought along too quickly." That summer Miss Brunton acted in Norwich, Bath, Bristol, Birmingham and Liverpool. In late August she traveled to Cork and made her Irish debut there on 14 August 1786. The following season at Covent Garden she essayed several new roles in tragedy, but the critics continued to have reservations about her youth.

Miss Brunton made her Smock Alley debut on 19 June 1787 billed as "from the Theatre Royal, Covent Garden, first appearance on this stage." In the weeks that followed she played most of the roles for which she had won praise in London. Dublin audiences marveled at her range and power. *The Hibernian Magazine* for July 1787 included a memoir and portrait of Miss Brunton.

As soon as she had finished her Dublin engagement, Miss Brunton traveled to Belfast in August 1787 and was received enthusiastically. A correspondent in *BNL* gave her high praise: "Though the combined effect of so much youth, beauty, and grace, interests every auditor in her favour, it is no more than a just, though high, compliment to allege, that her style of acting is, in an uncommon degree, simple unaffected and natural. In tender passages she has a softness and delicacy of manner which cannot fail to please the most rigid critic."

After leaving Belfast Miss Brunton returned to Covent Garden from 1787–88 until February 1792. She married the poet Robert Merry in 1791 and evidently retired from the stage for a time at the instance of his family. The couple went to France, but the excesses of the Reign of Terror forced their return to London. At that time Mrs. Merry met Thomas Wignell, the manager of the Philadelphia theatre, who was on a recruiting visit to London. She signed with Wignell and sailed for America in September 1796. Mrs. Merry made her successful Philadelphia debut at the Chestnut Street Theatre on 5 December 1796. She traveled to Baltimore and New York in the next months and was always warmly applauded.

After her husband Robert died on 24 December 1798 Mrs. Merry toured the major American cities for several years. According to the *BD* by 1792 "she was probably the dominant actress on the American stage and perhaps the most gracious." In January 1803 she married the Philadelphia manager Thomas Wignell, who died a short seven weeks later. She was now co-proprietor of the Chestnut Street theatre and acted there for the ensuing seasons. On 28 August 1806 she married her manager William Warren.

Mrs. Warren gave her final performance on 23 May 1808. A few weeks later she "was seized with a violent illness" of the brain, had a miscarriage, and died on 28 June 1808 at Alexandria, Virginia. One obituary said: "In her death the American stage has been deprived of its brightest ornament. . . ."

Repertory, October 1786–August 1787

Leonard McNally's *Fashionable Levities* had premiered in Dublin in April 1786. It was remarkable only insofar as it was written by an Irishman. Miles P. Andrews's play, *The Reparation,* was performed only once and is one of the few plays performed in Belfast that was evidently not performed in Dublin beforehand. Sheridan's *A Trip to Scarborough* had been acted in Dublin since May 1781. Nothing is known about the play, *The World,* written by the Belfast teacher, Mr. Eccles. From the mid-1750s a William Eccles operated a grocery store where he gave lessons in writing. In the 1760s Eccles gave up the grocery and dedicated himself to teaching ladies and gentlemen to write French. He died sometime between this year and February 1800, when his widow, "the relict of William Eccles," died. Arthur Murphy's farce *The Upholsterer* had been acted in Dublin since 1758 but evidently not in Belfast.

Total Performances: 27 of 19 different plays; 24 of 13 different named afterpieces.
        Shakespeare: 4.

New Mainpieces: 3.
New Afterpieces: 1.

(For a key to repertory symbols see above, page 11)

Mainpieces: *As You Like It; The Constant Couple; The Fair Penitent; Fashionable Levities*; The Grecian Daughter; Hamlet; The Jealous Wife; Lionel and Clarissa; The Maid of the Mill; A Man of the World*†; *Much Ado About Nothing* (2); *The Orphan; The Reparation*†; *Robin Hood*†; *The Roman Father* (2); *Romeo and Juliet*(2); *Rule a Wife; A Trip to Scarborough**; Unspecified "play"(2); *The World* Θ.

Afterpieces: *The Agreeable Surprise* (2); *All in the Wrong; The Contrivances; The Critic; The Deserter; The Devil to Pay; The Fairy of the Rock*†; *Florizel and Perdita; High Life Below Stairs; Midas; Rosina* (5); *The Sultan* (2); Unspecified "farce"(5); *The Upholsterer**.

Entr'acte entertainments: Singing: 2. Dancing:

Benefits (16): Mrs. Achmet (2); Atkins; Miss Brunton; Byrne; Mrs. Collins; Mrs. [George] Dawson; Eccles (playwright); Fotteral (2); Mrs. Hoskins; Lee Lewes (2); the Performers; Tyrrell; Mrs. Ward.

October 1786

The New Theatre of Belfast [in Rosemary Lane] will be opened early in October next. Atkins is happy to embrace every means of convincing the polite and liberal audience of Belfast, of his gratitude and respect, has engaged the celebrated Mrs. Achmet, the first female ornament of the Irish stage, a lady possessed of most uncommon abilities for a number of nights. He also engaged that most excellent comedian Lee Lewes from the Theatre-Royal, Covent Garden, Fotteral from the Theatre-Royal, Smock Alley, Freeman and Mrs. Freeman from the Theatre-Royal, York, and other respectable performers. He flatters himself that there never was such a company in point of merit yet seen in the North of Ireland and he makes no doubt of their meeting with that candour and encouragement that the town of Belfast are at all times ready and willing to bestow. Source: 29 Sept.–3 Oct. 1786

23 Mon. *Rule a Wife and Have a Wife.* Copper Captain–Lee Lewes (from Theatre Royal London); Estifania–Mrs. Achmet (from the Theatre Royal, Smock Alley) their first appearance on this stage. With a farce as will be expressed in the Bills. Half price will not be taken during the whole performance. Source: 17–20 Oct. 1786

November 1786

17 Fri. Mrs. Achmet's night. *The Constant Couple.* Sir Harry Wildair–Mrs. Achmet. Part of the pit will be railed in as boxes. [Clark 1965, 259 mistakenly ascribes this benefit performance to 11 November]. Source: 14–17 Nov. 1786

23 Thurs. *"Original Lecture Upon Heads"* with all its whimsical apparatus which he purchased for the sum of two hundred pounds of the late George Alexander Stevens which with the additional expence of one hundred pounds in modern characters heads, wigs, pictures he lately revived at the Theatre Royal, Covent Garden, with so much approbation and success that in four nights his receipts were £335. 10s. 6d. The treasurer's accounts to Lewes on each night may be seen by any gentleman at Magee's printer. Lewes mentions this circumstance being very desirous not to be thought obtruding too much when he invites the public to the theatre at the usual prices on play nights. He is ambitious to approve himself worthy their countenance and hopes the above night's exhibition of wit and humour, satire and sentiment with a new occasional prologue never spoken before will secure to him their future patronage. [In his listing of known performances of *"The Lecture on Heads"* Gerald Kahan, (*George Alexander Stevens and 'The Lecture on Heads'.* Athens, Ga.: U of Georgia P, 1984), seems unaware of this series by Lewes]. Source: 14–17 Nov. 1786

30 Thurs. By particular desire. *"Lecture upon Heads."* Boxes 3s. 3d., Pit 2s. 2d., Gallery 1s. 1d. Source: 24–28 Nov. 1786

December 1786

4 Mon. [Program unavailable]. Atkins informs ladies and gentlemen Belfast and its vicinity that Mrs. Achmet has renewed her engagement for six nights more which will be positively the last of her appearance here this season. She plays a principal tragic character on Monday next. Source: 28 Nov.–1 Dec. 1786

20 Wed. Benefit of Lee Lewes. *As You Like It.* Rosalind–A Lady [Mrs. Lee Lewes] (first appearance on any stage); Touchstone–Lewes. End of Act 1 Lewes will recite *"The Whimsical Journey of John Gilpin."* End of the play by particular desire the Mock Musical Cantata from the *"Lecture upon Heads."* With a farce never performed here called *The Upholsterer; or, What News?* [In the source issue a review is favorable to the performance, but notes that some ladies in the elevated seats and boxes had complained about the chandeliers]. Source: 12–15 Dec. 1786

29 Fri.   Mrs. Achmet's night. Last of her public appearances here. *Lionel and Clarissa.* Jessamy–Mrs. Achmet and the farce of *The Sultan.* Rosaland–Mrs. Achmet. Source: 19–22 Dec. 1786

January 1787

1 Mon. [Mainpiece unavailable] and *The Sultan.* Source: 19–22 Dec. 1786

11 Thurs. The last night of Lee Lewes. *"Lecture Upon Heads."* With additions, particularly a new ode by Pilon called *The Order of St. Patrick;* end of Act 4 *"A Military Hero."* Lewes is happy to inform the ladies and gentlemen that on the above night he will be indulged with the military band. Source: 29 Dec. 1786–2 Jan. 1787

12 Fri.   *"Lecture upon Heads."* Lee Lewes returns his most grateful thanks to the public for the very great encouragement and approbation they have been pleased to bestow on his lecture. It is during his present engagement at the Theatre totally withdrawn if at any future period he should have the honor of appearing before them on that or a similar capacity he will be careful to be provided with that novelty which he presumes to hope will entitle him to their further patronage. Source: 9–12 Jan. 1787

15 Mon. [Program unavailable]. Benefit of the Poorhouse and Infirmary. Mrs. Achmet is to perform a part. It is hoped no lady or gentleman will suffer private engagements to interfere. [Mrs. Achmet certainly performed more frequently during her stay in Belfast than the record indicates. *The Hibernian Magazine* of May 1788 praises her Belfast portrayals of Estifania (see 23 Oct. 1786), Euphrasia (in *The Grecian Daughter*), Polly (in *The Beggar's Opera*), Juliet ("particularly capital"), Sigismunda (in *Tancred and Sigismunda*), Sir Harry Wildair (in the play of the same title), Calista (in *The Fair Penitent*), and Monimia (in *The Orphan*)]. Source: 9–12 Jan. 1787

19 Wed. *A Man of the World.* Sir Pertinax MacSycophant–Cherry and *The Agreeable Surprise.* Lingo–Cherry. [This is probably an error. The Cherrys were both performing regularly at Smock Alley this season, Andrew on 15 and 22 Jan.]. Source: *Londonderry Journal* 30 Jan. 1787.

February 1787

19 Mon. Mrs. Ward's night. *All in the Wrong.* Sir John Restless–Lee Lewes; Belinda–Mrs. [Thomas] Ward. End Acts 1 and 2 Mrs. Ward will introduce the much admired Scotch ballads of *"Auld Robin Gray"* and *"How sweet's the love that meets return;"* end Acts 3 and 4 by particular desire the favourite hunting cantata *"Diana"* and the celebrated song of *"The Soldier Tired."* To which will be added the musical entertainment of *The Deserter*. Henry (for that night only)–Mrs. [Thomas] Ward. Source: 13–16 Feb. 1787

23 Fri.   Benefit of Miss Hoskins. Never acted here. *The Reparation*. The characters cast to the utmost strength of the company. With several entertainments. To which will be added Sheridan's much applauded dramatic piece called *The Critic*. Source: 16–20 Feb. 1787

26 Mon.   Fotteral's benefit. Never performed here. *Fashionable Levities*. With a musical farce and other entertainments. Source: 16–20 Feb. 1787

March 1787

2   Fri.   Lee Lewes's night. *The Jealous Wife*. Mrs. Oakly (for that night only)–Mrs. Lewes; Oakly–Tyrrell; Lord Trinket–Lee Lewes. Two favourite songs, by particular desire, Mrs. Ward. With (positively for that last time) the pantomime of *The Fairy of the Rock* with additional scene as performed by Lee Lewes in London in the pantomime of *Harlequin Dr. Faustus*. With the original prologue in the character of Harlequin written purposely for Lewes by the late Goldsmith which concludes with an escape through a tub on a man's head as in the pantomime of *Mother Shipton*. Source: 23–27 Feb. 1787

9   Fri.   Tyrrell's benefit. Never performed here. *A Trip to Scarborough* and *Rosina*. Source: 2–6 Mar. 1787

12 Mon.   Mrs. Dawson's benefit. [Program unavailable]. Source: 2–6 Mar. 1787

21 Wed.   As the play and farce advertised Benefit of Atkins do not prove agreeable to a number of his friends he takes the liberty of informing the ladies and gentlemen of Belfast that on Wednesday next will be presented *The Trip to Scarborough* and the musical entertainment of *Rosina*. Singing between the acts by Atkins and Mrs. Ward. Source: 16–20 Mar. 1787

30 Fri.   Byrne's night. *The Maid of the Mill* and *The Devil to Pay*. Byrne humbly hopes his friends will not impute the shortness of the notice to the least disrespect as the real cause is his not being permitted to advertise his night sooner. Source: 27–30 Mar. 1787

April 1787

9 Mon. Benefit of Fotteral. *Hamlet.* Hamlet–Fotteral; Ghost–Atkins; Ophelia–Mrs. [Thomas] Ward. With a favourite musical farce. This being Passion Week there will be no play till the above night. Source: 30 Mar.–3 Apr. 1787

13 Fri.   By particular desire of several persons of distinction. Benefit of Mrs. Collins. *Robin Hood of Sherwood Forest.* End Act 1 an address written by a lady and to be spoken by Master Collins a child of 5 years old which he concludes with a favourite song. Between the play and farce *"The Humours of Tipperary"* to be sung by Master Collins and after the farce the celebrated epilogue of *"Belles Have at you All"* which she concludes with the favourite hunting song of *"The High Mount."* With a much-admired musical entertainment called *The Agreeable Surprise.* Source: 10–13 Apr. 1787

25 Wed. *The World.* We are informed that *The World* by Mr. Eccles, a new opera, will be performed on Wednesday for the benefit of the Comedians and on Friday next for the benefit of the author who has upwards of thirty years filled a very useful department in the education of youth in this town. As the inhabitants seem already so desirous to express their regard for the person who has produced the piece no further encomium is thought necessary. Source: 24 Apr. 1787.

27 Fri.   *The World.* On Wednesday last the opera of *The World* written by Mr. Eccles of Belfast was performed in this theatre and on Friday it will be performed for the benefit of the author. It was well attended the first night and received with a very general plaudit. Source: 24 Apr. 1787.

May 1787

30 Wed. *Eidouranion: or, Large Transparent Orrery.* On this elaborate and splendid machine which is fifteen feet diameter and has been exhibited three seasons in the Theatre-Royal, Haymarket, London, in all the principal towns of England and Scotland and last in Dublin where this lecture was read fifty times to brilliant and crowded audiences who have bestowed on it the most flattering encomiums. Walker, Jr., son of Mr. Walker, lecturer on philosophy London, the inventor of this machine and who read several courses of his philosophy in Belfast about nineteen years ago, will deliver his astronomical lecture on Wednesday and Friday evening next May 30 and June 1 in the Theatre, Belfast. Scene 1 exhibits the earth in annual and diurnal motion; day, night, twilight, long and short days in this scene are so obvious that a bare inspection of the machine explains the reasons of these phaenomena even to those who may have never thought on the subject. Scene 2 consists of the sun, the earth, and the moon the intention is to shew the cause and effect of the moon's phases or different appearances her eclipses and those of the sun. Scene 3 shews the threefold motion of the earth, viz. that on its axis to produce day and night that round the sun to produce the seasons and that round the centre of gravity with the moon to produce spring and nap tides. Scene 4 exhibits every planet and sattellite in annual and diurnal motion; at once a comet descends in the parabolic curve from the top of the machine and turning round the sun ascends in like manner its motions being accelerated and retarded according to the laws of planetary motion. Scene 5 the plurality of systems agreeable to the ideas of Fontenelle, every motion in this complex variety seems without cause of support the sublime and awful simplicity of nature is daringly imitated and the *georgium sipus* or new planet, the appearance of the fixed stars and other recent discoveries made through a telescope magnifying 6,500 times by Herchell are all interwoven in this lecture and exhibition which is assisted by a great variety of auxiliary scenes. The celestina stop being a sister invention of Walker a few notes will be introduced on that instrument in the intervals of the lecture. Boxes 3s. pit 2s. gallery 1s. English. Tickets and books of the lecture may be had of Mrs. Smith at the coffee-house and on the days of exhibition at the theatre where places for the boxes may be taken doors open at six and the lecture begins at seven. Source: 25–28 May 1787

June 1787

1 Fri. *Eidouranion.* See performance of 30 May.

August 1787

3 Fri. *The Roman Father.* Horatia–Miss Brunton. With *Rosina.* Boxes 5s. 5d., pit 3s. 3d., gallery 2s. 2d. 6–10 July 1787 Atkins begs leave to inform the ladies and gentlemen of Belfast and its vicinity that he has engaged the celebrated Miss Brunton for ten nights who will make her first appearance in the beginning of August. He is also in treaty with a gentleman of the first abilities in his profession to support the principal tragic characters. Source: 31 July–3 Aug. 1787

6 Mon. *The Grecian Daughter.* Euphrasia–Miss Brunton. Source: 7–10 Aug. 1787

8 Wed. *Romeo and Juliet.* Juliet–Miss Brunton. With a farce. Boxes 5s. 5d., pit 3s. 3d., gallery 2s. 2d. Source: 3–7 Aug. 1787

10 Fri. By desire. *The Fair Penitent.* Calista–Miss Brunton. With *Rosina*. Source: 7–10 Aug. 1787

15 Wed. *Much Ado about Nothing.* Beatrice–Miss Brunton. With *High Life Below Stairs.* Source: 10–14 Aug. 1787

17 Fri. *Romeo and Juliet.* Juliet–Miss Brunton. With *Rosina*. Source: 14–17 Aug. 1787

20 Mon. Benefit of Miss Brunton. *The Roman Father.* Horatia–Miss Brunton. With *Florizel and Perdita.* Perdita–Miss Brunton. Source: 14–17 Aug. 1787

22 Wed. Last night but one of Miss Brunton's engagement. *Much Ado about Nothing.* Beatrice–Miss Brunton. With *Midas.* Source: 17–21 Aug. 1787

24 Fri. Last night of Miss Brunton's engagement. *The Orphan.* Monimia–Miss Brunton. With *The Contrivances.* Source: 21–24 Aug. 1787

1787–1788 SEASON

The Rosemary Lane Theatre was dark for the 1787–88 season. The company performed in Derry in the early spring.

1788–1789 SEASON

Venue: Rosemary Lane Theatre.
Company: Atkins; Miss Bradbury [often Bradberry]; Mr. and Mrs. James Chalmers (from Crow Street, Dublin); Corry; Mr. and Mrs. Freeman; Joseph Holman; Mrs. and Miss Hoskins; Miss Maria Hughes; [George?] King; Mr. and Mrs. Lynch; Mrs. Francis Molloy; Pye; Mr. and Mrs. Remington; Rowe; Tyrrell; Miss Valois.

For biography of **Michael Atkins** see the 1767–68 season.

The **Miss Bradbury** who made her stage debut at Belfast on 16 Jan. 1789 as Miss Hardcastle in *She Stoops to Conquer* seems to have been a local amateur. This is the only record of her performing.

The **Mrs. Chalmers** who made her Irish debut at Crow Street on 13 November 1758 playing Athenais in *Theodosius* was almost certainly Mrs. James (Sarah) Chalmers. She and her husband, James, acted at Crow Street for that season only. Subsequently, they played at Norwich in the 1760s and 1770s. Mrs. Chalmers and her husband were the parents of James Chalmers, Jr. who, by 1780, was already an accomplished harlequin at York. James Chalmers married Eleanor Mills, also a member of the York company, by the 1781–82 season.

Eleanor Mills came from a large acting family and performed as a child at Norwich as early as 1775, when James Chalmers, the elder, and his wife were also with the company. Before her marriage in 1781 Miss Mills had appeared in Edinburgh (1775, 1778 and 1779) Norwich (1776 and 1778), York (1780) and at Hull (1780).

James Chalmers, Jr. and his wife acted together at York through the 1782–83 season, when they tried their fortunes in London. Mrs. Chalmers made her debut at Covent Garden on 19 September 1783. Chalmers made his debut at Covent Garden on 8 October 1783 with some success, but by mid-October 1784 James had left London for an engagement at Smock Alley. Before the end of the 1784–85 season James was back at Covent Garden for a few months. In March Mrs. Chalmers joined the Fishamble Street theatre, billed as "the late Columbine of the Theatre Royal, Covent Garden."

Mr. and Mrs. Chalmers were engaged by Daly at Smock Alley for the 1786–87 season, she making her Smock Alley debut on 22 November 1786. On the same night James made "his first appearance these two years." The following season Mr. and Mrs. Chalmers continued at Crow Street. Chalmers premiered another original pantomime *Harlequin Shepherd; or, The Fair Italian* on 15 April 1788. A correspondent in the *FDJ* 17–19 Apr. 1788 observed: " The pantomime performed on Tuesday evening is much spoken of by the audience who participated in the pleasures resulting from its exhibition. The incidents are unexpected and whimsical; the pastry cook's shop, the smith's forge, the oven scene, the nunnery, and the temple of Hymen, which is particularly brilliant, afford attraction, that in our opinion can not be resisted." For his own benefit Chalmers appeared in (his own pantomime?) *Columbine Statue; or, Harlequin's Visit to and Flight from the Gods*. The pantomime was to conclude with Chalmers flying "from the back of the stage to the back of the upper gallery and return head foremost."

During their Smock Alley engagement the Chalmers also traveled with the Smock Alley company to Daly's provincial theatres before the opening of the Theatre Royal: to Waterford, Limerick and Cork in 1786 and to Kilkenny in 1787. Then Chalmers and his wife joined Atkins's Belfast company for the 1787–88 season and performed there with considerable success.

Thereafter, the Chalmers returned to York for two seasons, playing also at Weymouth. On 31 December 1791 Chalmers returned to Crow Street, billed as his first appearance there "these three years." Mrs. Chalmers is not found in the bills that season, perhaps she was already ill, for the *FDJ* of 24 May 1792 contains a notice of a performance deferral "on account of the sudden death of Mrs. Chalmers."

Chalmers appeared briefly in Birmingham in 1793, but then signed with Thomas Wignell of the Philadelphia theatre and performed there, in New York, and in Annapolis, Maryland. In 1796 he acted in Charleston but his engagement was a disaster due to a contract dispute with the manager. He remained in America, acting mainly in Philadelphia through the 1802–03 season. Thereafter, he returned to England and is found at Plymouth, Edinburgh and, perhaps, Manchester. He returned to America for a brief time in the autumn of 1804 but he returned home in 1805. Chalmers may have acted at Norwich thereafter but there is no record. On 22 August 1810 he died in Worcester, evidently of apoplexy.

According to Clark (1965, 354) a **"Mr. Corry"** traveled to Belfast and appeared with Michael Atkins's company for the 1788–89 season, but I am unable to find any record of Corry's association with this company.

For biographies of **Mr.** and **Mrs. Freeman** see the 1786–87 season.

Joseph George Holman was one of the most important figures of the London and Dublin stages of the later eighteenth and early nineteenth centuries. Born the son of an officer in the British army in 1764, he was raised by an uncle who sent him to the acting academy in Soho run by Dr. Barrow. He evidently was not attracted to the stage at that time, went to Oxford with plans to study for the clergy, but gave up that idea and made his stage debut at Covent Garden as Romeo on 25 October 1784. Playing a series of capital roles, such as Macbeth, Don Felix in *The Wonder*, Achmet in *Barbarossa*, Richard III, and Hamlet, he was immediately encouraged by the critics and engaged to perform at Covent Garden the following season.

In the summer of 1785 Holman paid his first visit to Ireland, making his debut at Smock Alley on 7 June 1785 in Hamlet and billed as "from the Theatre Royal, Covent Garden, his first appearance in this kingdom." The newspapers observed that on this night there attended "One of the most splendid and crowded audiences that ever filled our theatre royal." In addition to Hamlet, Holman performed many of the roles that he attracted attention in London and was warmly received in all of them. After leaving Dublin he traveled to Limerick and Cork where he appeared in August with equal success.

For the next two years Holman visited Ireland after Covent Garden closed for the season. He acted at Crow Street in June–July 1787 with Mrs. Melmoth and Miss Brunton and then traveled again to Cork in the early autumn before returning to London. However, Holman and Harris had a dispute over salary at the beginning of the 1787–88 season, and Holman returned to Crow Street where, according to *DEP* 27 Nov. 1787 Daly engaged Holman at a salary of 30 guineas per week, "a salary scarcely known in the London Theatres." During this time Holman began his four-year affair with the novice actress, Maria Hughes, who was to bear him two children. Again that summer Holman (and Miss Hughes) went with the Crow Street company to perform in Cork.

At the beginning of the 1788-89 season Holman engaged to perform with Atkins's company in Belfast for a few months. With him was Miss Maria Hughes and together they packed the houses there through December 1788. Thereafter, Holman (and, evidently Miss Hughes) played at Edinburgh, and, in May, in Manchester. Holman then returned to Oxford for a term in the spring of 1789, but was lured back to Covent Garden by Harris at a salary of £11 a week. He continued there (and twice briefly at Drury Lane) playing many leading roles in comedy and tragedy through 1799–1800.

Holman visited Ireland during the summer of 1793–94 but remained in London until the winter of the 1800–01 season. Holman married Jane Hamilton in February 1798 but the marriage was an unhappy one and they soon separated. She died in 1810. Holman's play *Abroad and at Home* premiered at Covent Garden in October 1793 and was very successful in London and Dublin. His second play, *The Votary of Wealth*, which premiered at Covent Garden in 1799, was an even bigger success. His adaptation of Shiller's *Die Rauber*, entitled *The Red Cross Knight* (Covent Garden, 1799), was only moderately popular.

In the 1799–1800 season at Covent Garden, Holman and other actors fell out with the managers of Covent Garden over free tickets and when the dispute was decided in favor of the managers, Holman evidently resigned from the theatre in favor of a Dublin engagement. He was never again to perform in a London winter season.

His first performance at Crow Street that December was advertised as his first "these six years." Frederick Jones had approached Holman about becoming the acting manager at Crow Street, and *The Monthly Mirror* for May 1801 reported that Holman had been offered £1,000 per year at Dublin "for his exertions as actor and manager, besides the profits of a benefit." Evidently, Holman was encouraged to remain in Dublin by what he construed to be Jones's offer to hand over management of the Theatre Royal to him at the end of the season. That season too Holman performed at Belfast for a short engagement in the spring and at Limerick and Cork in April with a company under his own management, including Macready, Hickey, and Mrs. Kniveton.

The Monthly Mirror for August 1801 announced that "The rumour gains ground that Mr. Holman is likely soon to conclude his engagement with Mr. Jones for the propriety of this theatre, and he has the earnest wishes of the inhabitants of Dublin, as well as of every admirer of professional talent and gentlemanly conduct, for his success. Mr. Holman is at present in London." Holman assumed these duties in the following season when Jacob Hammerton took himself to Belfast, having become unpopular with the Dublin University students.

Holman functioned as acting manager of Crow Street theatre from 1801–02 through 1802–03, after which he entered semi-retirement, spending long periods on his farm. The *DEP* 4 Dec. 1804 reported that Holman "has arrived from London to resume his post as Acting Manager at the theatre." He performed at Crow Street for the first time in two years in December 1804. He again became acting manager in place of Frederick Jones and held that position through the 1807–08 season, a fact not noticed by the *BD*.

On 22 February 1808 a Miss Holman made her Crow Street debut for her father's benefit. Her success was such that her portrait as Adeline in her maiden play of *Fontainville Forest* was published in Walker's *Hibernian Magazine* for February 1808. This young lady was Agnes, now about 18 years old, and a daughter of Joseph Holman and Miss Hughes.

In July 1808 Holman was slandered in "advertisements in the form of playbills" in the newspapers. Evidently, a cabal had been formed against him with the object of driving him out of Dublin. Holman offered a reward of £50 for the identity of the printer of the spurious playbills. *DEP* 30 Apr.

1808 contains an item condemning the activities of this cabal, calling their actions "contemptible," "effeminate," and "despicable." W. J. Lawrence (58:119), believes the cabal was a clique supported by Crampton and Dalton who were trying to get rid of Holman at all costs, hoping to wrest full control of the theatre from Jones, their partner.

The cabal evidently succeeded in their plot, but Holman was not to be kept out of Dublin and he returned for a limited engagement in the winter of 1809. *The Cyclopedian Magazine* for February 1809 reported that, after ten years in Dublin, Holman had taken up an engagement in London after his last performance in Dublin that season. In fact, Holman went first to Edinburgh and Glasgow with his daughter Agnes and remained there for the season, returning to Crow Street as the acting manager the following fall. At this time another cabal, led by John Magee the publisher of the *Dublin Evening Post*, had risen against the proprietorship of Frederick Jones and anyone associated with him. One of Magee's tactics was to salt the Theatre Royal audiences with disruptive elements. When Holman had one of these *agent provocateur* arrested, Magee launched a vicious campaign against him in his newspaper. At the end of the season Holman, whose first benefit was miserably attended, and whose second fared little better, left Dublin for good.

The Hibernian Magazine for March, 1810, reports that Holman had experienced the organized opposition of the Crow Street galleries: "The decline of this actor's popularity can scarcely be accounted for on any fair motives. It is certain that Mrs. Edwin left our stage in disgust at the shameless conduct of a gang of the 'private players,' (as they impudently term themselves) in the galleries, joined by a few jackeens of the pit, with their whistles—And perhaps (to what a despicable origin may we not trace some events!) Mr. Holman may have been 'cuckooed' out of his popularity by a wretched combination of Drury-lane spouters, with a typographical mimic at their head."

In the summer of 1811 Holman performed at the Haymarket Theatre for a few weeks. Joseph Holman and his daughter Agnes then traveled to New York where he made his debut in October 1812. Later that year they played in Philadelphia and in 1813 in Boston. Holman took over as manager of the Charleston theatre in the 1815–16 season. He returned to London that summer on a recruiting visit but gave up the Charleston venture at the end of the 1816–17 season.

Holman then made plans to open a new theatre in Richmond, Virginia, after marrying Miss Lattimore, one of his recruits from the Liverpool theatre on 22 August 1817. He died two days later at the age of 53 of a fever at Rockaway, Long Island, New York.

For the biographies of **Mrs.** and **Miss Hoskins** see the 1782–83 season.

Miss Maria Hughes never acted in London, but the *BD* gives the important events of her life, including the details of the termination of her affair with Joseph Holman, which may be found in the *BD* entry on Holman. She was born in 1761 to an Irish country squire at Thurles, Co. Tipperary. When her father died, she inherited his entire fortune and managed to squander it in a short time.

She made her stage debut in Dublin on 10 April 1788 as Euphrasia in *The Grecian Daughter*. At that time she met the Covent Garden actor Joseph Holman and was to be his mistress for about four years, giving birth to two children. Such was her popularity in her first Dublin season that a portrait of Miss Hughes in the character of Lady Townly was printed in Walker's *Hibernian Magazine* for June 1788.

She accompanied Holman to Belfast for a few months in the autumn of 1788 and then to Edinburgh later that season. Although Holman was engaged at Covent Garden during the entire decade of the 1790s, Miss Hughes had an independent career. She appeared for a few nights at Crow Street in February and March 1791.

In October 1792 Holman and Miss Hughes separated. She claimed that they had been married and he denied it. Holman did, however, continue to provide for their two children and eventually fostered his daughters' careers on the stage. After getting rid of Holman, she married the very wealthy Major Scott-Waring, former chief lieutenant in India to Warren Hastings, and became a London socialite. Interestingly, when Maria Hughes died in 1812 (of a broken neck from falling down her own stairs after a masked ball in honor of the Prince Regent), the Major almost immediately married another actress active in Dublin, Mrs. Harriet Esten.

The **"Mr. King"** who performed in Belfast this season was certainly not the popular London actor Thomas King, who, coincidentally, was visiting Dublin during this period. The manuscript diary that Thomas King kept during his tour indicates that on the nights that "Mr. King" was performing in Belfast, Thomas King was otherwise engaged in Dublin. Our King was probably George King, who acted in secondary roles in Ireland and elsewhere during this period.

For biographies of **Mr.** and **Mrs. John Lynch** see the 1771–72 season.

Mrs. Francis Molloy, late Miss Eliza Wheeler, was possibly related to the Wheeler who performed at Smock Alley in tertiary roles from the 1775–76 season. Eliza Wheeler, billed as "from Venice, her first appearance on an English stage," made her Dublin debut on 18 December 1783 in the Capel Street Opera House production of the Giordani opera of *Gibraltar. The Volunteer Evening Post* of 6–8 January 1784 observed: "The music is in the highest stile of possible perfection; particularly the sprightly air in the first act by Miss Wheeler, and a song in the last act by the same."

Following her successful Dublin debut season, Miss Wheeler was engaged at Covent Garden where she made her debut on 22 September 1784 as Rosetta in *Love in a Village*. The next summer Miss Wheeler performed at the Dublin Rotunda concerts, also with great success. During the 1785–86 season she sang and acted occasionally at Covent Garden and later was a member of the opera company at the King's Theatre. Miss Wheeler spent the 1786–87 season at Smock Alley where she made her "first appearance these two years." In the summer she again sang at the Rotunda concerts.

She married Francis Molloy on 28 September 1786 and thereafter she played at Smock Alley in 1787–88, at Crow Street and Belfast in 1788–89, and in Bath in October 1789. When her husband was arrested for highway robbery in March 1791, Mrs. Molloy assumed the stage name of Mrs. Murray. She subsequently performed at Richmond in 1791 and at Liverpool in 1792, before returning to Dublin in June 1792 (some confusion arises from the fact that a Mr. Murray and another Mrs. Murray were also appearing at Crow Street from this season until 1798–99, in minor roles).

Mrs. Murray subsequently retired from the stage, perhaps remarried or simply took the name Mrs. Cotter. She died at Chelsea on 21 November 1794.

For a biography of **Pye** see the 1768–69 season.

For biographies of **Mr.** and **Mrs. Remington** see the 1762–63 season.

For a biography of **Rowe** see the 1777–78 season.

For a biography of **Tyrrell** see the 1781–82 season.

The only record of the dancer named **Miss Valois**, who performed in Belfast with the touring company from Dublin which included Joseph Holman, is during the 1788–89 season.

Repertory, 1788–1789 Season

Judging from the surviving playbills Atkins presented very little that was new or unusual in Belfast during this period. Only one play, Elizabeth Inchbald's farce, *The Midnight Hour*, was advertised as new to the Belfast stage. The piece had premiered in Dublin in December 1788.

Total Performances (including summer season): 44 of 31 different named mainpieces; 34 of 15 different named afterpieces.
  Shakespeare: 3.
  New Mainpieces: 0.
  New Afterpieces: 1.

(For a key to repertory symbols see above, page 11)

Mainpieces: *All in the Wrong; The Beggar's Opera; The Brothers(2); The Chapter of Accidents; The Distrest Mother(2); The Foundling; The Gamester; Hamlet(2); The Heiress*†(2); *The Hypocrite; The Imposters*†; *The Inconstant*■; *Inkle and Yarico* [as a mainpiece]†(2); *Lionel and Clarissa(2); The London Merchant; More Ways Than One*†; *Much Ado About Nothing; Neck or Nothing*†; *Othello; The Provoked Husband; The Rivals(2); Romeo and Juliet* (2); *She Stoops to Conquer; Such Things Are*†; *The Suspicious Husband; Tancred and Sigismunda*†; *A Trip to Scarborough;* Unspecified mainpiece(6); *Venice Preserved; The West Indian.*

Afterpieces: *Catherine and Petruchio(5); Comus; The Critic; The Deserter; The Devil to Pay; The Farmer*†; *The Jubilee; The Midnight Hour**; *Poor Vulcan; Prometheus*†(2); *Rosina(2); The Son-in-Law; Three Weeks After Marriage*†; *The True Born Irishman*†; Unspecified "farce"(13).

Interlude: *Harlequin Gardener*†.
Afterlude: *The Poor Soldier.*

Entr'acte entertainment: Singing: 1. Dancing: 3.

Benefits (27): Atkins (2); Miss Bradbury; Chalmers(2); Mrs. Chalmers; Freeman; Mrs. Freeman; Holman; Mrs. Hoskins; Miss Hoskins(2); Miss Hughes(2); King(2); Lynch(2); Mrs. Lynch and Remington; Mrs. Molloy(2); Mrs. Remington(2); Rowe; Tyrrell; Miss Valois(2).

October 1788

20 Mon. On Monday last our Theatre was opened for the first time this season. *The Suspicious Husband.* Ranger–Chalmers; Clarinda–Mrs. Chalmers. Source: 21–24 Oct. 1788

29 Wed. [*Lionel and Clarissa; or,*] *A School for Fathers.* Clarissa–Mrs. Molloy (late Miss Wheeler). [The afterpiece may have been *Catherine and Petruchio* as is suggested in a review of this performance in 28–31 Oct. 1788]. Source: 24–28 Oct. 1788

November 1788

10 Mon. *Othello.* Othello–Chalmers. Also a farce with Mrs. Chalmers and Rowe. Source: 11–14 Nov. 1788

12 Wed. Benefit of Mrs. Molloy. *The Beggar's Opera.* Macheath–Mrs. Chalmers; Lucy–Mrs. Freeman; Polly–Mrs. Molloy. With the admired musical entertainment of *Rosina.* Belville–Atkins; Rosina–Mrs. Molloy. Source: 4–7 Nov. 1788

19 Wed. *Hamlet.* Hamlet–Holman (from the Theatres-Royal of London and Dublin). With *The Poor Soldier.* Source: 14–18 Nov. 1788

21 Fri. *The Provoked Husband.* Lady Townly–Miss Hughes (from the Theatre-Royal Dublin). With a farce as will be expressed in the Bills. Boxes 5s. 5d., Pit 3s. 3d., Gallery 2s. 2d. Subscribers tickets will be admitted. No half price during the whole performance. Source: 14–18 Nov. 1788

24 Mon. *Romeo and Juliet.* Romeo–Holman; Juliet–Miss Hughes. Source: 18 Nov. 1788.

26 *Wed.* *Tancred and Sigismunda.* Tancred–Holman; Sigismunda–Miss Hughes. [Published in Belfast by James Magee in 1745]. Source: 18 Nov. 1788.

28 Fri. Benefit Mrs. Molloy. Positively the last night of her performance this season. *Lionel and Clarissa.* Lionel–Tyrrell; Jessamy–Mrs. Chalmers; Clarissa–Mrs. Molloy. In the course of which will be sung and accompanied on the Piano Forte by Mrs. Molloy the favourite song called *"The Mansion of Peace."* To which will be added for the first time this season the musical farce of *Poor Vulcan.* Vulcan–Rowe; Venus–Mrs. Molloy. Source: 21–25 Nov. 1788

December 1788

1 Mon. *The West Indian.* Belcour–Holman; Charlotte–Miss Hughes. With *Catherine and Petruchio.* Petruchio–Chalmers; Catherine–Mrs. Chalmers. Source: 25–28 Nov. 1788

3 Wed. *The Distrest Mother.* Orestes–Holman; Hermione–Miss Hughes. Collins's *"Ode on the Passions"* for that night only spoken by Miss Hughes. With *Catherine and Petruchio.* Source: 28 Nov.–2 Dec. 1788

5 Fri. *Romeo and Juliet.* Source: 28 Nov.–2 Dec. 1788

8 Mon. [Second benefit for Miss Hughes]. *The Distrest Mother.* With *Catherine and Petruchio* and Collins's *"Ode on the Passions."* Source: 12–16 Dec. 1788

12 Fri. Holman's second appearance. *Hamlet.* Hamlet–Holman; Ophelia–Mrs. Chalmers. Source: 12–16 Dec. 1788

15 Mon. Holman's benefit, being the last night but one of his performance. *Venice Preserved.* Jaffier–Holman; Belvidera–Miss Hughes. With *Catherine and Petruchio.* Petruchio–Holman; Catherine–Mrs. Chalmers. Source: 9–12 Dec. 1788

17 Wed. Miss Hughes's benefit. *The Gamester.* Beverley–Holman (last night of his performing); Lewson–Tyrrell; Jervis–Atkins; Bates–Pye; Dawson–[George?] King; Stukely–Rowe; Charlotte–Miss Hoskins; Mrs. Beverly–Miss Hughes (last night of her performing). With the masque of *Comus.* Comus–Holman; Lady–Miss Hughes; Brother–Remington; Brother–Pye; Bachanal–Atkins; Bachanal–Tyrrell; Bachanal–Rowe; Bachanal–Lynch; Bachanal–Freeman; Bachanal–Chalmers; Euphrosyne–Mrs. Chalmers; Pastoral Nymph–Miss Valois; Bacchant–Mrs. Hoskins; Bacchant–Miss Hoskins; Bacchant–Mrs. Remington; Bacchant–Mrs. Lynch; Principal Bacchant (with the song of *"Sweet Echo")*–Mrs. Freeman. Source: 12–16 Dec. 1788

19 Fri. *Inkle and Yarico.* Sir Christopher–Rowe; Trudge–Remington; Campley–Lynch. Source: 26–30 Dec. 1788

January 1789

16 Fri. *She Stoops to Conquer.* Miss Hardcastle–Young Lady [Miss Bradbury] (first time). With the pantomime *Prometheus; or, Harlequin's Animation.* Harlequin–Chalmers. At the request of a reader the following remarks are inserted. The scenery in the pantomime does great credit to the manager particularly that of the churchyard and the last scene temple of Hymen. Source: 16–20 Jan. 1789

26 Mon. Benefit of Chalmers. *A Trip to Scarborough.* Lord Foppington–Chalmers; Hoyden–Mrs. Chalmers. With the pantomime of *Prometheus; or, Harlequin's Animation.* Harlequin–Chalmers (by particular desire he will introduce the Dying Scene and a leap through a brilliant sun of variegated fire and display of fireworks). With alterations and additions. Source: 20–23 Jan. 1789

29 Wed. Benefit of Mrs. Hoskins. *The Chapter of Accidents* with *The Jubilee.* Source: 20–23 Jan. 1789

30 Fri. Benefit Atkins. *The Hypocrite.* With a variety of entertainments and *Three Weeks After Marriage.* Source: 23–27 Jan. 1789

February 1789

2 Mon. Benefit of King. *The Rivals.* End of the play Collins's *"Ode on the Passions"* to be recited by King. With a new farce called *The Midnight Hour.* Source: 27–30 Jan. 1789

4 Wed. Mrs. Freeman's benefit. *The Heiress.* [Published in Belfast by James Magee in 1786]. During the evening an entertainment called *The School of Harmony* in which will be introduced the following favourite songs of *"To the Greenwood Gang,"* *"Bright Phoebus,"* *"The Soldier Tired,"* and *"How Sweet the Love."* With a favourite farce. Source: 27–30 Jan. 1789

6 Fri. Benefit of Mrs. Remington. Not acted here these three years. *More Ways Than One to Win Her.* With a farce and entertainments as will be expressed in the bills. Source: 30 Jan.–3 Feb. 1789

9 Mon. Benefit of Rowe. *The Rivals.* With *Rosina.* Source: 3–6 Feb. 1789

11 Wed. Benefit of Mrs. Chalmers. *Much Ado About Nothing.* Benedick–Chalmers; Beatrice–Mrs. Chalmers. With a farce as will be expressed in the bills of the day. With a pantomimic afterlude called *Harlequin Gardener.* Harlequin–Chalmers; Colombine (for that night)–Mrs. Chalmers. Preceding which Chalmers will speak Harlequin's prologue with a leap through fire and water. The whole to conclude with a front leap through a brilliant sun of variegated fire and grand display of fireworks. Source: 3–6 Feb. 1789

13 Fri. Tyrrell's benefit. [Play and farce. No other details of program available]. Source: 10–13 Feb. 1789

18 Wed. Pye's benefit. *The Brothers* with the farce of *The Devil to Pay.* Source: 10–13 Feb. 1789

20 Fri. Lynch's benefit. Not acted this season. *All in the Wrong.* After the play by particular desire and for the last time this season an Allemande and double hornpipe by Miss Valois and Lynch. With a farce as will be expressed in the bills. Source: 13–17 Feb. 1789

23 Mon. Miss Hoskin's benefit. [Play and farce. No other details of the program available]. Source: 13–17 Feb. 1789

27 Fri. Remington's benefit. *Such Things Are* with the farce of *The Critic.* Source: 20–24 Feb. 1789

March 1789

2 Mon. Benefit of Freeman. Not performed here these five years. *The Inconstant.* The following favourite songs by Mrs. Freeman: *"Hoot awa ye Loon,"* a new hunting cantata *"Let fame sound the trumpet,"* and The new *"Highland Laddie."* With a musical farce called *The Deserter.* To which will be added an afterlude called *The Poor Soldier.* Pat–Mrs. Freeman. The whole to conclude with an occasional address to the town written and to be spoken by Mrs. Freeman. Source: 20–24 Feb. 1789

4 Wed. King's benefit. Comedy, farce and entertainments. Source: 24–27 Feb. 1789.

6 Fri. Benefit of Mrs. Remington who having unfortunately failed in her former attempt. [Play, farce and entertainments. No other details of program available]. Source: 27 Feb.–3 Mar. 1789

9 Mon. Benefit of Miss Valois. *The Heiress.* Between the acts for this night only the following entertainments: End of Act 3 an allamonde by Lynch and Miss Valois; end of the play a double hornpipe by Lynch and Miss Valois. And a farce as will be expressed in the bills. Source: 27 Feb.–3 Mar. 1789

11 Wed. Lynch's second benefit. *The Brothers* and the musical farce of *The Farmer.* Source: 3–6 Mar. 1789

18 Wed. Second benefit for Chalmers. *Neck or Nothing; or, Harlequin's Flight from the Gods.* With exhibitions of flying by Chalmers. Source: 17 Mar. 1789

30 Mon. Miss Hoskin's benefit. [Play, farce and entertainments. No other details of program available]. Deferred from 13 Mar. Source: 17 Mar. 1789

April 1789

13 Mon. Benefit of Mrs. Lynch and Remington. *The London Merchant.* Maria (by particular desire)–Young Lady who performed Miss Hardcastle [i.e., Miss Bradbury] being her second appearance on any stage. With the following entertainments: an hornpipe blindfold over twelve eggs by Lynch; a Lilliputian dance in which the characters will change from men of three feet high to women of six by Remington and Lynch; a dance composed by Sig. Placido and the Little Devil called *"La Fricasse."* Source: 3–7 Apr. 1789

15 Wed. Miss Bradbury's benefit. Not acted here this season. *The Foundling.* With a farce and a variety of entertainments as will be expressed in the bills. Source: 7–10 Apr. 1789

24 Fri.   [Program unavailable]. The wetness of Wednesday night having occasioned Rowe's benefit to be postponed till Friday, this evening the entertainment that every person who attends the Theatre has repeatedly experienced in his performance will no doubt be remembered on this occasion and bring him a full house as a mark of the taste of the town and its regard for a good actor. [Rowe's benefit was deferred twice]. Source: 21–24 Apr. 1789

25 Wed.   Benefit of Miss Valois by particular desire. *Inkle and Yarico.* with entertainments of dancing by Lynch and Miss Valois. With the favourite farce of *The Son-in-Law.* Source: 21–24 Apr. 1789

27 Mon. The last night of this season. Benefit of Atkins. *The Imposters.* With *The True Born Irishman.* Source: 21–24 Apr. 1789

1789–1790 SEASON

[Belfast theatre dark. Atkins and his Rosemary Lane company spent the 1789–90 season in Derry].

1790–1791 SEASON

Venue: Rosemary Lane Theatre.

Company: Michael Atkins; Mrs. Elizabeth Coates; Mr. and Mrs. Godfrey; Griffith; Mrs. Hoskin; Lee; Lynch; Mrs. Mason (formerly Mrs. Booth); Mr. and Mrs. May; Mrs. Courtney Melmoth; Mrs. Power; Mr. and Mrs. Remington; Rowe; Stewart and Master Stewart. Summer: Thomas King (from Drury Lane).

For biography of **Michael Atkins** see the 1767–68 season.

The *BD* probably errs in saying the **Mrs. Elizabeth Coates** made her "professional debut" at Crow Street on 19 November 1789. The playbill for that performance says only that it is her "first appearance in this kingdom." An item in *FDJ* 5–7 Nov. 1789 stated that "Mrs. Kennedy from Theatre Royal, Covent Garden is engaged to perform a few nights. Miss Reynolds, Mrs. Coates, Mrs. Plomer, Miss Edmead and several other performers of eminence are also engaged," which certainly suggests that Mrs. Coates was at that time no stranger to the Dublin public. Indeed, she is probably the Mrs. Coates who had performed in Edinburgh and York during the 1788–89 season.

She was engaged at Crow Street for the 1789–90 season and played mainly secondary, but also several capital roles. She traveled with the Crow Street company to perform in Cork in the summer of 1790, and in October 1790 went to Belfast to act for "a few nights" at Atkins's Rosemary Lane Theatre (although she stayed on through January 1791 and returned in August, when the visiting Drury Lane actor Thomas King appeared for her benefit). She was with Atkins's company in Derry in the spring of 1791 and with the Crow Street company in Cork and Limerick that autumn. She was once more at Belfast January through March 1792 and at Newry that summer.

Mrs. Coates appeared regularly in capital roles at Crow Street during the 1792–93 season. That summer she traveled to Galway to perform. The following season she did not appear at Crow Street until March, and then for only one performance. Mrs. Coates then traveled to England and joined the Orchard Street Theatre in Bath for the 1793–94 season. She was again in Belfast from November 1794 until 2 January 1795.

She made her first appearance at Crow Street that season on 27 January and remained until the end of the 1794–95 season. Thereafter she is found at Manchester in January 1796, then Mrs. Coates and a Miss Coates, perhaps her daughter, are found at Crow Street with J. P. Kemble in the summer of 1796. The *BD* says that a Miss Coates had performed at Kilkenny in December 1790 and at Newry in August 1792, but I can find no record of these performances.

Mrs. Coates made her London debut at Covent Garden on 22 September 1797 as Clarinda in *The Suspicious Husband*; she was reengaged there and remained at Covent Garden until at least 1809. She was still alive in 1830.

The only record of **Mr.** and **Mrs. Godfrey** is in Ireland. Mrs. Godfrey acted in Derry with Atkins's company in the spring of 1790 and again with Atkins in Belfast for the 1799–91 season and at Derry that spring. No roles are listed for Mr. Godfrey although he received benefits.

Mr. Godfrey died sometime shortly before 16 August 1791 when his wife was given a benefit with the following explanation in *BNL*: "In consideration of the unprotected situation Mrs. Godfrey is unhappily left in from her recent loss, Atkins has kindly consented to allow her the use of the theatre on the above night." Mrs. Godfrey was reengaged by Atkins for the 1791–92 season at Belfast but thereafter disappears from the record.

The **Mr. Griffith** whose association with the Irish stage is confined in the main to Atkins's company in the north of Ireland between 1791 and 1798 first comes to notice in Belfast during the winter of 1790–91 (no roles are recorded for him that season). That summer he is found in Limerick, but he is acting with Atkins in Belfast and Derry in 1792, 1793, and 1794. In 1795 he is in Cork, but is back in the north for the 1795–96 season. He is last seen at Derry in April 1798, after which he disappears from the record.

For a biography of **Mrs. Hoskins** see the 1782–83 season.

Clark (1965, 365) identifies **Thomas Lee** as the actor who appeared at Belfast in the winter of 1791, in Wexford in October and December 1791, and in Limerick in October 1798. Nothing more is known about his career.

For biography of **John Lynch** see the 1771–72 season.

For biography of **Mrs. Mason** (formerly Mrs. Booth) see the 1775–76 season.

The acting careers of **Mr.** and **Mrs. James May** were evidently confined to provincial Ireland and largely to Michael Atkins's northern company. They are found acting in Belfast for the 1790–91 through the 1794–95 seasons. They also appeared in Derry in March–June 1791. Atkins appointed James May his deputy manager in Derry for the 1792–93 season while he remained in Belfast building the Arthur Street theatre. The Mays returned to Derry in January 1793 and April 1795, and May appeared in

Kilkenny in the autumn of 1795. They are not found in Dublin during this period and they have no *BD* entry.

Mrs. Courtney Melmoth was the wife of the actor, Courtney Melmoth, whose real name was Samuel Jackson Pratt. Pratt was the son of brewer of St. Ives. He was educated for the church but around 1771 he met and eloped to Dublin with a young boarding school girl, whose first name was Charlotte, and whose family name, the *BD* speculates, may have been Melmoth, the stage name they were to adopt.

Melmoth made his stage debut at Smock Alley in February 1773 billed as "The Young Gentleman of family and education lately from England who never yet performed on any stage, with a new occasional address written by him spoken by Ryder." He acted the role of Antony in *Julius Caesar* several times that season with considerable success. Mrs. Melmoth made her stage debut at Smock Alley later in the season on 8 May 1773 as Monimia in *The Orphan* for her husband's benefit. The benefit was disrupted however when members of the audience hissed another actor with whom they had a quarrel and about which Melmoth complained in the newspapers.

Melmoth must have had a little money for he went to Drogheda, built and opened a little theatre which, we are told, held £40. The venture was unsuccessful, and the Melmoths decided to try their fortunes in London. Mrs. Melmoth made her Covent Garden debut on 26 February 1774 and Melmoth made his the following season. Both debuts seem to have been successful, but later events suggest that Melmoth recognized that his wife's talent far exceeded his. As she become more popular he withdrew gradually from the stage and "lived off his wife's talents," according to a contemporary satire. In fact he took to writing plays but had little success.

The Melmoths' travels took them to Edinburgh in the autumn of 1776, and then to London, where Mrs. Melmoth made her Drury Lane debut as Lady Macbeth in November. She met with little encouragement there, however, and the Melmoths then traveled to Bath (1778–79), back to Edinburgh in 1779 and then, again, to Dublin. Mrs. Melmoth, but not her husband, was engaged at Smock Alley in capital roles for the 1780–81 season. She was especially successful in breeches parts, Macheath being one of her most popular. In the summer of 1781 Mrs. Melmoth moved to Crow Street for a few nights, remained there for 1781–82, but returned to Smock Alley for the summer season. Evidently the couple, who may never have had a marriage ceremony, parted sometime after 1781. Courtney Melmoth died in Birmingham on 4 October 1814.

When J. P. Kemble and West Digges came to Smock Alley for the 1782–83 season with Mrs. Inchbald, Mrs. Melmoth shared the status of leading lady. She is found for the first time as prima donna at Leoni's Capel Street English Opera House for the 1783–84 season. One critic observed: "When we consider Mrs. Melmoth's powers in tragedy, her excellence in genteel comedy and her consequence even in opèra, we may safely pronounce that she has no competitor whatever in this kingdom, and scarce an equal in so general a line of performance in any other."

Mrs. Melmoth appeared in most of the leading women's roles at Owenson's Fishamble Street theatre during the short 1784–85 season there. When Owenson's venture closed, Mrs. Melmoth returned to Smock Alley for the 1785–86, 1786–87 and the last half of the 1787–88 seasons. Mrs. Melmoth transferred back to Crow Street for the 1788–89 season at the end of which the *DEP* 14 July 1789 reported the retirement of Mrs. Charlotte Melmoth, who proposed to devote her future life "to the motivation of Ladies in the present fashionable amusement of Filagree; for which purpose she has taken an elegant house in this city, and is now in London collecting papers of the most exquisite colours. . . ."

Evidently, Mrs. Melmoth's filagree school was not very successful, for she is found acting, now in New York, in March 1793, billed as "from the Theatres Royal of London and Dublin." She also offered a program of recitations from Shakespeare's plays and other works at a New York hotel.

She spent the 1793–94 season as a member of Hodgkinson's company at the John Street Theatre and in the opinion of one critic was "the best tragic actress the inhabitants of New York, then living, had ever seen." She left John Street in 1798 and moved to the new Park Theatre. She also acted occasionally in Philadelphia and Hartford. In late 1811 she fractured her arm as a result of a carriage accident; the break did not heal properly, and she was forced to give up the stage. She was able to support herself with the proceeds of a tavern and a dairy farm she kept. She also started a school for elocution in New York.

The Thespian Dictionary says that Mrs. Melmoth converted to Roman Catholicism around 1786, according to them, for mercenary reasons. It seems more likely, however, that her conversion was genuine. Mrs. Melmoth died on 28 September 1823 and was buried in the graveyard of St. Patrick's Cathedral, New York.

A **Mr.** and **Mrs. Power** appeared in the Irish provincial theatres for about a decade near the end of the century. They have neither London nor

Dublin records. Power, whose *forte* seems to have been as a singer, is first noticed acting in Cork and Wexford in the autumn of 1788. Mr. and Mrs. Power acted together in Wexford in the winter of 1789 and in Kilkenny in the spring and summer of 1789. In 1790 they are found together in the summer and autumn in Waterford, Limerick and Ennis. Mrs. Power, but evidently not her husband, acted in Belfast during the early winter of the 1790–91 season. No roles have survived for her this season, but she shared a benefit with another actor.

The Powers returned to Limerick with Clinch's company in the winter of 1791, he making the "ordinary" actor's salary of £1. 1s. to £1. 11s. 6d. per week, she 10s. 6d. per week. Power, but not his wife, is found in Waterford in the winter of 1792 and in Derry in the spring of 1798. Mrs. Power, but not her husband, acted in Kilkenny in the spring of 1795. Thereafter, they disappear from the record.

Thomas King was one of the most popular and successful comic actors of the second half of the eighteenth century. As the *BD* observes, "Few players in the history of the London stage have come anywhere near playing so many excellent 'original' parts in comedy as Tom King did. Foremost among them were, in 1766, Lord Ogleby in *The Clandestine Marriage*, and, in 1777, Sir Peter Teazle in *The School for Scandal.*

King was born in London in 1730 to a successful merchant and his wife. At the age of 6 he was sent to a grammar school in Yorkshire and at 14 was articled to a solicitor where he stayed for three years before running off to join a strolling company in Tunbridge. He spent a short time with that company before setting up his own theatrical booth in Windsor in 1748.

There he was seen by David Garrick who had recently taken over the management of the Drury Lane theatre. Garrick engaged King in minor roles for the 1748–49 and 1749–50 seasons. King was attracted to Smock Alley by Sheridan for the 1750–51 season, and he remained there for the next four years. He spent the 1755–56 season in Bristol and then returned to Dublin through 1758–59, performing with the Smock Alley touring company at Cork in August 1757 and 1758.

King's wife, formerly Mary Baker, acted with him in Cork in the summers of 1757 and 1758. Miss Baker made her stage debut as a juvenile dancer at Goodman's Fields in October 1746 and performed there until moving to Covent Garden in 1748–49 and then to Drury Lane in 1749–50. She made her Smock Alley debut on 21 September 1750 dancing with Granier and others, and billed as "from the Theatre Royal, Drury Lane, first Time of her Appearance on this Stage." Later that season she danced in the Pantomime Ballet *"De Bucheuren en pas Deu trois Jalouise"* and a variety of other ballets with Billioni; Mlle. Pajot; Granier; Mlle. Granier and others.

Her first speaking part was as Juliet in March 1751. She remained at Smock Alley through the 1757–58 season (with the exception of 1755–56 when she may have been at Bath) and then moved to Crow Street for the 1758–59 season, acting with the Smock Alley company in Cork in the summers of 1757 and 1758.

Miss Baker returned to Drury Lane in 1759–60 and married Thomas King in 1766. She danced at Drury Lane until she withdrew from the stage after a salary dispute with Garrick in 1771–72. She died in 1813 at the age of 83.

King returned to Drury Lane in 1760 and he performed there for the next ten seasons. He returned to Dublin for an eight-night engagement at Smock Alley advertised from 21 May–3 June 1762. Wilkinson reveals that, despite the fact that King was "as great an established favourite as I ever remember in Dublin (not even Woodward excepted)," King's benefit was very poorly attended due to an influenza epidemic in Dublin. "Austin and I were in the middle gallery on his benefit night, when I do not believe there were twelve persons there besides, nor much more than £14. in the house." In June and July of 1768 King is found for a limited engagement in Dublin at Crow Street (not noticed by *BD*) and later that summer in Cork.

In addition to acting at Drury Lane, Thomas King also became co-manager of the theatre in Bristol and helped to direct a company that performed there in the summers until 1771 when he sold his share. Soon after that he purchased a share of the Sadler's Wells theatre, where he had performed as a clown and harlequin occasionally, and he was involved with that theatre until 1785, when he sold his interest.

According to the *BD*, by the time Garrick retired from the stage in 1776, "King had become Garrick's closest and most trusted professional friend." When Garrick died in 1779 and R. B. Sheridan took over the management of Drury Lane, King was soon brought in as deputy manager to reorganize the failing company. He tried, unsuccessfully, for three seasons to reverse the company's fortunes and declined signing with Sheridan for the 1783–84 season.

According to the *BD* King performed that season at Edinburgh, Glasgow, and Dublin; however, there is no record of King performing in Ireland during the 1783–84 season. Upon his return to London in September 1784 King resumed the deputy-management of Drury Lane and continued there through 1788–89. Evidently, exasperated by Sheridan's interference in theatrical matters, King again quit Drury Lane and set out on a year long acting tour which took him first to Ireland, returning to London via Glasgow, Edinburgh, Birmingham, York, and Leeds.

Back in London, King reached an agreement with Thomas Harris, proprietor of Covent Garden theatre, and he performed there, for the first time, during the 1789–90 season. However, he returned to Drury Lane for 1790–91 and remained with the company during the period it was being rebuilt and they acted at the King's Theatre in the Haymarket. In July and August 1791 Michael Atkins's engaged King for six nights each in Belfast and Derry, and again in May 1793 King appeared in Belfast. King spent the bulk of the 1793–94 season at Crow Street with Daly (billed as "from the Theatre Royal, Haymarket, his first appearance these two years"), but returned to Drury Lane in April. In an article on Richard Daly in *The Warder* of 1866 the following anecdote is recorded: "In 1794, King the renowned Lord Ogleby, played a most successful engagement. The houses were crowded nightly, almost beyond precedent. The manager and his star reaped a golden harvest. Some time after, one of the money-takers, when on his death-bed in the Marshalsea, sent for Daly and confessed that he, with his confederates, had filched £600 during that single engagement. Their word was, 'Boys, let us do the foreigner handsomely tonight.'"

King continued to perform at Drury Lane until he retired from the stage in late May 1802, when he played Sir Peter Teazle for the final time. He had been 56 years on the stage. He died in London on 11 December 1805.

For biographies of **Mr.** and **Mrs. Remington** see the 1762–63 season.

For a biography of **Rowe** see the 1777–78 season.

For biographies of **James Stewart** and **Master Stewart** see the 1769–70 season.

Repertory, 1790–1791 Season

Although the number of performance records is relatively large for this season, we see little that is novel or interesting in the repertory. The only new plays were two afterpieces: J. P. Kemble's *The Pannel*, which had premiered in Dublin in May 1790, and Joseph Reed's adaptation of

Fielding's farce *The Register Office*, which had been performed in Dublin since 1761, and probably had such drawing power as it did because of the popular Irish song it contained. The visit of the perennially popular English actor Thomas King drew audiences during the summer, although they were content to see King perform roles he had long before made his own.

Total Performances: 36 (including summer season)of 27 different named mainpieces; 33 of 19 different named afterpieces.
> Shakespeare: 6.
> New Mainpieces: 0.
> New Afterpieces: 2.

(For a key to repertory symbols see above, page 11)

Mainpieces: *All in the Wrong; As You Like It; The Belle's Stratagem; The Busy Body; The Clandestine Marriage*(2); *The Countess of Salisbury; Douglas*■; *The Earl of Essex; The Gamester* (2); *The Grecian Daughter; Hamlet* (2); *The Heiress; The Highland Reel*†; (2); *Isabella; Jane Shore; King Richard III*■; *Macbeth; The Merchant of Venice* (2); *The Mourning Bride; The Provoked Husband; The Rival Queens; Romeo and Juliet; The School for Scandal* (2); *The School for Wives; The Suspicious Husband;* Unspecified mainpiece(2); *Which is the Man?*†; *The Wonder.*

Afterpieces: *The Author; Bon Ton; The Citizen; The Critic* (2); *The Dead Alive* (2); *The Devil to Pay; Flora; Florizel and Perdita; High Life Below Stairs; The Honest Yorkshireman; The Lying Valet; Midas; The Miser*(2); *The Pannel**(2); *Peeping Tom; The Poor Soldier; The Quaker; The Register Office**; Unspecified "farce"(9); *The Way to Keep Him.*

Entr'acte entertainment: Singing: 1. Dancing: 1.

Benefits (24): Atkins; Mrs. Coates(3); Godfrey; Mrs. Godfrey(2); Griffith; Mrs. Hoskins; King; Lee and Power; Lynch; Mrs. Lynch; Mason; Mrs. Mason(2); May; Mrs. May; the Poor House and Infirmary; Pye; Remington; Mrs. Remington; Rowe; Stewart and Master Stewart.

September 1790

Mid-September 1790 Atkins will open theatre with an excellent Company the middle of next September. The usual number of tickets for the season will be disposed of application Atkins on his arrival in town. Source: 13–17 Aug. 1790

27 Mon. *The Gamester.* With a farce as will be expressed in the bills. Source: 21–24 Sept. 1790

October 1790

20 or **27** Wed. [Program not available]. Mrs. Coates is arrived in town from Dublin and is engaged by Atkins to perform for a few nights at the Belfast Theatre.

November 1790

10 Wed. *Jane Shore.* Jane Shore–Mrs. Coates. [Reviewed in source issue]. Source: 9–12 Nov. 1790

12 Fri. Mrs. Coates's benefit. *The Earl of Essex.* Essex–May; Southampton–Remington; Raleigh–Atkins; Burleigh–Rowe; Queen Elizabeth–Mrs. Melmoth; Rutland–Mrs. Coates. To which will be added the farce of *The Citizen.* Maria–Mrs. Coates. Source: 9–12 Nov. 1790

15 Mon. *Hamlet.* Hamlet–May; Ophelia–Mrs. Coates; Polonius–Rowe; Ghost–Stewart. [Reviewed in source issue]. Source: 9–12 Nov. 1790

19 Fri. *Douglas.* Not acted here these five years. With the farce of *The Dead Alive.* Source: 16–19 Nov. 1790

December 1790

3 Fri. Mrs. Mason, formerly known as Mrs. Booth, an old theatrical favourite of this town, made her appearance in *The Grecian Daughter.* Euphrasia–Mrs. Mason (after an absence of eleven years). [Reviewed in source issue]. Source: 3–7 Dec. 1790

20 Mon. *Isabella* and a farce expressed in the bills. Between the acts of the farce an address to the town written and spoken by Mrs. Melmoth. Source: 10–14 Dec. 1790

29 Wed. Benefit of Stewart and his son young Stewart. *The Merchant of Venice* and *Midas.* By desire Mrs. Melmoth will recite Collins's *"Ode on the Passions."* Between the acts: 1 *"Bucks Have at Ye All"* by young Stewart; 2 *"British Loyalty"* by Stewart. Source: 21–24 Dec. 1790

31 Fri. Benefit of Mrs. Remington. Not acted this season. *The Belle's Stratagem.* Letitia Hardy–Mrs. Coates. With the farce of *The Way to Keep Him.* With entertainments as expressed in the bills. Source: 24–28 Dec. 1790

January 1791

3 Mon. Benefit of Rowe. [Play and farce. Other details of program not available]. Source: 17–21 Dec. 1790

5 Wed. Benefit of Mrs. May. *Romeo and Juliet.* Romeo–May; Friar Laurence–Rowe;   Prince–Atkins;   Peter   and   Apothecary–Lynch; Mercutio–Remington; Nurse–Mrs. Remington; Lady Capulet–Mrs. Hoskin; Juliet–Mrs. Coates. In Act 5 will be introduced a grand solemn dirge. In the course of the evening May will recite Collins's *"Ode on the Passions,"* speak *"Bucks have at ye all"* and deliver Foote's poetical observation on criticism. With the comedy of *The Miser.* Lovegold–Rowe; Frederic–Lee; Starved Cook–Lynch; Ramillie–Remington; Mariana–Mrs. May; Mrs. Wisely–Mrs. Hoskin; Lappet–Mrs. Mason. Reduced into three acts. Source: 31 Dec. 1790–4 Jan. 1791

7 Fri. Pye's benefit. *The Highland Reel.* With a farce and entertainments as will be expressed in the bills. Source: 31 Dec. 1790–4 Jan. 1791

10 Mon. Benefit of Lynch. *The Heiress.* With a farce and entertainments as will be expressed in the bills. Source: 31 Dec. 1790–4 Jan. 1791

12 Wed. The manager's night. Benefit of Atkins. *The Mourning Bride.* With the farce of *The Devil to Pay.* Source: 4–7 Jan. 1791

14 Fri. Benefit Mrs. Godfrey. *The School for Wives.* Belville–May; Conolly–Rowe;   Leeson–Remington;   Torrington–Lynch;   Captain Savage–Lee; General Savage–Atkins; Mrs. Belville–Mrs. Melmoth; Miss Leeson–Mrs. Godfrey; Miss Walsingham–Mrs. Coates. With *The Poor Soldier.* Source: 7–11 Jan. 1791

17 Mon. Benefit of Mrs. Mason. *Which is the Man?* End of the play Mrs. Mason will recite the ode on the recovery of his Majesty as spoken by Mrs. Siddons at Brook's Gala in the character of Britannia. With a celebrated farce never acted here called *The Pannel.* A new scene painted for the occasion by Atkins. Source: 11–14 Jan. 1791

19 Wed. Benefit of Mrs. Hoskin. *The Highland Reel.* Between the acts of the opera May will recite Gray's *"Elegy in a Country Church-Yard,"* Collins's *"Ode on the Passions,"* and Foote's *"Poetical observations on criticism."* With the farce of *Florizel and Perdita.* Source: 11–14 Jan. 1791

21 Fri. Benefit of Griffith. *The Gamester.* With a farce and entertainments as will be expressed in the bills. Source: 14–18 Jan. 1791

24 Mon. Remington's benefit. Not acted these ten years. *King Richard III.* With entertainments as will be expressed in the bills and the farce of *Peeping Tom of Coventry.* Source: 14–18 Jan. 1791

26 Wed. Benefit [second] of Mrs. Coates. *The School for Scandal.* Sir Peter Teazle–Rowe; Joseph Surface–Remington; Sir Oliver Surface–Atkins; Crabtree–Lynch; Charles Surface–May; Mrs. Candour–Mrs. May; Maria–Mrs. Godfrey; Lady Sneerwell–Mrs. Hoskin; Lady Teazle–Mrs. Coates. With the farce of *High Life Below Stairs.* Kitty–Mrs. Coates (first appearance in that character). Source: 21–25 Jan. 1791

28 Fri.   May in his second appearance of *Hamlet,* for his own benefit did not forfeit the encomium on his former performance of that character. The receipt of the house was £69. 3s. Irish. Though rising merit such as May's in that favourite play of Shakespeare's deserved the reception it met with, we cannot avoid taking this opportunity of recommending it to the humane inhabitants of Belfast to shew at least an equal zeal in promoting a benefit which we hear is within a few days to be given. With the farce of [*Flora; or,*] *Hob in the Well* and an occasional address to be spoken by May. Source: 28 Jan.–1 Feb. 1791

31 Mon. Benefit of Godfrey. *Macbeth.* With the original music, scenery, and decorations. In Act 3 a grand banquet to which will be added the farce of *The Honest Yorkshireman.* Source: 21–25 Jan. 1791

February 1791

2 Wed. The last benefit. Benefit of Mason. *The Rival Queens.* With the farce of *The Miser.* Source: 25–28 Jan. 1791

4 Fri. Benefit of the Poorhouse and Infirmary. *The Provoked Husband* with a musical farce and other entertainments as will be expressed in the bills. Source: 28 Jan.–1 Feb. 1791

7 Mon. Lee and Mrs. Power's benefit. Positively the last night but one of the company performing this season. Not acted here these thirteen years. *The Countess of Salisbury* with the farce of *The Pannel* and other entertainments as will be expressed in the bills. Source: 28 Jan.–1 Feb. 1791

9 Wed. Benefit of Mrs. Lynch. Positively the last night of the company performing here this season. Not acted this season. *The Wonder, A Woman*

Keeps a Secret. With a farce and variety of entertainments of singing and dancing as will be expressed in the bills. Source: 1–4 Feb. 1791

July 1791

1 Fri.   On Friday evening last the Circus in Cunningham Greg's [lumber] yard was opened to a numerous and genteel audience. The performance throughout was received with universal applause. A short time after the performance had commenced part of a temporary gallery erected for the occasion fell by which a number of persons were considerably hurt and a boy had his leg fractured. (17–21 June 1791) Parker and Ricketts from their Circus Royal Edinburgh and now on their way to Dublin most respectfully beg leave to inform the ladies gentlemen and public in general of Belfast that their troops of equestrian and other performers consisting of fourteen of the first performers in Europe will display their unparalleled exhibitions for a few days in Belfast. Further particulars will be expressed and likewise the day of beginning in future handbills and advertisements. [The Parker and Ricketts Circus evidently performed, weather permitting, each evening from 1 July through Friday, 22 July. See 5–8 July 1791 and 15–19 July 1791. The headline performer would seem to be the William or possibly John Parker cited in *BD* 11, 208–209, equestrian, manager, and dancer, who is known to have died in 1858. Parker "was evidently an important figure in his own day and milieu, but information about him is extremely thin, especially compared to the copious accounts of his well-known second wife Sophia and his famous daughter Nannette." The authors of the *BD* were apparently unaware of Parker's connection with Rickets in Edinburgh, nor do they mention his visit to Belfast. The second partner in the circus was almost certainly John Bill Ricketts, equestrian and manager, who died in 1800 (see *BD* 12, 377–379). Again, the *BD* entry for Ricketts makes no mention of the Parker-Ricketts partnership. Rickets left Scotland for America in 1792. He settled in Philadelphia for nearly a decade and established a riding-school and amphitheatre there. Ricketts drowned when the ship in which he was returning to England foundered off Charleston, South Carolina. His son, Francis, performed in circuses in America in the nineteenth century]. Source: 1–5 July 1791

Summer Season

[The last recorded Belfast summer season before 1800].

18 Mon.   First of [Thomas] King's six nights. *The Clandestine Marriage.* Lord Ogleby–King (from the Theatre–Royal, Drury Lane). With a farce never acted here called *The Register Office*. Boxes 5s. 5d., pit 3s. 3d., gallery 1s. 1d. Source: 8–12 July 1791

Commentary: Atkins has the honour to inform his very liberal patrons of Belfast that he has engaged that great ornament of the stage King to perform at the theatre for six nights. Due notice will be given of his first appearance. Prices of admittance the same as in Dublin. No less than a whole row can be taken in the boxes and children and children only will be admitted at half price. The admirers of the drama will in the course of the ensuing month have an opportunity of seeing the celebrated King perform in this town as we are assured that Atkins has engaged him to play six nights in Derry and six in Belfast. 1–5 July 1791.

25 Mon. Atkins most respectfully informs the public that he has from Monday last by the advice and at the request of several ladies and gentlemen discontinued the performances intended for the week on account of the Maze races. The theatre will again be opened on Monday the 25th. *The School for Scandal.* Sir Peter Teasel–King. With the farce of *The Quaker*. King will also perform on Wednesday 27 and on Friday 29. There will not on Monday, August 1 on account of the review be any play. On Wednesday 3 August King will appear again which will be his last performance in this theatre. Source: 19–22 July 1791

27 Wed. Third of King's nights. *The Busy Body*. Marplot–King. To which will be added the farce of *The Lying Valet*. Sharp–King. Source: 22–26 July 1791

29 Fri.   Fourth of King's nights. *The Merchant of Venice*. Shylock–King. To which will be added the farce of *The Critic*. Puff–King. Source: 26–29 July 1791

August 1791

3 Wed. Benefit of King and the last night of his performing here. *All in the Wrong*. Sir John Restless–King. End of Act 4 King will deliver a serio-comic poetic prosaic Paraphrase of Shakespeare's *"Seven Ages"* written by George Alexander Stevens, and before the entertainments he will by desire recite Foote's poetical observations on criticism founded on the story of *"The Man, the Boy, and the Ass."* With a comedy of two acts called *Bon Ton*. Sir John Trotley–King. Source: 29 July–2 Aug. 1791

5   Fri.   The Maze races with other concurring circumstances having deprived a great part of the public of Belfast and its neighbourhood of the pleasure of seeing King in his much admired character of Lord Ogleby, Atkins by particular desire of several ladies and gentlemen, has made application to King on the occasion who has most readily consented to repeat it. *The Clandestine Marriage.* Lord Ogleby–King. With the farce of *The Dead Alive.*

Commentary: We only do justice to the taste of this town and neighbourhood in mentioning that the performance of King has given universal delight and convinced us that he is the first comedian at present on the stage. His Shylock was a piece of the first acting we have been witness to it was really the Jew that Shakespeare drew. In Puff and Lord Ogilby he has so long been admired that any compliment to his performance of those characters were unnecessary. As he generally takes the characters of the Jew and of Puff on the same night the versatility of his powers are very fully displayed as it is also in the parody on Shakespeare Seven Ages in which he discovers a wonderful command of the muscles and in the general expression of the face. Source: 2–5 Aug. 1791

8   Mon. *As You Like It.* Touchstone–King. And *The Critic.* Puff–King will positively conclude his engagement. Source: 2–5 Aug. 1791

10 Wed. Mrs. Coates's benefit. As King cannot depart till Thursday he has kindly offered his assistance in play and farce. *The Suspicious Husband.* Ranger–King; Clarinda–Mrs. Coates. With the entertainment of *The Author.* Cadwallader–King, who will by desire speak the original prologue thereto founded on the fable of *"The Man, The Boy, and the Ass."* The public may be assured this will be King's last performance at this theatre. As King is not to receive any emolument for his performance the prices will of course be as previous to his commencement: boxes 3s. 3d., pit 2s. 2d., gallery 1s. 1d. Source: 5–9 Aug. 1791

19 Fri.   Benefit of Mrs. Godfrey. [Play and farce. Other details of program unavailable]. In consideration of the unprotected situation Mrs. Godfrey is unhappily left in from her recent loss, Atkins has kindly consented to allow her the use of the theatre on the above night. Source: 12–16 Aug. 1791

1791–1792 SEASON

Venue: Rosemary Lane Theatre (last season there).
Company: Michael Atkins; Charles Bew; Mrs. Elizabeth Coates; Mrs. Fenner; Mrs. Godfrey; Griffith; Mrs. Hoskin; John Lynch; Mrs. Lynch;

Miss Lynch; Mrs. Mason; Mr. and Mrs. James May; Mrs. Melmoth; Miss O'Neil; Remington; Mrs. Remington; Richards; Rowe; Ryder; Miss E. Ryder; Miss R. Ryder; James B. Stewart.

For biography of **Michael Atkins** see the 1767–68 season.

The *BD* believes that the Mr. Bew who took a sole benefit (but for whom there is no performance record) in Belfast on 8 February 1792 was **Charles Bew**, the son of a London printer, who formerly had appeared at Norwich on 19 June 1791. At Norwich he was introduced as "a juvenile son of the buskin," a description which suggests that it is not likely to have been the same person.

For biography of **Mrs. Elizabeth Coates** see 1790–91 season.

The only record we have of a **Mrs. Fenner** is that she played two minor roles on one night in Belfast in February 1792 and shared a benefit with two other actors later that year. She may have been related to the "Mr. Fenner" who acted in a wide variety of tertiary roles at Crow Street during the 1775–76 season.

For biography of **Mrs. Godfrey** see 1790–91 season.

For biography of **Griffith** see 1790–91 season.

For a biography of **Mrs. Hoskins** see the 1782–83 season.

For biography of **John Lynch** and family see the 1771–72 season.

For biography of **Mrs. Mason** see the 1775–76 season.

For biographies of **Mr.** and **Mrs. James May** see 1790–91 season.

For biography of **Mrs. Melmoth** see 1790–91 season.

For biography of **Miss [Eliza] O'Neill** see the 1782–83 season.

For biographies of **Mr.** and **Mrs. Remington** see the 1762–63 season.

For biography of **Richards** see 1778–79 season.

For a biography of **Rowe** see the 1777–78 season.

For biographies of **Thomas Ryder, Miss E. Ryder** and **Miss R. Ryder** see 1769–70 season.

For biography of **James Stewart** see the 1769–70 season.

Repertory, 1791–1792 Season

Michael Atkins evidently made a considerable effort this season to bring new plays to Belfast. The calendar contains no fewer than nine plays that had never before appeared in Belfast playbills (although six of these make no claim for a first performance). The most important drawing cards of the season were John O'Keeffe's very popular comedy *Wild Oats,* which had premiered in Dublin two months earlier, in December 1791, and also his farce *Modern Antiques,* which had received its first Dublin performance in June 1791.

Total Performances: 40 of 24 different named mainpieces; 34 of 18 different named afterpieces.
    Shakespeare: 1.
    New Afterpieces: 1.
    New Afterpieces: 2.

(For a key to repertory symbols see above, page 11)

Mainpieces: *All in the Wrong; The Beggar's Opera; The Carmelite*†; *Cato; Chapter of Accidents; The Dramatist*†; *The Earl of Essex; Hamlet; He Would Be a Soldier*†; *The Heiress; The Highland Reel; Inkle and Yarico; Jane Shore; Lionel and Clarissa; Love in a Village; The Maid of the Mill; Next Door Neighbours*†; *The Revenge*■; *The Rival Queens; The School for Arrogance*†; *The Suspicious Husband*(2); Unspecified play(8); *The West Indian; Which is the Man?*(2); *Wild Oats**(4).

Afterpieces: *The Agreeable Surprise; Bon Ton; Barnaby Brittle;* [*The Death of*] *Captain Cook*†(4); *The Cheats of Scapin; The Devil to Pay; Florizel and Perdita; The Foundling; The Intriguing Chambermaid; The Midnight Hour; Modern Antiques**; *The Padlock; A Peep Behind the Curtain**(2); *The Provoked Husband; Rosina*(2); *The Sorcerers*†; *Thomas and Sally; Tit for Tat*†; Unspecified "farce"(11); *The Way to Keep Him.*

Prelude: *Regions of Accomplishment*†.

Entr'acte entertainments: Singing: 1. Dancing: 1.

Benefits (25): Atkins; Bew; Mrs. Coates(2); Mrs. Fenner, Miss Lynch and Miss O'Neill; Mrs. Godfrey; Griffith; Mrs. Hoskins; Lynch; Mrs. Lynch; Mrs. Mason; May; Mrs. May; Mrs. Melmoth; the Poor House; Remington(2); Mrs. Remington; Richards; Rowe; Ryder; Miss E. Ryder; Miss R. Ryder; Stewart.

September 1791

14 Wed. *All in The Wrong.* Sir John Restless–Ryder; Belinda–Miss E. Ryder. And *Rosina.* Phoebe–Miss E. Ryder; Rosina–Miss R. Ryder. Source: 9–13 Sept. 1791

16 Fri.   *The Highland Reel.* Jenny–Miss R. Ryder; Moggy McGilpin–Miss E. Ryder. With *Bon Ton.* Miss Tittup–Miss E. Ryder. Source: 13–16 Sept. 1791

21 Wed. *The Beggar's Opera.* Macheath–Miss E. Ryder; Polly–Miss R. Ryder. With a farce. Source: 16–20 Sept. 1791

23 Fri.   Benefit of Ryder. *The Maid of the Mill* with *The Cheats of Scapin.* Source: 16–20 Sept. 1791

30 Fri.   *Inkle and Yarico.* Wowskie–Miss E. Ryder; Yarico–Miss R. Ryder. With *Tit For Tat.* Source: 27–30 Sept. 1791

October 1791

3 Mon. Benefit of Miss R. Ryder. *Love in a Village* and *The Agreeable Surprise.* Source: 27–30 Sept. 1791

10 Mon. Benefit of Miss E. Ryder. *Lionel and Clarissa* and *The Intriguing Chambermaid.* Drunken Colonel–Ryder; Lettice–Miss E. Ryder. To conclude with the *"Minuet de la Cour"* by Miss E. Ryder and Miss R. Ryder. Source: 4–7 Oct. 1791

14 Fri.   *The Carmelite.* May–Rowe; Montgomeri–Remington; Lady Valeroi–Mrs. Melmoth. Source: 11–14 Oct. 1791

17 Mon. *Jane Shore.* Source: 11–14 Oct. 1791

19 Wed. Benefit of Mrs. Mason. *The Earl of Essex.* With a farce and entertainments. Source: 11–14 Oct. 1791

November 1791

2 Wed. *The School for Arrogance.* McDermot–Lynch; Lady Peckham–Mrs. Melmoth. Source: 1–4 Nov. 1791

30 Wed. By desire of 1st Belfast Volunteer Company. *Cato.* With *The Devil to Pay.* Source: 25–29 Nov. 1791

December 1791

2 Fri. *Which is the Man?* and *The Sorcerers; or, Harlequin Wizard,* with an entire new scene. Source: 29 Nov.–2 Dec. 1791

19 Mon. [Program unavailable]. Atkins and company take the earliest opportunity of returning their acknowledgements to the Belfast Volunteer Company in particular and the polite audience in general who honoured the theatre with their presence on Monday evening last. Source: 20–23 Dec. 1791

January 1792

early Jan. 1792 *The Suspicious Husband.* Ranger–May; Clarinda–Mrs. Coates. Source: 3–6 Jan. 1792

2 Mon. [Program unavailable]. Atkins and company take the earliest opportunity of returning their acknowledgements to the Belfast troop in particular and the polite audience in general who honoured the Theatre with their presence on Monday evening last. Source: 3–6 Jan. 1792

9 Mon. [Program unavailable]. Atkins and company takes the earliest opportunity of returning their acknowledgments to the officers of the 70th Regiment. Source: 10–13 Jan. 1792

13 Fri. By particular desire. Benefit of Rowe. Not acted this season. *The Foundling.* Between the play and farce a comic song by Lynch. With the farce of *Barnaby Brittle.* Rowe with the utmost respect and gratitude for favours past from an indulgent public humbly hopes his taking a benefit in his present situation will not be deemed an intrusion on their liberality especially as it is at the desire of several of his particular friends and of many ladies and gentlemen of the first consequence in Belfast. Source: 10–13 Jan. 1792

25 Wed. *The Foundling.* With for the last time this season the new serious pantomime called [*The Death of*] *Captain Cook.* Source: 20–24 Jan. 1792

30 Mon. Lynch's benefit. *He Would be a Soldier.* With a farce and entertainments as will be expressed in the bills. Source: 24–27 Jan. 1792

February 1792

1 Wed. Mrs. Coates benefit. *The West Indian.* Charlotte Rusport–Mrs. Coates. With *The Way to Keep Him.* Widow Belmore–Mrs. Coates. Source: 27–31 Jan. 1792

3 Fri. Mrs. Melmoth's benefit. [Play and farce. Other details of program unknown]. Source: 27–31 Jan. 1792

6 Mon. Mrs. May's benefit. *The Rival Queens.* Alexander–May; Lysimachus–Remington; Cassander–Griffith; Clytus–Atkins; Roxana–Mrs. Melmoth; Sysigambis–Mrs. Remington; Parisatis–Mrs. May; Statira–Mrs. Coates. In the course of the evening May will recite *"Alexander's Feast; or, the Power of Music an ode,"* Foote's poetical *"Observations on criticism"* and *"Bucks have at ye All."* To which will be added the musical entertainment of *Rosina.* Belville–Young gentleman (with favourite songs, first appearance on any stage). Source: 31 Jan.–3 Feb. 1792

8 Wed. Bew's benefit. [Play and farce. Other details of program unavailable]. Source: 31 Jan.–3 Feb. 1792

10 Fri. Benefit of Mrs. Hoskin. Not acted here these twelve years. *The Revenge.* With the farce as will be expressed in the bills of the day. Source: 3–7 Feb. 1792

15 Wed. Mrs. Remington's benefit. Never performed here. *Wild Oats.* The universal approbation this piece has met with in the Theatres Royal London and Dublin will it is hoped sufficiently recommend it to the attention of the polite audience of Belfast. With the farce of *Thomas and Sally.* Source: 10–14 Feb. 1792

17 Fri. Atkins's benefit. *Wild Oats.* Second time. With *The Padlock.* Source: 14–17 Feb. 1792

20 Mon. Mrs. Coates's benefit. [Play and farce. Other details of program unavailable]. Source: 10–14 Feb. 1792

24 Fri. May's benefit. *The Dramatist.* Vapid (with original epilogue)–May; Floriville–Remington; Ennui–Richards; Peter–Lynch; Willoughby–Griffith; Neville–Stewart; Lady Waitfort–Mrs. Remington; Letty–Mrs. Fenner; Miss Courtney–Mrs. Coates. Between the play and the farce an occasional address will be spoken and *"Bucks Have at Ye All"* recited by May. With the farce of [*The Sheep Shearing; or,*] *Florizel and Perdita.* Florizel–May; Camillo–Atkins; King–Griffith; Clown–Lynch;

Autolicus–Richards; Dorcas–Mrs. Fenner; Perdita–Mrs. Coates. Source: 14–17 Feb. 1792

27 Mon. Mrs. Godfrey's benefit. *Wild Oats.* Rover–May; John Dorey–Atkins; Ephraim Smooth–Lynch; Harry–Stewart; Sim–Remington; Sir George Thunder–Richards; Amelia–Mrs. May; Jane–Mrs. Godfrey; Lady Amaranth–Mrs. Coates. With the farce of the *Midnight Hour.* Source: 21–24 Feb. 1792

29 Wed. Remington's benefit. Not acted this season. *The Heiress.* With entertainments as will be expressed in the bills of the day. With a farce never performed here called *A Peep Behind the Curtain.* Source: 21–24 Feb. 1792

March 1792

2 Fri. Mrs. Lynch's benefit. *The Chapter of Accidents* and a new farce never performed here called *Modern Antiques; or, The Merry Mourners.* With a variety of entertainments as will be expressed in the bills. Source: 28 Feb.–2 Mar. 1792

5 Mon. Griffith's benefit. *Hamlet.* With a farce and entertainments as will be expressed in a future advertisement. Source: 28 Feb.–2 Mar. 1792

7 Wed. Stewart's benefit. [Play and farce. Other details of program unavailable]. Source: 28 Feb.–2 Mar. 1792

9 Fri. Remington's benefit. *Wild Oats* and a farce never performed here called *A Peep Behind the Curtain* [but see 29 February 1792]. Source: 6–9 Mar. 1792

19 Mon. On account of the very long and dangerous indisposition of Rowe a number of his friends have desired he should take another benefit. *The Provoked Husband.* With a farce and entertainments as will be expressed in the bills. As Rowe's indisposition renders him incapable of paying any attention to this business May has kindly undertaken to do it for him. [The veteran Belfast actor Richard Coxe Rowe died "after long languishing in a hopeless disorder" in Belfast on 7 May 1792]. Source: 13–16 Mar. 1792 and 8–11 May 1792

23 Fri. Benefit of Mrs. Fenner, Miss Lynch and Miss O'Neill. *Which is the Man?* And positively the last time the celebrated serious pantomime of [*The Death of*] *Captain Cook.* Source: 20–23 Mar. 1792

26 Mon. Benefit of the Poorhouse of this town. [Comedy and farce. Other details of program unavailable].Source: 20–23 Mar. 1792

28 Wed. Mrs. Coates's benefit. *The Suspicious Husband.* With the celebrated serious pantomime of [*The Death of*] *Captain Cook* and a variety of other entertainments as will be expressed in the bills. Last night but one of the company performing here this season. Source: 23–27 Mar. 1792

30 Fri.   The last night this season. Benefit of Richards. *Next Door Neighbours; or, The World As It Goes.* Preceding the play a prelude of one act called the *Regions of Accomplishment.* By R. B. Sheridan. After the comedy the celebrated serious pantomime of [*The Death of*] *Captain Cook.* Source: 27–30 Mar. 1792

1792–1793 SEASON

Venue: Arthur Street Theatre (opened 25 February 1793).
Company: Mrs. John Bernard; Miss Cranford; Thomas King; James May; James Middleton; Richards; Mrs. Stewart.

For biography of **Mrs. John Bernard** see the 1782–83 season.

The **Miss Cranford** who appeared with Michael Atkins's company in Derry at the beginning of the 1792–93 season and later that season in Belfast (April–May) is probably the same young woman who made her stage debut at Drury Lane on 7 January 1784 as a Spirit in a pantomime. She continued at Drury Lane in similar, minor roles, requiring some skill in singing and dancing, through the 1788–89 season.

Miss Cranford is found at the Haymarket Theatre in June 1786 and in each of the summer seasons thereafter until she was released in October 1789. The *BD* finds her still acting in the summer of 1792 at Richmond, after which she left England for Ireland for the 1792–93 season. She is found at the Theatre Royal, Windsor, in 1794 but thereafter she disappears from the record.

For biography of **Thomas King** see the 1790–91 season.

For biography of **James May** see 1790–91 season.

James Middleton was the stage name of James Magan, born in Dublin about 1769 and died 1799. Magan's father was an immanent Dublin surgeon who, after sending his son to Dr. Samuel Whyte's academy, intended him for the same profession. The stagestruck Magan, however, had other plans, and, in order to keep his aspirations secret until he had become a success, ran away to London. With the help of both Richard Daly, who was a relative, and the dramatist W. C. Oulton, Magan was given an audition by Harris at Covent Garden sometime in 1787. Harris agreed to engage Magan, who assumed the stage name of Middleton, again, presumably to disguise his identity, for the 1788–89 season, but suggested that he get some experience in the provinces, specifically at Bath. The *BD* reports that it was at about this time that Magan began to manifest the earliest reported signs of the mental instability that was to wreck his later life.

Middleton made his professional acting debut at Bath on 31 January 1788, as Othello, and the local critics were impressed. Later that winter he also performed at Bristol. The *BD* is unaware that in the summer of 1788 Middleton traveled to Dublin, where, using his stage name, on 16 June 1789 he made his Crow Street debut as Romeo and was billed as "from Covent Garden, his first appearance in his native kingdom." Middleton was to perform a variety of capital roles there that summer, and the Dublin audiences must certainly have been aware of Middleton's true identity for, as a part of his benefit in August, Middleton spoke "an address, written by Sam. Whyte, called "The Poetical Schoolmaster," which was published in *HJ* 5 Aug. 1789 and reprinted in Whyte's *Poems on Various Occasions.*

Middleton made his Covent Garden debut in September 1788 as Romeo, and he attempted several other capital parts that season with some success; however, he was not reengaged at Covent Garden, and, when his wife died suddenly, he returned to Ireland appearing with the Crow Street company during their annual visit to Cork and Waterford in the autumn of 1789. In January 1790 he was acting at Crow Street where he remained through the 1791–92 season, appearing again at Cork in the autumns of 1790 and 1791, and at Waterford in the autumn of 1792. On the 29 March 1792 he married Martha Ann Whyte (who evidently did not act), the daughter of his former schoolmaster.

After leaving Dublin in March 1792, Middleton traveled to Edinburgh and then returned to Ireland, to Belfast, for April and May 1793. Middleton then journeyed to London, where he was engaged for the 1793–94 Covent Garden season and where he remained through 1796–97. In August 1794 Middleton visited Derry with Atkins's company, the theatre in Belfast being closed because of civil disturbances. During the summers of 1795 and 1796 he acted in Birmingham.

By the winter of 1797 Middleton's mental illness and alcoholism was well advanced, quickly destroying his acting career. He was not reengaged at Covent Garden for the 1796–97 season because, among other things, he left the stage after his scene one night, went to a neighboring tavern, and refused to play any more that evening.

Middleton immediately left for Ireland and is found at Crow Street during the summer of 1797, acting in secondary roles with J. P. Kemble and Mrs. Yates and billed as "from the Theatre Royal, Covent Garden, first appearance these three years." He was engaged at Crow Street for the 1797–98 season, but his many irregularities of behavior caused the manager at Crow Street to cancel his engagement, and he disappears from the bills in March. Thereafter he traveled in the English provinces, appearing in Cheltenham and Gloucester.

Destitute and on his last legs, Middleton was taken back in at Drury Lane in the autumn of 1798, but on a much-reduced, daily salary. He survived the 1798–99 season, but was quickly losing his memory and self-control. He was imprisoned for debt for a time and then released when his friend Charles Kemble paid what was owing. The *BD* is not aware that in July 1799 Middleton is found with Kemble, Incledon, and Miss Gough at Crow Street for a brief engagement. Middleton did not act, but on 26 July he recited "Dryden's celebrated ode on Music called Alexander's Feast (his second appearance on this stage these four years)."

It was perhaps after his return to London that Middleton tried to eke out a living by giving recitations of his favorite roles from Shakespeare in a back-street theatre in Pimlico. He was found in an alcoholic stupor lying in a rainy street on 13 October 1799, and, despite the attempts of his friends to save his life, he died on 18 October 1799. The Drury Lane proprietors paid his funeral expenses. He was survived by his wife, from whom he had been separated for several years, two sons and a daughter.

For biography of **Richards** see 1778–79 season.

The **Mrs. Stewart** or Stuart who performed during the 1792–93 season at the new Arthur Street theatre in Belfast was probably too young to have been the wife of James Beatty Stewart, and Stewart's son would not marry until several years later. This Mrs. Stewart seems to have specialized in the singing of Scottish songs.

[Clark (1965, 354) errs in finding Andrew Cherry in Belfast on 24 October 1792].

Repertory, February–May 1793

Atkins evidently did not advertise his programs in the newspapers during this period and, despite recurring civil disturbances in Belfast, there were almost certainly many more performances than the sixteen of which we have record. Virtually all of the surviving performance information is from benefit performances the advertisements for which the recipients paid. With the exception of Mrs. Inchbald's *Every One Has Fault,* which had received its Dublin premiere only the previous July, the new mainpieces performed for the actors' benefits were not brought on to the Belfast stage in an especially timely fashion. Colman's *The Surrender of Calais* had received its first performance in Dublin in November 1791, Prince Hoare's farce *No Song, No Supper* in February 1791, and O'Keeffe's *The Young Quaker* in January 1784.

The Rev. Dr. Banbridge, the author of the new afterpiece, *The Guillotine,* with Atkins's tacit approval, evidently hoped to use the Belfast stage as a political forum and to draw a parallel between the unremedied popular grievances that led to the execution in January of Louis XVI, and the current political unrest in Ireland. Britain went to war with France in February, and the Belfast radicals who spoke in support of the French Revolution were considered by many little better than traitors. Banbridge's plan backfired and, as *The Northern Star,* the newspaper of the Belfast United Irishmen, reported on 29 May 1793, *The Guillotine* was shouted off of the stage, although the galleries demanded that it go forward. Atkins and Lynch both tried to restore order but the audience would not allow the program to continue. Atkins closed the theatre two days later and it was to remain closed for the next season.

Total Performances: 16 of 9 different named mainpieces; 13 of 7 different named afterpieces.
    Shakespeare: 2.
    New Mainpieces: 3.
    New Afterpieces: 2.

(For a key to repertory symbols see above, page 11)

Mainpieces: *The Chapter of Accidents; Every One Has His Fault**; *King Richard III; The Rival Queens; Robin Hood; Romeo and Juliet; Such Things Are; The Surrender of Calais**(2); Unspecified "play"(4); *The Young Quaker**(2);

Afterpieces: *The Apprentice; Comus; Cymon; The Guillotine*; High Life Below Stairs; No Song, No Supper**(3); *The Romp;* Unspecified "farce"(4).

Interlude: [*The Death of*] *Captain Cook.*

Entr'acte singing and dancing: 1.

Benefits (11): Atkins; Mrs. Bernard; Miss Cranford; Hurst; King; Lynch; Mr. and Mrs. May; Middleton; Remington; Richards; Mrs. Stewart.

February 1793

25 Mon. [Play. Other details of program unavailable]. Occasional address to be spoken on the opening of the new Theatre is written by Rev. Hugh George Macklin and spoken by May. [The text of this address and a brief account of the events of this evening may be found in *NS* 2 Mar. 1793]. Source: 19–22 Feb. 1793

April 1793

1 Mon. *Romeo and Juliet.* Romeo–Middleton. With *The Romp.* Source: 26–29 Mar. 1793

17 Wed. *The Rival Queens.* Alexander–Middleton; Roxana–Mrs. Bernard. In Act 2 the triumphal entry of Alexander into Babylon. The vocal parts by Mrs. Stewart, Richards, and Miss Cranford. In Act 4 a grand banquet. *The Apprentice.* Dick–Middleton. With the original prologue. Source: 12–16 Apr. 1793

26 Fri. Benefit of May. [Play, farce and entertainments. Other details of program unavailable]. Source: 16–19 Apr. 1793

May 1793

8 Wed. Benefit of Atkins. *The Chapter of Accidents.* Woodville–Middleton. Collins's *"Ode on the Passions"* by Middleton. To which will be added the new musical entertainment never performed here called *No Song, No Supper.* Source: 30 Apr.–3 May 1793

10 Fri. Middleton's night. *Every One has His Fault.* Irwin–Middleton; Edward–Miss Cranford; Lady Eleanor Irwin–Mrs. Bernard. Written by Mrs. Inchbald and now performing with universal applause at the Theatre-Royal, Covent Garden. The prologue to be spoken by King; the epilogue by Mrs. Bernard. Between the play and farce Middleton will recite an ode by Penrose *"To Madness."* With the farce of *High Life Below Stairs.* Duke's Servant–Middleton; Mrs. Kitty–Miss Cranford. A mock minuet by Middleton and Miss Cranford to conclude with *"That's Your Sort"* a farewell epilogue in the character of Goldfinch by Middleton. Source: 30 Apr.–3 May 1793

13 Mon. Benefit of Mrs. Bernard. Never performed here. *The Surrender of Calais.* To which will be added the Musical Romance of *Cymon.* Cymon (for that night only)–Mrs. Bernard. Source: 3–7 May 1793

15 Wed. Miss Cranford's benefit, having procured a perfect and correct manuscript copy the only one in this kingdom of the celebrated comedy of *The Young Quaker.* For that night only. With *No Song, No Supper.* Source: 7–10 May 1793

17 Fri. Mrs. Stuart's [Stewart] benefit. *Robin Hood; or, Sherwood Forest.* Clarinda–Mrs. Stuart. Mrs. Stuart will introduce the favourite Scots Song of *"Dee'l take the Wars," "The Soldier Tir'd,"* and the favourite harp song as introduced by the celebrated Madame Mara in *Artaxerxes.* With a farce and variety of entertainments. There will be no expense spared to render the nights entertainments worthy attention of the public. The band to be augmented. Source: 7–10 May 1793

20 Mon. Lynch's benefit. [Play and farce. Other details of program not available]. With a variety of entertainment singing and dancing. Source: 10–14 May 1793

22 Wed. Hurst's benefit. *King Richard III* with a variety of entertainments and a farce as will be expressed in the playbills. From the very flattering accounts of the attention paid to theatrical amusements at Belfast, Hurst has been induced to quit the respectable and profitable situation of deputy manager of the Theatre Royal in Dublin. Source: 14–17 May 1793

24 Fri. King's benefit. [Opera, farce, and entertainments. Other details of program not available]. Source: 17–21 May 1793

27 Mon. Benefit of Richards. *The Young Quaker.* To which will be added the much admired historical piece of two acts called *The Guillotine; or, The Death of Louis XVI.* This truly moral and instructive piece is selected and compiled by the Rev. Dr. Banbridge. The characters are highly drawn and masterly finished; the Reverend author has confined himself to facts and strictly avoids every idea of party and faction but gives plain historical account of that ever memorable transaction. [Not listed in Nicoll; no entry for this play in ESTC]. [Lynch performed a hornpipe]. Source: 21–24 May 1793

29 Wed.   Benefit of Mr. and Mrs. May. Never acted here [the same claim was made for the previous performance]. *The Surrender of Calais.* In the course of the evening an interlude taken from the celebrated pantomime [*The Death of*] *Captain Cook* consisting of his encounter with the Savages and Dying Scene and the favourite epilogue from *The Dramatist.* To which will be added *No Song, No Supper.* Source: 24–28 May 1793

30 Fri.   Remington's benefit. Not acted here these three years. *Such Things Are.* With *Comus.* Source: 24–28 May 1793

1793–1794 SEASON

Venue: The Exchange Room. The Arthur Street company did not perform this season because of the persisting disturbed conditions in Belfast associated with the United Irishmen. Evidently, James May, who had been with Atkins's company since 1790, decided to mount discreet performances in the Belfast Exchange Rooms during this time of trouble.

16 Mon.   Moss of the Theatre-Royal, Dublin is engaged by May to perform in the Exchange Room and for that night only in a dramatic entertainment called *The Wags and Oddities; or, Whim of the Moment.* [This piece is almost certainly Charles Dibdin's *The Oddities; or, Whim of the Moment*]. Source: 9–13 June 1794

1794–1795 SEASON

Venue: Arthur Street Theatre.
Company: Mr. and Mrs. Alexander Archer; Atkins; Mr. and Mrs. J. Brown; Master Henry Brown; Miss Campion; Andrew Cherry; Mrs. Elizabeth Coates; James Grant; Charles Lee Lewes; Mr. and Mrs. John Lynch; Miss Lynch; Mrs. Horatio Thomas McGeorge; Mr. and Mrs. Remington; John Richer; Mrs. Saunders; Mrs. Sinclair.

For a biography of the Belfast manager **Michael Atkins** see the 1767–68 season.

The *BD* misses the earliest known performance by **Alexander Archer**, which occurred at Smock Alley on 14 May 1781 when "Master Archer" played Fleance in *Macbeth.* It was his only performance that season. The following March Archer played another minor role at Smock Alley, and in October of 1782 he acted at Cork, both times billed as Master Archer.

The *BD* says that Archer made his adult debut in Dublin in 1786, but I can find no record of his having performed in Dublin in either the 1785–86 or 1786–87 seasons. He is next recorded in Edinburgh where he played from 1786 through 1792 in juvenile and young man's roles. According to the *BD*, Archer also acted in York, Wakefield, Hull, Pontefract and Leeds at various times in 1790, 1791, 1795, and 1796.

By the time he appeared in Belfast's Arthur Street Theatre in January 1795, Archer had married. He and his wife shared a benefit in Belfast, but no roles are listed for her. Archer then moved to Crow Street where he made his debut as Macduff in *Macbeth* on 22 June 1795, billed as "from the Theatre Royal, Edinburgh, his first appearance on this stage." Mrs. Archer evidently made her Dublin debut as Mrs. Coaxer in *The Beggar's Opera* on 1 July, but there is no comment about it being her first performance. It was her only appearance that summer.

Thereafter, the Archers traveled to England. Archer performed in Liverpool and Exeter in 1795 and at Brighton in 1796. He made his Drury Lane debut as Shylock on 13 December 1798, and he was encouraged by the audience. He was engaged at Drury Lane for the next three seasons at a salary of £3 per week. Archer co-leased the Brighton theatre during the summers of 1799 and 1800, gave up the lease, and acted at the Haymarket Theatre during the summers of 1803 and 1804.

Archer did not perform in London or Dublin again. In 1801 he was at Wolverhampton, and in Worcester in 1803–04. He became a regular member of the Edinburgh company in 1805–06 and acted there through 1814–15. Mrs. Archer is found in the Edinburgh bills from 1805 through 1807–08. She died in Edinburgh on 6 December 1814; he on 1 July 1817, at the age of 60.

The actor, acrobat and singer known only as **J. Brown** made his first recorded stage appearance, at Crow Street on 18 January 1776, billed as "A Gentleman" and singing the title part of Cymon. That he was not born in Ireland is suggested by the notice that this was his "first appearance in this Kingdom." Brown caught on with Dublin audiences that season, and he appeared in a wide variety of roles. Neither of the Mrs. Browns who were appearing in Dublin that season was Mrs. J. Brown.

Brown next traveled to Norwich from 1778 to 1782, returning to Ireland in the autumn of 1779 to act at Cork. In 1781 Brown married the widow of William Ross (d. February 1781), née Mills. She came from an acting family, and, as Mrs. Ross, had acted at Norwich from 1774 to 1780. She must have met Brown during their time together at Norwich (the *BD* and Clark err in finding Mrs. Ross at Crow Street in 1779; there is no record of her performing there during that year. Unsubstantiated, too, is Clark's assertion (1964, 352) that she performed in Cork in September 1779).

The J. Browns ventured to Dublin during the 1789–90 season and were generally well received. Although they had little to say of her husband's acting, reviewers in the Dublin newspapers were enthusiastic about Mrs. Brown's ability. The Browns returned to Covent Garden for a brief time at the end of 1788–89 but were not engaged there for the ensuing season. The "Mr. Browne" who performed at Crow Street during the 1789–90 season and later that year in Limerick and Ennis was probably J. Brown. His wife is also mentioned in the Ennis bills. The Browns acted at Crow Street the entire 1790–91 season (not noted in *BD*), and in the autumn they went with the company to Derry and Ennis; thereafter, they returned to England and joined the Norwich company, remaining with it until the autumn of 1794.

The Browns returned to Ireland for another visit in 1795, appearing briefly in Belfast. J. Brown disappears from the record after that season, but his wife continued on the stage, appearing in Ireland in March 1795 and in the 1795–96 and 1799–1800 seasons at Drogheda and Belfast. After that she too may have retired from the stage.

The Brown's son Henry, b. ca. 1788, made his stage debut and only known theatrical appearance at Belfast during the 1795–96 season.

Maria Ann Campion was born at Waterford in 1775. Her father, a merchant, died when she was about 17 years old, and Maria Ann, with no previous experience, took to the stage to support her mother and sister, who were destitute. She made her acting debut at Crow Street on 13 February 1790 in the leading role of Monimia in *The Orphan*, billed as a "Young Lady, her first appearance on any stage." Gilliland's *Dramatic Mirror* (1808, 901) relates the story of Miss Campion's extreme stagefright this evening.

Later that season Miss Campion played Juliet, Desdemona and Cordelia, in addition to a variety of other capital characters, to applause. At the end of the season, she took a sole benefit in her own name. She remained at Crow Street the following two seasons, increasing her repertoire of leading roles and singing occasionally. Favorites with Dublin audiences were her recitations of Collins's *"Ode to the Passions"* set to music by Giordani and of Dryden's *"Alexander's Feast."* Miss Campion traveled with the company to Cork in the autumns of 1790 and 1791.

On 28 July 1792 Miss Campion played Louisa Dudley in *The West Indian* and gave notice that it would be "positively the last night of her performing in this city." (The *BD* errs in saying that she left Crow Street in January 1792). Later that summer she was with the Crow Street company when it made its annual visit to Waterford, but her whereabouts for the months between September 1792 and March 1793, when she joined Frederick Jones's new Fishamble Street company, are unknown. July through September 1793 she spent at Galway, then she acted for a short time again at Fishamble Street in March 1794, but the record is silent as to her activities in the months between October and March

During her brief stay at Fishamble Street Miss Campion acted one night with a "Miss R. Campion," (not "Miss A. Campion" as the *BD* states). This young woman was almost certainly her sister. In June 1794 Miss Campion returned to Crow Street for the summer season, billed as "her first appearance here these three years." In July she is found in Derry and in August in Cork.

Miss Campion continued to perform at Crow Street as the company's leading lady through March 1795 at which time Charles Mathews wrote to a friend in a letter dated 31 March 1795 (Dickens 1879, 1: 143) that in addition to losing Mrs. Daly because of illness and Cooke, (because of drunkenness), "our greatest loss has happened since: Miss Campion has now left us. This is indeed a serious loss. There are very few such actresses to be met with. She possesses a very beautiful face, extremely elegant figure, and delightful voice; added to every advantage of nature in mental qualifications, and every accomplishment of education. No lady was ever a greater favourite in Dublin. The terms of her articles, I believe, expired March 10th. Daly could not prevail upon her to renew it; as I believe she has an engagement in Belfast."

Beginning on the 13 April 1795 Miss Campion appeared in Belfast for a one-month engagement (only two of her roles are recorded). There she was welcomed as "the first female ornament of the Irish stage." By 18 June she was again listed among the Crow Street company.

In early September 1795 Miss Campion was reported by the *Hibernian Journal* to have sailed for New York, but in fact she was then performing in

York and Hull, where, on 5 November 1795 she began to bill herself as Mrs. Spencer, although she is not known to have married. According to the *BD* she remained in York through 9 April 1796, when sudden illness prevented her appearing for her benefit. To complicate matters, the Crow Street playbills for 18 March 1796 list "Miss Campion" as playing the favorite role of Lady Eleanor Irwin in *Every One Has His Fault*, although that is the only record of her appearing in Dublin that season. She certainly appeared in Kilkenny in August 1796, before she returned to York for the 1796–97 season.

Mrs. Spencer made her London debut at Covent Garden on 13 October 1797 in her maiden role of Monimia. The London periodicals hailed her "a really great acquisition to the house." As the season progressed the accolades became more profuse. Then, on 24 January 1798, she married her colleague Alexander Pope. Mr. and Mrs. Pope remained at Covent Garden through the 1797–98 season and then went to Edinburgh for the summer. Mrs. Pope continued at Covent Garden through 1800–01, playing many original roles and being hailed as an actress second only to Mrs. Siddons (an exaggerated estimation of her talents, according to the *BD*).

The following season the Popes moved to Drury Lane, appearing in the summers in Nottingham, Brighton, Manchester, Hull, Sheffield, and Liverpool. They again spent the 1802–03 season at Drury Lane, but on 10 June 1803 Mrs. Pope fell ill in the third act of *Othello* and was unable to finish her performance. She suffered a stroke on 18 June and died, at the age of 28, leaving her husband and infant daughter.

For a biography of **Andrew Cherry** see the 1782–83 season.

For biography of **Mrs. Elizabeth Coates** see 1790–91 season.

According to Gilliland's *Dramatic Mirror* (1808, 947) **James Grant**, who later adopted the stage name of James Grant Raymond, was the son of a British army officer of Scottish descent who was killed fighting in the American revolution. James was trained for Anglican orders but ran away to sea as a midshipman, was befriended by an Irish gentleman who became his patron, and made his stage debut in *Oroonoko*, billed as "a young gentleman, his first appearance on any stage," at Smock Alley on 24 January 1792. His debut was reviewed favorably in *Rights of Irishmen* 28 January 1792. Gilliland also relates of James Grant's debut performance that "In the most interesting part of the last act, the misery in which he saw his adored Imoinda fixed itself with such strength in his tortured mind, that in a frenzy of love and despair, he applied his burnished cheek so closely to that of his unhappy princess as to leave half of his sooty complexion on her face. This awkward blunder convulsed the house with laughter; and it was some minutes before they could be restored to their proper tone of feeling. . . ."

Grant appeared three more times that season and took a sole benefit. A Miss Grant, a child of 6 years old, also made an appearance at the end of the season reciting a "Dissertation on Criticism, exemplified in the Grecian Fable of The Farmer, The Boy and the Ass, written by Samuel Foote." Perhaps she was one of Grant's four siblings or even his daughter.

In July 1792 Grant is found with the Newry company, then he (and Miss Grant) appeared at Crow Street, but only one time, during the 1792–93 season. He is thought to have married Frances Hannah Carmichael in 1792 and they were to have four children.

Grant's whereabouts are unknown for the regular 1793–94 season, although he is found in Derry in May of 1794. It is probably James Grant who acted with Atkins's company in Belfast during the 1794–95 season (Clark overlooks this engagement). Grant returned to Crow Street in June 1795 but only appeared one time that summer. He is listed as being at Derry in November 1795 and at Cork in March 1796 and August through October 1797.

Grant became Daly's acting manager at Crow Street from 1792 through about 1797. According to *BD*, Grant probably acted in Liverpool in December 1793. He was using the name of "James Raymond" by early May 1794, when on Mondays, Wednesdays and Fridays, he presented "*An Attick Evening's Entertainment; or, A Feast of Reason*" by permission of the Lord Mayor at the Attic Theatre, Exhibition-House, William Street. The offering was billed as being "In the manner of the late Mr. Sheridan's Readings, on the delivery of Written Language; performed at the Theatres, London and Edinburgh, and the Universities of Oxford and Cambridge. Compiled for the use of the Stage, the Pulpit, and the Bar in five parts by James Raymond with a prologue and epilogue."

When J. P. Kemble visited Crow Street in the 1794–95 summer season a "Mr. Raymond" is acting with him in secondary roles. Raymond appeared regularly at Crow Street during the 1795–96 season and on 3 March 1796 he took a benefit and the company performed his tragedy *The Indian Captive; or, The Death of Ducomar*. At the end of the play Raymond recited his own entertainment "*The Poet's Lamentation; or, a peep into the church, theatre, senate-house, bar, and college*," evidently an alteration of his "*Feast of Reason*."

Raymond again played at Crow Street for the 1797–98 season appearing in a wide variety of roles including King Louis XVI in the spectacle of *Democratic Rage,* written by William Preston. Also at about this time Raymond wrote a tragedy "founded on the death of the unfortunate Lewis the Sixteenth," which suggests that Raymond may have adapted Preston's 1793 play to the later period.

Raymond's name is found only once in the bills for the 1798–99 season, and it disappears from the Dublin bills thereafter. The *BD* finds him in Manchester in 1798 and in Lancaster 1799. "Mr. Raymond" made his London debut at Drury Lane as Osmond in *The Castle Spectre* on 26 September 1799. Reviewers were encouraging if not enthusiastic, likening his acting to that of Mossop. He remained at Drury Lane for the remainder of his career, playing a wide variety of mainly secondary roles.

During this period Raymond seems also to have turned his hand to biography and editing. The *CBEL* credits him with two books, *The Life of Thomas Dermody* (2 vols. 1806) and *The Harp of Erin, Containing the Poetical Works of the Late Thomas Dermody* (2 vols. 1807). It seems likely that Raymond and Dermody were friends.

After 1811 Raymond became a manager of the Drury Lane company and acted less often. He suffered a paralytic stroke and died, a moderately wealthy man, on 26 October 1817.

For a biography of **Charles Lee Lewes** see the 1786–87 season.

For biography of **John Lynch** and family see the 1771–72 season.

Mrs. McGeorge was the wife of Horatio Thomas McGeorge, the provincial actor who appeared in Dublin during the 1760–61 season but not thereafter. McGeorge was considered a very bad actor and seldom rose above tertiary roles wherever he acted, which included the Haymarket Theatre in 1770 and Bath, which was evidently his home. There is some question about whether or not McGeorge had died by 1795 or whether the McGeorge who acted at Derry in 1794 and advertised as "from Bath" was his son who had been acting since 1771.

Mrs. McGeorge was probably an actress before she met her husband, but we have no record of her maiden name. She and her husband were performing in Edinburgh in 1765 and at the Haymarket Theatre in 1766. In 1770–71 they were at Bath and at Derby in 1771–72. She continued with the Derby company off and on with one visit each to Drury Lane and to the Haymarket Theatre. She is found at Richmond in 1795 and at Belfast in 1795 and September 1796 after which she disappears from the record.

For biographies of **Mr.** and **Mrs. Remington** see the 1762–63 season.

John "Jack" Oliver Richer, whom contemporaries called "the best Rope Dancer then known," was one of a family of rope dancers and acrobats who performed in England, France, and continental Europe during the eighteenth century. John's father, Jacques (fl. 1772–1788), and grandfather, Charles-Toussaint Richer, had immigrated to London from Paris to Thomas King's Sadler's Wells theatre in 1772 as rope dancers and acrobats. During the 1770s they also performed with Philip Astley at his circus near Westminster Bridge and toured the northern provincial theatres. Mrs. Richer and two daughters also performed occasionally as rope dancers and wire walkers during these years.

John Richer was performing as a rope dancer at Sadler's Wells from at least 1788 when he is found with the premiere company of rope dancers of the era, which included his father, Paulo Redige ("The Little Devil"), Mrs. Redige ("La Belle Espagnole") and others. At about this time Jack, alone or in company with his family, traveled abroad to Russia, returning in 1793. Reviews of his performances after his coming back from St. Petersburgh praise his talent highly, one stating that his performances are "never equalled in this or any other country."

Richer remained at Sadler's Wells through the end of the century, making several tours in provincial England and Ireland. He made his Crow Street debut on 15 November 1793 when his bills advertised tightrope by Richer "his first appearance in this kingdom, who has been much followed in the capitals of Europe for five years past, and whose Performances at Sadler's Wells have been the theme of universal admiration during the whole of the last summer." He remained in Dublin until February 1794. Daly engaged Richer for the following season at Crow Street at a generous salary of £10 per week. Particularly popular that season was Richer's representation of William Tell in the new spectacle *William Tell; or, the Deliverer of his Country*. This season Richer remained in Dublin until the end of January 1795 after which he performed for a few nights in Belfast.

During the 1795–96 season Richer and a company traveled to Weymouth, Bristol and Bath. In March 1796 he was at York. When he is found again in Dublin, in December 1796, it is described as his "first appearance in this kingdom these two years." Richer performed at Sadler's Wells until the end of the summer season of 1801 when he announced that he was going to Russia "where he is to entertain his Imperial Majesty Alexander." By November 1802 he had returned to England and traveled in the English provinces for several seasons. He performed with the new Olympic Circus in Peter Street, Dublin, during June 1805 and, for the last time, the following summer and autumn.

By September 1806 Richer had joined the Royal Circus, London, and he followed its circuit to Manchester, Liverpool, Brighton, and Bristol between 1806 and 1813, when he disappears from the record.

Mrs. (Lucy?) Saunders was evidently the daughter of the musician George Frederick Pinto and the sister of the violinist George Frederick Pinto Saunders, who had a career as a musician under the name of Pinto. Mrs. Saunders, her son, "the young equestrian wonder, Master Saunders," and George Pinto Saunders, performed with Astley's Circus in Dublin in 1792, 1794, and 1796. Master Saunders is found there in 1802 and 1803, when he is also described as the "most complete tight rope dancer in the world." A Miss Saunders also performed that season for the first time.

The only record we have of **Mrs. Sinclair** is that she received a benefit at Belfast on 2 March 1795. No role is listed for her. Clark (1965, 373) seems to be in error when he says she also performed on 24 October 1794; I can find no evidence that she performed that night. Perhaps she was not a performer.

Repertory, 1794–1795 Season

The receipts for this season were inevitably hurt by the collapse of the theatre's pit floor on 7 November 1794. Although the damage was minor and soon repaired, theatre goers remained wary of the building for several weeks, despite testimonials from the architects vouching for its safety. At the beginning of this season, too, the political climate in Belfast remained heated despite the hope expressed by the *Northern Star* in September 1794 that "the revival of this elegant entertainment will not be attended with any of those rude intrusions, which, during the residence of *certain strangers* [radical republicans, such as Thomas Russell and Wolfe Tone], interrupted every pleasurable and social meeting, and that the inhabitants of this united place shall in future have an additional opportunity of coming together, as they have always done, with harmony and good humour." To help forestall trouble, Atkins banned all "boys" from admission to the gallery, and forbade his orchestra to play any songs other than those stated in the playbills.

Atkins presented a relatively large number of new mainpieces this season. Frederick Reynolds play *The Rage* had its Dublin premiere only three months before it was produced in Belfast. Francis Waldron's comedy *Heigh ho for a Husband* had received its Dublin premiere in April, and Cumberland's *The Jew* in August. The other mainpieces new to Belfast had been playing in Dublin for decades.

Atkins also produced a relatively large number of new afterpieces, most of which were current favorites in Dublin and London. Thomas Morton's very popular musical piece *The Children in the Wood* had premiered in Dublin in February 1792 and continued to be performed there frequently. Carlo Delpini's pantomime *Don Juan* also had enjoyed considerable success in Dublin since its premiere there in 1789. Atkins tried to satisfy the Belfast appetite for "Irish" plays, first, with Macready's *The Irishman in London*, which had been playing in Dublin since July. In the spring a favorite Belfast stage Irishman, Andrew Cherry, made a brief visit to Belfast and appeared in the new farce *Ways and Means*, to which was added what must have been a comic sketch written by Cherry expressly for the Belfast audience, *Poor Darty's Trip to Belfast*, in which he "introduced a serio-comic ballad descriptive of the town, public places, prevailing modes and fashion etc." Cross's *The Purse* had premiered in Dublin at Crow Street in April 1792. Nothing is known about the speaking pantomime called *Will o' the Wisp*, but it may have been composed by Brown.

Total Performances: 32 of 25 different named mainpieces; 23 of 15 different named afterpieces.
    Shakespeare: 5.
    New Mainpieces: 5.
    New Afterpieces: 6.

(For a key to repertory symbols see above, page 11)

Mainpieces: *Cato*; *Chrononhotonthologos*; Concert; *The Country Girl**; *Cymbeline*†; *The Fashionable Lover*■; *The Gamester*; *Hamlet*; *Heigho for a Husband**; *The Highland Reel*(2); *The Hypocrite*; *Isabella*■; *King Henry IV, Part One*; *Jane Shore*; *The Jew**; *Know Your Own Mind*; *Macbeth*; *The Man of the World*; *The Merry Wives of Windsor*; *Notoriety*†; *The Rage**; *Romeo and Juliet* (3); *Rule a Wife*; *The School for Scandal*; *Such Things Are*; Unspecified "play"(3); *Venice Preserved*.

Afterpieces: *All the World's a Stage*; [*The Death of*] *Captain Cook*; *The Children in the Wood**(3); *Don Juan**; *The Farmer*; *High Life Below Stairs*; *The Hotel* (2, once as first item on program); *Inkle and Yarico*; *The Irishman in London**; *The Jubilee*;

Peeping Tom; The Purse*; Rosina; The Spoiled Child†; Unspecified "farce"(4); Ways and Means*; Will o'the Wisp*.

Entr'acte entertainments: Singing: 4. Dancing: 1

Benefits (20): Archer and Mrs. Archer; Atkins; Mr. and Mrs. Brown; Master Brown; Miss Campion(2); Cherry; Mrs. Coates(2); Grant; Lee Lewes; Lynch; Mrs. Lynch; Mrs. McGeorge; the Poor; Remington; Mrs. Remington; Richer; Mrs. Saunders; Mrs. Sinclair.

Admission prices (benefit): Boxes. 3s. 3d., pit 2s. 2d., gallery 2s. 2d.

October 1794

13 Mon. *The School for Scandal* with the farce of *All the World's a Stage.* Boys of any description whatever will not be admitted to the gallery.

Commentary: From certain circumstances he [Atkins] has found it indispensable to take the direction of the orchestra entirely upon himself insomuch that no tune which is called for can be played and he is convinced that the well-known candor and good sense of a Belfast audience will excuse this necessity (3–6 Oct. 1794) . Source: 6–10 Oct. 1794

24 Fri.   It is several years since this town has been gratified by such excellent playing of Cherry as Lazarillo in Jepson's *The Hotel.* Lazarillo–Cherry; Borachio–Lynch. Also *Inkle and Yarico.* Trudge– Cherry. Source: 24–27 Oct. 1794

29 Wed.   Third night of Cherry's six nights. Never performed here. *The Jew; or, The Benevolent Hebrew.* Sheva–Cherry. With *Peeping Tom of Coventry.* Peeping Tom–Cherry. Source: 24–27 Oct. 1794

November 1794

5 Wed.   Cherry's sixth night. By particular desire. *The Jew.* With *The Hotel.* Source: 31 Oct.–3 Nov. 1794

7 Fri.   Cherry's benefit and the last night of his performing at this theatre this season. *The Highland Reel.* Shelty–Cherry. End of the opera an entire new comic sketch never performed called *Poor Darty's Trip to Belfast,* in which will be introduced a serio-comic ballad descriptive of the town, public places, prevailing modes and fashion etc. written to be recited and sung by Cherry. *"Belles Have at Ye All"* to be spoken by Mrs. Coates. A comic chaunt in the character of Dr. Grigsby called *"The Tippety Witchet"* to be sung by Cherry. With a celebrated new comedy in three acts never performed here called *Ways and Means; or, A Trip to Dover.* Sir David Dunder–Cherry. Source: 31 Oct.–3 Nov. 1794

Commentary: At Cherry's benefit play on Friday the Theatre being extremely crowded the flooring of a great part of the pit gave way and sunk to the level of the ground. The confusion occasioned by it in every part of the house may be easily conceived. Happily no limbs were broken though the risque was great. The passages leading to the boxes and gallery as well as the door into the pit should as far as possible be widened as a press of people in cases of alarm might have serious consequences. In the present instance the audience chiefly remained in their places. We cannot entertain a doubt that the pit will be rebuilt in such a manner as forever to prevent a similar disaster and we would think it advisable for the manager after it is done to publish the opinion of an architect as to the strength both of it and of the galleries for the purpose of doing away the fears of any who will not themselves examine them. It is alleged that the present gloom of the boxes might be removed by sinking the chandeliers some inches lower than their present stations (7–10 Nov. 1794).

10 Mon. *Hamlet.* With a new farce never performed here called *The Irishman in London.* Source: 3–7 Nov. 1794 [This performance probably did not take place due to the collapse of the pit floor the previous Friday].

19 Wed. *Jane Shore* and a celebrated new farce never performed here called *The Children in the Wood.* With new scenery and decorations. Source: 14–17 Nov. 1794

26 Wed. *Macbeth.* Lady Macbeth–Mrs. Coates. [Reviewed in source issue: Mrs. Coates's manner and her voice are "as happily suited to comedy as they are totally unfit for tragedy"]. Source: 24–28 Nov. 1794

December 1794

8 Mon. The first of Lee Lewes's six nights. *King Henry IV.* Falstaff–Lee Lewes (first appearance here these eight years). Source: 1–5 Dec. 1794

Commentary: Being called on to inspect into the security of the Belfast theatre and to give such instructions as we could see necessary for the safety of the audience, we now on a second examination find everything done according to the directions given. [signed] Roger Mulholland and Hugh Dunlap (28 Nov.–1 Dec. 1794).

Ca. 15 December 1794 *Romeo and Juliet.* [Reviewed in *NS* 18 Dec.1794. Mrs. Coates's Juliet was "a finished piece which rendered the audience incapable (more than once) of withholding the tear of sensibility"].

17 Wed. *Rule a Wife and Have a Wife.* Copper Captain–Lee Lewes; Estifania–Mrs. Coates.

Commentary: Colman's celebrated play of *The Mountaineers* is in rehearsal and Atkins is preparing to bring it forward with the advantages that scenery and decoration can give it. Many of our old plays some of them calculated for the dissolute age of Charles II and replete with humour indulge a loose and indecent vein which can never fail in representation to hurt the feelings of a modest audience. The manager who with his pen would expunge such expressions as are exceptionable would deserve the thanks of every auditor. Though the Belfast stage is as little liable to this charge as any other it would be to the credit of its manager were he to set an example to other stages in the point alluded to. The performance of Wednesday last in certain passages required his correction. Source: 12–15 Dec. 1794; 15–19 Dec. 1794

22 Mon. Lee Lewes's benefit. Never acted here. *The Merry Wives of Windsor.* Falstaff–Lee Lewes. To which will be added a farce and other comic entertainments as will be expressed in the bills of the day. Source: 12–15 Dec. 1794

29 Mon. Mrs. Coates's benefit. *Venice Preserved.* With (for the last time this season) *The Children in the Wood.* Source: 22–26 Dec. 1794

January 1795

2 Fri. Benefit of Mrs. Coates [second?] and the last night of her engagement. *The Gamester.* Beverly–Archer; Mrs. Beverly–Mrs. Coates(first appearance in that character). Between play and farce a favourite comic song by Lynch. With the farce of *High Life Below Stairs.* Kitty (with a song and mock minuet)–Mrs. Coates. Source: 26–29 Dec. 1794

16 Fri. [Play. Other details of program not available]. After the conclusion of the play the audience were entertained in the Belfast Theatre by the exhibition of Richer on the tight rope. Source: 16–19 Jan. 1795

30 Fri. Richer's benefit. [Program not available]. Last time of his appearance in this kingdom. Source: 23–26 Jan. 1795

February 1795

27 Fri.   Mrs. Brown's benefit. Never performed here. *The Country Girl.*
Country Girl–Mrs. Brown. End Act 3 a new song called *"The Downhill of Life
or Tomorrow"* by Mrs. Brown. Between the play and farce an occasional
address in character of Jenny Jumps, a staymaker, with a comic song giving
a description of the squinting, pinkeyed, stuttering, lisping, bawling,
minching, hook nosed, snub-nosed, straight back, hunch back, small rump,
cork rump damsels that were smitten with his person by Mrs. Brown. An
occasional address in the character of Moggy McGilpen in *The Highland
Reel.* To conclude with that much admired song of *"Although I am now a very
little lad"* by Brown. With a musical farce never performed here called *The
Purse; or, The Benevolent Tar.* Page–Master H. Brown (first appearance in this
kingdom). Source: 20–23 Feb. 1795

March 1795

2 Mon. Mrs. Sinclair's benefit. *The Man of the World.* Written by the
celebrated Macklin with a variety of entertainments between the acts. With
The Spoiled Child. Source: 23–27 Feb. 1795

4 Wed. Benefit of Mrs. Saunders. *Know Your Own Mind.* With a
dissertation on jealousy and its effects on Spanish, Dutch, Italian, French,
English, and Irish husbands to be spoken by Mrs. Saunders. With
O'Keeffe's musical entertainment of *The Farmer.* Source: 23–27 Feb. 1795

9 Mon. Atkins's benefit. Not performed here these eight years. *The
Fashionable Lover.* Collin M'Cloud–Mrs. Brown. After which will be revived
the much admired serious pantomime called [*The Death of*] *Captain Cook.*
With new scenery dresses and decorations. Source: 2–6 Mar. 1795

11 Wed. Lynch's benefit. Never performed here. *The Rage.* Written by
Thomas Holcroft [i.e., Frederick Reynolds. The bill misattributes
Reynolds's play to Holcroft. An earlier notice for the above benefit in 2–6
Mar. 1795 in addition to the above information cites for performance a
celebrated comedy never performed here called *Heigho for a Husband* by
Thomas Holcroft. Again, this is a misattribution of a play by Francis G.
Waldron]. A variety of singing and dancing by Lynch and Miss Lynch.
With a favourite farce. Source: 6–9 Mar. 1795

13 Fri.   Grant's benefit. *Cato.* With a farce and entertainment as will be
expressed in a future advertisement. Source: 6–9 Mar. 1795

15 Wed. Mrs. McGeorge's benefit. *Such Things Are.* With the farce of *Rosina.* William (for that night only)–Mrs. Brown. With an occasional address written and to be spoken by Mrs. McGeorge and other entertainments as will be expressed in the bills of the day. Source: 16–20 Mar. 1795

16 Mon. Remington's benefit. *Heigho for a Husband.* With *The Jubilee.* Source: 9–13 Mar. 1795

18 Wed. Benefit of Mr. and Mrs. Brown. *The Highland Reel.* Moggy McGilpin (with additional Scotch song)–Mrs. Brown. With a speaking pantomime called *Will o'th Wisp; or, Blue Beard.* Master H. Brown will perform a principal character. In the above piece Harlequin will take several flying leaps particularly over the back of a horse eighteen hands and a half high and afterwards down Blue Beard's throat. Source: 9–13 Mar. 1795

20 Fri.   Mr. and Mrs. Archer's benefit. *Cymbeline.* With a grand serious pantomime never performed here called *Don Juan; or, The Libertine Destroyed.* Source: 9–13 Mar. 1795

April 1795

6 Mon. Mrs. Remington's benefit. *Notoriety.* With a variety of entertainments to which will be added *Chrononhotonthologos.* King of Queerumania–Mrs. Remington. Source: 30 Mar.–3 Apr. 1795

13 Mon. Miss Campion, the first female ornament of the Irish stage, is engaged by Atkins to perform at the Theatre for a few nights previous to the closing of the season and will make her first appearance on Monday next in the tragedy of *Romeo and Juliet.* During the short period of her engagement Miss Campion will select her most approved and favourite characters for her performance. Source: 6–10 Apr. 1795

18 Wed. Benefit of Mrs. Lynch. *The Hypocrite.* With a variety of entertainment of singing and dancing and the favourite farce (for the last time) of *The Children in the Wood.* Source: 30 Mar.–3 Apr. 1795

22 Wed. Miss Campion's benefit. [Program unavailable]. Source: 17–20 Apr. 1795

29 Wed. Benefit of the Poor. *Romeo and Juliet.* Juliet–Miss Campion. With a farce and other entertainments as will be expressed in the bills. Boxes. 3s. 3d., pit 2s. 2d., gallery 2s. 2d.

Commentary: The handsome manner in which Miss Campion has engaged to perform Benefit of the Poor on Wednesday night deserves every acknowledgment. The theatrical talents of that lady will we hope be fully confessed by a crowded house on an occasion which has so just a claim upon the attention of the public. Source: 24–27 Apr. 1795

May 1795

8 Fri. By particular desire. Benefit of Miss Campion and positively the last night of her performance here. Not acted these five years. *Isabella*. Isabella–Miss Campion (her first appearance in that character). With a farce and entertainments as will be expressed in the bills. Source: 1–4 May 1795

July 1795

6 Mon. [Concert]. By permission of the Rev. William Bristow, Sovereign, on Monday evening 6 July Mr. Atkins informs the ladies and gentlemen of Belfast and its vicinity that there will be performed at the theatre for that night only a grand concert of vocal and instrumental music selected from the composition of the most eminent masters. Two gentlemen of the first abilities in the musical line have kindly offered their assistance in the instrumental part and the vocal parts by Bowles from the Theatre Royal Bath and Edinburgh. To begin precisely at 8 o'clock. Boxes 3s. 3d., pit 2s. 2d., gallery 1s. 1d. Source: 29 June–3 July 1795

1795–1796 SEASON

Venue: Arthur Street Theatre.
Company: Atkins (manager); Miss Bowles; Mrs. J. Brown and Master Henry Brown; Timothy Duncan; Maria Rebecca Duncan (from Crow Street); Miss Catherine Gough; Griffith; Henry Erskine Johnston (from Crow Street); Mr. and Mrs. Thomas Kennedy; Mr. and Mrs. John Lynch and Miss Lynch; Mrs. Horatio Thomas McGeorge; Mooney (boxkeeper); Reilly; Mr. and Mrs. Remington; Shannon (musician, Union pipes); R. Walker (from Crow Street); a young gentleman being his first appearance on any stage.

For a biography of the Belfast manager **Michael Atkins** see the 1767–68 season.

Miss Bowles is possibly the daughter of the minor actor Robert Bowles. In the 1794–95 season "Miss Bowles," billed as "from the Theatre Royal,

Norwich" played at Crow Street, mainly in young women's roles. Her last appearance was on 29 December 1794 for Richer's benefit. The only other record of her performing, if it is the same person, is in 29 May 1796 when Miss Bowles took a sole benefit at Atkins's Arthur Street theatre. No roles survive.

For biographies of **Mrs. J. Brown** and **Master Henry Brown** see the 1794–95 season.

For biographies of **Timothy Duncan** and **Maria Rebecca Duncan** see the 1783–84 season.

Catherine Gough tells us in her *memoirs* that she went onto the stage after her father had dissipated a fortune and left his family destitute. She was evidently born in Ireland, for she says that she received her early training on the stage in 1793 at Jones's Fishamble Street theatre, but there is no record of her performing there at that time, unless it was under another name.

She made her stage debut at Covent Garden on 22 October 1795 as Alicia in *Jane Shore* and was received with great enthusiasm, comparisons being made between her talent and that of Mrs. Siddons. Nevertheless, she was not reengaged at Covent Garden and returned to Ireland where she performed the role of Calista in *The Fair Penitent* on 21 April 1795, among others. In his advertisements for the ensuing summer season, Daly crowed about having acquired Miss Gough, "from the Theatre Royal, Covent Garden," and she began appearing as leading lady to J. P. Kemble on 1 July 1796. The *BD* places her also at Fishamble Street this summer, but I have no record of that theatre being open during this period.

Miss Gough then visited Edinburgh in the winter of 1796–97 where she was again enthusiastically received. She returned to Crow Street for the summer season and then took up an uneasy residence in Edinburgh, acting there through 1798–99, but playing briefly in Hull in January 1799 and in Bath and Bristol in 1798–99.

In 1798 she met Peter Galindo, a fencing master and actor who ran a fencing academy in Bristol at the time. Miss Gough returned to Crow Street and begun acting on 29 June 1799 when it was added that it was her "first appearance here these three years." Galindo, billed as from the Theatre Royal, Bath, began acting at Crow Street at the beginning of the 1799–1800 season. They did not marry the first year they performed together in Dublin but waited until the 1800–01 season had concluded, for it is not until the beginning of the 1801–02 season that she begins using his name in the playbills.

By the beginning of the 1802–03 season Miss Gough's (now Mrs. Galindo) preeminence in the Crow Street company began to slip. Mrs. Sarah Siddons paid a visit to Dublin, and Mrs. Galindo also had to share some of the leading roles with a new sensation, Miss Walstein. Mrs. Galindo and Mrs. Siddons soon became fast friends. A Dublin theatre goer reported that at this time Mrs. Galindo "lives in the same house with Mrs. Siddons, who has paid her some attention and, it is said, gives her much instruction."

At about this time a love affair began between Galindo and Mrs. Siddons of which Mrs. Galindo was unaware. Indeed, Mrs. Siddons acted as their first child's godmother in July 1803. She also arranged to have Harris engage Galindo, but not his wife, at Covent Garden for the 1803–04 season, although Mrs. Siddons brother, J. P. Kemble, objected to the impropriety and tried to have it canceled.

Mrs. Galindo followed her husband to Covent Garden for the 1804–05 season, and they remained there through 1807–08. When Catherine found out about the love affair is not known, but in 1809 she published an open letter to Mrs. Siddons laying the whole tawdry business before the public and accusing Mrs. Siddons of trying to ruin her husband and her children for his failure to repay to her a loan he had taken out in an unsuccessful attempt to manage the Manchester theatre.

Evidently, the Galindos did not separate, but they disappear from the performance record in 1809. She died on 18 January 1829 in Dublin at the age of 64.

For biography of **Griffith** see 1790–91 season.

Henry Erskine Johnston (in the early years of his career the name is spelled variously, Johnson and Johnstone, but here I will use the spelling settled on by the *BD*) was born in Edinburgh in May 1777. He was evidently stage struck at an early age but was apprenticed to a linen draper in this youth. At the benefit of a friend, in Edinburgh in 1794, he recited Collins's "*Ode on the Passions*," was noticed by Stephen Kemble, the Edinburgh manager, and offered a position there where he made his professional stage debut as Hamlet on 9 July 1794. In a performance later that season he played Douglas in Highland dress and thereby endeared himself to the audience.

Henry Johnston made his Irish debut at Crow Street on 5 January 1796 as Douglas and billed as "from the Theatre Royal, Edinburgh, first appearance in this kingdom." (There is no evidence to support Dibdin's claim that the debut took place in 1794). Critics called Johnston's Douglas "one of the best pieces of acting ever seen on the Irish stage," and he repeated it at least four times that season, by the end of which he was being billed as "The Scottish Roscius."

Johnston was engaged at Michael Atkins's Arthur Street Theatre in Belfast for a short engagement of six nights in March 1796, billed as "from the Theatres Royal in Edinburgh and Dublin." The reviewer in the *BNL* 4–7 Mar. 1796 observed that Johnston had only performed on any stage 35 times. His benefit was so crowded that he was forced to perform an additional night in order to accommodate all those who could not find seats on the first occasion.

Johnston returned to Edinburgh in April and remained there through the summer. In June he married the actress Nannette Parker, daughter of the equestrian producer William Parker, who was the proprietor of the Edinburgh Circus from 1788 to 1790. She had performed at Sadler's Wells and at the Royal Circus as a dancer in 1793 and 1795.

The couple went to Crow Street in January of the 1796–97 season for a limited engagement. His wife made her acting debut for his benefit on 15 February 1797 playing Lady Contest in the first Dublin staging of Mrs. Inchbald's *The Wedding Day*. That autumn Johnston performed in Cork for a few weeks and then the couple traveled to London, where Henry Johnston made his debut at Covent Garden on 23 October 1797 and was engaged at a weekly salary of £12 (his wife's was £3). Critics at the time had high praise for him, one observing that he had "finer requisites, figure excepted than any actor on the stage."

Johnston remained at Covent Garden as a leading man through the 1801–02 season, went over to Drury Lane for two seasons as the result of a contract dispute, then returned to Covent Garden for the 1805–1806 season. In the summers he and his wife acted at the Haymarket Theatre. At about this time Johnston got the urge to manage, and for a time proposed to take over the proprietorship of the Edinburgh theatre, promising to make it as good as any in the British Empire. His offer was not taken up, and he continued as an actor. H. E. Johnston appeared in Dublin for another limited engagement at Crow Street beginning on 2 July 1803, billed as his first appearance there in seven years. He returned to Dublin for yet another limited engagement at Crow Street in August 1806.

At the beginning of the 1809–10 season (not the 1811–12 season as *BD* states) H. E. Johnston took over the old Royal Amphitheatre in Peter Street, Dublin, and, according to the newspapers, "having been wholly new-modelled, painted, decorated and fitted up in a novel and elegant style, with the stage department of scenery, machinery, dresses, and decorations entirely new will be opened under the sanction of his Majesty's Patent by the name of The Royal Hibernian Theatre. Under the management and direction of Mr. Henry Johnston." The venture was praised by the critics for offering competition to the Crow Street house and thus forcing an improvement in the quality of performances there. Johnston was not successful, however, and discontinued playing at the Royal Hibernian Theatre after his benefit on 28 February 1811. He reopened the theatre for what was fated to be his final season at Peter Street in September 1811. After his benefit on 27 January 1812 he fled Ireland, leaving his children in the care of a Mrs. Dunne, to avoid his creditors. However, he was pursued and arrested for debt. At this time he had also invested heavily in several theatres in Scotland, including those in Glasgow, Aberdeen and Greenock. When Johnston was released from jail he took over the management of a company of players in Paisley and afterwards obtained the Montrose theatre.

Evidently, his multifarious theatrical ventures bankrupted him, and he returned to London as an actor and made his first appearance in twelve years at Covent Garden in December 1816. The following season he was at Drury Lane at £8 a week and he remained there through 1820–21. Thereafter, he was with the Olympic Theatre for a short time and then took over the management of the Caledonian Theatre until 1823. He disappears from the record for a time, though he probably acted in the provinces, and then he resurfaces at the Caledonian Theatre in 1830. He went to America in 1837 but was past his prime and returned to England the following year and evidently retired from the stage for good. He died in July 1845 being nearly 70 years old.

The Master Kennedy who played Tom Thumb at his mother's Smock Alley benefit on 1 April 1757 and who acted in minor roles (once or twice each season) was **Thomas Kennedy**, making his stage debut. The son of the actor Lawrence Kennedy and his wife (for their biographies see 1782–83 season), he traveled with the touring Smock Alley company to Cork in the autumns of 1756, 1757, and 1758. He may have performed occasionally with his parents in Scotland or England during the summer of 1759, but the record is otherwise silent until the family returned to Smock

Alley where they acted until the end of the 1759–60 Smock Alley season after which they traveled to London.

Master Thomas Kennedy appeared again at Smock Alley for the 1763–64 season (not noticed in *BD*). Mr. and Mrs. Kennedy returned with the Smock Alley company to Cork in the autumns of 1762, 1763, and 1764. The Kennedy family moved to Crow Street for the 1764–65 season but their whereabouts for the 1765–66 and 1766–67 seasons is not known. It is possibly one of these seasons to which the *BD* refers when it says that the Kennedys were engaged in Edinburgh "in 1764." They were certainly performing regularly in Dublin during the 1763–64 and 1764–65 seasons. Kennedy, Sr. was in Edinburgh for the 1767–68 season and a Kennedy acted once at Crow Street in November 1768. Kennedy is found in Stratford in the spring of 1771 and in 1772 he is known to have become manager of the new theatre in Gloucester, which also performed in Bristol in 1772 and the summer of 1773. The following year he managed the theatre in Richmond for a time, also acting at the Haymarket Theatre.

On 4 May 1774, while staying at their friend Younger's London home, a fire broke out and Mrs. Kennedy was killed. Kennedy, while attempting to save his wife, was severely burned and his face badly scarred thereafter.

Thomas Kennedy had, in the meantime, been maturing as a performer. Billed as "from the Theatre Royal, Richmond, first appearance in Ireland" on 22 November 1773, a Kennedy played at the new Capel Street theatre in young men's roles, some of them capital parts. He acted with some success at the Haymarket Theatre in the summer of 1774. Father and son returned to Dublin in the spring of 1775, and, billed as "Kennedy, Jr., his first appearance here" the younger Kennedy played a few nights at Smock Alley before the season ended. That summer and the next Thomas joined the Birmingham company and appeared there during the off-season. The Kennedys performed together at Crow Street during the 1775–76 season. The mention of an "E. Kennedy, Jr." in the bills of 1 November 1776 playing a spirit in *Comus* suggests that perhaps another Kennedy son may also have been performing there (or perhaps it is a compositor's error). The 1776–77 season Thomas Kennedy begins to perform regularly in dancing; his father's roles are now confined to the line of older men.

In July 1777 Thomas Kennedy eloped from Dublin with the wife of the actor Taplin. However, he abandoned Mrs. Taplin at Doncaster and soon married Agnes Holmes, a young actress with the York company. Miss Holmes's mother was a wardrobe keeper and dressmaker at Sadler's Wells and had made her stage debut at York in 1777. Mrs. Kennedy made her London debut at the Haymarket Theatre in 1779 summer season. Presumably Thomas was with her, but we have no record of his activities during this time.

When he resurfaces, he and Mrs. Kennedy are engaged at Covent Garden for the 1784–85 season (billed as from the theatre in Newcastle) playing secondary and tertiary roles at a salary of £2. 10s. a week. The Kennedys remained at Covent Garden through the 1786–1787 season, playing at the Haymarket Theatre in the summers. When their articles were not renewed there, they went to the provinces, playing at York, Manchester and Edinburgh to 1791.

Mr. and Mrs. Kennedy moved to Dublin's Crow Street theatre for the 1791–92 season, billed as "from the Theatre Royal, Covent Garden," and they continued to perform there as serviceable secondary actors through 1797–98. In March and April 1795 the Kennedys, accompanied by the eight-year-old Miss Kennedy, presumably a daughter, performed in Belfast and sporadically at Crow Street thereafter. Mr. and Mrs. Kennedy traveled with the Crow Street company on its annual circuit of provincial cities, appearing together in Cork in September 1792. Mrs. Kennedy is found in Limerick and Cork in the autumn of 1793, in Derry in November 1795 and January 1796, and in Cork again in August and October 1797 (with her husband).

Mr. and Mrs. Kennedy's movements thereafter are difficult to follow. They returned to Crow Street briefly in the summer of the 1798–99 season and may have been acting in Edinburgh in 1801 and perhaps in Liverpool, but then seem to have settled in Dublin and established themselves in business. Thomas Kennedy died in January 1808. After her husband's death, Mrs. Kennedy returned to the stage and acted at Covent Garden from 1815–16 through 1817–18 after which she retired for a time, but was called out of retirement to play at the Surrey Theatre in 1825. She died in May 1832 at the age of 93.

For biography of **John Lynch** and family see the 1771–72 season.

For a biography of **Mrs. Horatio Thomas McGeorge** see the 1794–95 season.

A tertiary actor named **Reilly** appeared in Dublin bills several times in the same role at Crow Street during the 1765–66 season. The next season he appeared once. It is unlikely that this is the same Reilly performing in Belfast in 1796 of whom nothing more is known.

For biographies of **Mr.** and **Mrs. Remington** see the 1762–63 season.

The only evidence we have of the piper named **Shannon** "who is engaged at Covent Garden Theatre to succeed the late [Denis] Courtney," is 9 and 18 May 1796 at the Arthur Street Theatre in Belfast when he played "favourite Scotch and Irish airs on the Union pipes: the Rondeau in *'Oscar and Malvina,' 'Carolan's Receipt,' 'Lango Lee,' 'So Vorreen Delish,' 'Moggy Lawder'* with variations, *'How oft Louisa,'* and *'The Lakes of Killarney'.*" There is no record of Shannon's performing in London.

R. Walker is first noticed in the Dublin playbills on 28 July 1795 singing the role of Dermot in *The Poor Soldier* at Crow Street. No comment is made about his playing such an important role, suggesting perhaps that he had been acting there for some time. A "Mr. Walker, from the Theatre Royal, Dublin," sang the same roles with Atkins's company in Belfast in March and April 1795. Walker played at Fishamble Street for the 1797–98 season, again singing a variety of capital roles.

Walker disappears from the record for several seasons, then he resurfaces at Crow Street at the beginning of the 1801–02 season, billed as "from the Theatre Royal, Haymarket, his first appearance here these four years." Again, he appeared in a variety of important singing roles. Walker may have returned to England after this season.

Repertory, February–July 1796

This season Atkins brought out two genuinely new pieces in Belfast. Richard Cumberland's comedy *The Wheel of Fortune* had its Dublin debut in May 1795, while Frederick Reynold's *Speculation* had premiered in Dublin in February 1796, only three months before it was staged in Belfast. This may also have been the first Belfast performance of the Miller-Hoadley tragedy *Mahomet.* Because of the potential of some lines to be construed as political allegory, this play had always had special significance in Ireland and had caused serious rioting in Dublin in 1753–54.

The sole new afterpiece to be performed was the relatively new comic opera of *The Cottagers*, by Miss Ross, the future Mrs. Anne (or Anna) Brunton (not to be confused with her aunt, the favorite American actress Anne Brunton, later Wignell), which she had written at the age of 15 and which premiered at Crow Street in May 1789. Miss Ross was the step-daughter of Mr. and

Mrs. J. Brown, and Mrs. Brown probably encouraged the presentation of this piece in Belfast. *The Deserter of Naples* would seem to be the new serious pantomime or ballet by Gardell and Delphini (Royalty, 1788) and not Dibdin's musical farce, which is billed simply as *The Deserter*. Of the new pantomime called *The Witches or, Harlequin Salamander* it can only be said that the piece does not seem to have been very "new": it was performed at Cork in 1778 and 1784, and again in Derry in 1796; it is apparently a different piece (perhaps composed by Atkins) from the pantomime staged in Belfast in 1773 and 1778 entitled *The Witches; or, Harlequin's Vagaries*.

Total Performances: 33 of 25 different named mainpieces; 24 of 12 different named afterpieces.
    Shakespeare: 4.
    New Mainpieces: 2.
    New Afterpieces: 1.

(For a key to repertory symbols see above, page 11)

Mainpieces: *The Belle's Stratagem; The Busy Body; Douglas*(2); *The Fair Penitent; The Foundling*■; *The Gamester; Hamlet* (2); *Inkle and Yarico* (2); *Isabella; King Henry IV, Part One; Know Your Own Mind; Lionel and Clarissa; Love in a Village; Macbeth; Mahomet*†; *The Maid of the Mill; The Rivals; The Road to Ruin*†; *Robin Hood; Romeo and Juliet; Rule a Wife; The School for Scandal; Speculation**; *Tancred and Sigismunda;* Unspecified "play"(3); *The Wheel of Fortune**.

Afterpieces*: All the World's a Stage; Catherine and Petruchio; The Cottagers** (2); *The Deserter of Naples*†; *Love a la Mode*■; *The Man of Quality; No Song, No Supper; The Padlock; Poor Vulcan; The True Born Irishman* (2); Unspecified "farce"(10); *Ways and Means; The Witches*†.

Interlude: *The Purse.*

Entr'acte entertainments: Singing: 1. Dancing: 2.

Admission Prices: Boxes 3s. 3d. , pit 2s. 2d., gallery 1s. 1d.

Benefits (15): Atkins; Miss Bowles; Mrs. Brown; Master Brown; Miss Duncan; Griffith; Kennedy; Mrs. Kennedy; Lee Lewes; Mrs. and Miss Lynch; Mrs. McGeorge; Poor House and Infirmary; Reilly; Remington; Mrs. Remington.

February 1796

[Evidently there were no earlier performances in Belfast this season. Atkins and his company acted in Derry during the autumn].

17 Wed. *Inkle and Yarico.* With *The True Born Irishman.* Atkins respectfully begs leave to inform the ladies and gentlemen of Belfast and its vicinity that he has concluded engagements with several performers of the first eminence whose appearance will be duly announced to the public. Source: 12–15 Feb. 1796

March 1796

2 Wed. First of Johnston's six nights. *Douglas.* Douglas–Johnston (from the Theatres Royal of Edinburgh and Dublin, his first appearance on this stage). With *Rosina.* Atkins respectfully begs leave to inform the ladies and gentlemen of Belfast and its vicinity that the celebrated Scotch Roscius, Henry Erskine Johnston is engaged to perform for six nights at this theatre and will make his first appearance in the course of the ensuing week in the character of Douglas (22–26 Feb. 1796). [Reviewed in the *NS* 3 Mar. 1796]. Source: 26–29 Feb. 1796

4 Fri. Second night of Johnston's engagement. *Hamlet.* Hamlet–Johnston; Ophelia–Miss Duncan. [Reviewed in the source issue, making the observations that Johnston has only appeared upon the stage 35 times]. Source: 4–7 Mar. 1796

7 Mon. Third of Johnston's six nights. *Romeo and Juliet.* Romeo–Johnston. With a farce as will be expressed in the bills. Source: 29 Feb.–4 Mar. 1796

10 Thur. Fourth of Johnston's six nights. *Douglas.* Douglas–Johnston. The character of Douglas was performed in this theatre last night by Johnston being the second appearance in that part. Source: 7–11 Mar. 1796

11 Fri. Fifth of Johnston's six nights. *Mahomet.* Zaphne–Johnston; Palmira–Miss Duncan. [Performance reviewed in the source issue]. Source: 11–14 Mar. 1796

14 Mon. Johnston's sixth night. ***Macbeth.*** Macbeth–Johnston (first attempt at that character and the last night but one of his performing here this season). Source: 7–11 Mar. 1796

16 Wed. *Tancred and Sigismunda.* Tancred–Johnston; Osmond–Young Gentleman (first appearance on any stage). With the farce of *Catherine and Petruchio.* Petruchio–Johnston. Being positively the last time of his performing here this season. [Receipts: £92. 12.s, but turned £20 away resulting in an additional performance on 18 March. Performance reviewed in 14–18 Mar. 1796 and *NS* 17 Mar.1796]. Source: 7–11 Mar. 1796

18 Fri.   *Hamlet.* Hamlet–Johnston. [This extra performance was given to allow persons holding outstanding benefit tickets to use them]. Source: 17 Mar. 1796

 28 Mon. *Lionel and Clarissa.* Lionel–Walker (from Theatre Royal Dublin his first appearance on this stage). With a farce as will be expressed in the bills. Source: 21–25 Mar. 1796

30 Wed. *The Belle's Stratagem.* Letitia Hardy–Mrs. Kennedy. Source: [Reviewed in1–4 April 1796].

April 1796

4   Mon. For the first time. *The Wheel of Fortune.* Eliza Tempest–Mrs. Kennedy. Source: 1–4 Apr. 1796

6   Wed. *Robin Hood.* With entire new scenery and decorations and a farce as will be expressed in the bills. [Reviewed in 15–18 Apr.1796]. Source: 1–4 Apr. 1796

18   Mon. First of Lee Lewes's nights. *The School for Scandal.* Sir Peter Teazle–Lee Lewes. With a farce as will be expressed in the bills. Source: 11–15 Apr. 1796

20 Wed. Mrs. Kennedy's benefit. *The Road to Ruin.* Goldfinch (for that night only)–Mrs. Kennedy. End of the play the epilogue of *"Belles Have at Ye All"* to be spoken by Miss Kennedy, a child of eight years old and being her second attempt on any stage. With the favourite Burletta of *Poor Vulcan.* Source: 15–18 Apr. 1796

21   Thur. *The Fair Penitent.* Calista–Miss Gough. This lady's merit is so universally acknowledged that we have only to express how very much her performance was esteemed by a genteel rather than a full house. Source: 22–25 Apr. 1796

22 Fri. *King Henry IV, Part One.* [The title of the mainpiece is not mentioned in any source, nor is it listed in Clark, but the fact that a brief review of Lewes's enactment of the role of Falstaff appeared in the source issue strongly suggests this play]. Source: 22–25 Apr. 1796

25 Mon. Second of Miss Gough's and third of Lee Lewes's nights. *The Gamester.* Mrs. Beverly–Miss Gough. With *Ways and Means.* Sir David Dunder–Lee Lewes. Source: 18–22 Apr. 1796

May 1796

2 Mon. Manager's night and positively the last of Miss Gough performing here this season. *Isabella.* Isabella–Miss Gough (first appearance in that character). With a farce in which Lee Lewes will perform. Source: 25–29 Apr. 1796

4 Wed. Kennedy's benefit. *Rule a Wife and Have a Wife.* Copper Captain–Lewes; Estifania–Mrs. Kennedy. Between the play and farce a favourite scene taken from *Harlequin's Invasion* with *The Sicilian Romance.* Lee Lewes will perform a principal character. Source: 29 Apr.–2 May 1796

9 Mon. Benefit of Lee Lewes. *The Busy Body.* Marplot–Lewes; Charles–Griffith; Sir Francis Gripe–Lynch; Sir Jealous Traffick–Duncan; Whisper–Kennedy; Sir George Airy–Remington; Isabinda–Mrs. McGeorge; Patch–Mrs. Remington; Miranda–Miss Duncan. A new prologue to be spoken by Lee Lewes: Hippisley's *"Drunken Man."* In the course of the evening Shannon, "who is engaged at Covent Garden Theatre to succeed the late Courtney, will play the following favourite Scotch and Irish airs on the Union pipes: the Rondeau in *'Oscar and Malvina,' 'Carolin's Receipt,' 'Lango Lee,' 'So Vorreen Delish,' 'Moggy Lawder'* with variations, *'How oft Louisa,'* and *'The Lakes of Killarney'."* Boxes 3s. 3d. , pit 2s. 2d., gallery 1s. 1d. With a farce not acted here these ten years called *Love a la Mode.* Squire Groom–Lee Lewes; Sir Theodore Goodchild–Griffith; Beau Mordecai–Lynch; Sir Callaghan O'Bralaghan–Duncan; Sir Archy Macsarcasm–Kennedy; Charlotte–Mrs. McGeorge. Source: 2–6 May 1796

16 Mon. Mrs. Brown's benefit. *The Rivals.* Sir Anthony Absolute–Lee Lewes. With a new farce called the *The Cottagers; or, the Female Metamorphosis.* Between the acts entertainments by Master H. Brown, including a recitation of *"New Brooms; or, Birch from Parnassus."* Source: 9–13 May 1796

18 Wed. Miss Duncan's benefit. Not acted this season. *Know Your Own Mind.* Dashwood–Lee Lewes; Lady Bell–Miss Duncan (first appearance in that character). Lewes, who originally performed the character in Covent Garden with the most distinguished applause, obligingly makes Miss Duncan the compliment to stay longer than he intended and being positively his last appearance this season. Shannon will for the last time this season perform several favourite airs on the Union pipes. Preceding the farce will be presented (for this night) only a new comic dance called *"The Merry Highlanders; or, Caledonian Lovers"* by Lynch, Miss Lynch and Miss Duncan. With the musical entertainment of *The Deserter of Naples*. Source: 9–13 May 1796

23 Mon. Mrs. McGeorge's benefit. *The Foundling.* Not performed here these five years. With *No Song, No Supper.* With other entertainments. Source: 16–20 May 1796

25 Wed. Remington's benefit. Never acted here. *Speculation.* With a variety of entertainments. With the farce called *The Man of Quality.* [This benefit evidently "failed." See his wife's benefit on 3 June below]. Source: 20–23 May 1796

27 Fri.   Lynch's benefit. [Comedy, farce, and entertainments. Other details of program not available]. Source: 16–20 May 1796 and 20–23 May 1796

29 Fri.   Miss Bowles's benefit. [Musical farce and entertainments. Other details of program not available]. In which Lee Lewes has kindly promised his assistance being positively his last appearance here this season. Source: 13–16 May 1796

30 Mon. Griffith's benefit. [Play, farce, and entertainments. Other details of program not available]. Source: 23–27 May 1796

June 1796

1 Wed. Benefit of Master Henry Brown and positively the last time of his performing this season by particular desire. The Musical piece in two acts called *The Cottagers*. Miss Mad Cap–Mrs. Brown. Preceding the opera a tragic comic operatic epilogue by Master Henry Brown in which he will personate the following characters: Hamlet, Romeo, Justice Woodcock, Scrub and Jacob Gawked with a comic song. End Act 1 *"Squire Groom's Dissertation on Hobbies"* by Master Henry Brown with the favourite song of *"Ding Dong Dash a Long"* after which a piece in one act called *The Purse*.

Page–Master Henry Brown. With *The Padlock*. Mungo–Master Henry Brown. Source: 23–27 May 1796

Commentary: The entertainments advertised for Wednesday evening next, benefit of Master Henry Brown, we have every reason to believe will be a real theatrical fete. In *The Cottagers; or, Female Metamorphosis* Mrs. Brown has certainly the best opportunity of displaying her comic abilities, the part of Miss Mad Cap being a character in which her powers must be exerted to the greatest advantage. The Child of Promise, Master Henry Brown, not eight year's old in the representation of the Page in *The Purse* last season shewed a degree of merit which was altogether wonderful (27–30 May 1796).

3 Fri. Benefit of Mrs. Remington. *Love in a Village*. Between the play and farce a much admired dance called *"The Merry Highlanders."* With a new pantomime called *The Witches; or, Harlequin Salamander*.

Commentary: The failure of the benefit of that truly deserving actor Remington which was owing to unavoidable accidents induces us to remind the lovers of the drama that his wife's benefit is announced for Friday next on which occasion we doubt not but a Belfast audience will evince their usual aptitude to reward modest merit. Remington has been long a favourite of the town and no performer can be at greater pains to conciliate the good will of the audience. Source: 27–30 May 1796

6 Mon. Reilly's benefit. *Inkle and Yarico*. With *The True Born Irishman*. Source: 30 May–3 June 1796

10 Fri. Benefit of the Poor-house and Infirmary of this town. *The Maid of the Mill*. With *All the World's a Stage*. Source: 3–6 June 1796

13 Mon. Mrs. Lynch and Miss Lynch's benefit. [Play, farce, and entertainment. Other details of program not available]. Being positively the last night of the Company's performing this season. Source: 3–6 June 1796

July 1796

11 Mon. Positively for one night only Lee Lewes Comedian will open the theatre with *Comic Sketches; or, Folly and Fashion*. Originally prepared partly written and wholly delivered by him at Calcutta in the province of Bengal and afterwards at the following Royal Theatres: Covent Garden, Drury

Lane, York, Edinburgh and Dublin. To begin precisely at half past seven o'clock. Boxes 3s. 3d., pit 2s. 2d., gallery 1s. 1d. Source: 4–8 July 1796

1796–1797 SEASON

The Arthur Street Theatre was closed for dramatic performances for the season due to continuing civil unrest.

1797–1798 SEASON

The Arthur Street Theatre was closed for the season due to continuing civil unrest. However, at least one concert was performed there during that time.

3 July 1797 By desire of Gen. Lake on Monday, 3 July will be performed a concert of vocal and instrumental music. The principal vocal part by Harris. Source: 30 June 1797

1798–1799 SEASON

Venue: Arthur Street Theatre was closed this season due to continuing civil unrest. However, several concerts were performed there.

December 1798

1   Sat.   Concert. On Saturday, 1 December will be performed a Grand Concert of Vocal and Instrumental Music to consist of three acts. The principal vocal parts by Martin, Freeman, and Miss Atkins, their first appearance in this Theatre. To begin at six and finish before nine. Boxes 3s. 3d. Pit 2s. 1d. Gallery 1s. 1d. Source: 27 Nov. 1798

August 1799

9   Fri.   Concert. Bianchi and Haigh's concert. Vocal and instrumental music by Master Moran. Source: 6 Aug. 1799

1799–1800 SEASON

The civil unrest having been suppressed, Atkins first took the Belfast company to Derry for the early months of this season, returning to Belfast in December.

Venue: Arthur Street theatre.

Company: Atkins; Atkins, Jr.; Mrs. Bevin; Biddy; Mrs. Boucheron; Mrs. J. Brown; Carlton; Davis; Miss Fairburn; Mr. and Mrs. Michael Fullam; Mr. and Mrs. Garvey; Joseph Dowling Herbert; Hilmer; Mr. and Mrs. Kelly; Charles Lee Lewes; John Lynch (died 13 February 1800); Macklin; Sheridan; Hugh(?) Sparks.

For a biographies of the Belfast manager **Michael Atkins** and his son see the 1767–68 season.

This is the only known dramatic activity of **Mr. Biddy.**

The **Mrs. Bevin** who sang tertiary roles at Belfast during 1799–1800 was probably the wife of the "Mr. Bevin" who sang at various Crow Street concerts during the 1797–98 season. I am unable to confirm Clark's (1965, 351) assertion that a Mr. Bevin was with his wife in Belfast during the 1799–1800 season.

Mrs. Boucheron was the daughter of the Belfast manager, Michael Atkins. Little is known of her career, although she certainly acted with her father's company at the Arthur Street Theatre in March 1800 and later in the Irish provinces until about 1803. She died in Newry in August 1807.

For biography of **Mrs. J. Brown** see the 1794–95 season.

The **Mr. Carlton** who appeared in one tertiary role at Belfast in March 1800 as a member of Atkins's Arthur Street company was probably the same actor who resurfaces in Dublin at Crow Street, again playing secondary and tertiary roles, for the 1807–08 season. On 12 December 1807 Carleton played in the role of Sir Arthur Tessel in *Time's a Tell-Tail.* A reviewer in *DEP* 15 Dec. 1807 makes a point of correcting Carleton in his mistaken belief that the applause given by the audience when he and Miss Walstein make their entrance together "could be meant for him." He disappears from the record at the end of the 1807–08 season.

A number of **Davises** appeared in Ireland between 1794 and 1815, and it is sometimes difficult to distinguish between their activities. A Davis, who is billed as "from the Theatre Royal, Edinburgh, his first appearance on this stage" and who appeared on 15 November 1794 as Spado in *The Castle of Andalusia* was a pantomimist and directed a new pantomime and performed as the Clown in *Harlequin in Persia; or, The Triumphs of Neptune.* Mrs. Davis, also from Theatre Royal, Edinburgh, made her Crow Street debut as Norah in *The Poor Soldier* in January 1795. They shared a benefit on 25 February 1795 and evidently then left Ireland for a time.

The Mr. Davis who (with Mrs. Davis) acted in Dublin in the entertainments of the Olympia Circus at Peter Street (headed at that time by William Davis) and later at Crow Street, billed in the 1799–1800 season as her "first appearance on this stage," may have been the same Davis who performed in tertiary roles at Belfast's Arthur Street Theatre during the 1799–1800 season.

The Davis family continued to act at Crow Street, she in secondary and he in tertiary roles from 1800–01 through 1802–03. At some time between the end of that season and the beginning of the 1803–04 season Mr. Davis died, for a benefit was given to his "widow and four children" on 16 December 1803. Mrs. Davis continued to perform at Crow Street as a principal member through the 1810–11 season. She was delayed in beginning the season, her first performance was not until March, because of "a severe indisposition." She disappears from the record thereafter; perhaps she died.

Clark (1965, 357) seems in error in crediting the activities of the child actor **Miss Fairburn** to "Master Fairborn."

For biographies of **Mr.** and **Mrs. Michael Fullam** see the 1768–69 season.

For biographies of **Capt.** and **Mrs. Garvey** see the 1781– 82 season.

Joseph Dowling Herbert may have acted in the Irish provinces for some years but he is first noticed acting in Cork in April 1789. His earliest association with the Dublin theatre seems to have been as a amateur with Frederick Jones's Fishamble Street Theatre in 1793 when, he tells us, he assisted Jones to find a venue for his projected theatre. Herbert, whose real name was Dowling, made his stage debut at Crow Street on 14 January 1799 as Osmond *The Castle Spectre* billed as a "Gentleman of this City, his first time on any stage." Herbert played a variety of principal roles that season and was a member of the committee for The Incorporated Musical Fund Society that year.

Herbert performed in the Irish provinces during the 1799–1800 season, first at Limerick in August 1799 and then in Belfast at Atkins's Arthur Street Theatre from February through April 1800. He was billed there as the actor "who last winter made his appearance at the Theatre Royal Dublin with such distinguished approbation." Herbert, who was also a painter of some repute, helped to paint the scenery of the Belfast production of *Pizarro*. In the bills for his benefit on 16 May Herbert announced that "Those ladies and gentlemen whose portraits he has begun he requests they will favour him with an opportunity of finishing their pictures previous to the 25th of May as his engagement in England will oblige him to leave Belfast on that day." Where he went in England and if he performed there is not known.

Herbert returned to Crow Street for the 1800–1801 season. A contemporary remarked in his diary at the time that he had attended Herbert's benefit play, *The Mountaineers*: "Herbert is a good player of the second class. His Octavian was copied in every gesture from Kemble. Equally passionate, but without the ease of the original. Having often admired the master, the pupil app[eare]d to great disadvantage."

Herbert's first appearance during the 1801–02 season was not until March when he played an unknown role in his own play, *Trial's All*. The play was evidently never published. At the beginning of the 1802–03 season Herbert revived *Trial's All* for three performances and then appeared no more in Dublin for the next seven seasons. According to Clark (1965, 361) Herbert made his Covent Garden debut in 1804. When he resurfaces at Crow Street on 29 March 1810 as Sheva in *The Jew* Herbert is billed as "from the Theatre Royal, Bath, his first appearance here these seven years." At the end of the 1809–10 season Herbert seems to have retired from the stage.

The only record of the stage activities of **Mr. Hilmer** is at Belfast this season when he played a few tertiary roles. Clearly, his principal vocation was that of a portrait painter for in the advertisements for his benefit he announces: "Hilmer's engagements as a drawing master utterly preclude the possibility of his paying his personal respects therefore takes this public method of soliciting the patronage of a public whose liberality he has experienced beyond his most sanguine hopes and to whom he pledges himself by every exertion as a drawing master to endeavour to merit a continuance of their favours. "

The identities of **Mr.** and **Mrs. Kelly** are unclear. Many Kellys were active on stage in Ireland and England at the end of the eighteenth century, including the singer-composer Michael, but judging from what we know about their biographies none of them can have been in Belfast at this time.

For a biography of **Charles Lee Lewes** see the 1786–87 season.

For biography of **John Lynch**, who died this season, see the 1771–72 season.

A **Mr. Macklin** was active in the Irish provinces as an actor between 1790 and 1800. He is found in Ennis in the spring of 1790 and in Kilkenny for the 1790–91 season. He was in Ennis again in October 1791. The last record we have of him is performing in secondary roles at Michael Atkins's Arthur Street Theatre in the spring of 1799–1800.

The singer and actor named **Sheridan** who was active in the Irish provinces, but evidently not in London or Dublin, at the end of the eighteenth century, first appears in the record as "Master Sheridan" at Kilkenny in the spring and summer of 1789. The following year "Mr. Sheridan" acted during January and March in Ennis. Sheridan then disappears for a decade but resurfaces in Belfast with Michael Atkins's company in the winter of 1799–1800. Although he acted in two secondary roles, his *forte* seems to have been singing comic songs, several of which are specified in the Belfast playbills: *"The Country Club; or, Quisical Society," "Margery Topping," "What's a Woman Like," "Abraham Newland," "Tippy Bob," "Drimindugh," "Ben Bowsprit of Wapping"* and *"Murphy Delany."*

The **Mr. Sparks** who performed in Belfast at Michael Atkins's Arthur Street Theatre from February through early May 1800 is probably not Richard Sparks, as Clark (1965, 374) and the *BD* assert, but may have been the Drury Lane singer and minor actor G. Hugh Sparks, who is said to have been related to Isaac Sparks.

Hugh Sparks was born in Scotland in 1752 and left college to take to the stage. He made his acting debut in Dundee around 1769, and he remained there "for some years." He is found in Edinburgh in 1777, as prompter and actor. Evidently, he also performed briefly in Liverpool and Chester during the years between 1777 and 1797, when he and his wife made their London debuts at Drury Lane. Whatever his talents as an actor, Sparks and his wife were engaged regularly at Drury Lane from that time until his death in 1816 (she continued performing with success until 1820).

The *BD* finds the Sparkses in Birmingham in the summer of 1798. It was probably not Hugh Sparks, his wife and daughter, Miss Sparks, who performed for the first time at the Peter Street Amphitheatre in Dublin in the 1798–99 season, although the Drury Lane record indicates that were not performing there at that time. That Mrs. Sparks played younger women, and the *BD* tells us that by 1799 Mrs. Hugh Sparks was specializing in antiquated ladies.

Repertory, 1799–1800 Season

Atkins's, once again, did not advertise his plays in the newspapers this season. The surviving records makes it clear that many more plays were performed than the 39 of which we have record. The Belfast manager continued his policy of presenting a repertory consisting predominately of stock plays, interspersed with a few, recent Dublin and London productions. The fact that the Arthur Street Theatre had been closed for nearly threes seasons gave Atkins a host of new plays to choose from. Chief among the these was Lewes's wildly popular melodrama *The Castle Spectre*, which had first been staged in Dublin in January 1799, and Thomas Morton's *Secrets Worth Knowing*, which had premiered in Dublin in December 1798. In 1799, Reynolds's play, *Cheap Living*, had met with little success in either Dublin or London, but Atkins's brought it forward in Belfast anyway, perhaps because of the popularity of that playwright's *The Will*, which made its Dublin debut in November 1799 to crowded houses.

The three new afterpieces (*Animal Magnetism, My Grandmother, The Prize*) were more consistently successful plays in Dublin and London, each of which had premiered in Dublin within the last dozen years, but none accurately could be said to be "new."

Total Performances: 39 of 23 different named mainpieces; 30 of 22 different named afterpieces.
    Shakespeare: 3.
    New Mainpieces: 4.
    New Afterpieces: 3.

(For a key to repertory symbols see above, page 11)

Mainpieces: *The Beaux' Stratagem; The Castle Spectre**(3); *Cheap Living**; *Douglas; Every One Has His Fault; The Fair Penitent; The Fashionable Lover*■; *Hamlet; He Would Be a Soldier; The Highland Reel; Lovers' Vows*† (3); *The Mountaineers*†(2); *Pizarro*†(5); *The Revenge*■; *The Rivals; Robin Hood; Romeo and Juliet; Secrets Worth Knowing**; *The Stranger*†(2); *The Tempest;* Unspecified "play"(3); *The West Indian; The Will**; *The Wonder.*

Afterpieces: *The Agreeable Surprise* (2); *Animal Magnetism**; *The Belle's Stratagem; The Brothers; Catherine and Petruchio; The Children in the Wood; The Deuce is in Him; Inkle and Yarico; The Jew and the Doctor*†; *The Lying Valet* (2); *The Mayor of Garratt; The Merchant of Venice; The Midnight Hour; My Grandmother** (2); *No Song, No Supper; The Prize**; *Proteus*†; *The Register Office; The Romp; The Spoiled Child;* Unspecified "farce"(4); *The Village Lawyer*†(2); *The Wrangling Lovers.*

Entr'acte entertainments: Singing: 12. Dancing: 0.

Benefits (22): Atkins(2); The Belfast Repository; Mrs. Bevin; Biddy; Mrs. Boucheron; Davis; Freemasons; Mrs. Fullam; Mrs. Garvey; Herbert(2);

Hilmer; Kelly; Mrs. Kelly(2); Lee Lewes; Lynch; Poor House and Infirmary; Public Kitchen; Sheridan; Sparks.

December 1799

9   Mon.   [Comedy and farce. Other details of program unavailable]. The Theatre Belfast by Permission will be opened on Monday, 9 December with a comedy and farce as will be expressed in the bills Atkins informs the ladies and gentlemen of Belfast that particular care has been taken to have the Theatre well aired. There will be a play each evening during the races. Boys of any description will not be admitted to the gallery nor any person on any account whatever behind the scenes. Source: 6 Dec. 1799

January 1800

ca. 10   Herbert who last winter made his appearance at the Theatre Royal Dublin with such distinguished approbation is engaged for a few nights in Belfast. *Lovers' Vows.* Frederick–Herbert. Source: 10 Jan. 1800

22   Wed.   Fifth   of   Herbert's   six   nights.   *The   Mountaineers.* Octavian–Herbert. With a farce as will be expressed in the bills. Source: 21 Jan. 1800

24   Fri.   *Lovers' Vows.* Last time this season. Source: 21 Jan. 1800

27   Mon.   Herbert's benefit and last night of performance. Never acted here. *Secrets Worth Knowing.* End of the play *"Bucks have at ye all"* by Herbert after which Lee Lewes will recite a whimsical narrative concerning *"Benjamin Bolus; or, The Newcastle Apothecary"* written by Colman. With the farce of *Catherine and Petruchio.* Source: 24 Jan. 1800

29   Wed.   *He Would Be a Soldier.* With *The Agreeable Surprise.* Source: 28 Jan. 1800

31   Fri.   *The Tempest; or, the Enchanted Island* as altered by Kemble with new scenery machinery and decorations and the farce of the *Village Lawyer.* Source: 28 Jan. 1800

February 1800

3   Mon.   Benefit of Lee Lewes. *Romeo and Juliet.* Romeo (for that night only)–Herbert; Mercutio–Lewes; Juliet–Mrs. Fullam. with solemn dirge and funeral procession. In the course of the evening Lee Lewes will give the following comicallities and novelties unnatural and ridiculous gesticulation exemplified in the characters of a maiden lady Miss Priscilla Squeamish and her three female attendants viz., Penelope Pip, Esther Fidget and Grace Greasy. A parody on the sixteenth ode of second The Book of Horace. Bad reading of newspapers and of little boys and girls at school. A whimsical dissertation upon law. A scene recited out of *Pizarro*. After which Lee Lewes will give the audience a little slice of bread and butter nice. With *The Wrangling Lovers*. Source: 31 Jan. 1800

10 Mon. Benefit of Mrs. Fullam. Jones, manager of the Theatre-Royal Dublin, with that liberality which has always distinguished him as a leader of taste in the Metropolis having consented to give Fullam a week's absence he will make his appearance in this Theatre. *The Brothers*. Sir Benjamin Dove (for that night only)–Fullam; Capt. Ironsides–Lee Lewes (last night but two of his engagement). End of the play Lee Lewes will give *"A Dissertation on Matrimony."* After which Sheridan will sing an entire new comic song called *"More Grist to the Mill; or, All the World Turned Grinders."* Being a review of the fashionable grinders viz., the bothering grinder, physical grinder, gambling grinder, cabbaging grinder, humbugging grinder, Britain's grinder, Paddy's grinder, Scotch grinder, Snob's grinder, and the Devil's own grinder. Previous to the farce Lee Lewes will give Hippisley's *"Drunken Man."* To conclude With *The Lying Valet*. Sharp–Fullam. Source: 7 Feb. 1800

12 Wed. Lynch's benefit. *The Highland Reel*. With a farce and entertainments as will be expressed in future advertisements.

Commentary: Died on Thursday [13 February 1800] Mr. Lynch, comedian, whose death will be long regretted by the admirers of Dramatic merit. The liberality of a Belfast audience whose principal favourite he was for many years was amply evinced at his benefit the night preceding his final exit. He has left an afflicted wife and five children to mourn his loss. Source: 7 and 14 Feb. 1800

14 Fri. Herbert is engaged for the remainder of the season. *The Stranger*. Source: 14 Feb. 1800

24 Mon. Not acted here these twenty-five years. *The Revenge*. With a farce never acted here called *Animal Magnetism*. Source: 21 Feb. 1800

26 Wed. Last time this season. *The Stranger*. With a new pantomime entertainment called *Proteus; or, The Adventures of Harlequin*. Which pantomime will be repeated on Monday. Source: 25 Feb. 1800

28 Fri.   Benefit of Sparks. Never acted here. *The Will.* With the farce of *The Agreeable Surprise.* In the course of the evening Sparks will sing the two following songs: *"The Muffin Man"* and *"The A B C."* Sheridan will also sing a new comic song called *"The Country Club; or, Quisical Society."* Source: 25 Feb. 1800

March 1800

[During March there was repeated disruption of performances because of protests about singing *"God, Save the King"* after the second act].

10 Mon.   *The Castle Spectre.* Earl Osmond–Herbert; Father Philip–Atkins; Motley–Hilmer; Reginald–Kelly; Hassom–Sheridan; Kenrick–[Hugh?] Sparks; Saib–Atkins, Jr.; Muley–Macklin; Edric–Carlton; Allan–Biddy; Earl Percy–Davis; Evelina–Mrs. Garvey; Alice–Mrs. Kelly; Angela–Mrs. Boucheron. With entire new scenery and decorations. On account of the length of the above performance there will be no Farce nor any thing under full price during the evening. Source: 7 Mar. 1800

12 Wed.   *The Castle Spectre.* Source: 7 Mar. 1800

14 Fri.   *The Castle Spectre.* Source: 7 Mar. 1800

27 Thur.   Benefit of the Belfast Repository. *The Mountaineers.* Octavian–Herbert. Singing by Sparks and Sheridan. With *The Village Lawyer.* Boxes and Pit 3s. 3d., Gallery 1s. 1d.

Commentary: Atkins with that liberality for which he is so eminently distinguished not only granted the above benefit but insisted on the charity accepting a handsome sum for his own ticket. Indeed the manager's conduct in this and every other respect reflect honor on himself and cannot fail of having due weight with a judicious and generous public. In the course of the evening an occasional address written and to be spoken by Hilmer [printed in *BNL* 2 May 1800]. Source: 25 Mar. 1800

April 1800

14 Mon.   *Pizarro.* Pizarro–Kelly; Las Casas–Atkins; Davilla–Macklin; Gomez–Biddy; Valverede–Sheridan; Elvira–Mrs. Kelly; Alonzo–Davis; Atabila–Sparks; Orozimbo–Hilmer; Rolla–Herbert; Cora–Garvey; Priests and Virgins of the Sun: Atkins; Hilmer; Mrs. Bevin; Mrs. Brown; Mrs. Boucheron. With entire new scenery dresses and decorations. Act 1: The magnificent tent and pavillion of Pizarro with a distant view of the Peruvian camp. Act 2: The Temple of the Sun with a procession in order to a solemn sacrifice and consecration of banners before battle. Act 5: A rocky recess with a cascade down a precipice and the falling bridge. Paintings the figures by Herbert, the landscape Atkins, Jr. and the architecture by Atkins. On account of the very great expence attending the above performance nothing under full price can be taken. There will be no Farce. Source: 8 April 1800

16 Wed. *Pizarro.* Source: 8 Apr. 1800

18 Fri. *Pizarro.* Source: 8 Apr. 1800

21 Mon. Benefit of Atkins. Never acted here. *Cheap Living.* Singing by Sheridan and Mrs. Boucheron. With the farce of *The Mayor of Garratt.* [See comments 25 April which indicate that Atkins's benefit night was poorly attended]. Source: 18 Apr. 1800

23 Wed. Mrs. Garvey's benefit. *The Belle's Stratagem.* And the favourite farce of *The Midnight Hour.* With entertainments as will be expressed in the bills. [Reviewed in 25 Apr. 1800]. Source: 18 Apr. 1800

25 Fri. Benefit of Kelly. *Every One has His Fault.* With the comic opera of *Inkle and Yarico.* End of the play *"The Mirror or World as it goes,"* being a display of fashionable follies wherein every body may see their own faults and features by Mrs. Kelly. In the course of the evening the following entertainments: a divertissement comic, amusing, descriptive called *A Ramble Through Belfast.* Including 1. a description of the Academy and Church, Donegall Street arts, sciences, etc. 2. The Poor House—blessing arising from charity, etc. 3. The Exchange on a day of business—traffic, etc. 4. Rooms on a coterie night-music, taste, etc. 5. The Quay—shipping commerce and benefits arising therefrom. 6. The Linen-Hall and manufactory—the stable wealth of Ireland and comforts of industry. 7. a peep into the play-house—actors, critics, etc. 8. a tavern scene and nightly adventures of a buck. 9. To conclude with an eulogy on the town, trade, and commerce of Belfast. A comic song by Sheridan called *"Margery Topping."* Source: 22 Apr. 1800

28 Mon. Sheridan's benefit. Not acted here this season. *The Wonder, A Woman Keeps a Secret.* In the course of the evening Sheridan will sing the following new comic songs *"What's a Woman Like," "Abraham Newland,"* and *"Tippy Bob."* With a new musical farce never performed here called *The Prize; or, 2, 5, 3, 8.* Source: 22 Apr. 1800

30 Wed.   Mrs. Bevin's benefit. *Robin Hood.* With the much admired farce of *The Jew and the Doctor.* With entertainments as will be expressed in the bills. Source: 25 Apr. 1800

May 1800

2 Fri.   Mrs. Boucheron's night. *Lovers' Vows.* With a new farce never acted here called *My Grandmother.* Source: 25 Apr. 1800

5 Mon.   Hilmer's benefit. *The Fair Penitent.* With the much admired farce of *The Spoiled Child.* In the course of the evening an address to the audience written by Hilmer will be spoken by Miss Fairburn, aged six years. End Act 2 an occasional address written and to be spoken by Hilmer. Sheridan will sing *"Drimindugh."* Sparks a new comic medley. Hilmer's engagements as a drawing master utterly preclude the possibility of his paying his personal respects therefore takes this public method of soliciting the patronage of a public whose liberality he has experienced beyond his most sanguine hopes and to whom he pledges himself by every exertion as a drawing master to endeavour to merit a continuance of their favours. Source: 29 Apr. 1800

7 Wed.   Davis's benefit. *The Merchant of Venice.* After the play the following comic songs *"Ben Bowsprit of Wapping"* and *"Murphy Delany"* by Sheridan. to which will be added the musical farce of *No Song, No Supper.* Source: 2 May 1800

9 Fri.   Benefit of Mrs. Kelly. *The Rivals.* In the course of the evening *"A Ramble through Belfast"* as sung by Kelly with very great applause printed copies of which will be delivered gratis at the box pit and gallery doors on Friday night. With the farce called *The Deuce is in Him.* Source: 6 May 1800

14 Wed.   Atkins's benefit. *The West Indian* and the farce of *My Grandmother.* Source: 9 May 1800

16 Fri.   Last night of the benefits. Herbert's benefit. *Douglas.* Lady Randolph–Mrs. Garvey. After the play singing by Sheridan. To conclude with the farce of *The Register Office.* Paddy O'Carrol (with songs for that night only)–Herbert. Those ladies and gentlemen whose portraits he has begun he requests they will favour him with an opportunity of finishing their pictures previous to the 25th of May as his engagement in England will oblige him to leave Belfast on that day. Source: 13 May 1800

19 Mon.   *Pizarro.* Source: 13 May 1800

23 Fri.   *Pizarro.* For the last time this season. Half price will be admitted to the pit at the usual hour. Source: 20 May 1800

26 Mon.   Benefit of poor and distressed Free Masons their widows and orphans. *The Beaux' Stratagem* with the farce of *The Lying Valet.* The prologue by Herbert a song by Sheridan and the epilogue by Mrs. Garvey. Source: 20 May 1800

30 Fri.   [Play and farce. Other details of program not available]. Benefit of the Poor-House and Infirmary. Source: 27 May 1800

June 1800

2   Mon.   Benefit of the Public Kitchen. *Hamlet.* The principal characters by officers of the garrison who have humanely offered to undertake them for the advantage of this charitable institution. Source: 30 May 1800

6   Fri.   Biddy's benefit. The last night of performing this season. Not acted here these six years. *The Fashionable Lover.* With the much admired musical farce not acted this season called *The Children in the Wood.* Source: 3 June 1800

9   Mon.   Benefit of Mrs. Kelly, having failed in her first attempt. Positively the last night this season.[Unspecified play. Other details unavailable]. With *The Romp.* Source: 3 June 1800

WORKS CITED/SELECT BIBLIOGRAPHY

NEWSPAPERS AND PERIODICALS

The Belfast Mercury; or, Freeman's Chronicle.
The Belfast Newsletter.
The Dublin Evening Post.
The Dublin Gazette.
Faulkner's *Dublin Journal.*
The Hibernian Journal (Dublin).
The Hibernian Magazine.
The Londonderry Journal.
The Newry Chronicle and Universal Advertiser.
The Belfast *Northern Star.*
The Public Monitor (Dublin).
The Public Register; or, Freeman's Journal (Dublin).
Saunders's Newsletter (Dublin).
The Theatric Magazine (Dublin).
The Weekly Oracle (Dublin).

MANUSCRIPTS

Charlemont, Earl of "Original Correspondence of James, Late Earl of Charlemont." Royal Irish Academy.
"The Drennan Correspondence," Public Record Office of Northern Ireland, Belfast.
Lawrence, William J. "Annals of the Old Belfast Stage, 1731–1831." 1897. NLI Ms. 4291.
— Manuscript Notebooks (99 vols.) in U of Cincinnatti Library.

PLAYBILLS

The British Library, London.
Harvard Theatre Collection, Boston, Massachusetts.

OTHER PRINTED SOURCES

Bardon, Jonathan. *Belfast: An Illustrated History.* Dundonald: Blackstaff Press, 1982.

Bartlett, Thomas and Keith Jeffery. *A Military History of Ireland.* Cambridge: Cambridge Univ. Press, 1996.

Benn, George. *A History of the Town of Belfast from the Earliest Times to the Close of the Eighteenth Century.* Marcus Ward, 1877.

Bernard, John. *Retrospections of the Stage by the Late John Bernard.* 2 vols. London : H. Colburn and R. Bentley, 1830.

Brett, C. E. B. *Buildings of Belfast 1700-1914.* London: Weidenfild and Nicolson, 1967.

Broadbent, R. J. "Old Circuit Days: Austin and Whitlock's Circuit," *The Stage.* n.p. n.d.

Clark, William Smith. *The Irish Stage in the County Towns: 1720 to 1800.* Oxford: Clarendon Press, 1965.

Drennan Letters, ed. D. A. Chart. Belfast, 1931.

Garrick, David. *Letters of David Garrick.* Eds. David M. Little and George M. Hahrl, with Phoebe de K. Wilson. 3 vols. Cambridge, Mass.: Harvard Univ. Press, 1963.

Hitchcock, Robert. *An Historical View of the Irish Stage.* 2 vols. Dublin, 1788–1794.

Kahan, Gerald. *George Alexander Stevens and 'The Lecture on Heads'.* Athens, Ga.: Univ. of Georgia Press, 1984.

Lacy, Robin Thurlow. *A Biographical Dictionary of Scenographers: 500 B.C. to 1900 A.D.* New York: Greenwood Press, 1990.

Lawrence, William J. "The Old Belfast Stage: Its Glories and Romances," *The Irish News*, 21 Nov. 1895.

Lewes, Charles Lee. *Memoirs of Charles Lee Lewes*, 4 vols. London, 1805.

Millin, S. Shannon, "The Arthur Street Theatre," *The Belfast Telegraph*, 21 Apr. 1938.

O'Keeffe, John. *Recollections of the Life of John O'Keeffe, Written by Himself.* 2 vols. London: Henry Colburn, 1826.

The Thespian Dictionary (1805)

Town Book of the Corporation of Belfast (1613–1816). Ed. R. M. Young. Belfast, 1892.

Wilkinson, Tate. *Memoirs of his Own Life.* 4 vols. York: Wilson, Spence and Mawman, 1790.

——. *The Wandering Patentee; or, A History of the Yorkshire Theatres from 1770 to the Present Time.* 4 vols. Wilson, Spence and Mawman, York, 1795.

INDEX OF AUTHORS, PLAYS
AND PERFORMANCE DATES

315

—— *The Magical Soldier; or, Harlequin's Mouth Opened*: 18 Dec 1771

—— *The Mentalist; or, Doctor of the Passions*: 15 Nov 1771

—— *Neck or Nothing; or, Harlequin's Flight from the Gods*: 18 Mar 1789

—— *Poor Darty's Trip to Belfast*: 7 Nov 1794

—— *Prometheus; or, Harlequin's Animation*: 16 Jan 1789: 26 Jan 1789

—— *Proteus; or, the Adventures of Harlequin*: 26 Feb 1800

—— *The Revels; or, Harlequin Villager*: 16 Feb 1776

—— *The School of Harmony* (musical entertainment): 4 Feb 1789

—— *The Sorcerers; or, Harlequin Wizard*: 2 Dec 1791

—— *The Spell; or, Harlequin's Funeral*: 11 Feb 1778

—— *The Tavern Bilkers; or, Harlequin Rake*: 5 Feb 1779

—— *Twiss in Ireland; or, Fop in Disgrace*: 20 Apr 1778

—— *The Vintner in the Suds*: 22 June 1753

—— *The Wanton Wife; or, The Glassman Outwitted*: 6 Nov 1765: 15 Nov 1765: 13 Dec 1765

—— *The Wapping Landlady; or, The Humours of the Navy*: 3 Aug 1761: 7 Aug 1761

—— *Will o'th Wisp; or, Blue Beard*: 18 Mar 1795

—— *The Witches; or, Harlequin Salamander:* 3 May 1796

—— *The Witches; or, Harlequin's Vagaries*: 4 Nov 1773: 19 Nov 1773

The Apprentice. See Murphy, Arthur

As You Like It. See Shakespeare, William

Arne, Thomas A.*: Henry and Emma; or, the Nut Brown Maid*: 29 Mar 1776

The Author. See Foote, Samuel

Baker, Thomas*: Tunbridge Walks*: 11 Nov 1768

Bambridge, Rev. Dr.: *The Guillotine; or, the Death of Louis XVI*: 27 May 1793

Barbarossa. See Brown, John Dr.

Barnaby Brittle. See Anonymous

The Beaux' Stratagem. See Farquhar, George

The Beggar's Opera. See Gay, John

The Beggars' Wedding. See Coffey, Charles

The Belle's Stratagem. See Cowley, Hannah

Bickerstaffe, Isaac: *The Absent Man*: 13 Jan 1769

—— *Daphne and Amintor*: 9 May 1781

—— *The Ephesian Matron*: 16 Jan 1782

Captain Cook: see Collier, George Sir, *The Death of Captain Cook.*
The Careless Husband. See Cibber, Colley
Carey, Henry: ***Chrononhotonthologos***: 8 Nov 1765: 8 Jan 1766: 15 Jan 1766: 4 Aug 1770: 16 Jan 1778: 6 Apr 1795
—— ***The Contrivances***: 14 Mar 1763: 27 Nov 1765: 3 Jan 1766: 7 Feb 1766: 30 Dec 1768: 11 July 1770: 18 Sep 1771: 27 Mar 1776: 24 Aug 1787
—— ***The Honest Yorkshireman***: 1751–1752 Season: 3 July 1753: 4 Sep 1761: 16 Oct 1765: 2 Dec 1768: 10 Aug 1770: 2 Aug 1771: 22 Nov 1771: 17 Jan 1772: 1 Oct 1773: 31 Dec 1773: 24 Apr 1778: 8 Jan 1780: 31 Jan 1791
The Carmelite. See Cumberland, Richard
The Castle Spectre. See Lewis, Matthew G.
Catherine and Petruchio. See Garrick, David
Cato. See Addison, Joseph
Centlivre, Susannah: ***A Bold Stroke for a Wife***: 24 Feb 1758: 3 Mar 1763: 11 Dec 1765: 26 May 1784
—— ***The Busy Body***: 20 Nov 1754: 26 Jan 1763: 25 Mar 1763: 27 Nov 1765: 16 Oct 1771: 27 Dec 1771: 15 Dec 1773: 27 July 1791: 9 May 1796
—— ***The Wonder, A Woman Keeps a Secret***: 25 July 1770: 22 Nov 1775: 9 May 1781: 9 Feb 1791: 28 Apr 1800
The Chaplet. See Mendez, Moses
The Chapter of Accidents. See Lee, Sophia
Cheap Living. See Reynolds, Frederick
The Cheats of Scapin. See Otway, Thomas
The Children in the Wood. See Morton, Thomas
Chrononhotonthologos. See Carey, Henry
Cibber, Colley: ***The Careless Husband***: 7 Sep 1753: 5 Aug 1761: 6 Jan 1769
—— ***The Provoked Husband***: 31 Jan 1755: 15 Feb 1758: 26 May 1758: 17 July 1761: 28 Aug 1761: 21 Jan 1763: 4 Apr 1763: 16 Oct 1765: 1 Jan 1766: 13 Jan 1769: 9 Aug 1771: 2 Oct 1771: 7 Jan 1774: 15 Mar 1776: 21 Nov 1788: 4 Feb 1791: 19 Mar 1792
—— ***She Would and She Would Not***: 28 Aug 1753: 12 Aug 1761
—— ***Damon and Phillida***: 6 July 1753: 18 Nov 1754: 22 Nov 1754: 3 Mar 1755: 13 Feb 1758: 2 June 1758: 12 Aug 1761: 13 Nov 1765: 9 Aug 1771: 13 Dec 1775: 29 Mar 1776
—— ***Love Makes a Man***: 11 Dec 1754: 14 Aug 1761: 20 July 1770: 9 Feb 1774: 28 Feb 1776: 1 Apr 1778
—— ***The School Boy***: 27 Jan 1755

The Connaught Wife; or, The Honest Munster Man. See Ryder, Thomas

The Conscious Lovers. *See* Steele, Richard

The Constant Couple. See Farquhar, George

The Contrivances. See Carey, Henry

The Cottagers; or, The Female Metamorphosis. See Brunton, Anna

The Countess of Salisbury. See Hartson, Hall

The Country Girl. See Garrick, David

The Country Lasses. See Johnson, Charles

Cowley, Hannah: ***The Belle's Stratagem***: 7 Nov 1781: 14 Nov 1781: 4 Jan 1782: 31 Dec 1790: 30 Mar 1796: 23 Apr 1800

—— ***More Ways Than One to Win Her***: 6 Feb 1789

—— ***Which is the Man?***: 17 Jan 1791: 2 Dec 1791: 23 Mar 1792

The Critic. See Sheridan, Richard B.

Cross, John C.: ***The Purse; or, The Benevolent Tar***: 27 Feb 1795: 1 June 1796

Cross Purposes. See O'Brien, William

Cumberland, Richard: ***The Brothers***: 24 Jan 1776: 18 Feb 1789: 11 Mar 1789: 10 Feb 1800

—— ***The Carmelite***: 14 Oct 1791

—— ***The Fashionable Lover***: 24 Sep 1773: 29 Sep 1773: 15 Oct 1773: 12 Nov 1773: 29 Dec 1775: 20 Nov 1778: 30 May 1781: 9 Mar 1795: 6 June 1800

—— ***The Imposters***: 27 Apr 1789

—— ***The Jew; or, The Benevolent Hebrew***: 29 Oct 1794: 5 Nov 1794

—— ***The West Indian***: 28 Aug 1771: 27 Nov 1771: 17 Dec 1773: 2 Feb 1776: 11 Dec 1783: 3 Mar 1784: 1 Dec 1788: 1 Feb 1792: 14 May 1800

Cymbeline. See Shakespeare, William

Cymon. *See* Anonymous.

Damon and Phillida. See Cibber, Colley

Daphne and Amintor. See Bickerstaffe, Isaac

The Dead Alive. See O'Keeffe, John

The Death of Captain Cook. See Collier, George Sir

Delap, John: ***The Royal Suppliants***: 23 June 1784

The Deserter. See Dibdin, Charles

The Deserter of Naples. See Gardell and Delphini

The Deuce is in Him. See Colman, George the elder

The Devil To Pay. See Coffey, Charles

13 Dec 1771: 20 Oct 1773: 3 Jan 1774: 6 Dec 1775: 28 Oct 1778: 19 Mar 1779: 26 May 1800

—— *The Constant Couple*: 25 Nov 1754: 24 May 1758: 27 Jan 1766: 15 Aug 1770: 15 Nov 1771: 24 Jan 1772: 4 Nov 1773: 12 Jan 1776: 17 Nov 1786

—— *The Inconstant*: 6 Feb 1758: 10 Mar 1766: 4 Dec 1771: 6 Oct 1773: 2 Mar 1789

—— *The Recruiting Officer*: 6 Dec 1754: 20 Nov 1755: 10 Feb 1758: 13 Nov 1765: 28 Sep 1768: 15 Dec 1775: 13 July 1785

—— *Sir Harry Wildair*: 2 Aug 1753: 25 Nov 1754: 24 May 1758: 17 Nov 1786

—— *The Twin Rivals*: 10 Aug 1753: 24 July 1761: 21 Nov 1781

Fashionable Levities. See Macnally, Leonard

The Fashionable Lover. See Cumberland, Richard

The Fashionable Wife. See Anonymous

The Female Officer. See Anonymous

Fielding, Henry: *The Intriguing Chambermaid*: 7 Feb 1755: 21 Feb 1758: 28 July 1770: 10 Oct 1791

—— *The Lottery*: 17 Jan 1755: 15 Mar 1758: 16 July 1770: 19 Jan 1776: 1 Apr 1778: 21 Nov 1781

—— *The Miser*: 22 Aug 1753: 23 Feb 1763: 30 Dec 1768: 18 July 1770: 13 Sep 1771: 20 Dec 1771: 23 Sep 1773: 11 Feb 1774: 10 Apr 1776: 30 Oct 1778: 11 July 1780: 5 Jan 1791: 2 Feb 1791

—— *The Mock Doctor*: 14 Sep 1753: 20 Nov 1754: 5 Feb 1755: 14 Mar 1755: 10 Feb 1758: 30 Oct 1765: 23 Dec 1768: 30 Apr 1770: 11 Sep 1771: 6 Sep 1773: 8 Jan 1780: 30 May 1781

—— *The Register Office*: 18 July 1791: 16 May 1800

—— *Tom Thumb*: 4 June 1753: 6 June 1753: 1 Aug 1770

—— *The Virgin Unmasked*: 18 Dec 1751: 24 Aug 1753: 27 Nov 1754: 6 Dec 1754: 6 Feb 1758: 12 June 1758: 26 Aug 1761: 14 Jan 1763: 26 Jan 1763: 23 Oct 1765: 20 Dec 1765: 10 Jan 1766: 19 Feb 1766: 23 Jan 1772: 17 Sep 1773: 29 Dec 1775: 4 Dec 1778

Fletcher, John: *Rule a Wife and Have a Wife*: 1 Aug 1770: 23 Oct 1778: 23 Oct 1786: 17 Dec 1794: 4 May 1796

Flora; or, Hob in the Well. See Hippisley, John

Florizel and Perdita. See Morgan, McNamara

The Follies of a Day; or, The Marriage of Figaro. See Holcroft, Thomas

Foote, Samuel: *The Author*: 12 May 1758: 29 Jan 1779: 10 Aug 1791

—— *The Disappointment*: 16 July 1770: 28 July 1770

—— *Lady Pentweazle of Blowbladder Street*: 4 July 1770: 30 July 1770: 24 Apr 1778

—— *A Peep Behind the Curtain*: 29 Feb 1792: 9 Mar 1792
Gay, John: *The Beggar's Opera*: 29 Nov 1754: 8 Mar 1758: 27 Mar 1758: 9 July 1761: 28 Jan 1763: 15 Feb 1763: 15 Nov 1765: 23 Aug 1768: 1 June 1770: 6 July 1770: 20 Nov 1771: 4 Dec 1778: 24 Feb 1779: 12 Nov 1788: 21 Sep 1791
—— *The What D'Ye Call It*: 27 July 1753: 28 Aug 1753: 28 Feb 1755: 20 July 1770
The Genii; or, Harlequin Restored. See Anonymous
The Gentle Shepherd. See Ramsay, Allan
The Ghost. See Anonymous
The Giant's Causeway; or, A Trip to the Dargle. See O'Keeffe, John
Goldsmith, Oliver: *The Good Natured Man*: 7 Nov 1777
—— *She Stoops to Conquer*: 17 Sep 1773: 29 Dec 1773: 17 Jan 1776: 13 Nov 1778: 16 Jan 1789
The Good Natured Man. See Goldsmith, Oliver
The Governess. See Ryder, Thomas
The Grecian Daughter. See Murphy, Arthur
Griffith, Elizabeth: *The School for Rakes*: 27 Sep 1771
The Guardian. See Garrick, David
The Guillotine; or, the Death of Louis XVI. See Bambridge, Rev Dr
Gustavus Vasa. See Brooke, Henry

Hamlet. See Shakespeare, William
Harlequin Animated; or, Fairy Friendship. See Anonymous
Harlequin Gardener. See Anonymous
Harlequin in Derry; or, The Dutchman Outwitted. See Anonymous
Harlequin in the Shades. See Anonymous
Harlequin Skeleton. See Anonymous
Harlequin with Thurot; or, The Taking of Carrickfergus. See Ryder, Thomas
Hartson, Hall: *The Countess of Salisbury*: 9 May 1770: 23 Feb 1776: 7 Feb 1791
Heigho for a Husband. See Waldron, Francis G.
The Heiress. See Burgoyne, John Lt. Gen.
Henry and Emma; or, the Nut Brown Maid. See Arne, Thomas A.
The Hermit; or, Harlequin Victorious. See Anonymous
He Would be a Soldier. See Pilon, Frederick
The Highland Reel. See O'Keeffe, John
High Life Below Stairs. See Townley, James
Hippisley, John: *Flora; or, Hob in the Well*: 3 Jan 1750: 19 July 1753: 29 July 1761: 28 Aug 1761: 28 Jan 1791

Jephson, Robert: *The Hotel; or, Servant with Two Masters*: 24 Oct 1794: 5 Nov 1794
The Jew and the Doctor. See Dibdin, Thomas
The Jew; or, The Benevolent Hebrew. See Cumberland, Richard
Johnson, Charles: *The Country Lasses*: 10 Jan 1755
Jones, Henry: *The Earl of Essex*: 27 July 1753: 21 Oct 1768*: 6 Mar 1776*: 12 Nov 1790: 19 Oct 1791 [*possibly Henry Brooke's version of the play, see above].
Jonson, Ben: *Every Man in His Humour*: 11 July 1770
The Jovial Crew. See Brome, Richard Sir
The Jubilee. See Garrick, David
The Judgment of Midas. See O'Hara, Kane (*Midas*).
Julius Caesar. See Shakespeare, William

Kelly, Hugh: *Clementina*: 19 Nov 1773: 6 Feb 1774
—— *False Delicacy*: 31 Oct 1768: 6 Dec 1771
—— *The School for Wives*: 27 Mar 1776: 14 Jan 1791
—— *A Word to the Wise; or, All for the Best*: 1 Jan 1779: 8 Jan 1779: 23 Mar 1781: 21 Apr 1783
Kemble, John P.: *The Pannel*: 17 Jan 1791: 7 Feb 1791
The King and the Miller of Mansfield. See Dodsley, Robert
King Henry IV, Part One. See Shakespeare, William
King Henry V. See Shakespeare, William
King Lear. See Shakespeare, William
King Richard III. See Shakespeare, William
King, Thomas: *Wit's Last Stake*: 30 Aug 1771: 18 Dec 1771
Know Your Own Mind. See Murphy, Arthur

Lady Pentweazle of Blowbladder Street. See Foote, Samuel
"The Lecture Upon Heads." See Lewes, Lee
Lee, John: *The Man of Quality*: 10 Apr 1778: 25 May 1796
Lee, Nathaniel: *The Rival Queens*: 23 Nov 1768: 15 June 1770: 11 Sep 1771: 18 Dec 1771: 22 Dec 1775: 2 Feb 1791: 6 Feb 1792: 17 Apr 1793
—— *Theodosius*: 10 Apr 1758: 11 Oct 1765: 7 Aug 1770: 10 Nov 1777
Lee, Sophia: *The Chapter of Accidents*: 14 Mar 1783: 29 Jan 1789: 2 Mar 1792: 8 May 1793
Lethe; or, Aesop in The Shades. See Garrick, David
Lewes, Lee: *"The Lecture Upon Heads"*: 23 Nov 1786: 30 Nov 1786: 11 Jan 1787: 12 Jan 1787

Midas. See O'Hara, Kane
The Midnight Hour. See Inchbald, Elizabeth
Miller, James and John Hoadley: *Mahomet, the Impostor*: 11 Mar 1796
Milton, John: *Comus*: 18 May 1770: 17 Dec 1788: 30 May 1793
The Miraculous Cure; or, The Citizen Outwitted. See Forde, Brownlow
The Miser. See Fielding, Henry
Miss In Her Teens. See Garrick, David
The Mock Doctor. See Fielding, Henry
Modern Antiques; or, The Merry Mourners. See O'Keeffe, John
Moore, Edward: *The Foundling*: 19 May 1758: 4 July 1770: 25 Oct 1781: 15 Apr 1789: 13 Jan 1792: 25 Jan 1792: 23 May 1796
—— *The Gamester*: 3 July 1753: 6 July 1753: 24 Oct 1777: 15 June 1785: 17 Dec 1788: 27 Sep 1790: 21 Jan 1791: 2 Jan 1795: 25 Apr 1796
More, Hannah: *Percy Earl of Northumberland*: 20 Apr 1778
More Ways Than One. See Cowley, Hannah
Morgan, McNamara: *Florizel and Perdita*: 15 Feb 1758: 29 Feb 1758: 30 May 1770: 29 Nov 1771: 2 Dec 1778: 20 Aug 1787: 19 Jan 1791: 24 Feb 1792
Morton, Thomas: *The Children in the Wood*: 19 Nov 1794: 29 Dec 1794: 18 Apr 1795: 6 June 1800
—— *Secrets Worth Knowing*: 27 Jan 1800
The Mountaineers. See Colman, George the younger
The Mourning Bride. See Congreve, William
Mrs Cole the Methodist. See Foote, Samuel
Much Ado About Nothing. See Shakespeare, William
Murphy, Arthur: *All in the Wrong*: 30 May 1770: 18 Sep 1771: 28 Jan 1774: 19 Feb 1787: 20 Feb 1789: 3 Aug 1791: 14 Sep 1791
—— *The Apprentice*: 24 May 1758: 29 Oct 1773: 30 Dec 1778: 17 Apr 1793
—— *The Citizen*: 11 Oct 1765: 25 Oct 1765: 19 Nov 1765: 1 Jan 1766: 30 Nov 1768: 11 Aug 1770: 8 Nov 1771: 6 Dec 1771: 20 Oct 1773: 5 Jan 1776: 9 Dec 1778: 5 Feb 1779: 5 Mar 1779: 24 June 1785: 12 Nov 1790
—— *The Grecian Daughter*: 13 Oct 1773: 8 Dec 1773: 16 Feb 1774: 7 Sep 1781: 10 Dec 1784: 13 June 1785: 6 Aug 1787: 3 Dec 1790
—— *Know Your Own Mind*: 3 Mar 1779: 4 Mar 1795: 18 May 1796
—— *Marriage a la Mode*: 19 Jan 1774
—— *The Old Maid*: 2 Dec 1765: 11 Dec 1765: 18 Dec 1765: 4 Sep 1771: 20 Dec 1771: 15 Jan 1772: 1 Dec 1773: 8 Apr 1776: 24 Feb 1779
—— *Three Weeks After Marriage*: 30 Jan 1789

Otway, Thomas: *The Cheats of Scapin*: 27 Jan 1766: 4 May 1770: 23 Sep 1791
—— *The Orphan*: 27 Nov 1754: 17 Dec 1754: 5 Feb 1755: 12 May 1758: 2 Dec 1765: 5 Feb 1766: 3 Oct 1768: 11 Aug 1770: 24 Aug 1787
—— *Venice Preserved*: 15 June 1753: 7 Feb 1755: 22 Nov 1765: 19 Feb 1766: 2 Dec 1768: 30 July 1770: 19 July 1780: 6 June 1785: 22 June 1785: 15 Dec 1788: 29 Dec 1794

The Padlock. See Bickerstaffe, Isaac
The Pannel. See Kemble, John P
The Patriot King; or, Irish Chief. See Dobbs, Francis
A Peep Behind the Curtain. See Garrick, David
Peeping Tom of Coventry. See O'Keeffe, John
Percy, Earl of Northumberland. See More, Hannah
Philips, Ambrose: The *Distrest Mother*: 21 Apr 1758: 9 Mar 1763: 18 Oct 1765: 25 Oct 1765: 7 Oct 1768: 16 Aug 1771: 3 Dec 1788: 8 Dec 1788
Pilon, Frederick: *He Would be a Soldier:* 30 Jan 1792: 29 Jan 1800
Pizarro. See Sheridan, Richard B.
Polly Honeycombe. See Colman, George the elder
Poor Darty's Trip to Belfast: See Anonymous
The Poor Soldier. See O'Keeffe, John
Poor Vulcan. See Dibdin, Charles
The Prize. See Hoare, Prince
Prometheus; or, Harlequin's Animation. See Anonymous
Proteus; or, the Adventures of Harlequin. See Anonymous
The Provoked Husband. See Cibber, Colley
The Purse; or, The Benevolent Tar. See Cross, John C.

The Quaker. See Dibdin, Charles

The Rage. See Reynolds, Frederick
Ramsay, Allan: *The Gentle Shepherd*: 25 Nov 1768
Ravenscroft, Edward: *The Anatomist*: 6 Aug 1753: 10 Aug 1753: 31 Aug 1753: 27 Mar 1758: 20 Jan 1766: 5 Feb 1766: 3 Jan 1772: 24 Jan 1772: 22 Dec 1773: 6 Feb 1774: 6 Mar 1776
The Recruiting Officer. See Farquhar, George
The Recruiting Serjeant. See Bickerstaffe, Isaac
Reed, Joseph: *The Register Office* (see Fielding, Henry)
The Regions of Accomplishment. See Sheridan, Richard B.
The Register Office. See Fielding, Henry
Reparation. See Andrews, Miles P.

The Reprisal; or, The Tars of Old England. See Smollet, Tobias
The Revels; or, Harlequin Villager. See Anonymous
The Revenge. See Young, Edward
Reed, Joseph: *Tom Jones:* 30 Oct 1771: 1 Nov 1771
Reynolds, Frederick: *Cheap Living:* 21 Apr 1800
—— *Dramatist:* 24 Feb 1792
—— *Notoriety:* 6 Apr 1795
—— *The Rage:* 11 Mar 1795
—— *The Will:* 28 Feb 1800
The Rival Queens. See Lee, Nathaniel
The Rivals. See Sheridan, Richard B.
Robin Hood. See Macnally, Leonard
Robinson Crusoe; or, Harlequin Friday. See Anonymous
The Roman Father. See Whitehead, William
Romeo and Juliet. See Shakespeare, William
The Romp. See Lloyd, T. A.
Rosina. See Brooke, Frances
Rowe, Nicholas: *The Fair Penitent:* 4 June 1753: 14 Sep 1753: 18
Nov 1754: 8 Feb 1758: 14 Jan 1763: 4 Dec 1765: 17 Oct 1768: 4 Aug
1770: 25 Sep 1771: 16 Feb 1776: 2 Dec 1778: 5 May 1784: 10 Aug
1787: 21 Apr 1796: 5 May 1800
—— *Jane Shore:* 18 Dec 1751: 22 Nov 1754: 18 Jan 1755: 8 Aug 1770:
9 Oct 1771: 5 Jan 1776: 10 Apr 1778: 10 June 1785: 10 Nov 1790: 17
Oct 1791: 19 Nov 1794
—— *Tamerlane:* 13 July 1753: 13 Dec 1754: 19 Mar 1755: 19 Nov
1765: 5 Nov 1768: 4 Nov 1771: 1 Jan 1772: 31 Dec 1773: 24 Nov 1775:
26 Jan 1776: 4 Nov 1778: 19 Feb 1779: 4 Nov 1779
The Royal Suppliants. See Delap, John
Rule a Wife and Have a Wife. See Fletcher, John
Ryder, Thomas: *The Connaught Wife; or, The Honest Munster
Man:* 9 July 1770
—— *The Governess:* 14 Jan 1778: 16 Jan 1778: 28 Jan 1778: 11 Feb
1778: 13 Jan 1779
—— *Harlequin with Thurot; or, The Taking of Carrickfergus[?]:*
31 July 1770

The School Boy. See Cibber, Colley
The School for Arrogance. See Holcroft, Thomas
The School for Rakes. See Griffith, Elizabeth
The School for Scandal. See Sheridan, Richard B.
The School for Wives. See Kelly, Hugh
The School of Harmony. See Anonymous

Secrets Worth Knowing. See Morton, Thomas

Shakespeare, William: *As You Like It*: 23 July 1753: 22 Mar 1776: 12 Dec 1777: 5 Mar 1779: 3 Mar 1780: 20 Dec 1786: 8 Aug 1791

—— *Cymbeline*: 20 Mar 1795

—— *Hamlet*: 6 Aug 1753: 7 Jan 1755: 5 Apr. 1758: 10 July 1761: 28 Feb 1766: 23 Sept 1768: 5 June 1770: 2 Aug 1770: 27 Oct 1773: 13 Dec 1775: 29 Jan 1779: 9 Apr 1787: 19 Nov 1788: 12 Dec 1788: 15 Nov 1790: 28 Jan 1791: 5 Mar 1792: 10 Nov 1794: 4 Mar 1796: 18 Mar 1796: 2 June 1800

—— *Julius Caesar*: 27 Jan 1755

—— *King Henry IV, Part One*: 14 Mar 1755: 3 July 1761: 25 Oct 1771: 7 Feb 1776: 21 Nov 1777: 8 Dec 1794: 22 Apr 1796

—— *King Henry V*: 3 Apr 1758: 6 Sep 1771

—— *King Lear*: 18 June 1770: 26 Feb 1779

—— *King Richard III*: 14 Aug 1753: 13 Feb 1758: 29 July 1761: 28 Feb 1763: 1 Nov 1765: 31 Jan 1766: 7 Feb 1766: 7 Sep 1768: 15 Jan 1772: 19 Jan 1774: 1 Dec 1775: 8 Apr 1776: 24 Jan 1791: 22 May 1793

—— *Macbeth*: 27 Dec 1765: 8 Jan 1766: 2 Aug 1771: 7 Jan 1778: 27 Apr 1778: 1 Mar 1780: 27 June 1785: 31 Jan 1791: 26 Nov 1794: 14 Mar 1796

—— *The Merchant of Venice*: 19 Apr 1758: 16 July 1770: 22 Nov 1771: 17 Nov 1773: 22 Jan 1779: 29 Dec 1790: 29 July 1791: 7 May 1800

—— *The Merry Wives of Windsor*: 1751–1752 Season: 22 Dec 1794

—— *Much Ado About Nothing*: 25 Nov 1778: 10 Mar 1780: 15 Aug 1787: 22 Aug 1787: 11 Feb 1789

—— *Othello*: 11 Sep 1753: 8 July 1761: 15 July 1761: 7 Oct 1765: 29 Nov 1765: 29 Mar 1776: 28 Dec 1778: 10 Nov 1788

—— *Romeo and Juliet*: 22 June 1753: 28 Feb 1755: 15 Mar 1758: 20 Mar 1758: 26 Aug 1761: 29 Mar 1763: 20 Dec 1765: 21 Feb 1766: 2 Sep 1768: 2 May 1770: 4 Oct 1771: 5 Nov 1773: 8 Aug 1787: 17 Aug 1787: 24 Nov 1788: 5 Dec 1788: 5 Jan 1791: 1 Apr 1793: ca. 15 Dec. 1794: 13 Apr 1795: 29 Apr 1795: 7 Mar 1796: 3 Feb 1800

—— *The Tempest*: 24 Apr 1758: 25 June 1784: 31 Jan 1800

She Stoops to Conquer. See Goldsmith, Oliver

She Would and She Would Not. See Cibber, Colley

Sheridan, Richard B.: *The Critic*: 21 Apr 1783: 23 Feb 1787: 27 Feb 1789: 29 July 1791: 8 Aug 1791

—— *Pizarro*: 14 Apr 1800: 16 Apr 1800: 18 Apr 1800: 19 May 1800: 23 May 1800

—— *The Regions of Accomplishment*: 30 Mar 1792

Thomas and Sally. See Bickerstaffe, Isaac

Thompson, Benjamin: *The Stranger*: 14 Feb 1800: 26 Feb 1800

Thomson, James: *Tancred and Sigismunda*: 26 Nov 1788: 16 Mar 1796

Three Weeks After Marriage. See Murphy, Arthur

Tit For Tat. See Colman, George the elder

Tom Jones. See Reed, Joseph

Tom Thumb. See Fielding, Henry

Townley, James: *High Life Below Stairs*: 22 July 1761: 24 July 1761: 28 Jan 1763: 28 Feb 1763: 7 Oct 1765: 29 Nov 1765: 1 Nov 1771: 28 Jan 1774: 16 Feb 1774: 8 Mar 1776: 15 Aug 1787: 26 Jan 1791: 10 May 1793: 2 Jan 1795

The Trip to Portsmouth. See Stevens, George A.

The Trip to Scarborough. See Sheridan, Richard B.

The Trip to Scotland. See Whitehead, William

The True Born Irishman. See Macklin, Charles

Tunbridge Walks. See Baker, Thomas

The Twin Rivals. See Farquhar, George

Twiss in Ireland; or, Fop in Disgrace. See Anonymous

Unspecified "comedy": 4 Mar 1789: 26 Mar 1792: 27 May 1796: 9 Dec 1799

Unspecified "farce": 2 Aug 1753: 1 July 1761: 15 July 1761: 26 Sep 1768: 3 Oct 1768: 17 Oct 1768: 31 Oct 1768: 21 Nov 1768: 28 Nov 1768: 29 July 1771: 28 Aug 1771: 17 Jan 1776: 10 Nov 1777: 15 Dec 1777: 25 Nov 1778: 13 Jan 1779: 27 Jan 1779: 4 Nov 1779: 7 Nov 1781: 19 July 1784: 19 Jan 1785: 23 Oct 1786: 8 Aug 1787: 10 Nov 1788: 21 Nov 1788: 4 Feb 1789: 6 Feb 1789: 11 Feb 1789: 13 Feb 1789: 20 Feb 1789: 23 Feb 1789: 4 Mar 1789: 6 Mar 1789: 9 Mar 1789: 30 Mar 1789: 15 Apr 1789: 27 Sep 1790: 20 Dec 1790: 3 Jan 1791: 7 Jan 1791: 10 Jan 1791: 21 Jan 1791: 9 Feb 1791: 19 Aug 1791: 21 Sep 1791: 19 Oct 1791: 30 Jan 1792: 3 Feb 1792: 8 Feb 1792: 10 Feb 1792: 20 Feb 1792: 5 Mar 1792: 7 Mar 1792: 19 Mar 1792: 26 Mar 1792: 26 Apr 1793: 17 May 1793: 20 May 1793: 22 May 1793: 24 May 1793: 22 Dec 1794: 11 Mar 1795: 13 Mar 1795: 29 Apr 1795: 8 May 1795: 7 Mar 1796: 28 Mar 1796: 6 Apr 1796: 18 Apr 1796: 2 May 1796: 27 May 1796: 30 May 1796: 13 June 1796: 6 Dec 1799: 22 Jan 1800: 12 Feb 1800: 30 May 1800

Unspecified "musical farce": 26 Feb 1787: 9 Apr 1787: 4 Feb 1791: 29 May 1796

Unspecified "opera": 24 May 1793

Unspecified "play": 28 Nov 1768: 30 Nov 1768: 16 May 1783: 19 May 1783: 19 July 1784: 19 Jan 1785: 14 July 1785: 15 July 1785: 16

The World. See Eccles, Mr.
The Wrangling Lovers. See Vanbrugh, John Sir

Young, Edward: *The Revenge*: 31 Aug 1753: 28 Apr 1758: 13 Dec 1765: 18 Dec 1765: 15 Jan 1766: 25 May 1770: 6 Aug 1770: 13 Mar 1776: 10 Feb 1792: 24 Feb 1800
The Young Quaker. See O'Keeffe, John

INDEX OF ACTORS, ROLES, AND PLAYS

(listed chronologically by dates of performance).
PC = Unspecified "Principal Character"

Achmet, Mrs Estifania *Rule a Wife and Have a Wife* 23 Oct 1786
—— Sir Harry Wildair *Constant Couple* 17 Nov 1786
—— Jessamy *Lionel and Clarissa* 29 Dec1786
—— Rosaland *Sultan* 29 Dec 1786
Aickin, Francis Young Mirabel *Inconstant* 6 Feb 1758
—— Horatio *Fair Penitent* 8 Feb 1758
—— Capt Plume *Recruiting Officer* 10 Feb 1758
—— Earl of Richmond *King Richard III* 13 Feb 1758
—— Lord Townly *Provoked Husband* 15 Feb 1758
—— Young Norval *Douglas* 21 Feb 1758
—— Florizel *Sheep Shearing* 29 Feb 1758
—— Mercutio *Romeo and Juliet* 15 Mar 1758
—— Frankly *Suspicious Husband* 31 Mar 1758
—— Bevil Junior *Conscious Lovers* 7 Apr 1758
—— Lysander *Aegis* 14 Apr 1758
—— Bassanio *Merchant of Venice* 19 Apr 1758
—— Pyrrhus *Distrest Mother* 21 Apr 1758
—— Don Carlos *Revenge* 28 Apr 1758
—— Southampton *Earl of Essex* 5 May 1758
—— Sharp *Lying Valet* 5 May 1758
—— Castalio *Orphan* 12 May 1758
—— Young Cape *Author* 12 May 1758
—— Sir Charles Raymond *Foundling* 19 May 1758
—— Oberon *Oracle* 19 May 1758
—— Col Standard *Constant Couple* 24 May 1758
—— Lord Townly *Provoked Husband* 26 May 1758
—— Sharp *Lying Valet* 26 May 1758
—— Young Norval *Douglas* 2 June 1758
—— Barnwell *London Merchant* 12 June 1758
Aickin, Mrs Francis (Mary) Miss Biddy *Miss in Her Teens* 8 Mar 1758
—— Peggy *King and the Miller of Mansfield* 21 Apr 1758
—— Miss Harriet *Reprisal* 28 Apr 1758
—— Phillida *Damon and Phillida* 2 June 1758
Allen Montano *Othello* 7 Oct 1765

337

Archer Beverly *Gamester* 2 Jan 1795
Atkins, Michael King *King and Miller of Mansfield* 23 Aug 1768
—— Young Bevil *Conscious Lovers* 26 Aug 1768
—— Romeo *Romeo and Juliet* 2 Sep 1768
—— Richard *King Richard III* 7 Sep 1768
—— Sir John Melvil *Clandestine Marriage* 14 Sep 1768
—— Damaetas *Judgment of Midas* 21 Sep 1768
—— Capt Plume *Recruiting Officer* 28 Sep 1768
—— Reynold *Tunbridge Walks* 11 Nov 1768
—— Osmyn *Mourning Bride* 16 Nov 1768
—— Colonel *Spanish Fryar* 18 Nov 1768
—— Young Wilding *Citizen* 30 Nov 1768
—— Orestes *Distrest Mother* 16 Aug 1771
—— Archer *Beaux' Stratagem* 4 Sep 1771
—— PC *Mentalist or, Doctor of the Passions* 15 Nov 1771
—— Lionel *Lionel and Clarissa* 17 Jan 1772
—— Douglas *Douglas* 6 Sep 1773
—— Lionel *Lionel and Clarissa* 8 Sep 1773
—— Linco *Linco's Travels* 28 Feb 1776
—— Lord Hastings *Jane Shore* 10 Apr 1778
—— Ghost *Hamlet* 9 Apr 1787
—— Belville *Rosina* 12 Nov 1788
—— Jervis *Gamester* 17 Dec 1788
—— Bachanal *Comus* 17 Dec 1788
—— Raleigh *Earl of Essex* 12 Nov 1790
—— Prince *Romeo and Juliet* 5 Jan 1791
—— Gen Savage *School for Wives* 14 Jan 1791
—— Sir Oliver Surface *School for Scandal* 26 Jan 1791
—— Clytus *Rival Queens* 6 Feb 1792
—— Camillo *Florizel and Perdita* 24 Feb 1792
—— John Dorey *Wild Oats* 27 Feb 1792
—— Father Philip *Castle Spectre* 10 Mar 1800
—— Priest *Pizarro* 14 Apr 1800
—— Las Casas *Pizarro* 14 Apr 1800
Atkins, Miss Vocal Part *Concert* 1 Dec 1798
Atkins, Charles Saib *Castle Spectre* 10 Mar 1800

Baker, David Erskine Champignon *Reprisal* 28 Apr 1758
—— Polydore *Orphan* 12 May 1758
—— Cadwallader *Author* 12 May 1758
—— Faddle *Foundling* 19 May 1758
—— Manly *Provoked Husband* 26 May 1758

Banford Bagshot *Beaux' Stratagem* 1 July 1761
—— Senator *Othello* 15 July 1761
—— Poet *Twin Rivals* 24 July 1761
—— Printer *Oroonoko* 7 Aug 1761
—— Priest *Love Makes a Man* 14 Aug 1761
—— Friar John *Romeo and Juliet* 26 Aug 1761
—— Conspirator *Cato* 4 Sep 1761
Barron, John O'Blunder *Brave Irishman* 23 Feb 1776
—— Capt O'Cutter *Jealous Wife* 3 Apr 1776
—— Matthew Mug *Mayor of Garratt* 3 Apr 1776
Bath Barbarossa *Barbarossa* 29 Feb 1758
—— Macheath *Beggar's Opera* 8 Mar 1758
—— Macheath *Beggar's Opera* 27 Mar 1758
—— Joe *King and the Miller of Mansfield* 21 Apr 1758
—— Damon *Damon and Phillida* 2 June 1758
Bernard, John Charles Surface *School for Scandal* 27 Jan 1783
—— Belcour *West Indian* 3 Mar 1784
Bernard, Mrs John Lady Teazle *School for Scandal* 27 Jan 1783
—— Charlotte *West Indian* 3 Mar 1784
—— Marcia *Cato* 7 May 1784
—— Roxana *Rival Queens* 17 Apr 1793
—— Lady Eleanor Irwin *Every Man has His Fault* 10 May 1793
—— Cymon *Cymon* 13 May 1793
Berry, Francis Brabantio *Othello* 7 Oct 1765
—— Jobson *Devil to Pay* 18 Oct 1765
Berry, Mrs Francis Emilia *Othello* 7 Oct 1765
—— Andromache *Distrest Mother* 18 Oct 1765
Betterton, Thomas Joseph Surface *School for Scandal* 12 Feb 1779
—— Solyman *Sultan* 19 Mar 1779
Betterton, Mrs Thomas Maid *School for Scandal* 12 Feb 1779
Bevan, Mrs Virgin *Pizarro* 14 Apr 1800
Biddy Allan *Castle Spectre* 10 Mar 1800
—— Gomez *Pizarro* 14 Apr 1800
Bisset *Equilibres* 23 Oct 1776
—— *Equilibres* 23 Feb 1779
—— *Equilibres* 2 Mar 1779
Blackler Hounslow *Beaux' Stratagem* 1 July 1761
—— Montano *Othello* 3 July 1761
—— Guildenstern *Hamlet* 10 July 1761
—— Montano *Othello* 15 July 1761
—— James *Provoked Husband* 17 July 1761
—— Constable *Twin Rivals* 24 July 1761

—— Blunt *King Richard III* 29 July 1761
—— Governor *Oroonoko* 7 Aug 1761
—— Lawyer *Love Makes a Man* 14 Aug 1761
—— Ragozin *Cleone* 24 Aug 1761
—— Benvolio *Romeo and Juliet* 26 Aug 1761
—— James *Provoked Husband* 28 Aug 1761
—— Conspirator *Cato* 4 Sep 1761
Bloomer Lothario *Fair Penitent* 14 Jan 1763
—— Lord Randolph *Douglas* 19 Jan 1763
—— John Moody *Provoked Husband* 21 Jan 1763
—— Matt o' th' Mint *Beggar's Opera* 15 Feb 1763
—— King Henry *King Richard III* 28 Feb 1763
—— Sackbut *Bold Stroke for a Wife* 3 Mar 1763
—— Bertram *Spanish Fryar* 14 Mar 1763
—— Fryar Laurence *Romeo and Juliet* 29 Mar 1763
Bloomer, Mrs Calista *Fair Penitent* 14 Jan 1763
—— Lady Townly *Provoked Husband* 21 Jan 1763
—— Lucy Lockit *Beggar's Opera* 15 Feb 1763
—— Marianne *Miser* 23 Feb 1763
—— Lady Ann *King Richard III* 28 Feb 1763
—— Anne Lovely *Bold Stroke for a Wife* 3 Mar 1763
—— Hermione *Distrest Mother* 9 Mar 1763
—— Elvira *Spanish Fryar* 14 Mar 1763
—— Juliet *Romeo and Juliet* 29 Mar 1763
Booth Moses *School for Scandal* 12 Feb 1779
Booth, Mrs (later Mrs Mason) Alicia *Jane Shore* 10 Apr 1778
—— Lady Teazle *School for Scandal* 12 Feb 1779
—— Roxalana *Sultan* 19 Mar 1779
—— Euphrasia *Grecian Daughter* 3 Dec 1790 (as Mrs Mason)
—— Lappet *Miser* 5 Jan 1791 (as Mrs Mason)
Boucheron, Mrs Angela *Castle Spectre* 10 Mar 1800
—— Virgin *Pizarro* 14 Apr 1800
Bradbury, Miss Miss Hardcastle *She Stoops to Conquer* 16 Jan 1789
—— Maria *London Merchant* 13 Apr 1789
Bridges, Mrs (Fredericka?) Mrs Strictland *Suspicious Husband* 30 Apr 1770
—— Irene *Barbarossa* 28 July 1770
—— Lettice *Intriguing Chambermaid* 28 July 1770
—— Maria *Citizen* 11 Aug 1770
Bridges, Miss Tom Thumb *Tom Thumb the Great* 1 Aug 1770
Brooks, Master Brazen *Recruiting Officer* 20 Nov 1755
Brown, Henry Page *Merry Wives of Windsor* 1751–1752 Season

—— Wat Dreary *Beggar's Opera* 23 Aug 1768
—— Coachman *Devil to Pay* 26 Aug 1768
—— Shepherd *Judgment of Midas* 21 Sep 1768
Brown, Mrs J Country Girl *Country Girl* 27 Feb 1795
—— Collin M'Cloud *Fashionable Lover* 9 Mar 1795
—— William *Rosina* 15 Mar 1795
—— Moggy McGilpin *Highland Reel* 18 Mar 1795
—— Miss Mad Cap *Cottagers* 1 June 1796
—— Virgin of the Sun *Pizarro* 14 Apr 1800
Brown, Master Henry Page *Purse* 27 Feb 1795
—— PC *Will o'th Wisp* 18 Mar 1795
—— Page *Purse* 1 June 1796
—— Mungo *Padlock* 1 June 1796
Brunton, Miss Anne Horatia *Roman Father* 3 Aug 1787
—— Euphrasia *Grecian Daughter* 6 Aug 1787
—— Juliet *Romeo and Juliet* 8 Aug 1787
—— Calista *Fair Penitent* 10 Aug 1787
—— Beatrice *Much Ado about Nothing* 15 Aug 1787
—— Juliet *Romeo and Juliet* 17 Aug 1787
—— Horatia *Roman Father* 20 Aug 1787
—— Perdita *Florizel and Perdita* 20 Aug 1787
—— Beatrice *Much Ado about Nothing* 22 Aug 1787
—— Monimia *The Orphan* 24 Aug 1787
Bullock Lockit *Beggar's Opera* 23 Aug 1768
—— Sir John Bevil *Conscious Lovers* 26 Aug 1768
—— Conjurer *Devil to Pay* 26 Aug 1768
—— Fryar Lawrence *Romeo and Juliet* 2 Sep 1768
—— Sir Peter Pride *Fashionable Wife* 2 Sep 1768
—— Stanley *King Richard III* 7 Sep 1768
—— Jupiter *Judgment of Midas* 21 Sep 1768
—— Sir Jasper *Citizen* 30 Nov 1768
Burden, W Sullen *Beaux' Stratagem* 4 Sep 1771
—— Supple *Tom Jones* 30 Oct 1771
—— PC *Mentalist or, Doctor of the Passions* 15 Nov 1771
Burden, Mrs PC *Mentalist or, Doctor of the Passions* 15 Nov 1771
—— Female Officer *Female Officer* 20 Nov 1771
Burdett, Mrs Rosetta *Love in a Village* 8 Dec 1775
Bushby Simple *Merry Wives of Windsor* 1751–1752 Season
—— Servant *Honest Yorkshireman* 1751–1752 Season

Caddell, Master Serjeant Kite *Recruiting Officer* 20 Nov 1755
Campion, Miss Maria Ann Juliet *Romeo and Juliet* 13 Apr 1795

—— Juliet *Romeo and Juliet* 29 Apr 1795
—— Isabella *Isabella* 8 May 1795
Carlton Edric *Castle Spectre* 10 Mar 1800
Carthy Priest *Hamlet* 10 July 1761
—— Senator *Othello* 15 July 1761
—— Hotman *Oroonoko* 7 Aug 1761
—— Antonio *Love Makes a Man* 14 Aug 1761
—— Montague *Romeo and Juliet* 26 Aug 1761
—— Poundage *Provoked Husband* 28 Aug 1761
—— Decius *Cato* 4 Sep 1761
Chalmers, James Ranger *Suspicious Husband* 20 Oct 1788
—— Othello *Othello* 10 Nov 1788
—— Petruchio *Catherine and Petruchio* 1 Dec 1788
—— Bachanal *Comus* 17 Dec 1788
—— Harlequin *Prometheus* 16 Jan 1789
—— Lord Foppington *Trip to Scarborough* 26 Jan 1789
—— Harlequin *Prometheus or Harlequin's Animation* 26 Jan 1789
—— Benedick *Much Ado About Nothing* 11 Feb 1789
—— Harlequin *Harlequin Gardener* 11 Feb 1789
Chalmers, Mrs James Clarinda *Suspicious Husband* 20 Oct 1788
—— Macheath *Beggar's Opera* 12 Nov 1788
—— Jessamy *Lionel and Clarissa* 28 Nov 1788
—— Catherine *Catherine and Petruchio* 1 Dec 1788
—— Ophelia *Hamlet* 12 Dec 1788
—— Catherine *Catherine and Petruchio* 15 Dec 1788
—— Euphrosyne *Comus* 17 Dec 1788
—— Hoyden *Trip to Scarborough* 26 Jan 1789
—— Beatrice *Much Ado About Nothing* 11 Feb 1789
—— Colombine *Harlequin Gardener* 11 Feb 1789
Cherry, Andrew Crabtree *School for Scandal* 27 Jan 1783
—— Varland *West Indian* 3 Mar 1784
—— MacSycophant *Man of the World* 19 Jan 1787[?]
—— Lingo *Agreeable Surprise* 19 Jan 1787[?]
—— Lazarillo *Hotel* 24 Oct 1794
—— Trudge *Inkle and Yarico* 24 Oct 1794
—— Sheva *Jew or, The Benevolent Hebrew* 29 Oct 1794
—— Peeping Tom *Peeping Tom of Coventry* 29 Oct 1794
—— Shelty *Highland Reel* 7 Nov 1794
—— Sir David Dunder *Ways and Means* 7 Nov 1794
Coates, Mrs Elizabeth Jane Shore *Jane Shore* 10 Nov 1790
—— Countess of Rutland *Earl of Essex* 12 Nov 1790
—— Maria *Citizen* 12 Nov 1790

—— Ophelia *Hamlet* 15 Nov 1790
—— Letitia Hardy *Belle's Stratagem* 31 Dec 1790
——Juliet *Romeo and Juliet* 5 Jan 1791
—— Miss Walsingham *School for Wives* 14 Jan 1791
—— Lady Teazle *School for Scandal* 26 Jan 1791
—— Kitty *High Life Below Stairs* 26 Jan 1791
—— Clarinda *Suspicious Husband* 10 Aug 1791
—— Clarinda *Suspicious Husband* early Jan 1792
—— Charlotte Rusport *West Indian* 1 Feb 1792
—— Widow Belmore *Way to Keep Him* 1 Feb 1792
—— Statira *Rival Queens* 6 Feb 1792
—— Miss Courtney *Dramatist* 24 Feb 1792
—— Perdita *Florizel and Perdita* 24 Feb 1792
—— Lady Amaranth *Wild Oats* 27 Feb 1792
—— Lady Macbeth *Macbeth* 26 Nov 1794
——Juliet *Romeo and Juliet* ca 15 Dec 1794
—— Estifania *Rule a Wife and Have a Wife* 17 Dec 1794
—— Mrs Beverly *Gamester* 2 Jan 1795
—— Kitty *High Life Below Stairs* 2 Jan 1795
Coghlan Rossano *Fair Penitent* 14 Jan 1763
—— Filch *Beggar's Opera* 15 Feb 1763
——James *Miser* 23 Feb 1763
—— Lord Stanley *King Richard III* 28 Feb 1763
—— Tradelove *Bold Stroke for a Wife* 3 Mar 1763
—— Alphonso *Spanish Fryar* 14 Mar 1763
Collins, John Maj O'Flaherty *West Indian* 2 Feb 1776
—— Falstaff *King Henry IV* 7 Feb 1776
—— Collin Macleod *Fashionable Lover* 30 May 1781
—— Mock Doctor *Mock Doctor* 30 May 1781
Comerford, Miss Rosetta Sylvia *Recruiting Officer* 10 Feb 1758
—— Dorcas *Mock Doctor* 10 Feb 1758
—— Lettice *Intriguing Chambermaid* 21 Feb 1758
—— Anne Lovely *Bold Stroke for a Wife* 24 Feb 1758
—— Lucy *Beggar's Opera* 8 Mar 1758
—— Lady Lace *Lottery* 15 Mar 1758
—— Lucy *Beggar's Opera* 27 Mar 1758
—— Ophelia *Hamlet* 5 Apr 1758
—— Sandane *Aegis* 14 Apr 1758
—— Nerissa *Merchant of Venice* 19 Apr 1758
—— Rosetta *Foundling* 19 May 1758
—— Melissa *Lying Valet* 26 May 1758
(for further performances see Ryder, Mrs Thomas, below)

Cranford, Miss Edward *Every Man has His Fault* 10 May 1793
—— Mrs Kitty *High Life Below Stairs* 10 May 1793

Davis Earl Percy *Castle Spectre* 10 Mar 1800
—— Alonzo *Pizarro* 14 Apr 1800
Dawson, Mrs George (later wife of Master Dawson below) Venus *Poor Vulcan* 8 Dec 1784
Dawson, Master George Young Sifroy *Cleone* 24 Aug 1761
Dawson, William Don Octavio *She Wou'd and She Wou'd Not* 28 Aug 1753
—— Scrub *Beaux' Stratagem* 1 July 1761
—— Cassio *Othello* 8 July 1761
—— Polonius *Hamlet* 10 July 1761
—— Cassio *Othello* 15 July 1761
—— Sir Francis *Provoked Husband* 17 July 1761
—— Glenalvon *Douglas* 22 July 1761
—— Subtleman *Twin Rivals* 24 July 1761
—— King Henry *Richard III* 29 July 1761
—— Vizard *Vintner Tricked* 31 July 1761
—— Daniel *Oroonoko* 7 Aug 1761
—— Trapanti *She Would and She Would Not* 12 Aug 1761
—— Sancho *Love Makes a Man* 14 Aug 1761
—— Sir Francis *Provoked Husband* 28 Aug 1761
—— Dick *Flora* 28 Aug 1761
—— Portius *Cato* 4 Sep 1761
—— Guard *Barbarossa* 28 July 1770
—— French Soldier *Harlequin with Thurot* 31 July 1770
Dawson, Mrs William (see Lewis, Mrs William for earlier roles)
—— Lady Bountiful *Beaux' Stratagem* 1 July 1761
—— Amelia *Othello* 8 July 1761
—— Amelia *Othello* 15 July 1761
—— Lady Wronghead *Provoked Husband* 17 July 1761
—— Mrs Midnight *Twin Rivals* 24 July 1761
—— Duchess of York *Richard III* 29 July 1761
—— Mrs Mixum *Vintner Tricked* 31 July 1761
—— Widow Lackit *Oroonoko* 7 Aug 1761
—— Honorio *Love Makes a Man* 14 Aug 1761
—— Isabell *Cleone* 24 Aug 1761
—— Nurse *Romeo and Juliet* 26 Aug 1761
—— Lady Wronghead *Provoked Husband* 28 Aug 1761
—— Juba *Cato* 4 Sep 1761
Day, George Tom Jones *Tom Jones* 30 Oct 1771
—— Jessamy *Lionel and Clarissa* 17 Jan 1772

—— Bellmour *Jane Shore* 22 Nov 1754
—— Clincher Jr *Constant Couple* 25 Nov 1754
—— Chaplain *Orphan* 27 Nov 1754
—— Nimming Ned *Beggar's Opera* 29 Nov 1754
—— Worthy *Recruiting Officer* 6 Dec 1754
—— Sancho *Love Makes a Man* 11 Dec 1754
—— Dervise *Tamerlane* 13 Dec 1754
—— Chaplain *Orphan* 17 Dec 1754
—— Sir John Bevil *Conscious Lovers* 3 Jan 1755
—— Horatio *Hamlet* 7 Jan 1755
—— Lurcher *Country Lasses* 10 Jan 1755
—— Bellmour *Jane Shore* 18 Jan 1755
—— Bellamy *Suspicious Husband* 24 Jan 1755
—— Julius Caesar *Julius Caesar* 27 Jan 1755
—— James *Provoked Husband* 31 Jan 1755
—— Bedamar *Venice Preserved* 7 Feb 1755
—— Sir Paul Pliant *Double Dealer* 24 Feb 1755
—— Benvolio *Romeo and Juliet* 28 Feb 1755
—— Scandal *Love for Love* late Feb or Mar 1755
Elrington, Richard Horatio *Fair Penitent* 18 Nov 1754
—— Mopsus *Damon and Phillida* 18 Nov 1754
—— Sir George *Busy Body* 20 Nov 1754
—— Duke of Gloster *Jane Shore* 22 Nov 1754
—— Clincher Senior *Constant Couple* 25 Nov 1754
—— Castalio *Orphan* 27 Nov 1754
—— Peachum *Beggar's Opera* 29 Nov 1754
—— Kite *Recruiting Officer* 6 Dec 1754
—— Don Lewis *Love Makes a Man* 11 Dec 1754
—— Bajazet *Tamerlane* 13 Dec 1754
—— Castalio *Orphan* 17 Dec 1754
—— Hamlet *Hamlet* 7 Jan 1755
—— Sir John English *Country Lasses* 10 Jan 1755
—— Archer *Beaux' Stratagem* 17 Jan 1755
—— Duke of Gloster *Jane Shore* 18 Jan 1755
—— Jack Meggot *Suspicious Husband* 24 Jan 1755
—— Brutus *Julius Caesar* 27 Jan 1755
—— Lord Townly *Provoked Husband* 31 Jan 1755
—— Pierre *Venice Preserved* 7 Feb 1755
—— Melefont *Double Dealer* 24 Feb 1755
—— Romeo *Romeo and Juliet* 28 Feb 1755
—— Valentine *Love for Love* late Feb or Mar 1755
—— Essex *Earl of Essex* 7 Mar 1755

—— Hotspur *King Henry IV* 14 Mar 1755
Elrington, Mrs Richard Calista *Fair Penitent* 18 Nov 1754
—— Damon *Damon and Phillida* 18 Nov 1754
—— Isabinda *Busy Body* 20 Nov 1754
—— Alicia *Jane Shore* 22 Nov 1754
—— Lady Lurewell *Constant Couple* 25 Nov 1754
—— Serina *Orphan* 27 Nov 1754
—— Lucy *Beggar's Opera* 29 Nov 1754
—— Silvia *Recruiting Officer* 6 Dec 1754
—— Angelina *Love Makes a Man* 11 Dec 1754
—— Indiana *Conscious Lovers* 3 Jan 1755
—— Aura *Country Lasses* 10 Jan 1755
—— Cherry *Beaux' Stratagem* 17 Jan 1755
—— Jacintha *Suspicious Husband* 24 Jan 1755
—— Page *Julius Caesar* 27 Jan 1755
—— Lady Townly *Provoked Husband* 31 Jan 1755
—— Lady Pliant *Double Dealer* 24 Feb 1755
—— Juliet *Romeo and Juliet* 28 Feb 1755
—— Queen Elizabeth *Earl of Essex* 7 Mar 1755
Elrington, Master Richard Page *Love Makes a Man* 11 Dec 1754
—— Page *Orphan* 17 Dec 1754

Farrell, Thomas Foigard *Beaux' Stratagem* 4 Sep 1771
—— Sportsman *Tom Jones* 30 Oct 1771
—— Jenkins *Lionel and Clarissa* 8 Sep 1773
—— Haly Hassan *Sultan* 19 Mar 1779
Farrell, Mrs Thomas (Elizabeth) Jenny *Beggar's Opera* 23 Aug 1768
—— Madge *King and Miller of Mansfield* 23 Aug 1768
—— Mrs Sealand *Conscious Lovers* 26 Aug 1768
—— Lucy *Devil to Pay* 26 Aug 1768
—— Prince *Romeo and Juliet* 2 Sep 1768
—— Lady Pride *Fashionable Wife* 2 Sep 1768
—— Shepherdess *Judgment of Midas* 21 Sep 1768
—— Cephisa *Distrest Mother* 16 Aug 1771
—— Lady Bountiful *Beaux' Stratagem* 4 Sep 1771
—— Landlady *Tom Jones* 30 Oct 1771
—— Lady Mary Oldboy *Lionel and Clarissa* 17 Jan 1772
—— Lady Mary Oldboy *Lionel and Clarissa* 8 Sep 1773
—— Elmira *Sultan* 19 Mar 1779
Farrell, Miss L Servant *Lionel and Clarissa* 8 Sep 1773
—— Maria *School for Scandal* 12 Feb 1779
Fenner, Mrs Letty *Dramatist* 24 Feb 1792

—— Dorcas *Florizel and Perdita* 24 Feb 1792
Fisher, Alexander Iago *Othello* 7 Oct 1765
—— Orestes *Distrest Mother* 18 Oct 1765
—— Aboan *Oroonoko* 23 Oct 1765
Fisher, Mrs Alexander Hermione *Distrest Mother* 18 Oct 1765
—— Imoinda *Oroonoko* 23 Oct 1765
Fisher, Master Roderigo *Othello* 7 Oct 1765
Fleming, Miss Dorinda *Beaux' Stratagem* 17 Jan 1755
—— Alicia *Jane Shore* 18 Jan 1755
—— Mrs Strickland *Suspicious Husband* 24 Jan 1755
—— Calphurnia *Julius Caesar* 27 Jan 1755
—— Lady Grace *Provoked Husband* 31 Jan 1755
—— Cinthia *Double Dealer* 24 Feb 1755
—— Lady Capulet *Romeo and Juliet* 28 Feb 1755
—— Mrs Foresight *Love for Love* late Feb or Mar 1755
—— Countess of Nottingham *Earl of Essex* 7 Mar 1755
Forde, Brownlow Scrub *Beaux' Stratagem* 4 Sep 1771
—— PC *Mentalist or, Doctor of the Passions* 15 Nov 1771
Forde, Master Capt Plume *Recruiting Officer* 20 Nov 1755
Fotteral, James Strictland *Suspicious Husband* 30 Apr 1770
—— King *Mourning Bride* 14 July 1770
—— Othman *Barbarossa* 28 July 1770
—— Puff *Intriguing Chambermaid* 28 July 1770
—— Thurot *Harlequin with Thurot* 31 July 1770
—— Pyrrhus *Distrest Mother* 16 Aug 1771
—— Aimwell *Beaux' Stratagem* 4 Sep 1771
—— Alworthy *Tom Jones* 30 Oct 1771
—— Sir John Flowerdale *Lionel and Clarissa* 17 Jan 1772
—— Hamlet *Hamlet* 9 Apr 1787
Freeman Bachanal *Comus* 17 Dec 1788
—— Vocal Part *Concert* 1 Dec 1798
Freeman, Mrs Lucy *Beggar's Opera* 12 Nov 1788
—— Principal Bachant *Comus* 17 Dec 1788
—— Pat *Poor Soldier* 2 Mar 1789
Fullam, Michael Jaffier *Venice Preserved* 2 Dec 1768
—— Sir Benjamin Dove *Brothers* 10 Feb 1800
—— Sharp *Lying Valet* 10 Feb 1800
Fullam, Mrs Michael Juliet *Romeo and Juliet* 3 Feb 1800

Garvey, Captain Careless *School for Scandal* 27 Jan 1783
—— Cora *Pizarro* 14 Apr 1800
Garvey, Mrs Evelina *Castle Spectre* 10 Mar 1800

—— Jane *Wild Oats* 27 Feb 1792
Gough, Miss Catherine Calista *Fair Penitent* 21 Apr 1796
—— Mrs Beverly *Gamester* 25 Apr 1796
—— Isabella *Isabella* 2 May 1796
Griffith Cassander *Rival Queens* 6 Feb 1792
—— Willoughby *Dramatist* 24 Feb 1792
—— King *Florizel and Perdita* 24 Feb 1792
—— Charles *Busy Body* 9 May 1796
—— Sir Theodore Goodchild *Love a la Mode* 9 May 1796
Guitar, William Dr Caius *Merry Wives of Windsor* 1751–1752 Season

Hamilton, Myrton Filch *Beggar's Opera* 23 Aug 1768
—— Cimberton *Conscious Lovers* 26 Aug 1768
—— Butler *Devil to Pay* 26 Aug 1768
—— Montague *Romeo and Juliet* 2 Sep 1768
—— Barnaby Brittle *Fashionable Wife* 2 Sep 1768
—— Catesby *King Richard III* 7 Sep 1768
—— Shark *Lying Valet* 14 Sep 1768
—— Midas *Judgment of Midas* 21 Sep 1768
—— Worthy *Recruiting Officer* 28 Sep 1768
—— Gomez *Spanish Fryar* 18 Nov 1768
—— Old Philpot *Citizen* 30 Nov 1768
—— Gibbet *Beaux' Stratagem* 4 Sep 1771
—— Sportsman *Tom Jones* 30 Oct 1771
—— PC *Mentalist or, Doctor of the Passions* 15 Nov 1771
—— Jenkins *Lionel and Clarissa* 17 Jan 1772
—— Old Shepherd *Douglas* 6 Sep 1773
—— Col Oldboy *Lionel and Clarissa* 8 Sep 1773
—— Don Diego *Padlock* 12 Feb 1779
Hamilton, William Scrub *Beaux' Stratagem* 19 Mar 1779
Harris Principal Vocal Part *Concert* 3 July 1797
Herbert [Dowling], Joseph Frederick *Lovers' Vows* ca 10 Jan 1800
—— Octavian *Mountaineers* 22 Jan 1800
—— Romeo *Romeo and Juliet* 3 Feb 1800
—— PC *Stranger* 14 Feb 1800
—— Earl Osmond *Castle Spectre* 10 Mar 1800
—— Octavian *Mountaineers* 27 Mar 1800
—— Rolla *Pizarro* 14 Apr 1800
—— Paddy O'Carrol *Register Office* 16 May 1800
Hern [or Herne], Miss Jacintha *Suspicious Husband* 30 Apr 1770
—— Colombine *Harlequin in Derry* 9 May 1770
—— Almeria *Mourning Bride* 14 July 1770

—— Portia *Merchant of Venice* 16 July 1770
—— Zaphira *Barbarossa* 28 July 1770
—— Colombine *Harlequin with Thurot* 31 July 1770
—— Estifania *Rule a Wife and Have a Wife* 1 Aug 1770
—— Ophelia *Hamlet* 2 Aug 1770
—— Leonora *Revenge* 6 Aug 1770
—— Jane Shore *Jane Shore* 8 Aug 1770
—— Monimia *Orphan* 11 Aug 1770
Hilmer Motley *Castle Spectre* 10 Mar 1800
—— Orozimbo *Pizarro* 14 Apr 1800
—— Priest *Pizarro* 14 Apr 1800
Hinde, Edward Lord Townly *Provoked Husband* 21 Jan 1763
—— Peachum *Beggar's Opera* 15 Feb 1763
—— King Richard *King Richard III* 28 Feb 1763
—— Sir Philip Modelove *Bold Stroke for a Wife* 3 Mar 1763
—— Pyrrhus *Distrest Mother* 9 Mar 1763
—— Pylades *Distrest Mother* 9 Mar 1763
—— King *King and the Miller of Mansfield* 9 Mar 1763
—— Fryar Dominick *Spanish Fryar* 14 Mar 1763
Hinde, Mrs Edward Lavinia *Fair Penitent* 14 Jan 1763
—— Lady Wronghead *Provoked Husband* 21 Jan 1763
—— Mrs Peachum and Diane Trapes *Beggar's Opera* 15 Feb 1763
—— Harriet *Miser* 23 Feb 1763
—— Lappit *Miser* 23 Feb 1763
—— Queen Elizabeth *King Richard III* 28 Feb 1763
—— Sarah Prim *Bold Stroke for a Wife* 3 Mar 1763
—— Queen Leonora *Spanish Fryar* 14 Mar 1763
Hinde, Miss Miss Jenny *Provoked Husband* 21 Jan 1763
—— Cynthia *Oracle* 21 Jan 1763
—— Mrs Coaxer *Beggar's Opera* 15 Feb 1763
—— Prince Edward *King Richard III* 28 Feb 1763
—— Peggy *King and the Miller of Mansfield* 9 Mar 1763
—— Vocal Part *Romeo and Juliet* 29 Mar 1763
Hinde, Master Squire Richard *Provoked Husband* 21 Jan 1763
—— Oberon *Oracle* 21 Jan 1763
—— Duke of York *King Richard III* 28 Feb 1763
Holman, Joseph George Hamlet *Hamlet* 19 Nov 1788
—— Romeo *Romeo and Juliet* 24 Nov 1788
—— Tancred *Tancred and Sigismunda* 26 Nov 1788
—— Belcour *West Indian* 1 Dec 1788
—— Orestes *Distrest Mother* 3 Dec 1788
—— Hamlet *Hamlet* 12 Dec 1788

—— Jaffier *Venice Preserved* 15 Dec 1788
—— Petruchio *Catherine and Petruchio* 15 Dec 1788
—— Beverly *Gamester* 17 Dec 1788
—— Comus *Comus* 17 Dec 1788
Hopkins, William King Henry *King Richard III* 13 Feb 1758
—— Mr Strickland *Suspicious Husband* 31 Mar 1758
—— Antonio *Merchant of Venice* 19 Apr 1758
—— Sir Francis Wronghead *Provoked Husband* 26 May 1758
Hopkins, Mrs William Bisarre *Inconstant* 6 Feb 1758
—— Calista *Fair Penitent* 8 Feb 1758
—— Melinda *Recruiting Officer* 10 Feb 1758
—— Lady Anne *King Richard III* 13 Feb 1758
—— Autolicus *Sheep Shearing* 15 Feb 1758
—— Lady Randolph *Douglas* 21 Feb 1758
—— Irene *Barbarossa* 29 Feb 1758
—— Perdita *Sheep Shearing* 29 Feb 1758
—— Polly *Beggar's Opera* 8 Mar 1758
—— Clarinda *Suspicious Husband* 17 Mar 1758
—— Polly *Beggar's Opera* 27 Mar 1758
—— Clarinda *Suspicious Husband* 31 Mar 1758
—— Indiana *Conscious Lovers* 7 Apr 1758
—— Euanthe *Aegis* 14 Apr 1758
—— Hermione *Distrest Mother* 21 Apr 1758
—— Leonora *Revenge* 28 Apr 1758
—— Almeria *Mourning Bride* 3 May 1758
—— Rutland *Earl of Essex* 5 May 1758
—— Monimia *Orphan* 12 May 1758
—— Mrs Cadwallader *Author* 12 May 1758
—— Cinthia *Oracle* 19 May 1758
—— Lady Lurewell *Constant Couple* 24 May 1758
—— Lady Randolph *Douglas* 2 June 1758
—— Maria *London Merchant* 12 June 1758
Hoskins, Mrs Charles Bachant *Comus* 17 Dec 1788
—— Lady Capulet *Romeo and Juliet* 5 Jan 1791
—— Mrs Wisely *Miser* 5 Jan 1791
—— Lady Sneerwell *School for Scandal* 26 Jan 1791
Hoskins, Miss Charlotte *Gamester* 17 Dec 1788
—— Bachant *Comus* 17 Dec 1788
Howard Fenton *Merry Wives of Windsor* 1751–1752 Season
Hughes, Miss Maria Lady Townly *Provoked Husband* 21 Nov 1788
—— Juliet *Romeo and Juliet* 24 Nov 1788
—— Sigismunda *Tancred and Sigismunda* 26 Nov 1788

—— Charlotte *West Indian* 1 Dec 1788
—— Hermione *Distrest Mother* 3 Dec 1788
—— Belvidera *Venice Preserved* 15 Dec 1788
—— Mrs Beverly *Gamester* 17 Dec 1788
—— Lady *Comus* 17 Dec 1788

Jackson, John Ben Budge *Beggar's Opera* 23 Aug 1768
—— Cook *Devil to Pay* 26 Aug 1768
—— Friar John *Romeo and Juliet* 2 Sep 1768
—— Shepherd *Judgment of Midas* 21 Sep 1768
—— Quilldrive *Citizen* 30 Nov 1768
Johnson Dick *Apprentice* 24 May 1758
Johnston, Henry Erskine Douglas *Douglas* 2 Mar 1796
—— Hamlet *Hamlet* 4 Mar 1796
—— Romeo *Romeo and Juliet* 7 Mar 1796
—— Douglas *Douglas* 10 Mar 1796
—— Zaphne *Mahomet* 11 Mar 1796
—— Macbeth *Macbeth* 14 Mar 1796
—— Tancred *Tancred and Sigismunda* 16 Mar 1796
—— Petruchio *Catherine and Petruchio* 16 Mar 1796
—— Hamlet *Hamlet* 18 Mar 1796

Kane, John Boniface *Beaux' Stratagem* 4 Sep 1771
—— Old Nightingale *Tom Jones* 30 Oct 1771
—— PC *Mentalist or, Doctor of the Passions* 15 Nov 1771
—— Sciolto *Fair Penitent* 2 Dec 1778
—— Rowley *School for Scandal* 12 Feb 1779
—— Old Dudley *West Indian* 3 Mar 1784
Kelly Reginald *Castle Spectre* 10 Mar 1800
—— Pizzaro *Pizarro* 14 Apr 1800
Kelly, Mrs Alice *Castle Spectre* 10 Mar 1800
—— Elvira *Pizarro* 14 Apr 1800
Kemble, Miss Anne Julia Almeria *Mourning Bride* 8 June 1785
—— Alicia *Jane Shore* 10 June 1785
—— Charlotte *Gamester* 15 June 1785
—— Maria *Citizen* 24 June 1785
Kennedy, Lawrence Whisper *Busy Body* 9 May 1796
—— Sir Archy Macsarcasm *Love a la Mode* 9 May 1796
Kennedy, Mrs Lawrence Letitia Hardy *Belle's Stratagem* 30 Mar 1796
—— Eliza Tempest *Wheel of Fortune* 4 Apr 1796
—— Goldfinch *Road to Ruin* 20 Apr 1796
—— Estifania *Rule a Wife* 4 May 1796

King, [George?] Dawson *Gamester* 17 Dec 1788
King, Thomas Lord Ogleby *Clandestine Marriage* 18 July 1791
—— Sir Peter Teazle *School for Scandal* 25 July 1791
—— Marplot *Busy Body* 27 July 1791
—— Sharp *Lying Valet* 27 July 1791
—— Shylock *Merchant of Venice* 29 July 1791
—— Puff *Critic* 29 July 1791
—— Sir John Restless *All in the Wrong* 3 Aug 1791
—— Sir John Trotley *Bon Ton* 3 Aug 1791
—— Lord Ogleby *Clandestine Marriage* 5 Aug 1791
—— Touchstone *As You Like It* 8 Aug 1791
—— Puff *Critic* 8 Aug 1791
—— Ranger *Suspicious Husband* 10 Aug 1791
—— Cadwallader *Author* 10 Aug 1791
Knipe, Richard William Othello *Othello* 7 Oct 1765
—— Pyrrhus *Distrest Mother* 18 Oct 1765
—— Oroonoko *Oroonoko* 23 Oct 1765
—— Hamlet *Hamlet* 28 Feb 1766
Knipe, Mrs Richard William Desdemona *Othello* 7 Oct 1765
—— Nell *Devil to Pay* 18 Oct 1765
—— Charlotte Weldon *Oroonoko* 23 Oct 1765
Knipe, Miss (see Cherry, Mrs Andrew)
Kniveton, Thomas Aimwell *Beaux' Stratagem* 1 July 1761
—— Iago *Othello* 8 July 1761
—— Hamlet *Hamlet* 10 July 1761
—— Roderigo *Othello* 15 July 1761
—— Manly *Provoked Husband* 17 July 1761
—— Old Norval *Douglas* 22 July 1761
—— Young Wouldbe *Twin Rivals* 24 July 1761
—— Richmond *Richard III* 29 July 1761
—— Lord Morelove *Careless Husband* 5 Aug 1761
—— Oroonoko *Oroonoko* 7 Aug 1761
—— Don Duarte *Love Makes a Man* 14 Aug 1761
—— Glanville *Cleone* 24 Aug 1761
—— Friar Lawrence *Romeo and Juliet* 26 Aug 1761
—— Manly *Provoked Husband* 28 Aug 1761
—— Sempronius *Cato* 4 Sep 1761

Layfield, Mrs Robert Nottingham *Earl of Essex* 27 July 1753
—— Mother Midnight *Twin Rivals* 10 Aug 1753
—— Lavinia *Fair Penitent* 14 Sep 1753
Lebrun Crabtree *School for Scandal* 12 Feb 1779

—— Scholar *Padlock* 12 Feb 1779
—— Grand Carver *Sultan* 19 Mar 1779
Lee Frederick *Miser* 5 Jan 1791
—— Capt Savage *School for Wives* 14 Jan 1791
Leech Dicky *Constant Couple* 25 Nov 1754
—— Watt Dreary *Beggar's Opera* 29 Nov 1754
—— Jaquez *Love Makes a Man* 11 Dec 1754
—— Haly *Tamerlane* 13 Dec 1754
—— Servant *Conscious Lovers* 3 Jan 1755
—— Bernardo *Hamlet* 7 Jan 1755
—— Sneak *Country Lasses* 10 Jan 1755
—— Bagshot *Beaux' Stratagem* 17 Jan 1755
—— Cinna *Julius Caesar* 27 Jan 1755
—— Constable *Provoked Husband* 31 Jan 1755
—— Eliot *Venice Preserved* 7 Feb 1755
—— Apothecary *Romeo and Juliet* 28 Feb 1755
Lewes, Charles Lee Copper Captain *Rule a Wife and Have a Wife* 23 Oct 1786
—— *"Lecture Upon Heads"* 23 Nov 1786
—— *"Lecture Upon Heads"* 30 Nov 1786
—— Touchstone *As You Like It* 20 Dec 1786
—— *"Lecture Upon Heads"* 11 Jan 1787
—— *"Lecture Upon Heads"* 12 Jan 1787
—— Sir John Restless *All in the Wrong* 19 Feb 1787
—— Lord Trinket *Jealous Wife* 2 Mar 1787
—— Falstaff *King Henry IV* 8 Dec 1794
—— Copper Captain *Rule a Wife and Have a Wife* 17 Dec 1794
—— Falstaff *Merry Wives of Windsor* 22 Dec 1794
—— Sir Peter Teazle *School for Scandal* 18 Apr 1796
—— Falstaff *King Henry IV* 22 Apr 1796
—— Sir David Dunder *Ways and Means* 25 Apr 1796
—— Copper Captain *Rule a Wife* 4 May 1796
—— PC *Sicilian Romance* 4 May 1796
—— Marplot *Busy Body* 9 May 1796
—— Squire Groom *Love a la Mode* 9 May 1796
—— Sir Anthony Absolute *Rivals* 16 May 1796
—— Dashwood *Know Your Own Mind* 18 May 1796
—— Mercutio *Romeo and Juliet* 3 Feb 1800
—— Capt Ironsides *Brothers* 10 Feb 1800
Lewes, Mrs Charles Lee Rosalind *As You Like It* 20 Dec 1786
—— Mrs Oakly *Jealous Wife* 2 Mar 1787
Lewis, Philip Shallow *Merry Wives of Windsor* 1751–1752 Season

—— Muckworm *Honest Yorkshireman* 1751–1752 Season
—— King *Mourning Bride* 6 June 1753
—— Touchstone *As You Like It* 23 July 1753
—— Southampton *Earl of Essex* 27 July 1753
—— Don Manuel *She Wou'd and She Wou'd Not* 28 Aug 1753
—— Don Alverez *Revenge* 31 Aug 1753
—— Jago *Othello* 11 Sep 1753
—— Sciolto *Fair Penitent* 14 Sep 1753
Lewis, William Hugh Evans *Merry Wives of Windsor* 1751–1752 Season
—— Gaylove *Honest Yorkshireman* 1751–1752 Season
—— PC *Jane Shore* 18 Dec 1751
—— PC *Virgin Unmasked* 18 Dec 1751
—— Pierre *Venice Preserved* 15 June 1753
—— Gomez *Spanish Fryar* 29 June 1753
Lewis, Mrs William Mrs Ford *Merry Wives of Windsor* 1751–1752 Season
—— PC *Jane Shore* 18 Dec 1751
—— PC *Virgin Unmasked* 18 Dec 1751
—— Charlotte *Gamester* 3 July 1753
—— Charlotte Welldon *Oroonoko* 19 July 1753
—— Emilia *Othello* 11 Sep 1753
(See Dawson, Mrs William for later roles)
Lewis, Master William Robin *Merry Wives of Windsor* 1751–1752 Season
—— Duke of York *King Richard III* 14 Aug 1753
—— Ostrick *Hamlet* 10 July 1761
—— Page *Twin Rivals* 24 July 1761
—— Duke of York *Richard III* 29 July 1761
—— Page *Love Makes a Man* 14 Aug 1761
—— Peter *Romeo and Juliet* 26 Aug 1761
—— Richard *Provoked Husband* 28 Aug 1761
Logan Simon *Suspicious Husband* 30 Apr 1770
—— Harlequin *Harlequin in Derry* 9 May 1770
—— Harlequin *Harlequin with Thurot* 31 July 1770
Logan, Mrs Lucetta *Suspicious Husband* 30 Apr 1770
—— Country Lass *Harlequin in Derry* 9 May 1770
—— Female Slave *Barbarossa* 28 July 1770
—— Mrs Macklin *Disappointment* 28 July 1770
—— Mrs Highman *Intriguing Chambermaid* 28 July 1770
Longfield Scialto *Fair Penitent* 18 Nov 1754
—— Coridon *Damon and Phillida* 18 Nov 1754
—— Sir Jealous Traffick *Busy Body* 20 Nov 1754
—— Shore *Jane Shore* 22 Nov 1754
—— Col Standard *Constant Couple* 25 Nov 1754

—— Cook *Miser* 5 Jan 1791
—— Torrington *School for Wives* 14 Jan 1791
—— Crabtree *School for Scandal* 26 Jan 1791
—— M'Dermot *School for Arrogance* 2 Nov 1791
—— Peter *Dramatist* 24 Feb 1792
—— Clown *Sheep Shearing* 24 Feb 1792
—— Ephraim Smooth *Wild Oats* 27 Feb 1792
—— Borachio *Hotel* 24 Oct 1794
—— Sir Francis Gripe *Busy Body* 9 May 1796
—— Beau Mordecai *Love a la Mode* 9 May 1796
Lynch, Mrs Bachant *Comus* 17 Dec 1788
Lyons, Thomas Master Lucy *Recruiting Officer* 20 Nov 1755

Macartney, Ar Master Castor Pearmain *Recruiting Officer* 20 Nov 1755
—— Justice Scale *Recruiting Officer* 20 Nov 1755
Macartney, Geo Master Worthy *Recruiting Officer* 20 Nov 1755
Macartney, Jo Master Justice Scruple *Recruiting Officer* 20 Nov 1755
Macklin Muley *Castle Spectre* 10 Mar 1800
—— Davilla *Pizarro* 14 Apr 1800
Magee, Master Justice Ballance *Recruiting Officer* 20 Nov 1755
Mahon Sullen *Beaux' Stratagem* 1 July 1761
—— Gratiano *Othello* 8 July 1761
—— Rosencrans *Hamlet* 10 July 1761
—— Gratiano *Othello* 15 July 1761
—— Constable *Provoked Husband* 17 July 1761
—— Officer *Douglas* 22 July 1761
—— Clear Account *Twin Rivals* 24 July 1761
—— Ratcliffe *King Richard III* 29 July 1761
—— Stanmore *Oroonoko* 7 Aug 1761
—— Charino *Love Makes a Man* 14 Aug 1761
—— Paulet *Cleone* 24 Aug 1761
—— Capulet *Romeo and Juliet* 26 Aug 1761
—— Constable *Provoked Husband* 28 Aug 1761
—— Lucius *Cato* 4 Sep 1761
Manwaring Francisco *Hamlet* 10 July 1761
—— Senator *Othello* 15 July 1761
—— Oxford *King Richard III* 29 July 1761
—— Printer *Oroonoko* 7 Aug 1761
—— Abram *Romeo and Juliet* 26 Aug 1761
—— Conspirator *Cato* 4 Sep 1761
—— Duke *Othello* 7 Oct 1765
Martin Vocal Part Concert 1 Dec 1798

Mason, Mrs See Mrs Booth
Maurice Friar Laurence *Romeo and Juliet* 22 June 1753
—— Stukely *Gamester* 3 July 1753
—— Bajazet *Tamerlane* 13 July 1753
—— Aboan *Oroonoko* 19 July 1753
—— Jaques *As You Like It* 23 July 1753
—— Burleigh *Earl of Essex* 27 July 1753
—— Col Standard *Sir Harry Wildair* 2 Aug 1753
—— Younger Woudbe *Twin Rivals* 10 Aug 1753
—— Richmond *King Richard III* 14 Aug 1753
—— Zanga *Revenge* 31 Aug 1753
—— Monsieur Le Medicine *Anatomist* 31 Aug 1753
—— Sir Charles Easy *Careless Husband* 7 Sep 1753
—— Capt Flash *Miss in Her Teens* 7 Sep 1753
—— Lodovico *Othello* 11 Sep 1753
—— Horatio *Fair Penitent* 14 Sep 1753
Maxwell, Mrs Mrs Slammakin *Beggar's Opera* 23 Aug 1768
—— Peggy *King and Miller of Mansfield* 23 Aug 1768
—— Lucinda *Conscious Lovers* 26 Aug 1768
—— Lady Loverule *Devil to Pay* 26 Aug 1768
—— Paris *Romeo and Juliet* 2 Sep 1768
—— Damaris *Fashionable Wife* 2 Sep 1768
—— Lady Ann *King Richard III* 7 Sep 1768
—— Melissa *Lying Valet* 14 Sep 1768
—— Juno *Judgment of Midas* 21 Sep 1768
—— Sylvia *Recruiting Officer* 28 Sep 1768
—— Belinda *Tunbridge Walks* 11 Nov 1768
—— Zara *Mourning Bride* 16 Nov 1768
—— Teresa *Spanish Fryar* 18 Nov 1768
—— Corinna *Citizen* 30 Nov 1768
—— Landlady *Suspicious Husband* 30 Apr 1770
—— Country Lass *Harlequin in Derry* 9 May 1770
—— Charlotte *Intriguing Chambermaid* 28 July 1770
May, James Essex *Earl of Essex* 12 Nov 1790
—— Hamlet *Hamlet* 15 Nov 1790
—— Romeo *Romeo and Juliet* 5 Jan 1791
—— Belville *School for Wives* 14 Jan 1791
—— Charles Surface *School for Scandal* 26 Jan 1791
—— Hamlet *Hamlet* 28 Jan 1791
—— Ranger *Suspicious Husband* early Jan 1792
—— Alexander *Rival Queens* 6 Feb 1792
—— Vapid *Dramatist* 24 Feb 1792

—— Florizel *Florizel and Perdita* 24 Feb 1792
—— Rover *Wild Oats* 27 Feb 1792
May, Mrs James Mariana *Miser* 5 Jan 1791
—— Mrs Candour *School for Scandal* 26 Jan 1791
—— Parisatis *Rival Queens* 6 Feb 1792
—— Amelia *Wild Oats* 27 Feb 1792
McCarthy Buckle *Suspicious Husband* 30 Apr 1770
—— Country Lad *Harlequin in Derry* 9 May 1770
—— Slave *Barbarossa* 28 July 1770
—— Trusty *Intriguing Chambermaid* 28 July 1770
—— French Soldier *Harlequin with Thurot* 31 July 1770
Macready, William Joseph Surface *School for Scandal* 27 Jan 1783
McGeorge, Mrs Isabinda *Busy Body* 9 May 1796
—— Charlotte *Love a la Mode* 9 May 1796
Melmoth, Mrs Charlotte Queen Elizabeth *Earl of Essex* 12 Nov 1790
—— Mrs Belville *School for Wives* 14 Jan 1791
—— Lady St Valeroi *Carmelite* 14 Oct 1791
—— Lady Peckham *School for Arrogance* 2 Nov 1791
—— Roxana *Rival Queens* 6 Feb 1792
Middleton [Magan], James Romeo *Romeo and Juliet* 1 Apr 1793
—— Alexander *Rival Queens* 17 Apr 1793
—— Dick *Apprentice* 17 Apr 1793
—— Woodville *Chapter of Accidents* 8 May 1793
—— Irwin *Every Man has His Fault* 10 May 1793
—— Duke's Servant *High Life Below Stairs* 10 May 1793
Molloy, Mrs Francis Clarissa *Lionel and Clarissa* 29 Oct 1788
—— Polly *Beggar's Opera* 12 Nov 1788
—— Clarissa *Lionel and Clarissa* 29 Oct 1788
—— Rosina *Rosina* 12 Nov 1788
—— Clarissa *Lionel and Clarissa* 28 Nov 1788
—— Venus *Poor Vulcan* 28 Nov 1788
Mozeen, Mrs Thomas Lavinia *Fair Penitent* 18 Nov 1754
—— Phillida *Damon and Phillida* 18 Nov 1754
—— Miranda *Busy Body* 20 Nov 1754
—— Jane Shore *Jane Shore* 22 Nov 1754
—— Angelica *Constant Couple* 25 Nov 1754
—— Monimia *Orphan* 27 Nov 1754
—— Polly *Beggar's Opera* 29 Nov 1754
—— Rose *Recruiting Officer* 6 Dec 1754
—— Louisa *Love Makes a Man* 11 Dec 1754
—— Arpasia *Tamerlane* 13 Dec 1754
—— Monimia *Orphan* 17 Dec 1754

—— Phillis *Conscious Lovers* 3 Jan 1755
—— Ophelia *Hamlet* 7 Jan 1755
—— Flora *Country Lasses* 10 Jan 1755
—— Mrs Sullen *Beaux' Stratagem* 17 Jan 1755
—— Jane Shore *Jane Shore* 18 Jan 1755
—— Clarinda *Suspicious Husband* 24 Jan 1755
—— Portia *Julius Caesar* 27 Jan 1755
—— Miss Jenny *Provoked Husband* 31 Jan 1755
—— Belvidera *Venice Preserved* 7 Feb 1755
—— Lady Froth *Double Dealer* 24 Feb 1755
—— Angelica *Love for Love* late Feb or Mar 1755
—— Countess of Rutland *Earl of Essex* 7 Mar 1755
—— Prince John *King Henry IV* 14 Mar 1755
—— Polly *Beggar's Opera* 23 Aug 1768
—— Indiana *Conscious Lovers* 26 Aug 1768
—— Juliet *Romeo and Juliet* 2 Sep 1768
—— Prince Edward *King Richard III* 7 Sep 1768
—— Miss Sterling *Clandestine Marriage* 14 Sep 1768
—— Nisa *Judgment of Midas* 21 Sep 1768
—— Melinda *Recruiting Officer* 28 Sep 1768
—— Maiden *Tunbridge Walks* 11 Nov 1768
—— Queen *Spanish Fryar* 18 Nov 1768
—— Andromache *Distrest Mother* 16 Aug 1771
—— Mrs Sullen *Beaux' Stratagem* 4 Sep 1771
—— Honor *Tom Jones* 30 Oct 1771
—— PC *Mentalist or, Doctor of the Passions* 15 Nov 1771
—— Clarissa *Lionel and Clarissa* 17 Jan 1772

Nugent Country Lad *Harlequin in Derry* 9 May 1770

O'Keeffe, John Frankly *Suspicious Husband* 30 Apr 1770
—— Dundspate Dismal *Harlequin in Derry* 9 May 1770
—— Cormin *Lady Pentweazle* 4 July 1770
—— Linco *Linco's Travels* 18 July 1770
—— Thomas Filbert *What D'Ye Call It* 20 July 1770
—— Hearty *Jovial Crew* 26 July 1770
—— Jerry Sneak *Mayor of Garratt* 26 July 1770
—— Lord Pride *Intriguing Chambermaid* 28 July 1770
—— Jaffier *Venice Preserved* 30 July 1770
—— Carmine *Lady Pentweazle* 30 July 1770
—— Jeremy Divil *Harlequin with Thurot* 31 July 1770
—— Colin *Colin's Welcome* 11 Aug 1770

O'Neil O'Blunder *Brave Irishman* 8 Feb 1758
—— Mock Doctor *Mock Doctor* 10 Feb 1758
—— Sir Francis Wronghead *Provoked Husband* 15 Feb 1758
—— Cassio *Othello* 7 Oct 1765
Owen Antonio *Love Makes a Man* 11 Dec 1754
—— Omar *Tamerlane* 13 Dec 1754
—— Myrtle *Conscious Lovers* 3 Jan 1755
—— Polonius *Hamlet* 7 Jan 1755
—— Double Jugg *Country Lasses* 10 Jan 1755
—— Gibbet *Beaux' Stratagem* 17 Jan 1755
—— Ratcliffe *Jane Shore* 18 Jan 1755
—— Buckle *Suspicious Husband* 24 Jan 1755
—— Octavius Caesar *Julius Caesar* 27 Jan 1755
—— Count Basset *Provoked Husband* 31 Jan 1755
—— Spinosa *Venice Preserved* 7 Feb 1755
—— Lord Touchwood *Double Dealer* 24 Feb 1755
—— Friar Lawrence *Romeo and Juliet* 28 Feb 1755
—— Jeremy *Love for Love* late Feb or Mar 1755
Owens, John Linegar, Sr Achmet *Barbarossa* 28 July 1770
—— Valentine *Intriguing Chambermaid* 28 July 1770
—— French Soldier *Harlequin with Thurot* 31 July 1770
—— Castalio *Orphan* 11 Aug 1770
—— Young Wilding *Citizen* 11 Aug 1770

Parker, James Macheath *Beggar's Opera* 23 Aug 1768
—— Tom *Conscious Lovers* 26 Aug 1768
—— Mercutio *Romeo and Juliet* 2 Sep 1768
—— Clodpole *Fashionable Wife* 2 Sep 1768
—— Buckingham *King Richard III* 7 Sep 1768
—— Sterling *Clandestine Marriage* 14 Sep 1768
—— Sileno *Judgment of Midas* 21 Sep 1768
—— Capt Brazen *Recruiting Officer* 28 Sep 1768
—— Woodcock *Tunbridge Walks* 11 Nov 1768
—— Gonsalez *Mourning Bride* 16 Nov 1768
—— Fryar *Spanish Fryar* 18 Nov 1768
—— Citizen *Citizen* 30 Nov 1768
—— Squire Western *Tom Jones* 30 Oct 1771
—— Col Oldboy *Lionel and Clarissa* 17 Jan 1772
Parks Sciolto *Fair Penitent* 14 Jan 1763
—— Count Basset *Provoked Husband* 21 Jan 1763
—— Macheath *Beggar's Opera* 28 Jan 1763
—— Macheath *Beggar's Opera* 15 Feb 1763

—— Prince of Wales *King Henry IV* 14 Mar 1755
Pye Mat o' the Mint *Beggar's Opera* 23 Aug 1768
—— Myrtle *Conscious Lovers* 26 Aug 1768
—— Sir John Loverule *Devil to Pay* 26 Aug 1768
—— Benvolio *Romeo and Juliet* 2 Sep 1768
—— Lovemore *Fashionable Wife* 2 Sep 1768
—— Richmond *King Richard III* 7 Sep 1768
—— Apollo *Judgment of Midas* 21 Sep 1768
—— Beaufort *Citizen* 30 Nov 1768
—— Pylades *Distrest Mother* 16 Aug 1771
—— Sir Charles Freeman *Beaux' Stratagem* 4 Sep 1771
—— Young Nightingale *Tom Jones* 30 Oct 1771
—— PC *Mentalist or, Doctor of the Passions* 15 Nov 1771
—— Harman *Lionel and Clarissa* 17 Jan 1772
—— Lord Randolph Douglas 6 Sep 1773
—— Harman Lionel and Clarissa 8 Sep 1773
—— Sir Benjamin Backbite *School for Scandal* 12 Feb 1779
—— Leander *Padlock* 12 Feb 1779
—— Bates *Gamester* 17 Dec 1788
—— Brother *Comus* 17 Dec 1788
Pye, Mrs Lucy and Mrs Peachum *Beggar's Opera* 23 Aug 1768
—— Kate *King and Miller of Mansfield* 23 Aug 1768
—— Phillis *Conscious Lovers* 26 Aug 1768
—— Nell *Devil to Pay* 26 Aug 1768
—— Nurse *Romeo and Juliet* 2 Sep 1768
—— Mrs Brittle *Fashionable Wife* 2 Sep 1768
—— Queen *King Richard III* 7 Sep 1768
—— Mrs Heidelberg *Clandestine Marriage* 14 Sep 1768
—— Kitty *Lying Valet* 14 Sep 1768
—— Daphne *Judgment of Midas* 21 Sep 1768
—— Rose *Recruiting Officer* 28 Sep 1768
—— Hillaria *Tunbridge Walks* 11 Nov 1768
—— Almeria *Mourning Bride* 16 Nov 1768
—— Elvira *Spanish Fryar* 18 Nov 1768
—— Maria *Citizen* 30 Nov 1768
—— Hermione *Distrest Mother* 16 Aug 1771
—— Cherry *Beaux' Stratagem* 4 Sep 1771
—— Mrs Western *Tom Jones* 30 Oct 1771
—— PC *Mentalist or, Doctor of the Passions* 15 Nov 1771
—— Diana *Lionel and Clarissa* 17 Jan 1772
—— Dorcas *Mock Doctor* 6 Sep 1773
—— Diana *Lionel and Clarissa* 8 Sep 1773

—— Leeson *School for Wives* 14 Jan 1791
—— Joseph Surface *School for Scandal* 26 Jan 1791
—— Hildebrand Montgomeri *Carmelite* 14 Oct 1791
—— Lysimachus *Rival Queens* 6 Feb 1792
—— Floriville *Dramatist* 24 Feb 1792
—— Sim *Wild Oats* 27 Feb 1792
—— Sir George Airy *Busy Body* 9 May 1796

Remington, Mrs James Lucilia *Fair Penitent* 14 Jan 1763
—— Lady Randolph *Douglas* 19 Jan 1763
—— Myrtilla *Provoked Husband* 21 Jan 1763
—— Fairy Queen *Oracle* 21 Jan 1763
—— Polly Peachum *Beggar's Opera* 15 Feb 1763
—— Biddy Bellair *Miss in Her Teens* 15 Feb 1763
—— Wheedle *Miser* 23 Feb 1763
—— Kitty *Lying Valet* 23 Feb 1763
—— Teresa *Spanish Fryar* 14 Mar 1763
—— Vocal Part *Romeo and Juliet* 29 Mar 1763
—— Bachant *Comus* 17 Dec 1788
—— Nurse *Romeo and Juliet* 5 Jan 1791
—— Sysigambis *Rival Queens* 6 Feb 1792
—— Lady Waitfort *Dramatist* 24 Feb 1792
—— King of Queerumania *Chrononhotonthologos* 6 Apr 1795
—— Patch *Busy Body* 9 May 1796

Richards, William Talbot Macheath *Beggar's Opera* 4 Dec 1778
—— Lionel *Lionel and Clarissa* 9 Dec 1778
—— Sir Peter Teazle *School for Scandal* 12 Feb 1779
—— Mungo *Padlock* 12 Feb 1779
—— Watty Cockney *Romp* 12 Mar 1779
—— Osmyn *Sultan* 19 Mar 1779
—— Ennui *Dramatist* 24 Feb 1792
—— Autolicus *Florizel and Perdita* 24 Feb 1792
—— Sir George Thunder *Wild Oats* 27 Feb 1792

Richards, Mrs William Talbot Polly *Beggar's Opera* 4 Dec 1778
—— Miss Lucy *Virgin Unmasked* 4 Dec 1778
—— Diana *Lionel and Clarissa* 9 Dec 1778
—— Leonora *Padlock* 11 Dec 1778
—— Leonora *Padlock* 12 Feb 1779
—— Louisa *Deserter* 26 Feb 1779
—— Rosetta *Love in a Village* 12 Mar 1779
—— Priscilla Tomboy *Romp* 12 Mar 1779
—— Ismene *Sultan* 19 Mar 1779
—— Priscilla *Romp or A Cure for the Spleen* 23 Mar 1779

—— Lovegold *Miser* 18 July 1770
—— Ensign Maclamore *Reprisal* 18 July 1770
—— Clodio *Love Makes a Man* 20 July 1770
—— Timothy Peascod *What D'Ye Call It* 20 July 1770
—— Lissardo *Wonder* 25 July 1770
—— Sharp *Lying Valet* 25 July 1770
—— Oliver *Jovial Crew* 26 July 1770
—— Maj Sturgeon *Mayor of Garratt* 26 July 1770
—— Mrs Cole *Mrs Cole the Methodist* 26 July 1770
—— Sadi *Barbarossa* 28 July 1770
— — Widow Lovitt *Disappointment* 28 July 1770
—— Drunken Colonel *Intriguing Chambermaid* 28 July 1770
—— Pierre *Venice Preserved* 30 July 1770
—— Lady Pentweazle *Lady Pentweazle* 30 July 1770
—— Commodore *Harlequin with Thurot* 31 July 1770
—— Copper Captain *Rule a Wife and Have a Wife* 1 Aug 1770
—— Hamlet *Hamlet Prince of Denmark* 2 Aug 1770
—— Ensign Maclamore *Reprisal* 2 Aug 1770
—— Lothario *Fair Penitent* 4 Aug 1770
—— Zanga *Revenge* 6 Aug 1770
—— Varanes *Theodosius* 7 Aug 1770
—— Vizard *Vintner Tricked* 7 Aug 1770
—— Lord Hastings *Jane Shore* 8 Aug 1770
—— Douglas *Douglas* 10 Aug 1770
—— Chamont *Orphan* 11 Aug 1770
—— Young Philpot *Citizen* 11 Aug 1770
—— Sir John Restless *All In The Wrong* 14 Sep 1791
—— Drunken Colonel *Intriguing Chambermaid* 10 Oct 1791
Ryder, Mrs Thomas [see also Comerford, Rosetta] Clarida
Suspicious Husband   30 Apr 1770
—— Countess Salisbury *Countess of Salisbury* 9 May 1770
—— Rosetta *Foundling* 4 July 1770
—— Mrs Kitely *Every Man in his Humour* 11 July 1770
—— Zara *Mourning Bride* 14 July 1770
—— Chloe *Lottery* 16 July 1770
—— Belvidera *Venice Preserved* 30 July 1770
—— Queen *Hamlet* 2 Aug 1770
—— Alicia *Jane Shore* 8 Aug 1770
—— Lady Randolph *Douglas* 10 Aug 1770
Ryder, E Miss Belinda *All In The Wrong* 14 Sep 1791
—— Phoebe *Rosina* 14 Sep 1791
—— Moggy McGilpin *Highland Reel* 16 Sep 1791

—— Miss Tittup *Bon Ton* 16 Sep 1791
—— Macheath *Beggar's Opera* 21 Sep 1791
—— Wowskie *Inkle and Yarico* 30 Sep 1791
—— Lettice *Intriguing Chambermaid* 10 Oct 1791
Ryder, Miss Rose Rosina *Rosina* 14 Sep 1791
—— Jenny *Highland Reel* 16 Sep 1791
—— Polly *Beggar's Opera* 21 Sep 1791
—— Yarico *Inkle and Yarico* 30 Sep 1791
Ryder, Samuel Tester *Suspicious Husband* 30 Apr 1770
—— Scaramouch *Harlequin in Derry* 9 May 1770
—— Aladin *Barbarossa* 28 July 1770
—— Pimplenose *Disappointment* 28 July 1770
—— Slap *Intriguing Chambermaid* 28 July 1770
—— English Officer *Harlequin with Thurot* 31 July 1770
Ryder, Mrs Samuel Harriet *Reprisal* 2 Aug 1770

Sennet, Master Rugby *Merry Wives of Windsor* 1751–1752 Season
Sheridan Hassom *Castle Spectre* 10 Mar 1800
—— Valverede *Pizarro* 14 Apr 1800
Sherriffe Osmyn *Mourning Bride* 6 June 1753
—— Jaffier *Venice Preserved* 15 June 1753
—— Romeo *Romeo and Juliet* 22 June 1753
—— Torrismond *Spanish Fryar* 29 June 1753
—— Beverly *Gamester* 3 July 1753
—— Beverly *Gamester* 6 July 1753
—— Tamerlane *Tamerlane* 13 July 1753
—— Oroonoko *Oroonoko* 19 July 1753
—— Orlando *As You Like It* 23 July 1753
—— Essex *Earl of Essex* 27 July 1753
—— Sir Harry Wildair *Sir Harry Wildair* 2 Aug 1753
—— Capt Trueman *Twin Rivals* 10 Aug 1753
—— King Richard *King Richard III* 14 Aug 1753
—— Don Philip *She Wou'd and She Wou'd Not* 28 Aug 1753
—— Don Alonzo *Revenge* 31 Aug 1753
—— Chrispin *Anatomist* 31 Aug 1753
—— Lord Foppington *Careless Husband* 7 Sep 1753
—— Fribble *Miss in Her Teens* 7 Sep 1753
—— Othello *Othello* 11 Sep 1753
—— Capt Duretete *Inconstant* 6 Feb 1758
—— Lothario *Fair Penitent* 8 Feb 1758
—— Capt Brazen *Recruiting Officer* 10 Feb 1758
—— King Richard *King Richard III* 13 Feb 1758

—— Count Basset *Provoked Husband* 15 Feb 1758
—— Old Norval *Douglas* 21 Feb 1758
—— Drunken Colonel *Intriguing Chambermaid* 21 Feb 1758
—— Col Fainwell *Bold Stroke for a Wife* 24 Feb 1758
—— Achmet *Barbarossa* 29 Feb 1758
—— Autolicus *Sheep Shearing* 29 Feb 1758
—— Romeo *Romeo and Juliet* 15 Mar 1758
—— Ranger *Suspicious Husband* 17 Mar 1758
—— Mat of the Mint *Beggar's Opera* 27 Mar 1758
—— Ranger *Suspicious Husband* 31 Mar 1758
—— Hamlet *Hamlet* 5 Apr 1758
—— Tom *Conscious Lovers* 7 Apr 1758
—— Varannes *Theodosius* 10 Apr 1758
—— Agis *Aegis* 14 Apr 1758
—— Shylock *Merchant of Venice* 19 Apr 1758
—— Orestes *Distrest Mother* 21 Apr 1758
—— King *King and the Miller of Mansfield* 21 Apr 1758
—— Zanga *Revenge* 28 Apr 1758
—— Ben Block *Reprisal* 28 Apr 1758
—— Osmyn *Mourning Bride* 3 May 1758
—— Essex *Earl of Essex* 5 May 1758
—— Chamount *Orphan* 12 May 1758
—— Young Belmont *Foundling* 19 May 1758
—— Beau Clincher *Constant Couple* 24 May 1758
—— Count Basset *Provoked Husband* 26 May 1758
—— Old Norval *Douglas* 2 June 1758
—— Trueman *London Merchant* 12 June 1758
Sherriffe, Mrs Almeria *Mourning Bride* 6 June 1753
—— Belvidera *Venice Preserved* 15 June 1753
—— Juliet *Romeo and Juliet* 22 June 1753
—— Queen *Spanish Fryar* 29 June 1753
—— Mrs Beverly *Gamester* 3 July 1753
—— Arpasia *Tamerlane* 13 July 1753
—— Imoinda *Oroonoko* 19 July 1753
—— Rosalind *As You Like It* 23 July 1753
—— Rutland *Earl of Essex* 27 July 1753
—— Lady Lurewell *Sir Harry Wildair* 2 Aug 1753
—— Aurelia *Twin Rivals* 10 Aug 1753
—— Lady Ann *King Richard III* 14 Aug 1753
—— Mariana *Miser* 22 Aug 1753
—— Hypolita *She Wou'd and She Wou'd Not* 28 Aug 1753
—— Leonora *Revenge* 31 Aug 1753

—— O'Blunder *Brave Irishman* 8 July 1761
—— Gravedigger *Hamlet* 10 July 1761
—— O'Blunder *Brave Irishman* 10 July 1761
—— Duke *Othello* 15 July 1761
—— John Moody *Provoked Husband* 17 July 1761
—— O'Blunder *Brave Irishman* 17 July 1761
—— Teague *Twin Rivals* 24 July 1761
—— Lord Mayor *Richard III* 29 July 1761
—— Mixum *Vintner Tricked* 31 July 1761
—— Patrick O'Monaghan *Wapping Landlady* 3 Aug 1761
—— Capt Driver *Oroonoko* 7 Aug 1761
—— Patrick O'Monaghan *Wapping Landlady* 7 Aug 1761
—— Don Manuel *She Would and She Would Not* 12 Aug 1761
—— Don Lewis *Love Makes a Man* 14 Aug 1761
—— O'Blunder *Brave Irishman* 14 Aug 1761
—— Grumio *Catherine and Petruchio* 24 Aug 1761
—— John Moody *Provoked Husband* 28 Aug 1761
—— Hob *Flora* 28 Aug 1761
—— Syphax *Cato* 4 Sep 1761
Stewart, James Beatty Dutchman *Harlequin in Derry* 9 May 1770
—— Don Lewis *Love makes a Man* 20 July 1770
—— Barbarossa *Barbarossa* 28 July 1770
—— Oldcastle *Intriguing Chambermaid* 28 July 1770
—— Scarecrow *Harlequin with Thurot* 31 July 1770
—— Ghost *Hamlet* 15 Nov 1790
—— Neville *Dramatist* 24 Feb 1792
—— Harry *Wild Oats* 27 Feb 1792
Stewart, [Stuart?]Mrs Clarinda *Robin Hood* 17 May 1793
Swindall, Mrs James Isabella *Isabella* 8 Dec 1784

Tisdall, Mrs Clarissa *Lionel and Clarissa* 30 Dec 1778
Trevillian, Mrs Dorinda *Beaux' Stratagem* 1 July 1761
—— Desdemona *Othello* 8 July 1761
—— Ophelia *Hamlet* 10 July 1761
—— Lady Grace *Provoked Husband* 17 July 1761
—— Anna *Douglas* 22 July 1761
—— Constance *Twin Rivals* 24 July 1761
—— Lady Anne *King Richard III* 29 July 1761
—— Lady Easy *Careless Husband* 5 Aug 1761
—— Charlotte Weldon *Oroonoko* 7 Aug 1761
—— Angelina *Love Makes a Man* 14 Aug 1761
—— Lady Capulet *Romeo and Juliet* 26 Aug 1761

—— Lady Grace *Provoked Husband* 28 Aug 1761
—— Flora *Flora* 28 Aug 1761
—— Marcia *Cato* 4 Sep 1761
Tyrer, Samuel Host *Merry Wives of Windsor* 1751–1752 Season
—— Sapscull *Honest Yorkshireman* 1751–1752 Season
—— PC *Jane Shore* 18 Dec 1751
—— Fryar *Spanish Fryar* 29 June 1753
—— Beau Clincher *Sir Harry Wildair* 2 Aug 1753
—— Teague *Twin Rivals* 10 Aug 1753
—— Cassio *Othello* 11 Sep 1753
Tyrer, Mrs Samuel Mrs Page *Merry Wives of Windsor* 1751–1752 Season
—— PC *Jane Shore* 18 Dec 1751
Tyrrell Oakly *Jealous Wife* 2 Mar 1787
—— Lionel *Lionel and Clarissa* 28 Nov 1788
—— Lewson *Gamester* 17 Dec 1788
—— Bachanal *Comus* 17 Dec 1788

Usher, Howard Archer *Beaux' Stratagem* 1 July 1761
—— Othello *Othello* 3 July 1761
—— Horatio *Hamlet* 10 July 1761
—— Othello *Othello* 15 July 1761
—— Lord Townly *Provoked Husband* 17 July 1761
—— Douglas *Douglas* 22 July 1761
—— Wouldbe *Twin Rivals* 24 July 1761
—— Richard *King Richard III* 29 July 1761
—— Douglas *Douglas* 31 July 1761
—— Sir Charles *Careless Husband* 5 Aug 1761
—— Don Philip *She Would and She Would Not* 12 Aug 1761
—— Carlos *Love Makes a Man* 14 Aug 1761
—— Sifroy *Cleone* 24 Aug 1761
—— Petruchio *Catherine and Petruchio* 24 Aug 1761
—— Romeo *Romeo and Juliet* 26 July 1761
—— Lord Townly *Provoked Husband* 28 Aug 1761
—— Friendly *Flora* 28 Aug 1761
—— Cato *Cato* 4 Sep 1761
Usher, Mrs Mrs Sullen *Beaux' Stratagem* 1 July 1761
—— Queen Gertrude *Hamlet* 10 July 1761
—— Desdemona *Othello* 15 July 1761
—— Lady Townly *Provoked Husband* 17 July 1761
—— Lady Randolph *Douglas* 22 July 1761
—— Amelia *Twin Rivals* 24 July 1761
—— Queen *King Richard III* 29 July 1761

—— Lady Randolph *Douglas* 31 July 1761
—— Lady Betty Modish *Careless Husband* 5 Aug 1761
—— Imoinda *Oroonoko* 7 Aug 1761
—— Louisa *Love Makes a Man* 14 Aug 1761
—— Cleone *Cleone* 24 Aug 1761
—— Catherine *Catherine and Petruchio* 24 Aug 1761
—— Juliet *Romeo and Juliet* 26 Aug 1761
—— Lady Townly *Provoked Husband* 28 Aug 1761
—— Lucia *Cato* 4 Sep 1761
Usher, Miss Euphrasia *Grecian Daughter* 10 Dec 1784

Valois, Miss Pastoral Nymph *Comus* 17 Dec 1788
Vernel, John Freeman *Beaux' Stratagem* 1 July 1761
—— Lodovico *Othello* 8 July 1761
—— Marcellus *Hamlet* 10 July 1761
—— Lodovico *Othello* 15 July 1761
—— Servant *Douglas* 22 July 1761
—— Richmore *Twin Rivals* 24 July 1761
—— Lieutenant *King Richard III* 29 July 1761
—— Blanford *Oroonoko* 7 Aug 1761
—— Governor *Love Makes a Man* 14 Aug 1761
—— Old Beaufort *Cleone* 24 Aug 1761
—— Tibalt *Romeo and Juliet* 26 Aug 1761
—— Marcus *Cato* 4 Sep 1761

Waker, Joseph Peachum *Beggar's Opera* 23 Aug 1768
—— Miller *King and Miller of Mansfield* 23 Aug 1768
—— Sealand *Conscious Lovers* 26 Aug 1768
—— Jobson *Devil to Pay* 26 Aug 1768
—— Capulet *Romeo and Juliet* 2 Sep 1768
—— King Henry *King Richard III* 7 Sep 1768
—— Mock Doctor *Mock Doctor* 6 Sep 1773
—— Sir John Flowerdale *Lionel and Clarissa* 8 Sep 1773
—— Scrub *Beaux' Stratagem* 3 Jan 1774
—— Roger *Ghost* 3 Jan 1774
Waker, Mrs Joseph Dolly Trull *Beggar's Opera* 23 Aug 1768
—— Isabella *Conscious Lovers* 26 Aug 1768
—— Lady Capulet *Romeo and Juliet* 2 Sep 1768
—— Duchess of York *King Richard III* 7 Sep 1768
—— Anna *Douglas* 6 Sep 1773
—— Margery *Lionel and Clarissa* 8 Sep 1773
Walker, R Lionel *Lionel and Clarissa* 28 Mar 1796

Walkinshaw, Master Thomas Appletree *Recruiting Officer* 20 Nov 1755
Walsh Mungo *Padlock* 10 Mar 1780
Ward, Henry Sir Francis Gripe *Busy Body* 20 Nov 1754
—— Alderman Smuggler *Constant Couple* 25 Nov 1754
—— Ernesto *Orphan* 27 Nov 1754
—— Ben Budge *Beggar's Opera* 29 Nov 1754
—— Bullock *Recruiting Officer* 6 Dec 1754
—— Charino *Love Makes a Man* 11 Dec 1754
—— Ernesto *Orphan* 17 Dec 1754
—— Cimberton *Conscious Lovers* 3 Jan 1755
—— Lucianus *Hamlet* 7 Jan 1755
—— Shacklefigure *Country Lasses* 10 Jan 1755
—— Hounslow *Beaux' Stratagem* 17 Jan 1755
—— Tester *Suspicious Husband* 24 Jan 1755
—— Artemidorus *Julius Caesar* 27 Jan 1755
—— John Moody *Provoked Husband* 31 Jan 1755
—— Lord Froth *Double Dealer* 24 Feb 1755
—— Friar John *Romeo and Juliet* 28 Feb 1755
—— Foresight *Love for Love* late Feb or Mar 1755
Ward, Henry (Sarah Achurch) Mrs Lucilla *Fair Penitent* 18 Nov 1754
—— Patch *Busy Body* 20 Nov 1754
—— Lady Darling *Constant Couple* 25 Nov 1754
—— Florella *Orphan* 27 Nov 1754
—— Mrs Peachum *Beggar's Opera* 29 Nov 1754
—— Melinda *Recruiting Officer* 6 Dec 1754
—— Elvina *Love Makes a Man* 11 Dec 1754
—— Selima *Tamerlane* 13 Dec 1754
—— Serina *Orphan* 17 Dec 1754
—— Mrs Sealand *Conscious Lovers* 3 Jan 1755
—— Queen *Hamlet* 7 Jan 1755
—— Lady Bountiful *Beaux' Stratagem* 17 Jan 1755
—— Lucette *Suspicious Husband* 24 Jan 1755
—— Metellus Cimber *Julius Caesar* 27 Jan 1755
—— Lady Wronghead *Provoked Husband* 31 Jan 1755
—— Lady Touchwood *Double Dealer* 24 Feb 1755
—— Nurse *Romeo and Juliet* 28 Feb 1755
—— Mrs Frail *Love for Love* late Feb or Mar 1755
Ward, Mrs Thomas Belinda *All in the Wrong* 19 Feb 1787
—— Henry *Deserter* 19 Feb 1787
—— Ophelia *Hamlet* 9 Apr 1787
Ward, Master Cha Bullock *Recruiting Officer* 20 Nov 1755
Ward, Master Ralph Silvia *Recruiting Officer* 20 Nov 1755

White Altamont *Fair Penitent* 18 Nov 1754
—— Charles *Busy Body* 20 Nov 1754
—— Catesby *Jane Shore* 22 Nov 1754
—— Vizard *Constant Couple* 25 Nov 1754
—— Polydore *Orphan* 27 Nov 1754
—— Macheath *Beggar's Opera* 29 Nov 1754
—— Governour *Love Makes a Man* 11 Dec 1754
—— Axalla *Tamerlane* 13 Dec 1754
—— Polydore *Orphan* 17 Dec 1754
—— Young Bevil *Conscious Lovers* 3 Jan 1755
—— Ostrick *Hamlet* 7 Jan 1755
—— Heartwell *Country Lasses* 10 Jan 1755
—— Aimwell *Beaux' Stratagem* 17 Jan 1755
—— Catesby *Jane Shore* 18 Jan 1755
—— Frankly *Suspicious Husband* 24 Jan 1755
—— Casca *Julius Caesar* 27 Jan 1755
—— Manly *Provoked Husband* 31 Jan 1755
—— Theodore *Venice Preserved* 7 Feb 1755
—— Careless *Double Dealer* 24 Feb 1755
—— Paris *Romeo and Juliet* 28 Feb 1755
—— Tattle *Love for Love* late Feb or Mar 1755
—— Raleigh *Earl of Essex* 7 Mar 1755
—— King Henry *King Henry IV* 14 Mar 1755
Whitmore, Miss Country Lass *Harlequin in Derry* 9 May 1770
Willis, Mrs Cherry *Beaux' Stratagem* 1 July 1761
—— Player Queen *Hamlet* 10 July 1761
—— Jenny *Provoked Husband* 17 July 1761
—— Prince Edward *King Richard III* 29 July 1761
—— Edging *Careless Husband* 5 Aug 1761
—— Lucy Weldon *Oroonoko* 7 Aug 1761
—— Elvira *Love Makes a Man* 14 Aug 1761
—— Jenny *Provoked Husband* 28 Aug 1761
Wilmot Sir Tunbelly Clumsey *A Man of Quality* 10 Apr 1778
—— Carmine *Lady Pentweazel* 24 Apr 1778
Wilmot, Mrs Jane Shore *Jane Shore* 10 Apr 1778
—— Miss Hoyden *A Man of Quality* 10 Apr 1778
Wilson Guard *Barbarossa* 28 July 1770
—— English Soldier *Harlequin with Thurot* 31 July 1770
—— Altamont *Fair Penitent* 4 Aug 1770
Wright, Mrs Diana Trapes *Beggar's Opera* 23 Aug 1768
—— Lettice *Devil to Pay* 26 Aug 1768
—— Shepherdess *Judgment of Midas* 21 Sep 1768

GENERAL INDEX

This index includes items discussed in the text of the general introduction, seasonal introductions, and materials in the calendar that are not incorporated into the other indexes. No effort is made here to list the many references to Belfast. Locations of biographical sketches of stage personnel active in Belfast during this period are indicted in bold type.